PROTESTANTISM

A SYMPOSIUM

EDITED BY

WILLIAM K. ANDERSON

Essay Index Reprint Series

BOOKS FOR LIBRARIES PRESS
FREEPORT, NEW YORK

STANDARD BOOK NUMBER:
8369-1018-4

LIBRARY OF CONGRESS CATALOG CARD NUMBER:
69-18918

PRINTED IN THE UNITED STATES OF AMERICA

PROTESTANTISM

A SYMPOSIUM

CONTENTS

INTRODUCTION

Samuel McCrea Cavert

The hour has struck for a strong reaffirmation of the basic principles of the Protestant Reformation. One reason for this is the crucial importance today of freedom and democracy, which have been historically associated in the modern world with the Protestant spirit. Another reason is the present challenge to Protestantism in Roman Catholic circles. The Roman Catholic hierarchy in America, for example, has recently made the open claim that their church should have an exclusive right to religious activity in Latin America. Their general point of view seems to be that the "Good Neighbor" policy requires a recognition of Roman Catholicism as the bond of mutual understanding between North America and the republics to the South. This is one of several factors impelling Protestants to rethink their own heritage, to gain a deeper insight into its significance for our own time, and to unite in making that significance more widely appreciated.

This situation lends timeliness to the chapters in this volume. Written by highly qualified scholars, they constitute a body of material for which all Protestants should be grateful because of their immediate relevance to present discussions as well as their permanent and intrinsic worth.

The word "Protestant" unfortunately has a negative sound. But the genius of the Protestant movement, as this book abundantly shows, is positive and creative. The Reformation was not merely an episode in history; it initiated a process that is still going on. It should be regarded less as a consummation than as a beginning. By its fresh recovery of vital aspects of the Christian gospel, it released a new spirit that has been and still is a powerful ferment not only in the Church but also in society at large. The central insights of the Reformation are a continuing part both of dynamic Christianity and of the cultural heritage of the Western world.

To a superficial view Protestantism often looks like a mere conglomerate of diverse ideas and organizations, with no unifying principle and little capacity for cohesion. Nevertheless, a real unity of spirit and outlook characterizes the Protestant movement as a historical force. It may readily be admitted that the temptation of Protestantism has always been to magnify freedom at the expense of unity. The temptation of Roman Catholicism, on the other hand, has been to magnify unity at the expense of freedom. The great need of Protestants today is a fuller realization that in the midst of their diversity there is an essential oneness and that they possess a common heritage in which they should all rejoice.

To interpret this common heritage is a part of the function of the

1

chapters that follow. It is in order here, however, to suggest briefly some of the basic insights that give inner unity and coherence to Protestantism as a whole:

1. Protestantism, in all its historic forms, insists upon the immediacy of man's relation with God. That relation rests on the unmerited grace of God, revealed to men in Jesus Christ and appropriated by them through faith in him. Man's reconciliation with God is something man does not initiate but joyously accepts as the freely offered gift of God.

2. Protestantism, in its many diverse expressions, holds that the Scriptures provide the decisive norm of spiritual authority. Read with the eye of faith and illumined by the guidance of the Holy Spirit, they offer to the individual Christian a saving knowledge of God and his will for human life.

3. All Protestants agree that there is a universal priesthood of believers. Since every Christian may receive in faith the gift of God's redeeming love in Christ, as recorded in the Scriptures, he is not dependent on priest or ecclesiastical rites but may exercise the right and duty of private judgment. This means a high emphasis upon the principle of individuality.

4. All Protestants stress the importance of religious freedom. They resist coercion, whether by political or ecclesiastical power, in matters of religious faith and practice. This makes Protestantism especially congenial to democracy. Both require the free assent of the individual.

Two further points, less widely recognized, call for special attention:

1. Protestantism tends to place a new valuation upon common life and labor. It recognizes no basic separation between the "religious" and the "secular" vocation. It regards all men as equally called to serve God in their daily occupations. It thus stresses the principle of Christian stewardship in all earthly callings.

2. Protestantism believes in the Church. The charge is often made that Protestantism so overemphasizes the individual as to produce an atomistic result, with no real doctrine of the Church. It must be acknowledged that this is the point at which Protestants have been weakest. The full synthesis of liberty and unity has never been achieved by either Catholicism or Protestantism. But the ecumenical movement of today is a clear indication that Protestantism cherishes the ideal of *community* as well as of *individuality*. If the note of the universal fellowship of all the people of Christ is late in coming to adequate embodiment, we can at least rejoice that it has now clearly emerged into the Protestant consciousness. Protestantism always leaves room for free criticism of the Church in the light of God's revelation of his will in Christ but at the same time struggles for the realization of the Christian community as one Body of Christ throughout the world.

If, as I believe will be the case, this book helps to reawaken a sense of our precious heritage in the Reformation and to make Protestants of every name more united in a common loyalty, it will serve our generation well.

2

Part 1

HISTORY

WAS THE REFORMATION NEEDED?

John T. McNeill

The Reformation was a hostile reaction to the late medieval church. It was more than this; perhaps it was not mainly this. But so often and so unreservedly did its leaders assail the unreformed hierarchical church as to leave no doubt of their deep revulsion from it. They thought the papacy a colossal misrepresentation of the religion of which it professed to be the authoritative exponent. This is the basis of their own argument that the Reformation in which they were engaged was necessary.

Their specific charges are too numerous to recite. They fall naturally into several categories. The Reformers denied the claims of papal and hierarchical authority. The assumption of power by the popes was, they declared, a usurpation. They subjected the teaching of the Scholastics to drastic revision. Especially was this the case with respect to the doctrines of the Eucharist, of Scripture, and of faith and works. They rejected as idolatrous much of the accumulated ritual and ceremonial. And most vehemently they cried out against the teeming abuses of ecclesiastical life, which had become increasingly scandalous in the days of the Renaissance popes. Along with their own doctrinal affirmations their criticisms of the old ecclesiastical order called forth a response that was to result in greater alteration of religion and society in the West than can be ascribed to any other historic crisis since Constantine emblazoned Christian symbols upon the imperial banners.

None of us thinks of any of the Reformers as infallible. While we recognize their greater familiarity with details of the scene than we can attain, historical research enables us to judge their times (if we are not blinded by prejudice) somewhat more philosophically than they possibly could. We have—or ought to have—a somewhat clearer view of the historical causes of the Reformation and of its background than these harassed and overworked leaders of a world-changing movement were able to acquire. We may well acknowledge the limitations of their views and the defective constructions they sometimes put upon the motives and ideas of their opponents. We cannot, for example, share all their judgments of the Scholastic writers, whose sincere attempt to build a system of reasoned thought around the dogmas of the church was worthy of more respect than it received from our Protestant founders. Nor can we, with them, look upon the medieval development of papal power, when we consider its undesirable alternatives, as a wholly deplorable chapter in the history of Europe. On the other hand, we ought not to be befuddled by the partisan and superlative laudation which papal theocracy and scholastic philosophy receive in some quarters today. The world moves, and these served their day. The church is never so wrong as when she declines to be changed.

THE TESTIMONY OF WITNESSES

It is charged against the Reformers that if they were sincere, they ought to have worked within the old order, applying themselves to its inward purification and regeneration; whereas in fact they were reckless revolutionaries and schismatics. Such a view has to assume that the old church was reformable without structural and doctrinal alteration. I do not think we can fairly deny the revolutionary character of the Reformation. Its sponsors viewed it as a revolution against an intolerable regime. In the history of states there may come crises in which a revolution is the only way to decent government, the only political salvation of a people. In such cases we have a right to call the leaders of the revolution patriots and not traitors. Is the case of the Reformers parallel to this or not? Constantly and with one voice they affirmed their love of the church. The one end for which they labored was the restoration of the church to spiritual efficiency. It is important to observe that they did not seek to make converts, one by one, to a sect, but to transform the church as a whole in each community. It was the church of which they were "Reformers," not merely individuals and not merely theology.

Was it, then, the duty of sincere seekers of reform to work within the old system? It should be remembered that this was not an untried effort. The attempt to reform the hierarchical church was as old as its formation. Men of energy and devotion had worked at it. It had been the perennial theme of discussion and of legislation in diocesan and provincial synods and in general councils. Reform of discipline had been accomplished a thousand times—on parchment. The spurt of power in the starter was never enough to get the engine of reform moving. The sum of all these efforts was failure.

It had long been evident that the Western church was moving morally on a downward curve. To be sure, it was not all corrupt. It is possible to describe any era of history in bright or dark colors simply by confining attention to one body of facts. If, in our view of the pre-Reformation age, we dwell upon the evidence of the growth of learning and education, the reform of a few of the monastic orders, the faithfulness of a few preachers, the interest in religion on the part of some of the northern humanists, the creative power of Renaissance art, and the rising literature of piety for the lay reader, we shall be made aware that some forces were at work from which men might take hope. We gladly welcome all the evidence of good in that untoward generation, and we acknowledge that the Reformers were generally disposed to overlook such evidence. Yet, so far as the organized church was concerned, these things were largely incidental. To claim that they were characteristic expressions of the life of the hierarchical church is far

6

from the truth of things, and the modern historians who enlarge upon these promising aspects of the times as if they offered a proof that the Reformation was needless and wicked are deceiving themselves and their readers. The piety of the fifteenth century did not center where the power of the church centered. J· was not fed by the hierarchy or inspired by the example of most of the clergy, monks, or friars. The most potent religious personality among the friars was Savonarola, and he was hanged and burned.

Those of the clergy and laity who deeply desired the well-being of the church and of the Christian society in that age habitually expressed themselves in the language of alarm, exasperation, or despair. If any testimony from men of worth in praise of the leaders of the church of that time is extant, I have not seen it cited. I would not press this point, for good men always criticize their own generation. I merely observe the singular unanimity of general and sweeping condemnation on the part of witnesses. Luther, Calvin, Tyndale, and Knox in their most vehement invectives never surpassed the scathing arraignments of the papal church uttered by men of unchallenged medieval orthodoxy in the fifteenth and the early sixteenth century. The criticism of the orthodox pre-Reformers—I am not here thinking of saintly heretics like Wyclif and Hus—differed from :hat of the Reformers, however, in this particular: the former in general wanted to amend and retain the papacy; the latter despaired of its redemption, despised its authority, and set out to reform the church without tarrying for the papacy.

I shall not describe the age before Luther by use of the language of Luther. It is needful that we see that age through the eyes of those who were then living and mingling with men and affairs. I cite some typical judgments expressed by such observers.

Dionysius the Carthusian was a monk, of the diocese of Liége, who died in 1471. He belonged to an order that among the numerous monastic connections enjoyed the reputation of a singular piety. He was an eminent theologian and something of a traveler, and he was associated with that great advocate of papal power—Nicholas of Cusa—after the latter had shifted from the conciliar to the papal party. Amid his voluminous writings there is a book called *On the Life of the Clergy*. In this he excoriates the bishops, admitting few exceptions among them from the general secularity that marks their behavior. They are in his view addicted to every sin: braggarts, flatterers, lustful, intemperate, and avaricious men, who make commerce of church appointments and take profits in dishonest business. He gives examples of these utterly unfaithful shepherds, naming names and recording their varied offenses and the startling numbers of their children. Unless the church obtains good bishops, there is no hope of reform. The lower clergy imitate the example set by the prelates. They are often drunken and scandalously unchaste. Such statements regarding the rank and file of priests are frequently met with. At the Council of Basle

7

the bishop of Lübeck urged the abolition of the rule of celibacy on the ground that not one priest in a thousand kept his vow—doubtless an exaggerated statement. The council took no action. Bishops were receiving fines for permitting priests to keep concubines.

Another Carthusian—Jacob of Jüterbock, a professor at Erfurt— wrote a tract *On the Negligence of Prelates* (1449). Jacob is almost hopeless. Things probably will go from bad to worse until God intervenes. One can hardly believe reform to be possible. The Pope ought to subject himself to the decision of a reforming council. St. Peter himself had to be reproved: why not his successor? This good monk is trying to revive the conciliarism of the previous generation. The Italian prelates, he says, tremble at the thought of a general council that would not spare their vices. Jacob speaks with equal severity of monks and clergy.

John of Wesel (d. 1479), a more valiant Erfurt theologian who ultimately came under suspicion of heresy, found abroad in the church impiety, pride, cold ceremonies, and vain superstitions. He lashed out against the traffic in indulgences. "Our souls will perish with hunger," he exclaims, unless "the yoke of our Babylonish captivity" is broken. In his book on *The Authority, Function, and Power of Pastors* he admonishes the bishops and the Pope, charging them with vainglory, ambition, and love of money.

In England there were similar criticisms. Thomas Gascoigne, Oxford scholar and chancellor of the university, wrote about 1450 *The Book of Truths*. Gascoigne, with frequent exclamations of sorrow and impatience, gives many startling examples of venality and neglect of duty on the part of Roman popes, cardinals, and clergy, and of the English bishops and abbots. He includes among the "seven rivers of Babylon," by which the church is defiled, the abuses connected with absolution, indulgences, and dispensations. He dwells upon the selfish aggression of the monks in the parishes. They appropriate the parish churches, mismanage the revenues, and compel the poor vicars to obligate themselves not to ask for an increase of their meager salaries. "In certain places," he observes,

virtually all the monks are great merchants and hold much private wealth in the hands of laymen. . . . Oh, how much good a good pope might do if he would send a good legate—one who yearns not for gifts but for the salvation of souls—with authority sufficient for the reform of the churches and kingdoms.

A generation later the clergy were under even more severe accusation. Writing in 1485 (when Luther was learning to walk), John Trithemius, abbot of Spannheim, charges that the priesthood is recruited from men who have neither learning nor conscience; who are more concerned to beget children than to buy books, addicted to drinking and gambling, and without the least fear of God. In Italy the charges of unfitness, immorality, and self-seeking are no less common. Sometimes the critics recognize the fact that classical learning may accompany ecclesiastical irresponsibility and ignorance of the Christian Scriptures.

"When I reflect upon the priests," declares Savonarola, "I am constrained to weep. . . . A terrible chastisement awaits them." At Rome the clergy mock at Christ. They traffic in the sacraments. Benefices are sold to the highest bidder. In a Lenten sermon in 1497 the zealous Dominican, with the eloquence of indignation, scourged the priests of Italy. They have withdrawn from God. They despise the Scriptures. They are profligate and no longer even pretend that their sons are nephews when they procure for them clerical offices. "O prostitute church," says this bold accuser, "thou hast displayed thy foulness to the whole world and stinkest unto heaven!" Yet he believes that the saints will intercede and that Christ has followers, in Germany, France, and Spain, who, responding to his call, will cause the corpse of the church to stir with life, as did that of Lazarus at the bidding of the Lord.

Greed Is an Old Sin

It will be observed that the charges made by would-be reformers among the clergy against their erring brethren imply that commercialism had laid hold of the system. Max Weber somewhat mistakenly held that the spirit of capitalism arose with Protestantism, and some have apparently inferred that the Reformation also gave birth to the spirit of greed. But greed has been with us from the beginnings of the human story; and it finds striking illustrations in the lives of bishops, cardinals, and popes in the days of the Borgias and the Medici. They had the mental attitudes of a trading class, and they brought these attitudes frankly into the ecclesiastical realm and trafficked in church offices in a large way. This evil, to be sure, was not new. It had never been wholly absent from the church since it was condemned in Simon Magus. But the rise of commerce and of a money economy caused it to abound. The church was aware of the danger. Three centuries earlier Francis of Assisi, espousing Lady Poverty, led a religious reaction against the commercial ideals of the town merchant class as represented by his father. That was in the beginning of the rise of business. A fairly advanced stage of development of commerce and banking had been reached when the new markets of the Renaissance gave new incitement and opportunity to such enterprise. The church had long assumed that all men were clerics, farmers, or fighters; and it had never made full adjustment to the existence of the rising bourgeoisie or brought a consistent moral discipline to bear upon business. It was helpless to resist the inroads of commercialism. Peter's successor could no longer say to Simon, "Thy money perish with thee!" Nay, he was himself a simoniac. Money was the password to advancement and wealth the prize of office. Men shamelessly bought their way to bishoprics and archbishoprics, to the cardinalate and the papacy. The lesser ecclesiastical offices were almost equally subject to the sway of simony. It became exceptional that a clerical appointment should be made without profit to those who made it.

It is not easy and it is not necessary to fix the blame upon individuals for this widespread flouting of the canon law. Men took their standards from their environment without too much anguish of conscience. But the significance of this condition for our question—"Was the Reformation needed?"—is inescapable. A fatal chain of evil had been established in the priesthood. This fact, too, was then recognized. It was pointed out, for instance, a century before the Reformation, by Matthew of Cracow, bishop of Worms, in a book on *The Filth of the Roman Curia (De squaloribus Romanae Curiae)*. Simoniacal appointment of the clergy, says this writer, "is the chief impediment to the promotion of able and honorable men." Such men will not stoop to such means. Those who do find admission are in too many instances "profligate and scandalous" in their lives. Many comparable utterances of the time indicate a growing apprehension among advocates of reform that the priesthood had been captured by unscrupulous traders and would be kept by their unscrupulous successors. Apostolic succession had yielded to simoniacal succession, which, apparently, nothing short of an ecclesiastical earthquake would disturb. "The canker had gone very deep," says the historian of the papacy—Ludwig Pastor.

Confirming this seemingly incurable abuse was the companion evil of nepotism—the preferment of the relatives and favorites of those who had offices in gift. Every man likes to help his poor relations. The temptation of the prelates was to use the ecclesiastical revenues to allay the often inordinate appetites of their kindred. The practice was widespread among the clergy and usual among the cardinals. Certain of the popes were the most scandalous offenders of all. A considerable proportion of the clergy were recruits from the flock of hungry aspirants to the favor of the prelates, consisting of their sons or relatives or persons who had some private claim upon them for service rendered.

The traffic in indulgences was in keeping with the general acceptance of money transactions in the realm of spiritual offices. This was a slow growth out of the notions of merit and satisfaction that were associated with penance. Indulgences, or exemptions from penance, were now scarcely at all a factor in the cure of souls; they were prized as a means of revenue to the papacy. They were peddled about by the pope's agents, often with the help of intermediaries. Prince Albert of Brandenburg, though under canonical age, purchased and obtained the important sees of Magdeburg, Halberstadt, and Mainz, obtaining for a large fee a dispensation from Leo X. This business put him very heavily in debt to the banking house of Fugger. To pay off this debt the simoniacal prince-archbishop entered into a bargain with the curia by which it was agreed to launch a sale of indulgences in Germany. It was announced that the funds raised would go to the Pope for building purposes; actually half of the proceeds was earmarked for a refund to the Fugger, whose agent was at hand to count the coin when the Dominican Tetzel, a loud-voiced salesman, had drawn the customers by his amazing claims. The official church was so implicated in this disgraceful deal with the bankers and the prelate that it was in no position to exercise upon Tetzel's selling talk any moral or theological restraint. The case is notorious because of Luther's protest, but it is by no means unique. In this matter of indulgences an inveterate abuse had become rooted and flourished without check in the pre-Reformation church.

THE PAPACY DEFEATS CONCILIAR REFORM

But it may be said: These evils were admittedly old, and the church had survived them. Why now make them the occasion of a separation? That the conditions were of long standing may be taken as an argument for a fourteenth-century Reformation rather than against a sixteenth-century one. I have already referred to earlier reform efforts. Apart from sectarian movements the greatest of these was the attempted conciliar reform. The primary aim of the conciliarists was to transform the structure of government in the church. They frankly attempted to reduce the absolute monarchy of the papacy to a limited monarchy. The supreme authority was to be vested in a representative general council. The movement developed its force under the leadership of university scholars during the period of the papal schism. The church was divided between contending popes, and the Council of Constance (1414-18) succeeded in the difficult task of reuniting the parts. This great parliament of the medieval church declared in strong language the conciliar principle: The Pope was to be subject to the general representative council, and such a council was to be summoned once every ten years. One of the slogans of the conciliar party was "reform of the church in head and members." Before the Council of Constance closed, it framed a somewhat extensive program of reform to cure the prevalent abuses and restore discipline. But by reuniting the papacy in Martin V it unintentionally gave to that Pope and his successors a new opportunity to assert monarchical power, which they exploited with enthusiasm. The popes set themselves against the conciliar plan of government. It was their bête noire. In the 1430's the Council of Basle reaffirmed in heightened language the declarations of Constance. But it was beaten by Pope Eugenius IV and by its own lack of sound leadership. Pius II execrated the doctrines of conciliarism (1459), and all who raised their voices in support of these ideas were marked for the enmity of the papacy. Yet the medieval dream of a representative system of government in the church did not entirely fade away. To many who grieved under ecclesiastical misrule the chief or the only hope of redress still lay in the possibility of a new series of general councils. Conciliar reform remained the theme of a number of propagandist writings. In the last year of his life Savonarola sent out an appeal to the princes of Europe to assemble a council in order to chasten Alexander VI. It is scarcely possible to see how else a general reform could have been undertaken. To the eve of the Reformation there were still a few

11

undiscouraged conciliarists. But Julius II gave them good reason for discouragement. Under pressure from France, Julius summoned a council—the Fifth Lateran—in 1512. The councils held earlier to reform the papacy had met, not in Rome, but in Pisa, Constance, and Basle. Julius and Leo X kept control of the Lateran Council, and in sessions spread over five years it accomplished no serious work of reform. A few months after its close in 1517 Luther posted his Ninety-five Theses.

The moral condition of the papacy in the fifteenth century is well known and scarcely any longer in dispute. The papacy was threatened by political forces; but, as Burckhardt points out, its greatest danger at the end of the century consisted in the characters of the popes themselves. If the age had been favored with a series of saintly or even of spiritually and morally competent popes, the whole situation would have been different. Between 1294 and 1566 Rome had no pontiff who later qualified for canonization. The lives of a number of the Renaissance popes were abhorrent to the saints, and this condition was not amended until staggering blows had been dealt by the Reformers. In its efforts to meet the rising strength of secular governments the papacy more and more took on the character of a secular state. It had territorial possessions, it formed and shifted alliances, it engaged in wars, and these and like matters became its main concerns. By Machiavelli it is frankly judged in accordance with the success or failure of its use of the methods of Realpolitik. He might have defended this basis of judgment by the fact that it accords with the manifest motives of such pontiffs as Alexander VI and Julius II, in whose days he lived and wrote.

Moral Bankruptcy of the Papal Church

It is true, of course, that the older affirmation of divine right—absolute power (*plenitudo potestatis*) in temporal as well as spiritual affairs—had not been withdrawn. The popes of an earlier age had assumed a role more pretentious, perhaps, than that of any series of rulers in the history of the world. It is thus not surprising that the later ones refused to be humbled by the councils. They still thought of their office as one of unlimited, divinely given power. But there was no blinking the fact that this power was impaired by circumstances. It had always been in actuality very much less than it claimed to be. Popes who made the loftiest claims (the thirteenth-century Innocents and Gregorys) were unable to control the turbulent forces of the world. There was no era of real social and political unification under the popes. There was no halcyon interval of European peace under papal sway, in the thirteenth century or later. When we speak of the Hundred Years' War, which ended in the middle of the fifteenth century, it is necessary to recall that every year of this period of history was a year of war. From Boniface VIII in 1300 to Alexander VI in 1500 war was always being waged in some considerable area of Europe.

But now the claim of universal dominion seemed more and more unreal. The popes could not command the rulers; at best they could form with them concordats by which power was shared. Amid a perpetual play of bargaining diplomacy, punctuated by moments of mutual defiance, these agreements were frequently violated and frequently altered. The popes were not men of vision for the church or for society. Save for a faint attempt to revive crusading against the Turk they did nothing to enlist loyalty to great causes and offered to their age no commanding idea that could challenge wonder and devotion. If men wondered at their deeds, it was at their misdeeds.

It is fair to observe here that the Renaissance popes were morally average men of the privileged classes in the Italy of their day. A strange moral indifference pervaded the Italian Renaissance. One might better call it a moral incapacity. A wit in Scotland said, in doggerel verse, of Cardinal Beaton, the persecutor of the Protestant Wishart, that of theology he knew "no more than does blind Allan of the moon." The comparison of a blind man's awareness of the moon might be applied to many of the gifted Italians of that age when we look for evidence of a moral consciousness in them. Not a few men with fine artistic or literary sensitiveness were morally inept or obtuse. Some were street brawlers or roués whose personal and social behavior seems never to have been disturbed by the promptings of a conscience. The unmoved tones (except where they recite their own grievances) in which writers like Platina, Infessura, Burchardus, and Machiavelli record the absorption of the popes in war and diplomacy and the enormities of their lives reflects this widespread vacancy of moral judgment. Though not universal, this condition is a mark of the Italian society with which the papacy was environed. If it cannot be fully explained, it may itself help to explain the irresponsible conduct of the popes. They did not fear, because they did not encounter, public moral indignation or private rebuke. There was no Nathan to confront David in his sin. In Rome no man censured the popes on high moral or religious grounds. Voices of rebuke and of complaint seemed faint and far away.

When, in 1450, Gascoigne wrote (as noted above) : "Oh, what good might be done by a good pope!" the reigning pope was Nicholas V, the least blameworthy of the series but without zeal except for books. His successor—Calixtus III (Alfonso Borgia) —on one day appointed two of his nephews to the cardinalate. Of these Rodrigo Borgia was forty years later to be Pope Alexander VI. Pius II was a humanist of easy morals, who as Pope tried in vain to organize a crusade. Paul II is depicted by Platina, who was tortured in the Pope's prison, as a cruel tyrant. There is no doubt of his love of fine food and fine jewels, and of processions in which his tall form appeared to advantage. He violated his election promise to hold a reforming council, but he avoided simony and nepotism in his own appointments. Sixtus IV, of the Rovere family, a well-educated Franciscan, appointed as cardinals his nephews Pietro Riario, a notorious spendthrift, adventurer, and gambler, and Giuliano della Rovere, who was later to be Pope Julius II. Innocent VIII gave his efforts largely to the task of providing for his numerous children. He created new offices by the hundred in order to sell them.

It was in Alexander VI (1492-1503) that the nadir of moral degradation was reached. By lavish bribery of influential cardinals he won the papal election. He sold twelve cardinal's hats for ten thousand florins each. He doted on his handsome, infamous sons and daughter. Of his sons Cesare gained a certain ascendancy over his father and became celebrated for his crimes, his conquests, and his treasons. Alexander disported himself amid scenes of splendor, indecent festivities, and deeds of turpitude that attest a cynical abandonment of moral and spiritual ideals. Hilaire Belloc, who minimizes the offenses and magnifies the virtues of other popes, remarks of Alexander that his conduct "shook the edifice of papal prestige" and that his eleven years of office "were of lamentable and permanent effect." Our reference to the councils has already shown the failure of Julius II to meet the need of reform. It was not without significance that Alexander and Julius bore as popes the names respectively of the Macedonian and of the Roman conqueror. Julius was called the "pontiff terrible" because of his reliance upon the sword. He had other faults a-plenty; but he "devoted himself," says Ranke, "to the gratification of that innate love of war and conquest which was indeed the ruling passion of his life." After him Leo X (1513-21), a son of Lorenzo de' Medici, "enjoyed the papacy" without caring to reform it and promoted members of the Medici clan. One of his nephews, though by illegitimacy disqualified from holy orders, became Pope Clement VII. But Leo's successors stand within the Reformation era.

Prior to the rise of Protestantism there was no real promise of a regeneration of the Western church. From papal election to papal election good men had waited for it in vain. The doors to reform were guarded by ecclesiastical careerists, who drew their livings and their power from the church's degradation. The seekers of reform were cheated and perplexed and well-nigh discouraged. The services were performed and the processions and apparel of the clergy were maintained, but spiritual vitality was so low as to make these things seem unreal. It was widely felt that something ominous was in the air. "O priests and friars," exclaimed Savonarola in 1497, "ye whose evil example has entombed this people in the sepulcher of ceremonial, I tell you, this sepulcher will burst asunder; for Christ will revive his Church in his spirit." Egidius of Viterbo, general of the Augustinians, at the opening of the Lateran Council in 1512 cried out in apostrophe to Christ: "Hear . . . into what a deep sea of evils the Church thou hast founded by thy blood has fallen." His prayer that this council might bring "the healing of all Christendom" remained unanswered. In the same year Lefèvre d'Etaples said to young Farel, "The church will be renovated, and you will live to see it." "Without doubt," wrote a

14

very different observer—Machiavelli, "either ruin or a scourge is now hanging over" the church. When the indulgence sales were being pushed in Germany in 1517, Erasmus wrote to his friend John Colet, "The court of Rome has lost all sense of shame." During these years apocalyptic agitators were traversing northern Italy with cries of alarm. That strange mania the dance of death was another popular reaction to the leaderless confusion of religion. By many tokens the time was ripe for sweeping change. It was the end of an era.

CATHOLIC REFORM FINALLY A RESULT OF THE REFORMATION

The turn toward moral seriousness in the papacy came with Paul III and his commission of newly appointed cardinals to report on the situation and propose reforms. Their report (*Advice for Reforming the Church*, 1537) is evidence enough that nothing substantial had yet been done to remove abuses. Some modern advocates of the papacy have gravely adopted what is really the cynical argument of Boccaccio's Jew. The papacy, they say, must have been divinely maintained, else it would have perished through its abominations. But if it was from God that it received a new lease of life, surely a secondary agency was employed in its restoration. There can be no doubt that the new spirit of gravity and responsibility that made possible the Counter Reformation was, in large measure at least, a response to the Reformation itself. Burckhardt's remark is justified: "The moral salvation of the papacy was due to its mortal enemies."

At the beginning of this discourse I called attention to some of the more favorable aspects of the pre-Reformation age. Professor Brunner insists that the Church is not an institution but only *has* an institution. It is a fact that no disorder of the institution can destroy Christianity itself. To destroy it men would have to efface every record that it had ever been. There was still in 1500 a great deal of Christianity upon which a reformer might count if once he could get a hearing. To appreciate this we should have to look at some of the confused flock of heretical sects persecuted by the Inquisition. We should have to see the practical service to their fellows of the men of the New Devotion in the Netherlands. We should have to observe the efforts to reform the Augustinians and the continued faithfulness of the small Carthusian order, which was so often pointed out as the exception to general monastic laxity. We should have to study the work of pastors and preachers distinguished for their faithfulness such as John Geiler of Kaisersberg (d. 1510), who through many years exercised a fruitful pastorate in Strassburg. We should have to read the sermons of John Colet, the *Enchiridion* of Erasmus, and his Introduction to the text of the New Testament. We should have to inquire into religion in family life, where, in some instances at least, we have evidence of careful instruction in those elementary documents the creed, the Lord's Prayer, and the Ten Commandments. We should need to examine some of the primers of instruction and little books of piety which were spread fairly widely among the literate lay people at the beginning of the age of printing. We should have to recognize that the possession, in however defective translations, of the vernacular Scriptures, by members of tenacious and active sects such as the Lollards and Waldenses exemplified a deep and wide craving for access to the Bible in the people's speech. The laity received from the ecclesiastics little encouragement to hope that they would be trusted to read the Scriptures for themselves. In this respect the attitude of the clergy was wholly opposed to that of the Church Fathers, who had encouraged free lay reading of the sacred books. But it ought to be remembered that the medieval church had never repudiated the authority of Scripture. By the appeal to this authority, which all Christians recognized, the Reformers, when once they resolved to defy the hierarchical opposition to reform, were able to by-pass it and to reach the willing ears of the people. It is important, too, that the northern humanists provided them with the tools and techniques of biblical scholarship.

As for theology it was not very sure of itself or capable of stanch defense of the traditional orthodoxy in which the doctrine of works and merit found support. Thomas Aquinas was a thinker of such stature as to be of importance for all later centuries. But in his own century men assailed his system. Soon it largely gave place to the widely variant teachings of Duns and later to those of Ockham. Such stout Augustinians as Thomas Bradwardine and Gregory of Rimini set the stage for that revival of Augustinianism which culminated in Luther. Theologically, then, the situation was insecure and, in some degree, inviting to the Protestant emphasis on grace and faith.

Such matters as these deserve thoughtful attention, since they offer partial explanation of the fact that an all-out effort to revive the church in defiance of the papacy was able to achieve incalculably important results. Political factors, too—national and territorial interests and taxation grievances—went far to condition the development of the Reformation. While not in itself nationalistic the movement fell into the mold set for it by the national and subnational states.

But the statement that the Reformers chose not to work within the church is an ambiguous one. They worked within that church which consisted of the baptized Christian people. They retained the parishes and, where possible, the priests. When bishops invited Luther's advice on the reform of the church in East Prussia, an episcopal Lutheran church was the result. A comparable development took place in Sweden and in England. Calvinist writers, too, freely admitted that episcopacy was not necessarily to be effaced from all churches that cast off the papacy. Where "God used the bishops" for reform, wrote Pierre du Moulin in 1658, "the name and rank of bishop have remained." The earlier conceptions of the conciliarists were in large part revived with the Protestant movement. In the year following the close of the futile Fifth Lateran Council, Martin Luther, using the very language of Constance, called for a free Christian council. He repeated his appeal in 1520, and (as I have elsewhere shown) he and his followers reiterated the demand many times in after years. Protestantism everywhere took on a conciliar as opposed to a monarchical form of organization. All these facts mean that the Reformers worked "within" as much of the church as they could get to join in reform. They assembled under their banners the vital forces in the tradition.

ANY OTHER TYPE OF REFORMATION IMPOSSIBLE

There are those who will say: Admitting that reform was needed is not the same as admitting that the Reformation was needed. The historical Reformation was needlessly rough and radical. They may so revolt from its roughness as to affirm that the cure was worse than the disease. People who take that view have perhaps not adequately diagnosed the disease. But many would have preferred an Erasmian to a Lutheran reformation. Erasmus appealed especially to the academic mind. A reform led by him would have been educational, gentle, and lighted by a gay humanist wit. But was an Erasmian reform a possibility? Erasmus rendered a great service to the Reformers, and he has been called with some reason a Reformer. I am not one of those who would minimize the religious significance of Erasmus. But Erasmus had no access to the common people either as a writer or as an orator. His table talk was in Latin. His appeal was to the well-educated minority. His message could only reach the people by intermediaries, as in part it did when his learned admirers, such as Melanchthon and Zwingli, became Reformers. The Protestant Reformers were men who had the rare combination of gifts that enabled them to lead both scholars and uneducated lay people. What Erasmus and his circle could of themselves bring to reform the church was too little and too late to ensure a smooth and orderly reformation. His English friend Colet had made a brave effort—he had a real concern for the people and sometimes employed the vernacular—but in 1517 he was old and sick and discouraged by harsh treatment from his bishop. Thomas More was to show a fear of the popular use of the Bible and, finally, to affirm with his life the cause of papal unity in Europe, as if the papacy had not sufficiently shown that it was incapable of bringing unity. An Erasmian reform? Would it have been better if John Wesley had settled down after 1738 in Oxford as a professor of theology, diffusing the light of God's love from a professorial chair and by means of Latin writings? He might have succeeded well in that role. But the Methodist movement would have been postponed a generation; and, rightly or wrongly, Wesley felt the need to be too urgent for such a course.

But these historical "ifs" may betray us into unprofitable speculations. Any number of varieties of reform are imaginable, but most of these varieties were in the circumstances precluded. Indubitably the Reformation was in part made by the psychological personalities of the Reformers, and it would have been different if they had been different. But in any case it would have required leaders who had conviction and

17

unhesitating determination—men who would take risks, even the risk of being rough and abrupt.

All in all, then, I think we may be assured that a reformation was needed, and that something a good deal like the historic Reformation was the only possible way out of the morass. This is not to say that the Reformers were always in the right or always admirable, or that Protestantism has always been good and beautiful. The Reformers might have made a better Reformation. The Protestant churches have their sins and need ever new reformations and reformers. Christianity is always finding ways of renewing itself. It would be sad indeed if we should study the pre-Reformation church merely to justify the Reformation. Its abiding lesson is that of a warning example of ecclesiastical power without the indwelling Spirit; from which condition, in every church, in every generation, Good Lord, deliver us!

PROTESTANTISM AND THE PRIMITIVE CHURCH

MARTIN RIST

SINCE the Christianity of the first two or three centuries and the Protestantism of modern times are two separate movements, we should be scrupulous lest we commit the historical error of telescoping the two, overlooking the intervening centuries; lest we be guilty of modernizing the one or antiquing the other.

On the other hand, there are marked similarities, which are more than coincidental. Different as the first century in the Mediterranean world was from the sixteenth century in Western Europe, these two historic periods, which produced such significant religious movements as primitive Christianity and Protestantism, have a great deal in common. For the spread of Hellenism throughout the Mediterranean in the earlier period is analogous to the rise of the Renaissance in Europe in the later. Nor is this surprising, for the Renaissance was to a considerable extent a conscious and deliberate revival of the ancient Greco-Roman culture and learning. In both periods of enlightenment— the early and the late—these similarities may be noted: an adventurous, creative spirit; an emphasis upon man and his needs; a stress upon freedom and individualism; a certain disregard for tradition and old landmarks; a desire for greater culture and learning; and a sincere quest for religious values and satisfactions. Just as Hellenism prepared the way for Christianity in regions bordering on the Mediterranean and was to some extent mirrored in evolving Christianity, in much the same way the Renaissance was a forerunner of Protestantism, being reflected by it. Indeed, it has been truly said that the Reformation was, in a great degree, the Renaissance as it was transformed when it reached the Germanic lands.

Furthermore, there was a conscious attempt on the part of the Reformers to return to the beliefs and patterns of the early Church in their revolt against Rome. Some of the early doctrines and practices, which had survived in one way or another through the centuries, were stripped of the encrustations they had accumulated and were given greater emphasis by the Reformers. In other instances the Reformers deliberately imitated the early Church, which they accepted as a norm. So the influence of the first Christians, and particularly of Paul, who became the apostle of the Protestants, as he had previously been of the Gentiles, is both evident and understandable.

All this helps to account for the admitted similarities between Protestantism and primitive Christianity. It also serves to explain why Protestantism, in several respects, more faithfully reflects the early Church than does Catholicism. On the other hand, we should, in all

19

honesty, admit that in some particulars Catholicism is the closer to the Christianity of the first centuries; that there are marked differences between the primitive Church and any modern form of the Christian religion; and that neither the presence nor the absence of a given religious belief or practice in the early Church is an absolute criterion of its validity and worth. We may be guided by the first Christians, but we are under no obligation to be controlled by them.

THE ROMAN AUTHORITY

With these preliminary considerations before us we should note that Protestantism was basically an attempt to redefine the concept of ecclesiastical authority. It was in this area that the major conflict with Rome developed, and it was here that the greatest contrast between Protestantism and Catholicism is to be seen. Following the triumph of the Church in the reign of Constantine—a triumph that in some respects was a Pyrrhic victory—Catholic Christianity became more and more closely integrated and organized and increasingly uniform in its liturgy and doctrines. During the Middle Ages, Latin Christianity in the West, with which we are primarily concerned, developed an amazingly uniform and authoritarian ecclesiasticism.

This religious authoritarianism, essentially totalitarian in its scope, was founded on a variety of instrumentalities. It was dependent, but only in part, on the acceptance of the Bible as the authoritative, revealed Word of God. But, even more, it was posited upon (1) a continuing revelation as this was expressed in the Fathers, in the creeds and dogmas of the Church, and in the decrees of councils and popes as these developed during the centuries; (2) upon an elaborate sacramental system, which controlled each Christian from the cradle to the grave and beyond; (3) upon a hierarchy set apart from the rest of the Christians by the sacrament of ordination, claiming divine authority through the mystery of apostolic succession, and possessing the power to administer or withhold the sacraments, through which salvation was obtained. In addition monasticism, paralleling the secular priesthood, added greatly to the control of the church through its various activities. Chief of all, the bishop of Rome had evolved into the Pope of all Christendom, the lineal descendant of the apostle Peter, upon whom the Church had purportedly been founded, and to whom the keys of heaven and hell had reputedly been entrusted. He claimed —and few had the wisdom or temerity to challenge him—to be the overlord of all Christendom, the vicegerent of Christ on earth, an absolute monarch independent of and superior to all earthly authorities, both spiritual and temporal.

Here, indeed, was a totalitarian superstate that actually embraced all of Latin Christianity and most of Western Europe under its theory of absolute control and authority. It was against this totalitarian authoritarianism that the Reformers rebelled, with leaders, princes, and laity united in a common cause (if from different motivations), giving expression to the spirit of the Renaissance, to the spirit of freedom, and, as they maintained, to the spirit of the early Church. Protestantism, then, was initially a revolt, a protest, and, as such, a negation. But the Reformers did not live wholly upon negations; on the contrary, they balanced them with positive affirmations and creative contributions. Moreover—and this is not always recognized—they retained more of Catholicism than they rejected, preserving that which they considered most valuable; for, after all, they were Reformers, not revolutionaries.

In this they were faithful to the attitude of Jesus and the early Christians. Jesus did not come to destroy the Law and the Prophets but to reinterpret and enrich them. Likewise, while his first followers criticized, denounced, and rejected certain aspects of Judaism, they preserved more than they repudiated, and upon this base they made their own positive contributions. The same attitude prevailed as Christianity became increasingly a religion of the Hellenistic world. While many of the views and practices of paganism were justly renounced as utterly sinful and idolatrous, much was retained and incorporated into evolving Christianity. Paul, for example, reflects the influence of Hellenistic religion and thought—an influence that becomes more marked in later Christian leaders of the second and third centuries—for example, Justin Martyr, Tertullian, Clement of Alexandria, and Origen. Clement, indeed, asserted that Plato spoke with some degree of divine inspiration, thereby preparing the ground for the appropriation of Platonism by Christian theology. It is this ceaseless process of testing and re-evaluation, of rejection and preservation, of improvement and innovation, which keeps a religion dynamic, vital, and meaningful.

THE BIBLE AS A NORM OF CRITICISM

With respect to the external authority of Scripture (as translated into the vernacular so that all might read) the Reformers restored it to the prominent position it enjoyed in the primitive church. For early Christianity, in the main, was bibliocentric, at first accepting the Jewish Bible as the inviolate word of God, his absolute will for mankind, and later on, toward the end of the second century, adding certain approved Christian writings as of equal authority with the Jewish canon. A certain flexibility, however, was provided by the use of allegorical interpretation, whereby all Scripture could be used "in teaching, in reproof, in correcting faults, and in training in uprightness" (II Timothy 3:16).

So with the Reformers: When they rejected papal authority, the Bible became the absolute, infallible word and revelation of God, the complete and perfect guide and norm of Christian belief and practice. That which could be shown to have biblical sanction was accepted; that which was nonbiblical might be rejected. However, as in the early Church, absolute rigidity was avoided by "modernizing" obscure or embarrassing passages through the means of allegorical interpretation, each Christian being theoretically permitted to rely on his private judgment. In extreme cases an entire book, like James, might be called non-apostolic, hence of dubious validity. This appeal to the authority of Scripture, which was typical of Protestantism, was in a real sense an appeal to the early Church; for the New Testament was the product of the early Christians and embodied their views. Moreover, not a little of the interpretation of Old Testament passages by the early Fathers, as well as their method, was appropriated by the exegetes of the Reformation as normative.

This elevation of the Bible to the position of supremacy was a master stroke; for in resorting to it in their rejection of ecclesiastical authority the Reformers were invoking an objective control, which even the sacerdotalism they were renouncing accepted, and which Christians in general were able to understand and appreciate as an absolute, objective norm, especially since it was soon made available in vernacular translations. As has been so often said, an infallible pope was replaced by an infallible Bible, which was indeed a significant change for the better.

Because of the passing of the emergency that caused the elevation of the Bible in the first place, but more definitely attributable to the research and study of generations of Christian scholars since the Reformation, the Bible has lost much of its pre-eminence as the complete and infallible authority for the Church and for the individual Christian, though at present there are indications in Protestantism of a return to a bibliocentric authority and all that this implies. The current ascendancy of apocalypticism in many areas of the Church, the rise of numerous Pentecostal and Holiness sects, the rapid spread of neo-orthodoxy (or Barthianism), and the revival of the demonology of the New Testament as an explanation of evil are disturbing trends in this direction. For while we should use the Scripture as a guide, mentor, and tutor, as Paul himself stated, we become involved in grave difficulties when we make ourselves subject to it as a complete, absolute, and infallible norm of belief and conduct.

The Break With the Hierarchy

In their resort to the supreme authority of the Bible the Reformers forged a potent weapon, despite its limitations, which they used in their repudiation of papal claims. For, notwithstanding the Catholic appeal to Matthew 16:17-19 and John 21:15-19, the Reformers ably contended that there was no scriptural basis for the papal office. They cited Church history as evidence that there was no pope at all in the early Church; that, in fact, no bishop was considered superior to any other bishop, all being thought of as equal. Thus, both Scripture and the primitive Church supported the Protestants in their rejection of the papacy and its grandiose claims. However, the Roman Church has never receded from its pretensions regarding the power of the papacy, and we should be more concerned than we are about current attempts to restore some of its lost temporal prestige and power.

The Reformers also cited the New Testament and the early Church

22

as authority for renouncing the entire Catholic hierarchy of cardinals, archbishops, bishops, and parish priests set apart and elevated by the sacrament of ordination, which stamped them with special powers and prerogatives as the reputed successors of the apostles. They showed that this hierarchy did not exist in the early Church and had little, if any, New Testament precedent, but was the end product of a long historical process.

In this they were right, for the first Christian communities lacked any formal organization, partly because the movement was new, partly because they were guided by the spirit, and partly because the end of this age was expected momentarily. Paul, even, experienced difficulty in asserting his control over some of the churches he himself had founded. Later, when bishops and elders, with the minor clergy, became an accepted feature, there was still no organized hierarchy, claiming ecumenical authority. Instead each local church or group of churches was practically autonomous, electing its own clergy and administering its own affairs. Bishops and elders of important churches, like Ignatius of Antioch and Clement and Victor of Rome, might admonish or advise other churches; but they could not order or command them. Still later one of the striking features of Christianity was the independence of the bishops. This reflected the independence of the local churches. Even some of the Church Fathers like Cyprian, who were supporters of an ecumenical Christianity, maintained the equality of all bishops.

The congregational type of organization, with its independence, facilitated local variations in belief and practice and accordingly greatly encouraged the rise of heterodoxy and heresy. Hence, the concept of a catholic, ecumenical church, with an organized clergy supporting a somewhat uniform body of doctrine and liturgy, was developed by the end of the second century to counteract the rise of heresies and sects that threatened the existence of the Church from within at a time when persecution was endangering it from without. But this early connectional organization, which conceivably saved the church in a time of grave danger, was far removed from the sacerdotalism of the later centuries. Some of the Protestant groups, like the Anabaptists, attempted to restore the congregationalism of primitive Christianity, whereas Calvin, going to the other extreme, succeeded in erecting an authoritarian theocracy at Geneva. But the majority wisely sought a *via media* between the extremes of authoritarianism and local autonomy. Even Luther, despite his emphasis upon the priesthood of all believers, saw the necessity for adopting a middle course—a view also exemplified in our Methodist connectionalism.

APOSTOLIC SUCCESSION AND MONASTICISM

In one major respect, at least, the Catholic Church had the support of the early Church—namely, in its reliance on the doctrine of apostolic succession. In the primitive Church the apostles had the first place. Paul, in establishing his authority, averred that he too was one of the apostles, though born out of time. In the pseudo-Pauline work called Ephesians the Church was assertedly built upon the apostles and the prophets as their foundation, while Clement of Rome and Ignatius of Antioch state the belief even more explicitly. It is also basic to the Church organization outlined in the Pastoral Epistles, which must be dated around the middle of the second century. By the end of the century the theory was more fully developed by leaders like Irenaeus and Tertullian, forming the basis of authority for the Catholic Church, which had its real beginning at this time. In keeping with this concept it was claimed that the chief churches of the orthodox (or Catholic) Christians had been founded by apostles; that their bishops were the direct spiritual descendants of the apostles, inheriting their purported authority; that the Catholic creeds and church orders had originated with the apostles; and that each writing included in the New Testament canon was reputedly composed by one of the apostolic group. Accordingly, through the application of this doctrine, early Catholicism become welded into a more compact, homogeneous organization far better equipped to withstand persecution from without and to counteract schisms and heresies within. Nevertheless, despite the effectiveness of this doctrine and its sanction by the early Church, we find ourselves in complete agreement with those Protestant churches which have abandoned it as a religious fiction that served its purpose in its day but has no validity for us.

The monastic system, which developed so remarkably during the Middle Ages, had great social, economic, philanthropic, and cultural as well as religious significance. Owing their primary allegiance to the Pope, the great orders had become important agencies in maintaining his prestige and power and in controlling heresy. Permeating the whole of society with their manifold activities, they touched the lives of most individuals in one way or another. There was much that was good in the monastic system; but for the Reformers—and we accept their judgment—the evil outweighed the good. Consequently, monasticism was disavowed and banished by the Protestants and, with it, the enforced celibacy of the secular clergy, which had been patterned after the monastic vow of chastity. In this they had the support of the primitive Church; for Christian monasticism, as such, did not appear until the third and fourth centuries in Egypt, with Anthony and Pachomius as the traditional founders, one of the eremitic, the other of the cenobitic type. Once begun, it spread with amazing rapidity throughout the Christian world, both East and West, and played an important role in the medieval period. However, we should note that the ascetic ideal, which is basic to monasticism, was not wholly absent from the early Church. While Jesus probably accepted the nonascetic, Jewish norm "of nothing too much," Paul and certain other early Christians inclined toward a limited asceticism. Indeed, certain Gnostics and other spiritists went to extremes, thereby laying the ground for the organized asceticism that followed. But the main body of Christians in the early

24

Church either rejected asceticism entirely or, like Paul, accepted a limited form of voluntary discipline and self-denial—an attitude we may well encourage in this day of comparative luxury and easy living.

THE SACRAMENTS

Logically, it would seem, the Reformers, with their emphasis upon an inward, subjective religious authority, should have discarded all external ceremonials, including the seven sacraments of the church; for it was through the custody of these sacraments that the hierarchy made their control over individual Christians immediately effective. To most people excommunication was a fearful punishment, for it excluded them from the benefits of salvation inherent in the various sacraments. Nevertheless, the Reformers retained two of these sacraments—baptism and the Eucharist—as essential to salvation; for these two had the undoubted sanction of the New Testament and of the early Church; while Luther desired to keep penance, though with certain modifications and reservations.

However, the sacraments retained were given a new interpretation in that they were not effective apart from the faith of the recipient. Luther stated the case with reference to baptism: "So faith clings to the water and believes that baptism confers salvation and life, not through the water (as has been stated), but because it embodies God's word and command and because his name is attached to it." In this Luther and other Reformers did not differ materially from Paul, who considered both baptism and faith as necessary for salvation. But Zwingli went still further in emphasizing the subjective rather than the objective character of baptism, which for him was only an "initiative sign," like a badge, symbolizing "that we are to conform our life to the rule of Christ." This does not differ greatly from Josephus' statement to the effect that the baptism of John the Baptist was not a means by which sin was removed from the candidate but a sign that he had previously repented of his sins.

As for the Eucharist, it was stripped of the doctrine of the Mass, which made it a repetition of the redeeming sacrifice on the Cross. This sacrificial view of the Eucharist was stated explicitly by Cyprian, the bishop of Carthage, who died a martyr in A.D. 258; and it may possibly be inferred in Hippolytus, who lived somewhat earlier. Some even discover the concept in Paul, who wrote, "For as often as ye eat this bread, and drink this cup, ye do shew the Lord's death till he come" (I Corinthians 11:26). On the other hand, Harnack and other scholars maintain that there is no clear indication of the doctrine of sacrifice, which became so prominent in the Mass, until the time of Cyprian, and that the Reformers had the sanction of the early Church in removing this accretion.

Despite their rejection of the sacrificial Mass most of the Reformers retained the Eucharist as an objective sacrament. Although they repudiated the doctrine of transubstantiation, they affirmed the real pres-

25

ence of the body and blood of Christ in the elements. Accordingly the communicant who partook of them by faith obtained forgiveness of his sins and became one body with Christ and with the saints in heaven and on earth. Thus, these Reformers were faithful to a Christian tradition and practice that go back to very early times—to Ignatius, Clement I, and Paul.

Zwingli, however, in his treatment of the Eucharist was consistent with his attitude toward baptism; for he affirmed that the bread and the wine merely *signified* the body and blood of Christ so that partaking of these elements can only *symbolize* the appropriation by faith of the salvation secured for man by Christ's atoning death.

In any case the Reformers, despite their reservations, modified or abandoned the sacraments to such an extent that they undermined the entire sacramental system of the church, thereby destroying the authoritatorian sacerdotalism that was dependent on it. While some may feel that in some respects they did not go far enough, even so we are forever indebted to them for freeing us, as they did, from sacramentalism and the authority inherent in it.

PREACHING AND WORSHIP

The decreased importance of the sacraments and the accompanying liturgy had another positive effect, for it served to restore the sermon to its earlier position of prominence. Preaching had been an important feature from the beginning. It was through preaching that both John the Baptist and Jesus had announced their message of the kingdom of God. It was through the preaching of the good news that Christianity was proclaimed throughout the Mediterranean world by the apostles and other early missionaries. Following the pattern of the synagogue service, the sermon became an integral and significant part of Christian worship; but with the increase of sacramentalism and liturgy in the Middle Ages it was relegated to a secondary position. However, preaching did not die out but was revived, from time to time, by monastic groups like the Dominicans and the Franciscans and by individual preachers of renown like Wyclif, Eckhart, Tauler, and Hus. Indeed, both Luther and Zwingli were popular as preachers before they attracted attention as Reformers. But it wasn't until the Reformation was under way that preaching in the vernacular regained its earlier position of importance in the worship service. It was through the effective use of this medium that the Reformers exerted their greatest influence over the masses. Despite this history of preaching there is a current tendency in Protestantism to minimize the sermon by subordinating it to an elaborate liturgy borrowed from the liturgical churches. We need much more form, order, and beauty in our church services, but it is a mistake to assume that we should provide this by imitating the high-church liturgy. What we introduce into our service of worship should be functional, reflecting the spirit and meeting the religious needs of our congregations.

In the early Church the worship service was conducted in the vernacular language of the worshipers, that all might participate with understanding. This practice was restored by the Reformers, who in this way made the church service more meaningful to those who were present. Also, the early Christians composed and sang new hymns which expressed the hopes and aspirations of this new religion. While this may be purely coincidental, it is noteworthy that the Reformers introduced many new hymns, which voiced the thought and spirit of the new movement.

MARY AND THE SAINTS

Turning to another subject, throughout the centuries the Catholic Church had acquired other bases for its authoritarianism, including the cultus of Mary and the saints, purgatory, the treasury of merits, indulgences, prayers for the dead, relics, and sacred shrines. None of these can be said to have been a characteristic of the early Church; they all had their rise and development in the Middle Ages. Nevertheless, the seeds of some of these ideas and practices were present in the early centuries. They needed only the proper soil and climate, such as were provided in the medieval period, to germinate and grow luxuriously.

For example, Mary is extolled to some extent in the birth narratives in Matthew and Luke. From this modest beginning she assumed an increasing importance in the second and third centuries. This foreshadowed her later exaltation. Similarly, according to Acts, the shadow of Peter and handkerchiefs and garments touched by Paul were used to heal the sick. Even more amazing supernatural powers were attributed to them and other of the apostles in the later apocryphal acts. Furthermore, the veneration accorded to confessors and martyrs during the periods of persecution anticipated their later elevation to sainthood. However, it was not until the Middle Ages that the cults of Mary and the saints, some of the latter substitutes for local deities, were fastened upon the Christian Church. In this period not only God but Christ as well had become so transcendent, so far removed from man and from earth, that Mary and the saints were increasingly appealed to as quasi-divinities, intercessors between man and his God.

The Reformers, who could find little or no sanction in the early Church for these accretions, did away with Mary and the saints as semi-divine intermediaries and helpers and eliminated not only the doctrine of their superabundant merits (but not those of Christ, it will be noted) but also rejected purgatory, indulgences, prayers for the dead, relics, and sacred sites. By doing so they struck another powerful blow against the sacerdotalism that had fattened upon these beliefs and the more-or-less superstitious practices associated with them.

THE POSITIVE SIDE

On the positive side the Reformers centered attention once more upon Christ as the one and only mediator between man and God.

thereby reviving the emphasis the early Christians had placed upon his mediating and saving work. This in turn stimulated Christological discussions and formulations such as characterized an earlier period in Christianity. However, as Dr. Bennett has noted in a recent number of *Religion in Life*, no wholly satisfactory statement concerning the person and work of Christ has as yet been formulated. We may not be ready to accept the Christology he proposes, but at least we may agree with him that here is an area of Christian doctrine which needs still further investigation and clarification.

These are among the more important points of contact between Protestantism and the primitive Church. They also mark the fundamental difference between Protestantism, a subjective religion of freedom, and Catholicism—an objective, authoritarian religion. The essential nature of Protestantism has been summed up by Luther in a simple but profound paradox, which is elaborated in his beautifully written treatise, dedicated to the Pope, *On Christian Liberty*: "A Christian man is a perfectly free lord of all, subject to none; a Christian man is a perfectly dutiful servant of all, subject to all."

This paradox, which Luther said comprised the essence of true religion, was professedly derived from Paul, who wrote to the Corinthians, "For though I am free from all, I have brought myself under bondage to all." This is indeed a characteristic teaching of Paul, who has perhaps stated it even more forcibly in his letter to the Galatians: "For you, brothers, have been called to freedom; only do not make your freedom an excuse for the flesh, but in love be slaves to one another."

Paul, we may recall, had proclaimed a religion of freedom from the externalities, ceremonials, and authoritarianism of traditional religion, not only Jewish but gentile as well. He had preached a subjective, inward religion, in which salvation was granted by God's grace to those who by faith confessed that Christ, whom God had raised from the grave, was Lord. However, all too many who gladly accepted this good news mistook the freedom Paul proclaimed for license and antinomianism, for freedom from personal and social duties and obligations. Accordingly these free souls, the radical *pneumatikoi*, or spiritists, were actually slaves to the flesh and its appetites, to immorality, idleness, and selfishness, even though they claimed to be controlled solely by the Spirit.

This was not the type of freedom Paul desired. In fact, he was greatly distressed by its evil manifestations in his churches. Instead he insisted that if those who claimed they were free were actually under the control of the indwelling Spirit, this would be shown by conduct marked by love, joy, peace, patience, kindness, goodness, faithfulness, meekness, and self-control. Further, they would be controlled not by self-interest but by the higher law summed up in the statement "You must love your neighbor as you do yourself." Accordingly, they would do nothing to cause their brothers to stumble. As members of one body they would be affectionate toward one another, preferring others to themselves. In conformity to this higher, inner law they would be bound to offer their bodies as living sacrifices, holy and acceptable to God.

Luther resolved this paradox of the mutual dependence of true freedom and obligation in much the same manner. Indeed, throughout his treatise he shows the influence of Paul. The Christian, he affirmed, was the freest of all men; was, in fact, his own priest, free from the sacerdotalism, ecclesiasticism, ceremonialism, and works of satisfaction which previously had enslaved him; for he has been justified through faith.

However, this newly acquired freedom places the Christian under greater bondage than ever before; for in his liberty he must empty himself, as Christ did, taking upon himself the form of a servant. Although good works do not make a man righteous, a righteous man is under obligation to perform good works. He will discipline his body, making it mirror the indwelling spirit and subject to its demands. Although, through faith, he has been created anew and restored, as it were, to Paradise, he must work, as Adam did before the fall, devoting the profits of his labors to the welfare of others; for a Christian lives not alone and for himself but for all men on earth. Nor is his liberty to be considered an end in itself; on the contrary, it is the means whereby he, in self-sacrifice and love, best serves others. Above all, the Christian is subject to the commandment of love. Luther also gives the practical advice that the Christian, although he is his own high priest, needs the ministrations of the church, which he should attend and support.

This, then, is the paradox of Protestantism as Luther derived it from Paul. In part it also corresponds to the familiar paradox in the Gospel that he who seeks to save his life will lose it, but he who loses his life will save it. It is the same paradox that today most clearly distinguishes Protestantism and differentiates it from a religion of authority, in which a minimum of individual freedom results in a minimum of personal responsibility.

In this paradoxical teaching is to be found both the strength and the weakness of Protestantism. In a democracy, the political analogy to Protestantism, extreme individualism weakens the nation and thereby destroys the freedom it guaranteed. But when the free citizens of a democracy assume the duties and responsibilities of their citizenship, not only do they become better citizens, but, also, they strengthen the State that granted freedom to them. So in Protestantism: There are those who accept the religious freedom it offers without assuming the corresponding obligations of self-discipline and of service to others. In their one-sidedness as Protestants they threaten the very existence of the religion that granted their freedom. But those who combine the exercise of their freedom with a deep sense of obligation not only develop into strong, full-rounded, integrated Christians, but, as such, strengthen Protestantism, making it a vital, dynamic religion, serving this present age. It is to the development of this type of Protestantism that we should devote and consecrate our lives and services as Protestant preachers and educators.

PROTESTANTISM BEFORE LUTHER

Edwin Prince Booth

In the strictly historical sense it is not possible to use the word "Protestantism" until the actual usage occurs in its own time and place. To do otherwise is to do violence to the actual. Yet, in the sense in which Protestantism is a culmination of historical movements, one has a right to seek out and study these movements as they are to be found prior to their coalescence. Protestantism is historically the result of a reform movement; it is not the reform movement itself. Yet lines of reform had been steadily evolving out of the climax of the medieval church, and many men had been working at the ideas and changes that finally came to life in the Protestant Reformation. In the normal law of organic life change is inevitable, and it seems that usually the most abrupt and decisive changes come at the moment when a given stage of development has reached its highest phase. All men who view the Middle Ages with affection are wont to contemplate with nostalgia the civilization of the thirteenth century. Then it was that the medieval Catholic idea had its full flowering. The names of Francis, Dominic, Innocent III, Thomas Aquinas, Dante, Mont St. Michel, and Chartres are sufficient to illustrate the exceptional beauty and strength of the century.

Yet, in true Hegelian fashion, the antithesis was even then at work, and every line of greatness carried its own decay within itself. Francis' mighty love of the Church Visible was accompanied by his own sovereign independence. Dante's matchless Latin was challenged by the mother tongue of Italy. Aquinas used the power of a vast and logical intellect to defend and explain the Church, but he trained a weapon as useful to opponent as to friend. The towering cathedrals inspired awe and reverence, but the contrast to the poverty of the homes of the people was a prelude to disaster. Innocent III carried papal power to "giddy and untenable heights," and the edifice swayed before the storm. Dominic wrought a uniformity among the heretics, but the fires he lighted in doing so were to burn for many a long day. And these are but symbols of the condition in every way of life. Vested interests of tremendous power existed in monastery and bishopric, but the "long, long patience of the plundered poor" could be heard by the waves of Lake Constance, calling for the Peasants' Revolt.

It is not possible to apply forms too readily to history, but it is the purpose of this present chapter to suggest that the roots of the Reformation be studied as thesis and antithesis, to which the Reformation itself will be seen as synthesis. The thesis is the medieval Catholic

Church in all its manifestations in society. The antithesis is the reform movement in all its branches, including the so-called Renaissance. Protestantism is a rejection of each in assimilating essentially true units of each into a new society. In a partial sense, but a very true one, the work of Ignatius Loyola belongs with that of Luther and Calvin, and the largest use of the word "Reformation" will include the traditionally called "Counter Reformation." Let us, then, consider the work of some men and movements, set in the centuries before Luther, tending toward the formation of the Protestant epoch.

THE CATHARI (ALBIGENSES)

By the year 1200 a widespread movement through northern Italy, southern France, and northern Spain (there were other branches in Bulgaria, et cetera, but we are dealing only with the Western church), known as the Cathari, had risen to challenge the power and the authority as well as the doctrinal truth of the church. The title comes from the Greek, meaning "pure." Much of the Catharist position showed little kinship with the lines of thought destined to win the future, but there was discernible a strong criticism of the wealth and power of the church, a rejection of the medieval sacraments in favor of baptism and the Lord's Supper, a high evaluation of the laity, the centrality of the sermon, and, most promising of all, a dependence on Scripture for authority. In this last they evidenced the coming of critical work by discriminating evaluations within Scripture. Nourished from the families of the poor, the movement was strongly anticlerical. Its many weaknesses must not be permitted to obscure the fact that its protest was popular, ethical, and biblical.

THE WALDENSES

Contemporary with the Cathari and with much more soundness of doctrine and practice, Peter Waldo carried out a great work, creating an organization that, alone of all Western medieval sects, still exists in unbroken organizational life. He was a rich merchant of Lyons, France, and was converted in 1176 by contemplation upon the words of Jesus: "If thou wilt be perfect, go, sell what thou hast, and give to the poor, and thou shalt have treasure in heaven; and come, follow me." He did just that. Taking the New Testament literally as his guide, he dressed and journeyed and preached as Jesus told his disciples to do. The better to understand it all, he used the New Testament in translation in French. Others joined him, and they applied to the third Lateran council (1179) for permission to preach. There the precedent was set which turned the tides of reforming strength away from the church, for Pope Alexander III refused the request. With his New Testament to support him Waldo saw this as the counsel of men against that of God. He continued to preach, and the church excommunicated him and his followers in 1184. The movement grew rapidly. It was based on many doctrines later to flower in Luther. Among the most important of

31

these was the rejection of masses, prayers for the dead, and the doctrine of purgatory, since these could not be found in the Scriptures. In positive realms the Waldenses stressed preaching by the laity, constant reading and memorization of the New Testament, and simple, ethical lives of piety and prayer.

The issue between the church and these two sects finally came to the stage of battle. After twenty years of "crusading" by the superior forces of the Roman Church and the French monarchy the Catharii were practically eliminated; but, hidden away in the valleys of the Italian and Swiss Alps, communities of Waldensians rode out the wars and operate today as one of the acknowledged branches of the Protestant church.

MARSILIUS OF PADUA AND OTHERS

The church suffered severe setbacks in the course of the fourteenth century. It is enough to recall the terrible period of the great schism, which followed, with an irony almost unparalleled in church history, immediately upon the *Unam Sanctam* of Boniface VIII. In this document stands the highest claim the papacy ever made for supremacy over Church and State. Yet within a decade the Church was captive to the State and rent asunder with internal schism. Against this black background one sees bursts of protesting light in the work of Dante, John of Paris, Catharine of Siena, Marsilius of Padua, and Petrarch. The *Defensor Pacis* of Marsilius is a worthy parent of Protestantism. He sees the whole people as the basis of all power; sees them organized as citizens in a State and as believers in a Church. They are the legislators. They possess the power. Working from the New Testament (the one binding thread in all protests), Marsilius denies the ordination of bishops, claiming all priests are equal; challenges the Petrine theory of supremacy at its roots; and maintains that only a representative general council of the whole company of believers could be the supreme authority in the Church. Most Protestant states and churches now rest upon this basis. Yet Marsilius and his coworkers were forced to seek safety in flight and were excommunicated.

Meanwhile the papacy, in captivity in Avignon, allowed worse and ever worse evils to fasten upon the church. Catharine of Siena cried out in spiritual anguish against it all but to little avail. All forms of financial corruption settled down upon the institution, not the least of which was the buying and selling of the spiritual office. All these are familiar to the vocabulary of ecclesiastical history under the word "simony." Seldom was that evil more flourishing than in the late fourteenth and throughout the fifteenth century.

As the situation worsened, the opposition strengthened, and soon the church was challenged by reformers from every area of her life. Gerhard Groot and the Brethren of the Common Life in the Lowlands, John Wyclif in England, John Hus in Bohemia, Savonarola in Italy, together with the full force of the conciliar movement and the nationalist hopes of all the reigning houses, faced the ancient church's papal authorities with demands for reform in all branches. Most "protestant" of all these were the demands that the laity be given voice in church control and that ethics be made a central issue in church management and life.

The movement known as the Renaissance was both ally and enemy to the reform movement. Ally it was in all that pertained to the awakening human interest in affairs of the mind and the life of man as a human being of this earth, but enemy it was in proportion as it recovered the mighty paganism of the Greco-Roman civilization. It was essentially foreign to the interests of the church in its artistic and literary revival in Italy, and the thesis that it furnished the model for the secularization and degradation of the papacy is defensible. There is a sense in which the Reformation is not the child of but rather the enemy of the Renaissance. It will be well seen in this light if we consider the name often given, for instance by Albert Hyma, to the great work of the Brethren of the Common Life—namely, the "Christian" Renaissance, thus distinguishing it from the movement elsewhere, which was truly a "pagan" or "classical" Renaissance. This is an important point and all too often forgotten by Protestant scholars. The movement headed by Luther, Calvin, and Loyola and resulting in the Reformed churches of the epoch now dying was a movement consciously antithetical to the Renaissance as such, though fed by many a spring that was also nourishing the revival of pagan antiquity.

Charles Homer Haskins has shown conclusively that the Renaissance had its primary origin in the cathedral schools of the waning Middle Ages. From that source it developed in two branches. The one recovered the earthly glory of the Greek and Roman classics and flowered in the literary and artistic revival in Italy, with all the consequent demoralization of the papacy. This has caused the historian to use the very name "the Renaissance papacy" to define the institution in the period of its utter worldliness. The other branch is best represented by the quiet, humble, strong growth in the cities and towns of the lowlands, flourishing in education and public piety from 1380 until the Reformation itself and placing under its ever-increasing influence the men who molded the finally reformed church: Luther, Calvin, Erasmus, Loyola, Sturm. It is doubted that many readers of this chapter can name any members of the Society of the Brethren of the Common Life save only Thomas à Kempis, whose *Imitation of Christ* is the sterile residue of a once-mighty teaching and practicing order.

GERHARD GROOT AND THE BRETHREN OF THE COMMON LIFE

Gerhard Groot was born in Deventer, Holland, in 1340 and educated for the Roman Catholic Church. He studied in Paris and Cologne and Prague. I have been unable, both as regards time and resources, to study much in the history of the church and university in Prague, but I wonder if there isn't some great teacher hidden away in the story of Prague. For Groot and Wyclif (exact contemporaries) and also Hus, with the whole Hussite movement, have roots reaching to Prague of the period of 1350-90. Groot was well educated and accepted in church life, having been to the papal court at Avignon (thus seeing its corruption) on an ecclesiastical mission.

Illness shocked Groot into a stern review of his life. Upon recovery he fled to the influence of the beloved Jan Ruysbroeck, best known of the "mystics" of the North. But mysticism was not for Groot. His heart was with the people and the church's great task of practical piety. He returned to public preaching and for some time exposed on every occasion the corruption of the higher clergy and the need of reform. Silenced by episcopal edict, he turned to spread his message by the written word. Hiring schoolboys as copyists, he was amazed at the ignorance and vice of the boys and saw quite clearly that religious education was the tool by which he might contribute to the improvement of the piety of the people of the Netherlands. Devoting himself to education and to social service, he gathered friends around him and formed a fellowship. Before this was finally under way, the plague of 1384, one of Europe's worst, came to Deventer. Groot, visiting the sufferers, contracted it and died, as he would have wished, in the service of that Master whom he so dearly loved. Florentius Radewyn, his friend and disciple, consummated the formation of the society and is often given as its founder. Nothing could be further from the truth. Gerhard Groot had one of the clear visions in Western Christendom—the vision of a trained and biblically ordered laity, obeying the ethical laws of the New Testament. And the spirit of the master Groot, dead at forty-four in the midst of plague sufferers, was the genius of the organization. The men who had loved him, humble and unknown, threw themselves into schoolteaching to create for the Lord a new generation. John Cele (1374-1417), teaching at Zwolle; Alexander Hegius (1433-98), at Deventer; Jakob Wimpfeling (1450-1528), at Basle, Erfurt, Heidelberg; Wessel Gansfort (1419-89), to whom Luther owed so much; and Jan Standonck (1450-1504), librarian of the Sorbonne, are names sufficient to indicate the work being discussed.

These men aimed above all else to match the pagan Renaissance with a renaissance of Christian antiquity. They made over the curriculum of the schools of the North in keeping with the new love of classical languages, but they never surrendered the central position of Christian character. "The kingdom of heaven consisteth not in knowledge and speech but in work and virtue," wrote John Cele. There was to be no mass education, but every boy was a unit in himself. Eight classes appeared as the best division for the elementary education, and for the upper two of these specialist teachers were to be used—the system we still use! And under Cele, in the city school at Zwolle, were enrolled in one year twelve hundred boys. The New Testament in the best Greek available, scorning the Latin of the Vulgate, became the central subject of study. It was in such a school that Erasmus learned his passionate love of the New Testament and from such men that he learned that attitude which was eventually to speak in the matchless preface to his own New Testament edition in Greek. "The better education of the young is the foundation of all true reform, ecclesiastical, national, and domestic," wrote Jakob Wimpfeling as he labored in the German universities for the preparation of teachers for the great work. And he laid into the spirit and the mood of the men of the classical Renaissance with sharpest attack as he enunciated the principles of the northern Renaissance: "Of what use are all the books in the world, the most learned writings, the most profound research, if they only minister to the vainglory of their authors and do not or cannot advance the good of mankind?" Again, "What profits all our learning if our characters be not correspondingly noble?" Yet again, "Let study be for the quickening of independent thought." All who know the work of Erasmus and the quiet, unfulfilled dream of the gentle John Calvin know full well how they were nurtured at the breast of this idealism of Jakob Wimpfeling, the first real "preceptor of Germany."

In all these schools Latin literature was subjected to the most exacting study, and to that study these teachers brought a full Christian influence. They set forth for Christian students the nobility of Cicero and Seneca and rejected the furious downward ethical pull of Ovid and of Terence, the influence of which had been so severely known and tested by St. Augustine centuries earlier. Yet these teachers of the Brethren set up the first printing presses for the education of the North, and from their press at Deventer came forth the first great series of printed textbooks the world had ever had. Before the year 1500 more than 450 different texts had come from the press at Zwolle and Deventer for use in their schools. Books printed by them were read by Ignatius Loyola in those bitter months of illness after Pamplona, and they set him out on his strong career. These were the teachers Luther knew in that first year away from home in Magdeburg. These were the men who set the immortal vision of the life of the Christian mind in the young Erasmus, which vision he carried to the halls of English study to have confirmed by the clear and eloquent Colet. These were the men in charge of the student lodginghouse when John Calvin went up to Paris a young and sensitive student; and to these men, too, Ignatius Loyola came as he entered Paris in the full determination of his life. These were the men who trained and set John Sturm, greatest schoolman of the Protestant North, in his lifework at Strassburg, under whom, also, Calvin taught for three happy years before the stern necessity of Geneva was laid upon him. These were the men who trained the generations that listened so gladly to the reform preaching when it came, and out from these lowlands villages came the first martyrs of the early Lutheran days—two young men for whom Martin Luther himself wrote the funeral ode, first of his Protestant hymns.

Yet they were all quiet and little-known men, possessing the final and authentic mark of the great teacher—the mark that causes a man to point to his own student, saying, "He must increase, but I must decrease." All of them stayed within the allegiance of the ancient church, because the bitter cleavage had not appeared. They pleaded for reform. Only when reform was finally and decisively refused was rebellion in order. These were the men who sowed for the generation that was to reap the mighty harvest of freedom.

John Wyclif (?-1384)

In John Wyclif all the elements of the final reform were present except the ripeness of the times in general. Of unknown birth and early training, Wyclif comes to prominence as a lecturer of clear and forceful style at Oxford. He was a churchman of stern and practical ethical life. He finally came into his position of national leadership with the lectures *On Civil Lordship*, delivered about 1376 at the university. Therein he claimed that all power, ecclesiastical and civil, is the gift of God, the great Overlord, and is dependent on the ethical and lawful performance of the obligations attaching to it. His attack upon the clergy in high places and upon papal interference in civil affairs was direct, simple, clear. Driven from this position to the deeper one concerning the source of authority, he entered more fully into New Testament studies and taught that Scripture is the only law of the Church, and that the Church itself is the whole body of believers and only in an earthly and historical sense subject to pope and priest. The papacy must of course be subject to the law of scriptural ethics, and any deviation from the same constitutes the abrogation of authority. The monastic orders, in his time the veritable infantry of the papacy, he attacked as without any basis in Scripture. However, taking the little scriptural authority that the orders could muster in defense of themselves, he organized his own preaching men, as Waldo and Francis had done before him. It should be remembered that Francis of Assisi wanted little or no organizational vows at the start of his movement, but that they were forced upon him by the power of the church.

The men whom Wyclif organized and sent over England were to "spread scriptural holiness throughout the land." For this purpose he and his associates prepared an English text of the Bible—another sure mark of the authentic reforming spirit. Finally, it became clear to him that the central doctrine of late medieval piety, the doctrine of transubstantiation, had no New Testament support, and he must attack it. This touched the heart of the great church organization, and he was forbidden to teach longer at Oxford but was permitted to continue in the quiet life of his pastorate at Lutterworth. For many years the church had wished to bring him to trial and to death, but the political support of John of Gaunt had kept him protected. Now he was removed from the office of teaching, but his work was done. His English people had seen the free spirit, they had heard the strong prophetic denunciation of wickedness in high places, they had been shown the ethical life of the simple and serene Christian, and they had the priceless gift of the Scripture in their mother tongue. He was quietly buried after his death in 1384; but by order of the Council of Constance (1415) the church exhumed his body, burned it, and cast the ashes upon the little river Swift, which flows into the Avon. Wyclif having been crowned with martyrdom, his work went on as quietly and as truly as the unknown poet sang it:

> The Avon to the Severn runs,
> The Severn to the sea;
> And Wyclif's dust shall spread abroad
> Wide as the waters be.

The influence of John Wyclif can hardly be overestimated in so far as England is concerned. The men of the great Reformation there were largely, if unconsciously, in his debt; and the long history of steady religious interest among the common people as evidenced by Puritanism, the Baptist movement, the work of Fox, and the work of Wesley testify to the thoroughness with which he planted. But on the continent he was to leave to other men speaking the native tongue of their own peoples the furtherance of the work.

JOHN HUS (ABOUT 1373-1415)

Chief among all the continental pre-Reformation reformers must always be counted John Hus, of Bohemia. Standing in his own right, independent of Wyclif, though influenced by him, he spoke a word of protest for Central Europe at the opening of the fifteenth century.

Independent of any other direct influence from European life, the Bohemians were emerging into an intensely nationalistic feeling as their king Charles IV, who was also the Holy Roman Emperor, did much for the advancement of the land. He it was who founded the University of Prague in 1348. Strong German elements, however, resisted the rising Slavic feeling. Church reform was evident early in the work of Conrad of Waldhausen (died 1369), Milicz of Kremsier (died 1374), Matthias of Janov (died 1394), and Thomas of Stitny (died 1401). To these men John of Husinetz worked in direct succession. He was a student in the University of Prague when English influences were felt. Those influences were due to the exchange of students between the nations when, in 1383, Ann of Bohemia married Richard II of England. But Hus's outlook was always distinctly Czech. After ordination he remained to teach at the university and to lead the Czech elements in the days when they fought themselves free of the Germanic elements in the university-governing body. He was rector of the university in 1404. Thoroughly familiar with the doctrines of Wyclif, now widely discussed on the continent, he defended many of them, never dreaming of heretical implications. His mastery of and publications upon the *Sentences* of Peter Lombard gave him his own place in the theological leadership of the day.

But the issues were more than theological. Imbued with the same deep piety that Wyclif had had and ordering his whole life on the New

Testament, Hus interested himself in the religious condition of the common people. He preached regularly in the Bethlehem Chapel, preached in the Bohemian language, preached the great and simple truths of New Testament piety. To do this it became more and more apparent that he must pass judgment upon the life of luxury and immorality so often practiced by the higher clergy. Eventually the issue came to the structure of the church and the power and rights of the papacy. Here Hus argued that only the elect constitute the Church, that no act of the visible church can change that fact. He boldly stood against what he considered to be unjust actions of the papacy in a matter concerning Pope John XXIII and the crusade he was attempting against the King of Naples. For all of this Hus was excommunicated, and Prague put under the interdict.

The whole matter was to be discussed and set forth at the Council of Constance, called to meet to settle the papal schism and all other matters of the deeply disturbed church. To this council Hus came under safe conduct from the Emperor Sigismund. There he was treated with the greatest indignities, made to live under most unhappy circumstances, refused permission to state his case, and steadily maneuvered toward death. He stood his ground magnificently. Letters he wrote home contain the martyr spirit in its most heroic mold. He died at the stake, abused by the council and its members, denied the right of defense, betrayed in the matter of the safe conduct, but with the "Kyrie Eleison" upon his lips and the spirit of the reform reborn in his death.

The Bohemian people rallied behind the spirit of their martyred leader and for bitter years defended with armies in the field their right to order the church as they saw fit. They were never completely rewon to the Roman Church and have contributed much to the progress of the Protestant faith in Europe. The contribution made by John Hus and the Hussite movement to the freedom of the northern peoples from Roman obedience is immense. Luther spoke of a great man, and he justly acknowledged that debt, when he quietly said to John Eck at Leipzig the day that gentleman first set the terrible name of "heretic" upon him, "But, good Master Eck, everything that Master John Hus said isn't wrong." Let John Hus be named as first of that mighty company heralding the reform.

THE CONCILIAR MOVEMENT

One of the most powerful influences marking the way for Protestantism was the idea that the final authority for the church rested in a general council. Even when not advanced in an extreme form but only to the point of pressing for the calling of a council for the correction of abuses, it still gave form to the growing interests of the laity. The papal schism was so manifest a scandal and so open a denial in practice of the very essence of Roman Catholic theory that all concerned realized that some way must be found for healing it. There was no hope from the rival claimants themselves, for no contending pope was willing to surrender the office. Sentiment for a council grew but slowly. The precedent of Nicea was not welcome, since the State (Constantine) had called and controlled that, and the Western Church had fought too long and too hard to establish its freedom from the secular. Yet the Holy Roman Emperor was a loyal Roman Catholic and could be of great service in the matter.

Finally, the cardinals of both popes met and called in their own names a council of the ranking churchmen with representatives of the secular princes. This first met in Leghorn, was then transferred to Pisa, and resulted in confusion, since it elected a new pope while neither of the existing two would accept its decisions. Yet the seed was sown, and other councils were to come. The emperor Sigismund called the next meeting for Constance. There the schism was healed in the deposition of all claimants and the election of Martin V. Unhappily this is the council that took so repressive and dogmatic a stand in the matter of the doctrinal and ethical issues fast arising and symbolized in the trial and death of Hus and the burning of the long-dead Wyclif. Still, it appeared that the church was well on the way toward the establishment of a type of constitutional monarchy for the papacy—an end greatly to be desired. The matter came to an abrupt end through the unwise and fruitless efforts of the Council of Basel, and from the middle of the century onward the unity of Western Christendom disintegrated.

France fought for her rights, as witness the "pragmatic sanctions." England laid the keels of her navy under Henry VII. Bohemia stood her ground around the Hussite flag. Every Italian city maintained an army and often fought the papacy, as under Julius II. Spain began its climb to power. Each independent unit of the powerful Germans guarded its right to be the master of its own destiny. The papacy became an Italian princedom in fact and theory and came, under Alexander VI, to a perilous secularization. All protest was in vain. Savonarola raised a noble voice in Florence in defense of Church and common people, only to be brought to death in the public square of his beloved city. Through all this men longed for some healing instrument of just government and remembered the hope of the general council of Christian leaders. It is not without historic cause that Luther's first great call to constructive action is entitled *To the Christian Nobility of the German Nation Concerning the Bettering of the State of the Church*. It was a call to general council, in which the lay rulers of the German people would institute the reforms the religious leaders refused.

THE OXFORD REFORMERS

The names of John Colet (?-1519), Thomas More (1478-1535), and Desiderius Erasmus (1466-1536) have long been associated with one another as coworkers in the reform of teaching and piety. Because of the place where they labored together they are called the Oxford

Reformers. Erasmus came out of the influence of the Brethren of the Common Life into the influence of Colet and More. Colet had been much interested in the Italian Renaissance and had spent some time in Italy, but he was first and foremost a Christian teacher and was busy at the work of reform in England. All three hoped for the success of the reform ideals by means of study and teaching and compromise with the existing authorities while the level of common piety was slowly lifted. Colet and More did great service to the cause in their native land. Erasmus transferred his activities to Switzerland, where he could work better with the printing houses of Basel. There he set himself to promote reform by writings in criticism and satire. At the same time he worked with considerable success to bring the best literature of the Christian past to the use of the scholars of his time. Luther was jubilant when, in 1516, he was able to take the Greek text of the New Testament edited by Erasmus to the lecture desk in the Wittenberg classroom.

Erasmus, as one of the ablest of the men of the Christian Renaissance, did much to set the mood for the Protestant experience; yet he himself was far from the position, either religiously or intellectually, of Luther or Calvin. The Reformation was not cradled in the Renaissance but was a parallel movement to it, evolving from the natural changes in society; and since it absorbed much of the old church and much of the Renaissance while rejecting much of each, it is properly seen as a synthesis. One must not say that the Renaissance is "Protestantism before Luther." It would be more accurate to say, "Protestantism is the antithesis to the Renaissance"; but it would be most accurate to say, "Protestantism is the synthesis of the Renaissance, the reform movement, and the ancient church."

OTHER TENDENCIES

There were many other reform tendencies at work in the years before Protestantism became a historic accomplishment. Much in common between the later theology of Luther and Melanchthon and that of the earlier German mystics can be seen. All the striving for personal communication between the believing soul and God, for which these northern mystics so fervently prayed, was a prelude to the strong and moving doctrine of the priesthood of all believers. To this same central Lutheran doctrine, also, much was contributed by associations within the church striving for the increase of personal piety by means of private prayer and the disciplined life.

In the sense also in which Protestantism is productive of social reform there were precursors of the work in all the reforming priests of the North who labored among the peasantry of the Teutonic lands. Hans Boheim, with the fearless New Testament preaching that led to the belief that the individual man is of worth and right in the sight of God and is therefore not to be exploited by the Church or State, prepared the way for that wave of protest which came to grief in the terrors of the Peasants' Revolt. Yet the grief is not to cloud the fact that great advance for the Christian cause was made in the very fact of the uprising.

In every field of Western Christian life the harvest was ready for Luther. The roots of life were all religious, and in every area of disaffection the Church was involved. Luther possessed a nature centrally and sincerely religious; and when he spoke in the early years of his leadership, he drew to him all the reform movements of Europe. As then it moved into constructive theology and organization, he held to himself only those elements which had at heart the same interests as himself. In the formation of Protestantism as such there is the growth of a new social experience, drawing many of its noblest elements directly from the past but recasting them all into a powerfully effective historic experience.

LUTHER AND HIS TRADITION

ABDEL ROSS WENTZ

IF WE would understand Martin Luther and his tradition, we must guard against two mistakes that are rather common in approaching the subject: One is the idea that Luther's movement was merely a turning back of the course of history for a thousand years to the purity of the primitive Christian age. The other misconception is that the heroic qualities of Martin Luther—his own giant stature and his own mighty achievements—account for the success of the Lutheran Reformation in the sixteenth century. It will give perspective to our study if we first clarify both of these points.

LINEAL CONTINUITY

Luther's movement was not a negative or reactionary movement; it was positive and progressive. It was not merely a sudden revolt against the immediate past, an impulsive throwing off of a mountain load of errors in the official ecclesiastical apparatus of salvation; on the contrary it was the logical outcome of the centuries, the continuation of the deepest and most vital elements in the Christian piety of the past.

The thought and practice of Christians in the Middle Ages oscillated about two poles: One was the showy external legalism of the official church, in which the grace of God disappeared under a vast ecclesiastical mechanism of salvation by ceremonial good works. The other was a stream of deep, quiet, evangelical piety, usually set in a framework of superstition and often hidden from general view but flowing along from generation to generation in obscure but saintly souls who felt the utter insufficiency of their own works and, for their comfort and satisfaction, went back to the grace of God in Christ Jesus. The Lutheran Reformation was the emergence of this hidden stream of genuine Christian piety upon the plain of general history, its legitimation before the empire alongside the old and official church. It was the expression in terms of the sixteenth century of a vital force that had been continuous since apostolic times, the flaming up of an unquenchable spark of divine truth that had smouldered for generations under the institutionalism and sacramentalism of the Orthodox and Roman Churches. The Reformation was the Anglo-Saxon expression of that timeless truth of the Christian gospel which had already ministered so abundantly to Jews and Greeks and Romans.

Because the official teachings of the Roman Catholic Church had so long obscured the evangelical elements in Christianity, the teachings of the sixteenth-century Reformers broke upon the minds of men with

42

the force of a revelation and wrought upon the old, corrupt church with the impact of a revolution. But, as a matter of fact, the essence of the Protestant Reformation was not a revolt, and its principles were no breach of continuity with the genuine Church of all ages.

It follows, therefore, that the names by which Luther's movement and tradition have been known are unfortunate and even misleading. Luther himself protested right strenuously against the use of his own name to designate the movement or the body of teachings which he and his colleagues championed. He wrote: "What is Luther? The teaching is not mine, nor have I been crucified for anyone. . . . In common with the congregation of God's people I hold the one common doctrine of Christ, who alone is our master." It is clear that "Lutheran" is a very inadequate name to give to a movement that is not limited to a person or an era but is as ecumenical and abiding as Christianity itself. And such negative terms as "Protestant" and "Reformation" are unhappy designations for a movement that in essence was not protest but affirmation, not reform but conservation, not reaction but propulsion. Its best name is "Evangelical." It stands in lineal continuity of the best apostolic succession through all Christian ages.

LATERAL UNITY

It is well also, before proceeding to Luther himself and his tradition, to understand that the genius of the man does not in itself account for his place in history. I would not, of course, subtract one cubit from the heroic stature that historians in general ascribe to him; for I regard him as the greatest Christian personality between St. Paul and our day with the possible exception of St. Augustine. But proper perspective requires that we recognize also the influences of the contemporary scene.

It would be a mistake to suppose that without Luther there would have been no Reformation of any kind in the sixteenth century, or that Luther, with all his superb qualities of leadership, could have stepped upon the stage of history at any time or in any land and could have called forth a Reformation movement. The great-man theory of history will no longer suffice as an explanation. Students of history and biography have learned that great men are not so much the makers as the products of their age. Their success is due to their representative quality. We should therefore think of Luther, not as the winged angel who comes out of the skies to proclaim a new heaven and a new earth nor yet as the great giant who strides through his generation with pompous pace, determined to overthrow the Pope and correct the glaring abuses of the church in his day; we should think of him rather as the unwitting leader of an unplanned movement, the accidental mouthpiece of a discontented generation that was groping for a really religious apprehension of Christianity. Luther became vocal in the world because his age provided him with a sounding board.

The sixteenth century in Western Europe was seething with change in every major social interest, and the movement that bears Luther's name was only one phase of a many-sided transition to the modern world. Preserved Smith has pointed out that the Reformation was the ideal expression of seven great changes that came over the people of Western Europe in the sixteenth century. Every one of them is a cultural parallel to Luther's movement in the sphere of religion. "And the earth helped the woman." There was the rising tide of nationalism and the increasing restlessness of Teutonic people under Latin dominion. And there was the growing power of the common people—a social revolution that abolished special privilege for the clergy as well as the nobility. This led to another general change—the growth of capitalism, the turn to industrial life, and the overthrow of the ascetic ideal in ethics. A fourth great change in the general spirit of the age was the recovery of the individual from the corporate and mass activity of the Middle Ages, opening the way for a religion of private judgment and the entire movement for toleration.

Parallel with all these was the intellectual advance, heralded by the Renaissance and now popularized and making untenable many of the medieval superstitions. The transition from feudal society to absolute monarchy is a seventh parallel; for in the sixteenth century neither God nor king any longer needed intermediaries to come between him and his people, and deposed saints took their place with deposed feudal barons.

When all these revolutions are added together, we see the magnitude of the change that took place in Luther's day. We realize that the Reformation was just the religious phase of one great general transition to a new age, and Luther was swept along by that transition quite as much as he helped to produce it. By the grace of God, Luther had the qualities to play the heroic part demanded for that hour, but it must not be overlooked that the stage of history was well set in his day for such a man as he was. For, in the providence of God, he lived and wrought as a representative of his age, the herald of a new stage in Christian history, and the eloquent mouthpiece of a more inclusive interpretation of the Christian gospel.

And now, having established Luther's lineal continuity with his Christian ancestors through fifteen centuries and his lateral unity with his contemporaries of the sixteenth century in every sphere of general culture, we approach our subject more closely and ask who Martin Luther was and how we are to understand his tradition in the total framework of Protestantism.

ADJUSTMENT THROUGH COMMITMENT

The most important thing about Luther is the fact that he was a man of very deep religious experience. This placed him under the impress of divine compulsion and made him in a real sense a prophet of God. Now, a prophet of God was the supreme need of the world in the beginning of the sixteenth century. The consciences of men were bound under a sense of sin. The only God they knew was a frowning, far-away God. The life of the average man was full of fear—fear of plague and pestilence, fear of the Turks, fear of death and judgment, fear of an angry God.

Martin Luther was born into a generation that longed for a sense of God's forgiveness. Men filled their days with penitential and other sacramental ceremonies. They traveled from shrine to shrine. They muttered prayers, paid for indulgences, maintained ignorant priests, and crowded into monasteries. But the sense of pardon did not come. God remained a far-away God. In vain did the humanists plead for a renovation of morals, public and private, and a reform of organizations, ecclesiastical and secular. In vain did men criticize the hierarchy and mock the stupidity of the popular religion. In vain did the scholars and the philosophers seek for a revival of learning and a reign of reason. What the times needed was a prophet—a man who had himself felt a commanding sense of pardon, one who knew from experience that they who worship God must worship him with the heart and with the life, one who could communicate his experience to his fellow men in terms they could understand.

Lindsay, in his volume on the Reformation in Germany (p. 190), says:

History knows no revivals of moral living apart from a new religious impulse. The motive power needed has always come through leaders who have had communion with the unseen. Humanism had supplied a superfluity of teachers; the times needed a prophet. They received one: a man of the people; bone of their bone and flesh of their flesh; one who had himself lived that popular religious life with all the thoroughness of a strong, earnest nature, who had sounded all its depths and tested its capacities and gained, in the end, no relief for his burdened conscience; who had at last found his way into the presence of God and who knew, by his own personal experience, that the Living God was accessible to every Christian.

The spiritual crisis in Luther's life, the one that finally made him a Reformer, grew out of a practical religious need. It did not arise out of any intellectual criticism of medieval doctrine, and its major result cannot be seen in any revision of the theological system. Luther's primary question was quite individual and practical: How can I get a merciful God? He was moved by the overwhelming pressure of anxiety to save his soul. Using the method most approved in that day, he entered a monastery. There he spent two years of anguish, battling with himself and with his sin. With all the force of a strong nature he applied himself to the complicated penitential system of the church. With punctilious exactitude he obeyed every order, observed every statute, and fulfilled every ceremony. But in vain he waited for the experience of God's favor. His sense of sin was not relieved. God remained far away. And Luther was too clear-sighted and too honest with himself to conceal his despair and pretend assurance when he had none.

At last, through fragments of the Scriptures which he chanced to read, he began to realize that what he was trying to do for himself Christ had already done for him, that God's pure righteousness might be appropriated by the sinner if he would simply trust in the merits of Christ rather than his own good deeds. "He who through faith is righteous shall live" (Romans 1:17). From that day Luther threw himself without reservation upon the atoning work of Christ, and there he found the comfort and peace of soul which he had been seeking in vain through all the labyrinth of monastic observances.

Thus Luther, in the quiet depths of his own profound soul, had experienced what is called justification by faith. His soul was adjusted to God because he trusted God. His heart was geared into the divine requirements through his personal commitment to Christ. For faith, says Luther, is "the heart's utter trust in Christ." He who has that has Christ's righteousness, and "he who through faith is righteous shall live." This experience of salvation solely by faith in Christ was the most important thing in Luther's life. It serves to explain every other important fact in his career as a Reformer.

A recent Roman Catholic writer on John Wesley refers again and again to Luther's doctrine as "salvation without works." He thereby shows that he does not understand what Luther meant either by justification or by faith. Justification our Roman author takes, not in the Pauline and Lutheran sense as forensic, but in the Augustinian sense as factual, confused with regeneration and sanctification. And faith he understands, not in the biblical and Protestant sense as confiding trust and personal commitment of the entire life, but in the scholastic and Tridentine sense as a form of knowledge, assent to doctrine, submission to an institution.

These distinctions are important for our understanding of the Lutheran tradition. Faith is a continuing act whereby the soul throws itself upon God and receives the smile of God, and that smile of a forgiving Father adjusts the entire life to a new obedience. Adjustment by faith through divine favor, as Luther experienced and taught it, is not negative, like "salvation without works"; it is a very positive and continuing experience of the love of God, which brings the assurance of forgiveness, transforms the well-springs of conduct, and gives a new quality to the whole of life.

A NEW LOYALTY

Luther reached his conviction concerning justification by faith not later than 1513, perhaps even as early as 1508; but eight or ten years passed before he emerged as a Reformer. Only gradually did he come to see the implications of his experience, its far-reaching import in practical affairs. Step by step, as he undertook increasing responsibilities in the church, first as priest and then as professor, he encountered increasing opposition in maintaining his position concerning justification and concerning faith. And step by step he was forced along the road that led to an open breach with Rome and the substitution of a new authority in matters of religion.

In 1517 Luther set up his ninety-five propositions for debate, intending only to use his right as a professor to proclaim his views in academic discussion. But such was the spirit of the times that his propositions attracted unusual attention. For he had attacked the sale of indulgences. This was one of the characteristic practices in that day. In theory an indulgence was a substitute for the ceremonial works required as a temporal penalty for sins that had been confessed and absolved, but in practice those who bought indulgences regarded them simply as pardons for sin. Against this practice Luther protested because of its dire spiritual effects upon men. He took the position that repentance means turning from sin to God; and that when a man does turn from sin and place his trust in God, his sins are immediately and entirely forgiven without the absolution of a priest or the indulgence of the Pope.

But when Luther attacked the sale of indulgences, without knowing it he really attacked the entire penitential system of the medieval church. And, what is more, he attacked the power of the Pope who proclaimed the indulgences. So his theses of 1517 kindled a great fire and began his own trek away from Rome. Two years later, in his famous debate with the Catholic theologian John Eck, Luther was forced by the very skill of his opponent to see for himself the consequences of the course upon which he had entered in 1517 and to come out with the clear and definite statement that popes are not infallible and that even church councils are not the ultimate authority over the soul.

This clarified the issues for Luther. He now realized that he had struck at the very heart of the church's system and that no change was to be expected of the Pope or the hierarchy. In the meantime he had been diligently studying and teaching the Bible and had become more deeply convinced than ever that salvation is alone through faith in Christ and that such salvation is full and free and present.

In 1520 Luther broadcast his case to the people. The broadcasting apparatus in those days was the newly invented printing press. He wrote three books that year. The most important in its influence was the one entitled *The Liberty of a Christian Man.* This was a clear, brief statement of the principles underlying Luther's whole position. It explained in a popular way that a man is justified by faith alone; that, therefore, every Christian is his own priest and has direct access to God; and that the man who trusts God need not fear the priests nor the church.

The Pope and his advisers now prepared extreme measures against Luther. Late in 1520 a papal bull was issued, condemning his views and works and threatening him with excommunication if he did not recant within sixty days. This threatening document Luther burned in public and with great formality. He needed no bridges behind him.

He accepted the role of heretic. This bold step electrified Germany and clarified the issue for the masses of the people.

Luther's local prince was favorable to him, and such was the political situation in the empire just at that juncture that the Emperor could not execute the "holy curse" upon Luther without giving him a hearing before the imperial diet. This brought the dramatic trial at Worms in 1521.

There, before a brilliant and august assemblage of Church and State potentates, the rugged monk of Wittenberg, his heart aflame with spiritual fire, his eyes flashing defiance, rises to the full height of his prophetic stature. Called upon to take back what he had said and what he had written, he exclaims in clear and earnest accents: "My conscience, my conscience, is bound to the Word of God. Unless convinced by clear arguments of reason based upon the Scriptures, I will not and cannot recant. God help me! Amen!" That splendid utterance of the dauntless monk strikes a responsive chord in the heart of every Protestant to this very day.

Conscience, reason, Scripture—it was public notice on the most conspicuous signpost in the world that a new force had stepped upon the stage of history. If eras can be dated, that was the beginning of the modern world—April, 1521. Up to that time there was an authority in the world that all men thought immovable. It consisted of pope, council, and emperor. Since that time there is a force in the world that all men know to be irresistible. It consists of Scripture, reason, and conscience.

Luther's successful impeachment of the old trinity of human authority and his substitution of the new trinity of spiritual power was the greatest moral triumph in his life. It was the logical outcome of his spiritual experience of justification years before. And it was the annunciation of another fundamental principle of the Protestant Reformation, the setting up of a new authority in matters of religion, the sole authority of the Bible.

Fifteen years before, in his terrific spiritual trials, Luther had found light and deliverance in the Scriptures. From that time forward he made the Bible the object of his study. When he found his doctrine of grace and faith opposed by representatives of the church, he entered the conflict with no other weapon than the Bible. When the churchmen likewise argued from Scripture but asserted the exclusive right of the Pope and his predecessors to interpret and apply the Scripture, Luther took a step forward and insisted that in matters of faith and the soul's salvation the Bible is clear and self-attesting and no tradition of pope or council can bind the individual conscience or take away the right of private judgment. This position on the Bible he took in his great writings of 1520, when he protested against unscriptural theories, extrascriptural sacraments, and practical abuses in the church unwarranted by the Bible.

Then, at Worms in 1521, Luther took the final step in the development of his attitude toward the Word. The church had fully opened his eyes to her own corruption and had placed him under the curse of excommunication. The empire, too, was about to pronounce the ban against him. So he fell back upon the Word with a devotion more exclusive than hitherto. Before this he had only contended against that which he saw to be in conflict with the contents of Scripture. Now he expressed the view that nothing belongs to saving truth except what is positively and clearly contained in Scripture. The Word as interpreted by the enlightened conscience, the common sense, and the private judgment of the individual Christian is the only supreme source of truth, the only infallible rule of faith and practice. And thus the second great principle of the Protestant Reformation was articulated—the authoritative character of the Word. Both logically and chronologically it was the outgrowth of the material principle of justification by faith alone.

A Conserving Tradition

Having laid these solid foundations in positive principles, Luther proceeded to build his Reformation along conservative lines. The events of the sobering decade that followed the Diet at Worms constituted a progressive definition of Luther's tradition as over against that of other Reformers, especially those of radical tendencies.

First in time and foremost in its significance was the new translation of the Bible. This was the next logical step, the practical outcome of his conviction about the Word and his bold stand at Worms. For Luther was a faithful priest. He wanted his people to experience Christ as he himself had experienced him. He wanted them to burst the shackles of priestly domination. He wanted all the people to accept the Bible alone as their guide in matters of religion. So he gave them the Bible in their own tongue.

Luther was thoroughly equipped for this important work of translation. He knew the contents of the Bible and knew them intimately. He had a profound experience of the central message of the Scriptures. He had a deep insight into the hearts of men and their modes of expression. And he knew the German tongue. He gave his translation a religious fervor and a literary flavor that no writer since his day has surpassed and few have equaled.

The translation of the Bible was Luther's most important single achievement for Protestantism as a movement. It was valuable not only for its own intrinsic worth but also for its pioneer character, because it blazed the way for more than a thousand similar undertakings in other modern tongues. It did more than any other one thing to conserve the two great principles of Protestantism—justification by faith and the supreme authority of the Word. It fixed the positive, conservative nature of the Lutheran tradition and determined the outstanding characteristics of the Church that bears his name. Concerning the high significance of this achievement I have said on another occasion:

Through his translation the lofty prophets of ancient Israel descended from the stately heights of oriental imagery, traveled to the Western world, entered the home of the simple peasant and humble laborer, and, without sacrificing one whit of their prophetic dignity, uttered their profound thoughts in the language of most tender familiarity. Through this new people's book the inspired Evangelists and devoted apostles of the first century leaped the intervening ages and spoke to the drab men and women of the sixteenth century in such real and vivid accents that it caught their imagination, fired their spirits, and led them to thrill with pentecostal enthusiasm. The fragrant flower of prophetic and apostolic message was transplanted to an entirely new soil with such deftness and such delicate and sympathetic handling that it lost almost nothing of its native fragrance and color and fruitfulness. Simple without ceasing to be elegant, plain without ceasing to be eloquent, and incisive without approaching the bizarre, Luther's Bible clearly marked a new era both in literature and in religion and, even after the lapse of four centuries, stands unapproached in its vital and compelling power.

Other events in that decade continued the process of defining Luther's movement in terms of conservation. When certain deluded fanatics came to Wittenberg, while Luther was absent in the Wartburg, and started to wrest the Reformation there into radical channels, Luther suddenly left his place of hiding, appeared upon the scene in Wittenberg, and with a series of vigorous sermons made it clear that the Lutheran Reformation was not to be a revolutionary movement but a conservative and evangelical one.

A few years later, when the downtrodden peasants in the name of the new movement arose against their oppressive lords and appealed to arms, Luther risked his life in an effort to restrain them from violence while he negotiated for their rights. Failing in that, he denounced in most vigorous terms any use of force on behalf of gospel truth. He was violently opposed to violence on behalf of the kingdom of God. This alienated a large element of the peasantry from Luther and his cause and helped to ally that cause with the political princes; but it made it clear that the great work of reform would be carried on with the sword of the Spirit and not with the sword of steel.

Shortly after that Luther and his colleagues became involved in a controversy with the Swiss theologians on the subject of the Lord's Supper. A conference of the two parties was held at Marburg in 1529. No agreement could be reached. This was due in part to the fact that Luther stood firm upon the Christology of Chalcedon but largely to the fact that he suspected the Swiss of political motives and radical tendencies. So it became clear that in the Lutheran tradition there would be no compromise of doctrine for the sake of external union, that unity of faith would be primary and union of organization very secondary in relations with other Protestants.

In the meantime Luther had married. In various other ways he had set himself against asceticism in ethics and the monastic ideal in the

50

religious life. Then, in 1529, came Luther's catechisms, calculated to suffuse family life with evangelical instruction; and, in 1530, the Augsburg Confession, which twenty-five years later proved to be the charter of a legalized Lutheran Church.

So the blueprint of the Lutheran tradition was complete. Its material is justification by faith. Its norm is the Bible. Its spirit is conservative. Its purpose is evangelical.

ZWINGLI AND THE REFORMED TRADITION

George W. Richards

Continental Protestantism in its formative stage crystallized into three distinct types: the Lutheran, the Reformed, and the Radical (Anabaptist, Mystic, and Socinian). The third type divided and subdivided, protesting against Roman Catholicism, against Lutheranism and Zwinglianism, and against one another. Bullinger, in his *History of the Reformation,* mentions thirteen different Anabaptist groups. Ortius, in his *Annals* (1772), writes of fifty-two sects. The three types agreed in their protest against the Roman Catholic Church, however much they differed among themselves. They protested against the Pope's claim to the headship of the Church by divine right, the clergy's exclusive prerogative to mediate grace and truth between Christ and the believer, the propitiating value of the Mass, almsgiving and pilgrimages as works of merit, veneration of Virgin and saints, and the religious superiority of the monastic over the social life.

Protestantism, however, was more than a critical and destructive opposition to Catholicism. The Reformers, excluded from the church of their fathers, were compelled to organize churches with doctrine, government, and worship corresponding to their experience of salvation and their interpretation of the New Testament.

A line of cleavage, however, appeared in conservative Protestantism in the first decade of the Reformation, when the effort was made to define the new faith and to organize new churches. In Wittenberg and in Zurich men at first friendly to Luther and Zwingli became dissatisfied with their conservatism and objected to their compromising attitude toward kings and princes as well as toward popes and bishops. They were restless, aggressive, radical, and asked for a reform "without tarrying for any" and without concessions to a corrupt Church or a secular State. Their avowed purpose was to complete the Reformation only partially finished by Luther and Zwingli. Karlstadt, Storch, and Muenzer in Saxony; Grebel, Manz, and Blaurock in Zurich, became the forerunners and founders of mystic and revolutionary circles variously called fanatics, dissenters, anti-Trinitarians, deformers, and by the generic term Anabaptists. They stood for conscious, personal regeneration and conversion of each Christian through the Holy Spirit; for freedom of conscience and worship; for separation of Church and State; for a holy congregation, excluding sinners by rigorous discipline; for admission to the congregation by believers, or adult baptism; for a fellowship of brethren, with a voluntary sharing of spiritual and temporal possessions, at times running into communism; for a refusal

52

to carry arms and to use force against enemies; for indifference to the legal authority of the government and to the culture of the school.

Conservative Protestantism divided under the leadership of Luther and Zwingli. The difference between the two men was at first hidden but could not be concealed when they began to interpret the gospel and to apply it in practice to the individual and social life. They agreed in finding salvation in God through Christ, but they differed in their views of the appropriation and the assurance of salvation. The first evidence of division came to light, therefore, in the definition of the sacraments or the means of grace, especially the doctrine of the Lord's Supper. The sacramental controversy, however, was not so much a cause of division as a symptom of a difference of national genius, training, and religious experience, which necessarily ended in separation. When, therefore, Luther and Zwingli parted after their first and only meeting at the Colloquy of Marburg (1529), two distinct Protestant churches followed in their wake—the Lutheran and the Reformed. Both are legitimate types of evangelical Christianity, not contradicting or excluding but completing each other.

THE EDUCATION OF ZWINGLI

Zwingli was born in the village of Wildhaus in the Toggenburg valley in German Switzerland. The day of his birth—January 1, 1484—was about seven weeks after Luther's—November 10, 1483. Zwingli came of a respectable family in comfortable though not affluent circumstances; in the language of Bullinger, "good, old, honest stock." Besides himself there were eight brothers and two sisters in the family. Both on the father's and the mother's side he had relatives who were either priests or monks.

At the age of nine Zwingli's paternal uncle—Bartholomew, the dean of Wesen—took the promising lad into his home and directed his education. He sent him at the early age of ten to a Latin school at Basle, taught by Gregory Buenzli, who afterward became a close friend and adviser of the Reformer. Four years later he entered the school of Heinrich Woelflin at Berne, the first school in Switzerland to adopt the humanistic methods of education. He continued the study of Latin, read the ancient classics, and developed musical talent of no mean order. He became an accomplished player of a number of instruments, among others the harp, violin, flute, and cornet. The Catholics, says Bullinger, referred to him afterward with a sneer as the "guitar player and evangelist upon the flute."

For some unknown reason Zwingli took up his abode in the Dominican monastery of Berne, perhaps for the training the monks promised him in music more than for any desire of the monastic life. Both his father and his uncle evidently feared the lure of the monks over the youth, so sent him to the University of Vienna, where his name is inscribed on the register as "Udalricus Zwinglin ex Lichtensteig," for the summer semester, 1500. There he remained two years and, in the words of Myconius, "included in his studies all that philosophy embraces." He doubtless came under the influence of the "arch-humanist" Conradus Celtis, who was then the ruling spirit of the university.

From 1502 to 1506 Zwingli continued and completed his studies in Basle, teaching at the same time in the school attached to St. Martin's Church. In addition to the arts course he studied theology and received the degree of B.A. in 1504 and of M.A. in 1506. At the close of that year he was called to the pastorate in the parish of Glarus.

A survey of Zwingli's education shows that from the time he left his father's house to his ordination to the priesthood he was under men of liberal culture, influenced by the new learning. His own father, his uncle, and his teachers were men with faces turned toward the coming rather than the passing age. Under their oversight he breathed in the spirit of independent investigation and free speech. He was deeply devoted to his fatherland, having nurtured his soul from childhood upon the exploits of Swiss heroes in battles for the freedom of the confederacy. Looking back over his student days, he said, "The Lord granted me the privilege from my youth up to devote myself to the reading of things divine and human."

Of special significance for Zwingli's future career was his contact with Thomas Wyttenbach, whose lectures on the "Sentences of Peter Lombard" he attended the last year of his course at Basle. Trained as a humanist, Zwingli was not favorably disposed to the study of the schoolmen, yet he desired a knowledge of their methods and doctrines. He learned, however, to appreciate his teacher more than the text. His master dropped into the student's heart seeds of heresy that bore fruit years afterward.

In 1523 Zwingli wrote, "I had already been taught what a cheat and delusion indulgences were by my master and beloved faithful teacher Dr. Thomas Wyttenbach." In 1527 he referred to him again as "the most learned and holiest of men," who taught him "that the death of Christ was the sole price of the remission of sin," that "faith is the key which unlocks to the soul the treasury of remission," that the "Bible is the supreme authority in faith and practice." Neither Zwingli nor Wyttenbach at the time understood the full significance of these statements. But to us, who look at the seed in the light of the full-grown fruit, they are essential principles of Protestantism.

In his last years at Basle, Zwingli also read the writings of the Italian humanist Pico della Mirandola, who died in Florence in 1494. Thirteen out of nine hundred theses, which Mirandola proposed to maintain against all comers, were condemned as especially heretical by Pope Innocent VIII. Zwingli approved of at least some of these theses, and Myconius tells us that on this account he was suspected of heresy. Of the theses in question the following may have had a bearing upon Zwingli's later views: "that neither the cross of Christ nor any image ought to be adored in the way of worship"; "that the words 'this is my body,' pronounced during the consecration of the bread, are to be taken as a mere recital, and not as denoting an actual fact."

THE PARISH PRIEST

It must have meant a struggle for the aspiring young student and teacher to break away from university circles to devote himself to the work of a parish priest. Zwingli's decision, however, to accept the call to Glarus had far-reaching consequences not only for himself but also for Switzerland and the modern age. Though only twenty-three years old when he was ordained, he was deeply sensible of the responsibility of his office. On his way to Glarus the young priest made a noble resolution: "I will be true and upright before God in every situation of life in which the hand of the Lord may place me."

Suiting his action to his word, Zwingli became both an ardent student and a busy pastor. He mingled freely with his parishioners in the home and on the market place. He rejoiced in their joys and grieved in their sorrows. His big heart won the Glareans for him as much as his brilliant intellect. When, at the close of a ten years' pastorate, he went to Einsiedeln, one of his pupils at Glarus wrote, "What could possibly have happened more saddening for our Glarus than to be bereft of so great a man?" In 1522 Zwingli himself referred to the pleasant relations with Glarus: "I lived in such a peaceful and friendly manner with my lords of Glarus that we never had the smallest difficulty, and I went away in such favor that they allowed me for two years to receive the income of the living."

Zwingli did not permit his pastoral work to interfere with his studies. With a view to effective preaching he read the classics, studied eloquence, and, for purposes of pulpit illustration, memorized the anecdotes collected by the Latin author Valerius Maximus. Of his preaching Myconius writes:

He began now, after the example of Christ, to denounce from the pulpit certain base vices that were then extremely prevalent, especially the taking of gifts from princes and baleful mercenary wars. He proclaimed evangelical truth without making any allusion to Romanish errors or with a very slight reference to them. He wished truth first to make its way to the hearts of his hearers; for, thought he, if the truth be once comprehended, the false will be easily detected as such.

That Zwingli had won considerable reputation as a preacher may be inferred from the fact that he was invited to preach at the festival of the "Angel Dedication" at Einsiedeln—an honor bestowed only upon those who had attained distinction in their art.

Zwingli never ceased to be a teacher while he was a pastor. Through his influence a Latin school was opened at Glarus. He taught the most promising youths of his parish, preparing them for the university. Some of these became men of note in literature and politics and ardent Reformers. They never ceased to admire the teacher of their youth.

as a number of glowing testimonials from their pens bear witness. Even the great Erasmus sent him a glowing tribute: "All hail! say I to the Swiss people, whose intellectual and moral qualities yourself and men such as yourself are training."

About 1513 Zwingli began the study of Greek without the aid of a teacher, that, as he said, "he might read the teaching of Jesus from the original sources." He copied with his own hand the Epistles of Paul in Greek and committed them to memory. The original manuscript, with numerous marginal notes, is preserved in the library at Zurich. As he became imbued with the teachings of the Bible, he turned more and more from the theology of the schoolmen to the simple truths of the apostles. "God is my witness," he wrote in 1527, "that I owe my knowledge of the essence and contents of the gospel to the reading of the writings of John and of Augustine, and with special attention the Epistles of Paul, a copy of which I made with my own hands eleven years ago."

Zwingli's emancipation from theology and philosophy, which marks a turning point in his life, like the experience of justification by grace in the life of Luther, is thus described at some length:

In my younger days I was as much devoted to worldly knowledge as any of my age; and when, seven or eight years ago, I gave myself up to the study of the Bible, I was completely under the power of the jarring philosophy and theology. But, led by the Scriptures and the word of God, I was forced to the conclusion: "You must leave them all alone and learn the meaning of the word out of the Word itself."

Two minor though not insignificant incidents made a lasting impression upon the young priest about this time. He found an old liturgy, in a town near Glarus, in which the Latin rubric required that both bread and wine be given to the communicants. This was contrary to the prevalent Catholic custom of permitting the laity to commune only in one kind, the cup being withheld from the people and reserved for the priest. Upon investigation he concluded that the custom of Communion in both kinds had been in vogue not later than two hundred years back. The second incident was the discovery in Italy that the Mass books did not agree exactly. The variations in the different copies were sufficient to disprove the claim of the Roman Church that her liturgy was the same in all times. Facts like these started trains of thought which in due time ended in protest.

The Patriot and Humanist

In two passages of his later writings we catch a glimpse of the patriotism even of the boy Zwingli. "When I was a child," he writes, "if anyone said a word against our fatherland, I bristled up instantly." Again, "From boyhood I have shown so great and eager and sincere love for an honorable confederacy that I trained myself diligently in every art and discipline for this end." His inborn love of the fatherland resented anything that injured his countrymen. He was no less a patriot because he became a priest. He was especially offended by the custom of Swiss soldiers serving in foreign armies for pay. "Every day we receive," he writes, "messengers from the Pope or the Emperor, the Milanese, the Venetians, the Savoyards, and the French, and send others to them." The purpose of these foreign emissaries to Glarus was to buy Swiss troops to serve under the standards of strange kings and princes.

Three times Zwingli went as chaplain with the Glarean soldiers on Italian campaigns. He saw with his own eyes the evil effects of mercenary service. It meant both a loss of men and a deterioration of character. He determined to "utterly root out the traffic" by pen and tongue. He wrote two tracts against it, the second much bolder in its opposition than the first. The one is entitled *The Labyrinth;* the other, *The Ox and Other Beasts.* These, so far as we know, are the firstfruits of his pen. A third composition from this period was a hastily written narrative recounting the deeds of the Swiss soldiers in Italy in 1512.

But more telling than Zwingli's tracts were the sermons he preached against receiving pensions from foreign princes and fighting in foreign armies for money. He gave offense to some of his more prominent parishioners, who profited in this traffic of men. He held them as unpatriotic and "un-Swiss," as dealers in human souls. Terms like these pricked their consciences, wounded their pride, and touched their pocketbooks. They determined to rid themselves of the young preacher, who would not confine himself to the gospel but was so injudicious as to apply it to the sins of his people. The people as a whole, however, stood by and applauded him. Yet the time came when, after ten years' service at Glarus, Zwingli felt constrained to accept a call to become people's priest in the abbey church at Einsiedeln (1516). Thus far in his ministry Zwingli was a scholarly humanist and an ardent patriot.

THE EVANGELICAL REFORMER

As pastor and patriot, Zwingli at first was a humanistic Reformer of the type of Erasmus. He shared the humanists' enthusiasm for the ancient classics and the study of the Bible in the original languages. He had also their antipathy toward the scholastic theology of Aquinas and Scotus and their admiration for the Fathers—Augustine, Ambrose, and Jerome. He sought the simple gospel of Jesus and its interpretation by the apostles, "the pure philosophy of Christ, straight from the fountain." In the words of his friend Rhenanus he refused "to bleat out nonsense about the power of the Pope, remission, purgatory, counterfeit miracles by the saints, vows, pains of the damned, and Antichrist."

From the beginning, however, Zwingli differed from the humanists, a difference that ended in a breach of friendship between Erasmus and himself. After Erasmus had read Zwingli's *True and False Religion* (1525), he exclaimed, "O good Zwingli! what dost thou write that I have not written before thee?" Whereupon Zwingli replied: "Oh, that Erasmus, in his fine style, had written my books! The whole world would have been convinced, and I should not have had to suffer so much hatred." The humanists were intellectual aristocrats with scant regard for the masses. Zwingli had a deep interest in the people of his parish and in the education of the youth of Glarus. The humanists professed a cosmopolitan or world-wide citizenship in place of national patriotism; Zwingli was a loyal Swiss, incessant in his labors for the advancement of his country. In these respects he was in close agreement with Luther, the prophet of the common people and the ardent German patriot.

Unlike Luther, however, Zwingli became Protestant and evangelical, not by a religious struggle and an almost sudden conversion, but by gradual illumination through patient study of the Scriptures and the discipline that came with his experiences in the pastorate.

Luther left the university and entered a monastery; Zwingli went from the university into a parish. Luther's purpose was to become righteous and to make God gracious; Zwingli was in quest of the way of life for his people. The one was concerned about his own salvation; the other, about the salvation of his parishioners. Luther solved his problem through his experience of justification by grace through faith; Zwingli found the way of life by turning from "jarring philosophy and theology" to the sacred Scriptures. Broadly speaking, Luther discovered the sole efficacy of faith, and Zwingli the sole sufficiency of the Scriptures. In time Luther accepted the Bible as the only authority in doctrine and in life, and Zwingli based salvation wholly upon grace through faith.

Three factors entered into making Zwingli an evangelical Reformer. Each of them became gradually operative in his life. The first was the Bible, the only rule of faith and conduct; the second, Christ, the only mediator between God and man; and the third, the grace of God, the only hope of salvation. The first impulse toward these religious ideas he received from different men and at different times.

Erasmus, more than anyone else, helped to free Zwingli from the bondage of doctrines and traditions of men and to convert him to the simple teaching of the New Testament. This change took place in his Glarean ministry, when he gave himself up to the study of the Bible and forsook the philosophers and schoolmen. His test of doctrine, tradition, and practice, was the question "Has Christ taught us this?" Whatever differed from the Bible he abolished; whatever conformed to the Bible he allowed to stand. Even before he knew and read Erasmus, his teacher Wyttenbach, at Basle, told him that the Bible was the supreme authority in faith and life.

While at Einsiedeln he could not help but be impressed by the worship of the Virgin and saints by the thousands of pilgrims who came there every year; for "more gracious than elsewhere," they were told, "is here the help of the Godhead, and more on her altars the presence of Mary works wonders." By reading a poem of Erasmus and by the study of the Bible he came to question saint worship and to preach boldly against it. At Einsiedeln also he talked with prominent cardinals, bishops, and prelates, discussing with them errors in doctrine and warning them that they must proceed to do away with abuses if they would not themselves perish in the great upheaval. He argued that the papacy was based on false foundations and supported his position from the Scriptures. To these facts he doubtless refers when, in 1523, he refers to his preaching at Einsiedeln, saying, "I began to preach the gospel of Christ in the year 1516, before anyone in my locality had so much as heard the name of Luther."

Zwingli tells us in a letter how Erasmus opened his eyes to the error of saint worship:

I will not withhold from you how I came to the opinion and pure belief that we require no other mediator than Christ; also, that between God and us no one can mediate except Christ alone. Eight or nine years ago I read a poem on the Lord Jesus, written by the profoundly learned Erasmus of Rotterdam, in which, with many very beautiful words, Jesus complains that men did not seek all good in him so that he might be to them a foundation of all good, a Saviour, comfort, and treasury of the soul. So I reflected, "Well, if it is really so, why, then, should we seek help of any creature?"

The last step toward evangelical doctrine was taken when Zwingli understood more clearly the doctrine of saving grace and the difference between law and gospel. This experience belongs to his pastorate at Zurich. It was the result of his own deep religious struggle, during a serious illness, of a study of the Epistles of Paul and of the reading of the writings of Luther, which then circulated widely in Switzerland and for which Zwingli had high regard. In 1527 he wrote, "The significance of the gospel I have learned from what I have read in the writings of John and Augustine and by the careful study of the Greek Epistles of Paul." Of Luther's works he said, "What I have read of his writings I find based on the word of God, and no creature can overthrow that."

Professor Lang, in his monograph on Zwingli and Calvin, says, "Around the year 1520, through personal experience in sickness and through the influence of Luther, Zwingli ceased to be merely an Erasmian Reformer and became an evangelical Reformer in the full sense of the term." Then Zwingli refused to receive the annual pension from the Pope, which he had taken since 1512. He began his criticism of the Roman Catholic Church until he was separated from its communion and, with Luther, became the founder of a reformed church. By 1523 he had become a full-fledged evangelical and, though proceeding with caution and moderation, was laying the foundation of a new order in the Canton of Zurich.

The Reformation in Zurich

Until 1523 the Reformation in Zurich was a theory and not a fact. It was put into practice from 1524 to 1525. Public sentiment had been so far educated in the simplicity of the gospel that men demanded changes both in the social order and in church worship.

On September 29, 1523, the council ordered

that henceforth no fees should be collected in the Great Muenster for baptism, the administration of the Eucharist, or burials without gravestones; that the use of candles at burials was not obligatory; that all the clergy of the Muenster should preach the word of God; that the unnecessary number of persons supported by the Muenster should be reduced gradually by not filling the places of those who died; that the Bible should be daily publicly read for an hour each in Hebrew, Greek, and Latin and at the same time explained; that a thorough education be given to all candidates for the ministry, and that the children be also specially cared for; that for educational purposes suitable buildings be provided; that holders of benefices should, as far as possible, discharge parish duties; that the cathedral surplus should be distributed to the poor under the care of a committee of which Zwingli was a member.

Perhaps more difficult to control than the Catholics were the men who became extremists in the work of reform. At first they were friendly to Zwingli, but afterward they bitterly opposed him because of the slowness of his procedure and of his spirit of compromise with the civil authorities. They detested the state church of Zwingli as much as the church State of Rome. Most of them were of the peasant and burgher class. They insisted on radical changes in the social as well as in the ecclesiastical order. Peasants refused to pay tithes for the support of the clergy. A bookseller named Andrew on Crutches held meetings of the people with lay preaching. These men spoke in sharp terms against the Catholic Mass and Communion in one kind; reviled the "stinking noblemen and magistrates"; and denounced the rich who, by trickery and craft, cared for their "smooth skins," while "the poor thieves are hanged." In vain did Zwingli try to silence these revolutionary voices in a sermon on "Divine and Human Righteousness," July 30, 1525.

The radicals came to be known as Anabaptists and appeared for the first time in the Second Disputation of 1523. They were represented by Simon Stumpf, Balthasar Hubmeier, and Conrad Grebel. Their aim was wholly to separate themselves from the ungodly, whether in the old church or in the old State, and to begin anew a church and people strictly according to God's word. They opposed the office of the ministry, the existing civil government, the taking of oaths; and advocated communism of goods and the baptism of believers (or adults) only. For the written Word they frequently substituted the Inner Light and awaited a visible kingdom, from on high, in which the saints would rule the world.

Among these radicals were the idol stormers or image breakers. They entered the churches, destroyed pictures and images, sacred lamps and crucifixes, and violently attacked the old order generally. They broke the fasts. They declared infant baptism unscriptural and a remnant of papal Catholicism. In January, 1523, while a small group was assembled in the town of Zollikon, in Chur, Conrad Grebel rebaptized George Blaurock by pouring water from a dipper upon his head. Afterward Blaurock rebaptized fifteen others. Then they celebrated the Lord's Supper. This was the first Baptist congregation in Switzerland.

It was on account of these outbreaks and disorderly proceedings that the Second Disputation (1523) was called by the council. While there were Catholic representatives present, and the subject of the sacraments was discussed, interest centered in the discussion of the use of images in the churches. The council decided that because the radicals were disturbing the peace of the community and wounding tender consciences, further changes should be made only after the people were properly educated for them. To this end Zwingli prepared *A Short Christian Introduction,* the purpose of which was "to teach the bishops who had hitherto either been ignorant of Christ or had been turning away from him." This document was sent to the bishops and to the cantons in the confederacy.

Thereupon the Swiss Diet, June 24, 1524, at Lucerne, voted to support the old church order of Rome and sent a commission to warn Zurich from further innovations. In March, 1524, the council replied that it would remain true to the confederacy but would not deviate from the word of God and the way of salvation. In the same year, by legal action, the number of holy days was reduced, and sacred processions, vestments, and fasting were abolished. On certain appointed days images and idols were removed from churches in an orderly way, were gathered together, and were burned. The monasteries were closed, and the property belonging to them was taken in charge by the council. With the innovations of 1524 the Reformation in Zurich was in principle completed.

The New Church Order

Pilgrimages, relics of the dead, masses for the dead, and numerous minor ceremonies of worship were no longer permitted. Instrumental and vocal music was suspended in the services. Convents and nunneries were turned into hospitals, poorhouses, and orphanages. Priests and nuns were married. Zwingli himself was secretly married in 1522. His marriage was publicly announced in 1524. His wife's name was Anna Rinehart, a widow and mother of three children.

New modes of worship were gradually introduced. A German baptismal service was published in 1523. The Lord's Supper was celebrated in an evangelical way in April, 1525, by the authority of the council. It was a simple biblical service in the Swiss language. In place

61

of an altar there was a table covered with a white linen cloth. Bread was served on wooden plates, and wine in wooden cups. The men were ranged on one side of the aisle, and the women on the other. Zwingli preached a sermon and offered prayer. A deacon read Paul's account of the institution of the Lord's Supper in I Corinthians 11:24. There was no singing. The elements were passed by the deacons to the people in the pews. The parts of the Sunday service were prayer, confession, the Lord's Prayer, the creed, the sermon, and the benediction. The ministers wore citizen's dress—a black coat and a white ruff. While the fashion of the people has changed, the ministers kept the original garb, which later became a clerical robe or gown.

The first part of Zwingli's Bible translation appeared in 1525. A theological statement of Reformed doctrine was published by Zwingli in the same year. It is entitled *On the True and False Religion*. It is similar to the *Loci Communes* of Melancthon and the *Institutes of the Christian Religion* of Calvin. Theses three were the great doctrinal treatises of the Reformation. For the training of preachers Zwingli established an institution called "The Prophecy." It was an assembly of students and ministers for the study of the Old Testament after the early sermon each day of the week except Friday. The expositions were based on the Hebrew and Greek texts. Leo Jude presented the substance in popular form to the congregation. Thus, the Scriptures, interpreted in a grammatical and historical way, were made the bases both for the religious and social life.

The government of the church was in control of the town council. But a distinct body, composed of ministers of the city and canton and two lay delegates of each parish, also four members of the small and four of the great council, constituted a synod. It met twice a year in the city hall of Zurich and had oversight of the doctrines and morals of the clergy. Intemperance, extravagance, and neglect of church ordinances by clergy or people were carefully noted and severely censured. Zwingli was the founder of the synod, while Calvin was the organizer of the consistory in the Reformed churches. These changes having been effected, the church of Zurich was reconstructed after the evangelical pattern and may be called the mother of the Reformed churches in all lands.

Distinctive Teachings

All the Reformers were Protestants in their attitude toward Roman Catholicism and evangelical in their attitude toward rationalism. They differed from one another, however, at many points when they came to define Christianity as they found it in the Bible. The distinctive characteristics of each original Reformer were due to differences in national genius, early training, religious experience, and method of approach to the New Testament. Zwingli found the standard of doctrine and life in the Bible. In this respect he agreed with Luther and differed from the Anabaptists. His conservatism appeared in his attitude to the Roman Catholic Church. His aim was to reform the old church in the light of the New Testament. The humanists were content simply to enlighten and purify the old church, opposing changes in its organization. The Anabaptists renounced and denounced the old church and insisted on establishing a *new* church. The mystics were prepared to abolish the old church and to have *no* church.

As a conservative Zwingli accepted two of the seven sacraments, including infant baptism; the official ministry; and a regular church government. He never questioned the ecumenical creeds, including the doctrines of the Trinity and the Incarnation. Notwithstanding the clearness of his thinking and the philosophical bent of his mind, he always remained a supernaturalist. He never was a rationalist in the modern sense of the term. The Anabaptists were indifferent and even hostile to State and school. Zwingli recognized both as serving a divine purpose in the kingdom of God. He considered patriotism and the duties of citizenship an inseparable part of Christian life. The school also was necessary to train youth for effective service in Church and State. He had no confidence in the dreams, the fancies, the Inner Light, of the radicals, nor in the blind acceptance of doctrine and law by tradition and ecclesiastical dictation.

All Reformers, conservative and radical—Luther and Zwingli, Hubmeier and Socinus, Erasmus and Denck—professed to follow the sacred Scriptures. Yet they differed both in their estimate of the Bible as a whole and in their interpretation of specific doctrines and precepts. Zwingli approached the Scriptures as a humanist, making it the sole authority in matters of faith and conduct. His test of doctrine or practice was contained in the question "Has Christ taught us this?" or "Is it clearly and certainly taught us in the Divine Word?" We must obey God and his eternal word, and not men and their changing opinions. Only that which was commanded in the Bible, either directly or by clear inference, should be permitted in the Church. All this a good humanist would have affirmed. Yet Zwingli differed from Erasmus and his kind in making the Bible, not simply a divinely revealed law or philosophy of life, but a gospel of salvation. In it he found, with the aid of the writings of Luther and through his personal experience, the doctrine of salvation by grace. On that account Christ became to him, as well as to Luther, the only comfort and treasure of his soul; and through Christ men are redeemed and reconciled unto God. This is the essence of evangelical in distinction from Catholic or humanistic Christianity.

Yet Zwingli's view of the Bible was different from that of Luther—a difference of emphasis and viewpoint perhaps more than of formal definition. True to his personal experience of salvation by grace, Luther made the gospel consist in the good news of redemption by grace and felt himself free from biblical and ecclesiastical laws and ordinances. Through the law men were convinced, while the gospel gave assurance of forgiveness and sonship. He valued most highly those books in the Bible which proclaimed salvation by grace through faith. On account of the absence of that doctrine in the Epistle of James he called it "a right strawy Epistle." Zwingli also found the doctrine of grace in the Bible, but for him it still remained the law of life for the saints as well as the manifestation of grace for the sinner. He did not make Luther's sharp distinction between the Old Testament and the New, law and gospel. He defined the word "gospel" as "everything that is made known of God to men, which instructs them and assures them of his will." In this sense of the term even pagans may have gospel—Seneca and Plato, for example. The Old Testament, no less than the New, is part of the gospel. Luther limited his definition of gospel to the Bible and especially to those parts of the Bible which revealed the grace of God in Christ Jesus. In the apology for the Augsburg Confession we are told, "Gospel properly is the promise of remission and justification on account of Christ."

Corresponding to these two views of gospel, there are two conceptions of faith. Zwingli defines it in the general sense as "absolute trust in God and his word without wavering." He correlates faith with the all-controlling providence of God. Faith, therefore, is not the cause of election but the effect of it. Luther defines it exclusively as trust in the pardoning grace of God revealed through Christ. It is constantly renewed through the use of the sacraments. What is sealed in baptism is reiterated in the Lord's Supper.

While Zwingli accepted the Bible as his rule of faith and conduct, he ventured beyond it in defining the nature and character of God. He did not have Luther's contempt for the natural reason. His idea of God, therefore, was far more philosophical and in some respects more modern. Professor McGiffert says:

He thought of the Deity in much more abstract terms than Luther. God was less a personal Father than the Creator and Ruler of the world, and the attributes which Zwingli ascribed to him were those of traditional theology, omnipotence and omniscience occupying a chief place. This is particularly manifest in connection with his doctrine of predestination, which finds its most elaborate and systematic expression in his work on the providence of God.[1]

Since Zwingli considered God as the all-controlling and absolute cause of everything, he traced even sin to the divine will, assuming that through it God revealed his justice in the punishment of the sinner and his grace in the salvation of the sinner. He based the assurance of salvation upon the election of grace, which is realized in the individual through Christ. The gracious operations of God he did not limit to the Bible and the Church. He believed that God was working in all men, even among the pagans, some of whom are elect

---

[1] Arthur C. McGiffert, *Protestant Thought Before Kant*, chap. III; Charles Scribner's Sons, publishers; used by permission.

and have a place in the heavenly kingdom. "If this be true," said Luther, "then the whole gospel is false." Luther made religious experience, the consciousness of divine forgiveness, central in his thought and work; while Zwingli made the absolute and unconditioned will of God central. The one was Christological, the other theological. The one was inclined to be more experimental, the other more ethical and doctrinal.

Zwingli was the creator of a new type of piety in Protestantism. He emphasized the believer's independence of human ordinance and traditions and his dependence on God alone. Since God alone creates, upholds, provides, saves, and sanctifies, to him alone must *honor* be given. God is honored by obedience to his will. Through obedience a man becomes sure of his divine election, and his salvation therefore rests, not upon the mutable feelings and works of men, but upon the eternal and unchangeable will of God.

Christians must oppose all forms of creature worship which detract from the honor due to the Creator. Accordingly Zwingli began the Reformation by preaching against the worship or veneration of Virgin and saints and by protesting against the substitution of human ordinances and traditions for the divine command. He would not even allow that grace is communicated through material sacramental channels. He relied for his assurance of salvation upon the direct and immediate operation of the Spirit through the Word. The marks of the Church are not merely the gospel truly preached and the sacraments rightly administered but also the application of the divine will to the individual and social life. The great ethical motive in Luther was to prove one's justification by patient endurance of the sorrows and ills of life; the ethical motive of Zwingli was to honor or glorify God by subduing the world to the will of God. The Church, therefore, is not simply an institution of salvation, with gospel and sacraments, but a fellowship of saints co-operating in converting individuals and in transforming human society.

Differences like these came to light when Luther and Zwingli met in 1529 at the Colloquy of Marburg. Neither of the men could have clearly defined the points of difference, yet each felt what Luther said before they separated: "You are of a different spirit from us." When they parted without shaking hands, each was true to his convictions. Not simply on account of stubbornness, personal ambition, or human arbitrariness did they become the leaders of two branches of Protestantism. Each represented a type of evangelical Christianity, and each was necessary to bring out the fullness of truth in Christ Jesus.

ZWINGLI'S DEATH

The doctrines of the Reformation divided the cantons of Switzerland into two groups—Roman Catholic and Protestant. The city cantons, as a rule, became Protestant; while the forest cantons remained Catholic. The confederacy was thus divided into hostile camps, each group preparing to fight out the religious question on the field of battle. The inevitable result was a war between the Catholics and the Protestants. In the second war, which followed the first after a brief armistice, Zwingli, as chaplain, accompanied the troops of Zurich to the battlefield of Kappel. The Catholics, however, were better prepared for the conflict and put the soldiers of Zurich to flight. Zwingli was wounded and fell to the ground. He was found by a Catholic soldier, who offered him the services of a priest for his dying hours, but Zwingli refused. Thus he was recognized as a Protestant. One of the Catholic soldiers drew his sword and pierced his body, saying, "Die, obstinate heretic!" While breathing his last Zwingli pronounced the memorable words: "They may kill the body, but the soul they cannot kill." His corpse was cut into four pieces by the hangman as a punishment for treason. The parts were burned into ashes as a punishment for heresy. The ashes were mixed with those of a swine and scattered to the four winds of heaven. Zwingli was a martyr on the battlefield for his country, and his body was burned to ashes for his Church. Thus, in death as in life, he bore testimony to the inspiring ideal of his ministry—the union of patriotism and Christianity.

CALVIN AND HIS TRADITION

GEORGIA HARKNESS

JOHN CALVIN was born at Noyon, Picardy, on July 10, 1509. He died in Geneva on May 27, 1564. Between these dates is compressed one of the most vigorous and influential lives in the history of the Christian Church. It is a life of many lights and shadows, of great faults and great virtues, lived powerfully for the glory of God.

THE MAN

Calvin's life, though full of battles, followed a relatively simple course in its external structure. As a schoolboy he was precocious, serious-minded, and censorious, winning from his schoolmates the nickname of "the accusative case." At fourteen he entered the University of Paris, where he displayed unusual skill in Latin and argumentation, thereby laying the foundations for his subsequent ability to write theology in Latin of remarkable clarity and vigor. At the desire of his father he took a course in law at Orleans, and this, by accentuating his naturally legalistic turn of mind, undoubtedly influenced the tenor of his later thought.

Though reared a Roman Catholic, Calvin became a Protestant while studying in Paris sometime between April, 1532, and November, 1533. Of the circumstances connected with this turning point in his life he gives no account in all his voluminous writings. It is in keeping with the God-centered character of his religion that in the few references he makes to his conversion to Protestantism he speaks of it as coming direct from God. It is probable that he was influenced by some Protestant friends and by the general unrest created throughout Western Europe by the preaching of Luther and Zwingli. He never met either of these leaders personally. Zwingli died in 1531, before Calvin's conversion. Luther lived till 1546, ten years after Calvin became the leader of the Geneva church, but streamlined Pullmans had not yet been dreamed of.

In March, 1536, while living in seclusion at Basel because of some flurries caused by his Protestant convictions, Calvin published the first edition of his great work *The Institutes of the Christian Religion*. Though this went through five editions in his lifetime and grew from six to eighty chapters, the general structure of his thought remained unchanged. This first edition shows amazing maturity for a youth of twenty-six.

The location of Calvin's lifework in Geneva came about by one of those minor circumstances which in retrospect can be viewed only as the leading of Providence. Called from Basel to Noyon to settle his father's estate, Calvin wished on his return to go to Strassburg. Finding the usual route blocked by war, he went by Geneva and stopped to spend the night. Geneva was already nominally Protestant, though far from unified. William Farel, the pastor, was having more than he could handle in this gay, pleasure-loving city, and he saw in Calvin the assistant he needed. Calvin, who was by nature studious and retiring, even shy, was reluctant to give up a quiet life of study for one of turbulent action. But Farel adduced one argument that was unanswerable: "I denounce unto you, in the name of Almighty God, that if, under the pretext of prosecuting your studies, you refuse to labor with us in this work of the Lord, the Lord will curse you as seeking yourself rather than Christ." Calvin yielded. In August, 1536, he began his ministry in Geneva, and Calvinism was born.

But not born without a struggle! We cannot here trace the details, but the outlines are essential to an understanding of the emergence of the Genevan theocracy. Calvin's major battle centered in a conflict of power between the civil and religious authorities. What he aimed to do was not to unite Church and State in an ecclesiastical absolutism but to make Geneva a city in which the word of God should be the absolute authority in morals and doctrine. This required rigid discipline. He conceived it to be the duty of the Church to interpret the word and to admonish offenders, but of the State to punish infractions. He therefore consented to and in part created a dual system. Political authority was centered in a council; religious authority in the consistory, with the ministers at its head, though the council retained the power of employing the ministers. In theory it was the function of the consistory, representing the Church, to determine what constituted purity of doctrine and morals; it was the function of the council, representing the State, to enforce such purity. In practice there was almost interminable conflict.

Even before Calvin's arrival the council had made attendance at the Protestant service compulsory. Enforcement of this edict and the passage of sumptuary legislation, anticipating the New England "blue laws," was abetted and further instigated by Calvin. However, it was soon apparent that a clash was inevitable, for the council insisted upon retaining the right of excommunication and of determining the form of the sacraments. When, in April, 1538, Calvin and Farel refused to accede to the council's demand for the use of unleavened bread, they were ordered to leave the city within three days. Calvin's comment reveals his spirit: "Well, indeed! If we had served men, we should have been ill rewarded; but we serve a Great Master, who will recompense us."

Thus ousted, Calvin spent the next three and a half years in Strassburg, where he lived in poverty but satisfying activity as preacher and professor of theology. He revised the form of public worship, introduced congregational singing, and established the sermon-centered type of Sunday service, which is used to the present in most of the non-liturgical churches. In this period he married a widow of his congregation, who until her death, nine years later, gave companionship to an otherwise lonely life.

Meanwhile Geneva, which had not been able to get along with Calvin, found that it could not get along without him. Confusion reigned with the hand of the master executive withdrawn, and the council made overtures to induce Calvin to return. Though reluctant to do so, he consented in order not to be one of "those who have more care for their own ease and profit than for the edification of the Church."

From the time of his return, in September, 1541, until 1555, Calvin's life was one of almost continual conflict. During the last nine years of his life he was the acknowledged head of the Genevan theocracy. He spent many more years fighting for power than in enjoying the fruits of victory. But one does not understand Calvin who fails to see how largely it was the authority of the Church, rather than his own power, that he was fighting to uphold. This is not to say that he was completely selfless, for he was inflexible, fully convinced that God had entrusted to him the truth; yet he was far less a personal dictator than he is commonly represented.

The opposition came in part from Roman Catholic sympathizers, but more from the Libertines, freethinkers, and free livers, who objected to the rigid policing of private morals. From time to time the Libertines got the ascendancy in the council, and in 1553 Calvin again almost lost his pulpit in a clash over the power of excommunication. Some of the offenses for which the consistory admonished and the council punished during this period were absence from church, dancing, playing cards on Sunday, spending time in taverns, betrothing one's daughter to a Catholic, eating fish on Good Friday, shaving the tonsure on a priest's head, having one's fortune told by gypsies, saying that there is no devil or hell, criticizing the doctrine of election, calling the Pope a good man, singing a song defamatory of Calvin. Other common offenses, such as theft and adultery, came in for their share of attention.

Such action was designed to preserve purity of morals. But it was purity of doctrine that mattered most, and the action taken against heretics is the chief stain on Calvin's memory. Though the events connected with the burning of the Spanish physician Michael Servetus for his unitarianism are very complicated, it is impossible to absolve Calvin from responsibility. The high-minded Sebastian Castellio was excluded from the Genevan ministry for questioning the inspiration of the Song of Solomon, and Jacques Gruet was beheaded for belittling the Mosaic law and writing "all nonsense" in one of Calvin's books. It is, however, necessary to understand why Calvin persecuted heretics. In part, he was the child of his age. In part, also, he believed it necessary to protect those who were being injured—not in body, but worse yet, in soul—by the virus of false doctrine. Supremely, he believed that heresy dishonored God, and that at any human cost God's honor must be upheld.

In 1555 the opposition of the Libertines was effectively put down, and the power of excommunication firmly lodged with the consistory. In 1559 Calvin's desire for an educated laity as well as ministry led to the opening of the University of Geneva, which has rendered distinguished service to the present. In this year also the council honored him by conferring citizenship upon him, for Geneva's foremost servant for twenty years had not heretofore been a citizen.

Always an indefatigable worker, Calvin increased his labors. His associate and first biographer—Theodore Beza—cites a statement that should give courage to any preacher of today who finds his study invaded by parish duties:

When the messenger called for my book, I had twenty sheets to revise, to preach, to read to the congregation, to write four letters, to attend to some controversies, and to return answers to more than ten persons who interrupted me in the midst of my labors for advice.

Calvin's writings fill the greater part of the fifty-nine quarto volumes of the *Calvini Opera.* Beza estimates that Calvin preached (always to the same congregation) 286 times a year and lectured on theology another 180 times. He was called upon to give advice on every human problem from the choice of stoves and of wives to the stabilization of the faithful throughout the Reformed churches of Western Europe. Many of his letters show a tenderness in personal relations not often associated with his name. Without limit he gave himself for the good of the people and the glory of God.

Never of robust health, Calvin wore himself out early and died at fifty-five. He continued to preach when he was too ill to walk and had to be carried to the pulpit in a chair. At his death he left a material estate of less than two thousand dollars and a spiritual inheritance of unestimated value.

One wonders what more Calvin would have accomplished had his life been spared, as Wesley's was, for another thirty years. Yet to few men is it given to round out one's lifework so completely. Before his death the morals of Geneva were firmly grounded on the word of God as he saw it. Heresy was stamped out. The ecclesiastical system was established. Commentaries had been written on nearly every book of the Bible. The final edition of the *Institutes* was published in 1559, the year the university was opened. Calvin's history-making work was done. His influence was in its genesis.

CALVINISM

When one speaks of Calvinism, one may mean a system of theology, a type of morals symbolized by the Puritan conscience, or a form of Church-State relation. The three are interrelated. All are traceable to Calvin's personality, and all have had an important influence in America. At the risk of oversimplification it is necessary to state the outlines of each.

1. *Theology.*—Calvin's theology was authoritarian, legalistic, logical, and biblical. The Bible was to him the sole authority in faith and morals. Its writers he believed to be verbally inspired, "the sure and authentic amanuenses of the Holy Spirit." Differences of interpretation were to be settled by ministers taught by the Holy Spirit; but not by all ministers, for only the elect were thus inwardly taught. As to who were of the elect no one could say of another with complete certainty, but one could be assured of his own election by an inner witness. Calvin never doubted that he was of the elect, and that God had called him to interpret the word of God to the people. It was this assurance, rather than personal bigotry and conceit, which made him adamant when any disagreement arose.

Unlike Luther, Calvin regarded all parts of the Bible as equally the word of God. However, he drew most of his texts from the Old Testament. The Decalogue, rather than the Sermon on the Mount, was the center of his faith. This accounts for the fact that Calvin's main emphasis falls, not on the love of God or his self-disclosure in Jesus, but on the sovereignty of God and his judgment upon sinners.

God to Calvin was triune, just, holy, the all-powerful Ruler and Governor. God's will is unconditioned. What God does is good, not because it satisfies man's moral expectations, but because God does it. Man cannot understand or explain the mysteries of Divine Providence, and to attempt to do so is blasphemy. Man's duty is to worship, trust, and obey a Sovereign Deity by whose will all things are determined.

The correlate of God's absolute sovereignty is man's utter helplessness. Made in the divine image, man lost this image through the Fall. Adam's sin has tainted the whole human race and robbed man both of his original goodness and his freedom. In this state man suffers from "an hereditary corruption and depravity of our nature." God has given man the law as his guide; but since man is unable to perform saving works, the law serves only to reveal to him his lost condition. Like Augustine, Calvin held that man is free to sin but not to do good. It was by this route that both avoided the conclusion that God is responsible for human sin.

Though man cannot save himself, God saves some. God in his mercy has sent the Eternal Son to enter into sinful flesh and suffer in man's stead. Christ's atoning work is wrought through his threefold office of prophet, priest, and king. As prophet he reveals God; as priest he atones by his obedience for man's sin and appeases God's wrath; as king he rules as the head of the Church of the elect whom he has thus redeemed.

Why not "whosoever will"? The doctrines of predestination and election, irresistible grace, and perseverance of the saints have always seemed to the Arminian branch of Protestantism an outrageous affront both to human freedom and to the inclusivenss of God's saving work

71

in Christ. Yet they follow consistently, not only from a literal reading of Romans 8:29-30, but from the doctrines of God's absolute sovereignty and man's helplessness. If God determines all events, even the most trivial, he surely determines the supreme event of a man's salvation. If man cannot save himself by electing to do so, then to be saved God must elect him. If God is truly sovereign, his grace is not only prevenient but also irresistible. Then, when God has chosen a soul for salvation, it is to question the wisdom and efficacy of the divine act to suppose that the choice is temporary.

Calvin's doctrine of predestination follows essentially the pattern set by Augustine and Luther, but with an important exception: both these men were warm-hearted mystics, who could never quite bring themselves to affirm double predestination—that is, the election by God of some to be damned. Calvin drew the logical conclusion. With Luther love is central to his idea of God; with Calvin, majesty. If a God of transcendent majesty chooses to leave some men to suffer the deserved penalty for their guilt, it is not for human minds, Calvin thought, to question the divine justice. The sun is not evil if its light, falling upon putrid flesh, causes foul odors to arise.

2. *Ethics.*—It has often seemed to outsiders that Calvinism ought to breed in its adherents a complete moral lethargy. Yet the Calvinists have been great activists in both religious and secular pursuits. The explanation lies, not in inconsistency, but in another strain of Calvin's thought.

Calvin never claimed that only the elect could be moral in the ordinary sense of refraining from theft, adultery, murder, and other offenses against society. What he did maintain was that such morality, whether in the form of abstinence or of positive good works, was unable to save a man. In fact, it was not true righteousness unless done for God's glory; for one might outwardly be virtuous while sacrilegiously affronting the majesty of God. But when one has been redeemed by God's grace, his morality takes on a new quality. He is not thereby excused from moral effort; on the contrary he is called to labor with untiring zeal for the glory of God and the service of men.

The Calvinists strove with terrible earnestness to make their calling and election sure. Though good works could not save a person, they could be a sign that God had saved him. Such activity took three main forms. One was the duty, through preaching and witness, to arouse others from complacency in sin by proclaiming the judgment of God. A second was the keeping of the Ten Commandments, applied to every detail of life. This included the obligation to cleanse the morals of the community by forcing others to keep them. A third was the obligation to be zealous in one's vocation, not merely serving God with resignation *in* one's calling, as Luther had enjoined, but actively seeking to serve God *through* it. One sees the effects of the first kind of works in Jonathan Edwards' famous sermon on "Sinners in the Hands of an Angry God"; of the second, in the inhibitions and imperatives of

72

the Puritan conscience; of the third, in the economic fruits of Calvinism, which is the theme of Max Weber's essay on *The Protestant Ethic and the Spirit of Capitalism.* Leaving the familiar first type, we must inquire what the second and third entailed.

The morality of keeping the commandments was predominantly, both for Calvin and his New England followers, a series of "thou shalt nots." Since God's glory was paramount, the worst offenses were sins against God—idolatry, blasphemy, and heresy. Roman Catholics were viewed as idolaters, and Calvin never tired of excoriating the papists and ridiculing their superstitions. Blasphemy was an offense to be punished by the civil authorities. The penalties for idolatry and blasphemy were variable but never more serious than exile. That Calvin invoked the death penalty for heresy indicates its greater seriousness in his estimate. Murder was the killing of the body, heresy the poisoning of the soul; and both seemed to him to demand a penalty of death for the protection of the innocent. One kills the wolf to save the sheep; one scotches the snake in the grass to save the children. Had nonconformity in doctrine been more common in Geneva, the Servetus affair might have been many times repeated.

It is in the ordinary relations of the Christian to his neighbor that the Puritan or middle-class virtues come into the foreground, linking Calvinistic ethics with economics. The elect Christian must honor God and prove his election by his industry, thrift, honesty, sobriety, chastity. Or, to put it negatively, the Christian community will not tolerate the idler, the spendthrift, the liar or thief, the drunkard, the adulterer. Regular attendance at the Sunday service and a pure use of the Lord's day is a duty owed both to God and man. Put these virtues together, and they do not add up to the type of ethics set forth in the Sermon on the Mount; but they do summarize the most conspicuous requirements both of Calvin's Geneva and of our founding fathers.

3. *Politics.*—We have seen how the theocracy came about as a form of power politics—an attempt to give divine sanction to civil affairs in the interests of personal righteousness. Calvin's political theory closely approximates that of Hildebrand but with the authority of the Bible replacing the power of the papacy. Church and State were conceived as two separate and distinct institutions but with the Church above the State because of its guardianship of the word of God. It is clear that such a structure could persist only on the fulfillment of two conditions: (*a*) the willingness of the people to be so governed and (*b*) a dominant personality to interpret the word of God so that his word was accepted as God's word. These conditions were met for a time in Geneva and in Puritan New England, but with increasing freedom of thought and the passing of the great divines the theocracy was bound to fall apart.

Another political influence stemming from Calvin has been far more permanent. On the surface there is little that looks like democracy in his absolutism; yet Calvinism was the foundation for the establishment of the Dutch republic, the revolt of the Scotch against Mary Stuart, the

Puritan revolution in England, and, in part, the American and French revolutions. It must not be forgotten that the movement for American independence was in large measure conceived and nourished in Calvinistic New England.

The sources of this democratic impulse from Calvin are twofold:

One is Calvin's doctrine of man. He would hardly have said that all men are created free and equal; yet he believed with his whole soul that all men, by the curse of Adam, are equally unfree. God is no respecter of persons, nor was Calvin. No rich reprobate in Geneva could escape the condemnation of God, the consistory, or the council. Calvin knew that no prerogative of class or economic standing, no man-made distinctions, will save a man. Before God we are all sinners. The doctrine of God's absolute sovereignty and man's total depravity and helplessness thus becomes a great leveler, a solvent to human pretensions, and a foundation stone for the democratizing of the social order.

The other main source of Calvin's democratic influence lies in his doctrine of resistance to tyranny. Like Paul and Luther he believed that the ruling powers are ordained of God. Like Luther he enjoins, in the *Institutes,* passive resistance. But there is little passive resistance in his own conduct, and in his sermons he goes far beyond Luther in sanctioning active resistance to civil authorities that defy God. In his commentary on Daniel 6:22 he writes:

Earthly princes lay aside all their power when they rise up against God and are unworthy to be reckoned in the number of mankind. We ought rather to spit on their heads than to obey them when they are so restive and wish to rob God of his rights.

Again, in a sermon on the same chapter, he says:

Even though they torture us bodily and use tyranny and cruelty toward us, it is necessary to bear all this, as St. Paul says. *But when they rise against God,* they must be put down and held of no more account than worn-out shoes.

Those who are familiar with Karl Barth's call to Christians to resist Nazi tyranny as a divine duty will find in it an almost exact replica of Calvin's position.

Calvin's Influence in America

We must now attempt to pull together various strands of Calvin's thought and make some estimate of his contemporary influence in America.

Calvinism came to our shores through several channels. The French Huguenots, fleeing from persecution after the massacre of St. Bartholomew's Eve and again after the revocation of the Edict of Nantes, settled all the way from the Canadian border to Florida but chiefly in North and South Carolina. Another line from Geneva to America is by way of the Netherlands. This comes most directly through the Dutch who settled in and about New York, but there was an interpenetration of Dutch and Puritan thought when the Dutch Calvinists fled to England to escape the persecutions of the Duke of Alva, and later our Pilgrim Fathers took refuge in Holland before coming to America. The third main line—that in which Calvinism is most fully preserved —is that of the Scotch and Scotch-Irish Presbyterians. Thrifty, canny, and resolute, they settled everywhere save for the fact that their brother Calvinists in New England gave them a cold shoulder and shoved them west. Though New York, New Jersey, and Pennsylvania became the main centers of settlement, they pushed southward to the warmth of the Carolinas and westward to become the main line of advance beyond the Alleghenies and in the second tier of colonies. The fourth channel is, of course, the Congregationalism of the Plymouth and Massachusetts Bay colonies, which came to dominate New England except for the Baptist stronghold in Rhode Island. Together these four groups formed the chief substructure for the erection of the American republic.

What have they given us? Though any evaluation must of necessity be a wholly inadequate summary, five contributions stand out:

1. *A type of character suggested by the phrase "the Puritan virtues."* —Common to both Puritan and Presbyterian strains (shared by the Dutch and Huguenot, though these are far less influential), these virtues became the implicit standard of respectability and decency in the American way of life. Though we are now far removed from the discipline of Geneva or Massachusetts Bay, it is still the assumption of the majority of our laity in American Protestantism that to be a Christian means to work hard, to save one's money, not to break the law, not to drink (perhaps, also, not to smoke), to be the faithful husband of one wife, and to attend church regularly on Sunday.

2. *A strong reinforcement to our capitalistic economy.*—Though I believe Weber overstates the case for regarding Calvinism as the chief foundation of capitalism, there can be no doubt that the Puritan virtues are primarily middle-class virtues. This conjunction goes far toward explaining why American Protestantism is, on the whole, on the side of capital rather than labor. It explains also why the churches have so firmly undergirded the morality of small-group relations while leaving almost untouched the wider Christian obligations regarding war, race, and economics. John Wesley saw that "religion must necessarily produce both industry and frugality, and these cannot but produce riches." To avoid the resulting corruption Christians, he thought, must be exhorted to gain all they can, to save all they can, to give all they can. Calvinists and Methodists alike have tended to follow this pattern, at least in its first two items. The result is that philanthropy rather than economic justice is the primary economic virtue in most of our churches.

Mention should also be made of Calvin's contribution to capitalism by another channel—the lifting of the medieval ban on usury. The sanction Calvin gave to the taking of interest on investments is regarded by R. H. Tawney as a watershed in the history of capitalism. Calvin did not materially change the practice, for money had been loaned at interest long before his time. What he did was to lift the ban and place responsibility upon the Christian conscience, shifting restraint from ecclesiastical prohibitions to the golden rule. The door was thus opened for those who wished to let conscience be their guide. This transition in economic practice was for the most part completed before the settlement of America.

3. *A foundation for American democracy.*—Our political theory stems from two main channels: (*a*) a Greek (primarily Stoic) conception of the natural rights of man, which came to America by way of the Enlightenment and had its chief exponents in Thomas Jefferson and Benjamin Franklin; (*b*) a Christian conception of the equality of all men before God. To the second Calvinism made a major contribution, though not by the route of the exaltation of human dignity, which is a familiar note in liberal preaching. The present-day call to repentance for our common sin as the basis of any right ordering of society is in keeping with Calvin's spirit. As for the Christian's duty to resist tyranny, a straight line runs from Calvin's Geneva to Cromwell's England, to the Boston Tea Party and to the interventionism of our time.

4. *Emphasis on an educated ministry and an educated laity.*—We have noted Calvin's concern to establish the university in Geneva. He would not countenance sloppy thinking; for one must offer his best, intellectually as morally, to the glory of God. This spirit was shared by our founding fathers.

Among the Puritans and Presbyterians who migrated to our shores the educational level was high. In New England, Oxford and Cambridge men were numerous, and a profound respect for learning was in the heritage of a Christian home. Harvard University was founded, primarily to prepare young men for the ministry, only sixteen years after the landing of the Pilgrims. By 1647 Massachusetts had made public instruction compulsory and had established an educational system extending from the elementary school to the university.

Among the Presbyterian frontier settlers the school had a place second only to the church. Their ministers were men of scholarship, often trained in Edinburgh or Aberdeen; and as the second and third generations came along, a great crop of Presbyterian colleges emerged to give higher education near the homes of the people. Their estimate of the importance of an educated ministry is evidenced by the fact that seminary training has long been required for ordination in the Presbyterian Church.

5. *A dogmatic but powerful theology based on the authority of the Bible.*—In Congregationalism predestination gave way before the claims of liberal thought; and, after being strongly influenced in New England by Unitarianism, the Congregational-Christian Church now stands for freedom of religious thought as of ecclesiastical structure. Presbyterian-

ism has followed a course much closer to the genius of Calvin. Though predestination has receded, theological rigor and biblical authority have not. As a consequence of the conjunction of these notes with insistence upon an educated ministry the Presbyterian Church has been more sharply divided by the fundamentalist-modernist controversy than has any other in our time. The liberalism of the clergy far outruns that of the laity. Though the theological stamp of the clergy varies greatly, depending not only on which seminary was attended but in which decade, Presbyterians can usually be counted on to have convictions.

The emergence of neo-orthodoxy is, for the most part, a reappearance of Calvinism but without Calvin's doctrine of election or his biblical literalism. Distinctions between Lutheran and Calvinist thought are less sharp than they once were, yet it is significant that the chief centers of neo-orthodox influence in this country are in seminaries that are Calvinist in background. Emphasis upon God's glory and sovereignty, the sinfulness and helplessness of man, the divine initiative in revelation and redemption, the saving work of Christ, the Bible as basis of religious knowledge—these concepts, though no exclusive prerogative of Calvin's, were central to his thought. The truth that lies in them is being increasingly recognized by those who stand outside the Calvinist tradition.

When Calvin died in 1564, his grave, by his own wish, was left unmarked, and "no man knoweth of his sepulcher unto this day." Yet, like Moses, with whose spirit he had much in common, he was permitted to catch a glimpse of the Promised Land. Neither could foresee to what magnitude his work was predestined to grow. They belong among the immortals because with total devotion they served God and his people, consenting to have no other gods before the Most High.

THE ANGLICAN TRADITION

Alexander C. Zabriskie

My task is to discuss the spirit of the Anglican tradition. My interpretation is obviously personal, not official. For the sake of emphasis and of brevity I shall confine myself to one point, omitting any consideration of other features we prize as well as of that church's particular limitations and faults, though I fully realize their existence. If I stress the value of its special characteristic, I trust you will not think that I am trying to disparage any other Christian church.

The Peculiar Genius of Anglicanism

The genius of the Anglican tradition is its holding together the *positive insights* of both Catholicism and Protestantism. It has never held them in balance. At times one has received the greater emphasis, at other times the other. But it insists on holding onto both, even at the cost of constant tension, and is therefore the most dialectical form of organized Christianity. Nor has it succeeded in harmonizing them into a neat synthesis; rather it affirms that both contain valid insights, and that these insights must be accepted even though the human mind is as yet unable to systematize them. It has, in fact, an inherent suspicion of all close-knit systems of theology. This suspicion is largely due to a third factor, which has greatly affected the specifically Anglican combination of Protestantism and Catholicism—namely, its legacy from the Christian humanists of the English Reformation. These men bequeathed to their successors an open-mindedness to new learning and an appeal to sound scholarship as the final arbiter in disputes over the interpretation of Scripture and doctrines; a functional rather than a dogmatic attitude toward the institutions of Chrisianity; an interest in philosophical theology as great as if not greater than in systematic; and an ineradicable strain of Platonism, with its trust in spiritual intuition as a surer guide to ultimate truth than logic.

Let me insert these parenthetical remarks:

First, the bulk of Anglicans have valued Catholicism and Protestantism not as closed systems but as series of great insights. They have held them together, that they might cross-fertilize each other. Some Anglicans have regarded them as complete and mutually exclusive systems: they have wanted their church to become one or the other, but they have never been able to thwart the efforts of those who tried to keep them together.

Secondly, until the middle of the nineteenth century Anglicans always distinguished sharply between Catholicism on the one hand

78

and Romanism or medievalism on the other. Jewell and Hooker, the theologians who in the sixteenth century marked off the position of Anglicanism *vis a vis* Rome and Puritanism, enunciated a view to which Anglicans tenaciously held—namely, that catholicity meant conformity to that which characterized the Church of the New Testament, the early Fathers, and the early councils. These writers regarded Rome as heretical and schismatical, because its medieval developments were contrary to these norms, and they thought sixteenth-century Protestantism a divinely sent protest against this perversion. Protestantism was the opposite not of Catholicism but of Romanism. Catholicity also means universality and wholeness: universality in including all races and nations and in extending to the whole known world; wholeness in maintaining the completeness of the faith and in existing uninterruptedly from the beginning. Rome contradicted vital parts of the faith by her medieval additions and sacrificed a rich fund of insights for a rigid system and an unscriptural tyranny that caused its break with the Eastern Orthodox Church and compelled the church to reform itself in various countries of Western Europe. This has been the view of the great bulk of Anglicans. Not till the nineteenth century did some men become enamored of the Middle Ages and look to Rome as the norm of Catholicism.

Thirdly, Anglicanism's development was not the result of deliberate advance planning but (like all great historical developments) of the interplay of historical forces which there is no time to discuss here.

THE PRAYER BOOK

The best way to illustrate the genius of Anglicanism is to study the *Book of Common Prayer* and the historic episcopate, because these have been the two chief factors binding it together through various ages, in different countries, and under considerable variations in its ecclesiastical government; and also because, in the judgment of many of us, they are the most significant contributions that Anglicanism has to make to the great Church of the future next to its contention that the Catholic and Protestant insights must be held together.

The importance of the *Prayer Book* demonstrates, first of all, that Anglicanism is a liturgical church rather than a confessional one.

Its members are not united by agreement to a confession of faith such as those of Augsburg and Westminster or the decrees of Trent. The only confession to which all Anglicans must subscribe is the Apostles' Creed. Subscription to the Thirty-nine Articles has never been demanded of candidates for confirmation. Today only clergymen subscribe to them, and only in the specifically English branches of Anglicanism; and among them it is understood that their subscription involves an acceptance of the general position outlined therein rather than of the details. They define the general boundaries of the Anglican position on the questions at issue in the middle of the sixteenth century. Do not misunderstand me: Anglicanism has never said that doctrine is unimportant. It is strongly doctrinal. It insists on the creeds. It has had heresy trials. But if its members accept the creeds, they do not have to subscribe to a detailed confession defining what the creeds mean.

Again, loyalty to a great human leader to whom they look back as, under God, the founder of their church means nothing to Anglicans in comparison with the importance attached to St. Peter, Luther, Calvin, Wesley, and other "founding fathers."

In having a common form of worship for its center of unity Anglicanism retained a Catholic insight. But, guided by Renaissance-inspired studies into the early Catholic Church, it also assimilated the correlative Protestant insight—namely, that worship must be intelligible (and therefore in language understanded of the people) and biblical. Gladly Cranmer and his colleagues used the common tongue, and gladly they drew upon the earlier liturgies. Anglicanism began its reformed career as a church united by a common form of worship in the vernacular, most of which comes directly from the Bible; and in every century and in many countries it has remained so.

Again, the *Prayer Book* clearly illustrates the combination of Catholic, Protestant, and Renaissance elements in its order for the celebration of the Holy Communion, especially if that is taken in conjunction with the twenty-fifth through the thirty-first Articles of Religion. Controversy between Protestants and Catholics over this sacrament was concerned then (as it still is) with the presence of Christ and the eucharistic sacrifice. The *Prayer Book* teaches that both groups have had valid insights, but that both systems, when considered as total systems, are in error.

The *Prayer Book* inculcates a doctrine of sacrifice. Note that the words of institution come in the prayer of consecration: they are said to God rather than to the people. The sacrifice of Christ is liturgically re-enacted by minister and congregation with God as the audience, if I may so put it. It is presented to God, not to the congregation. This rehearsal of Christ's passion and of the love for mankind it reveals is, in the prayer of humble access, avowed to be the basis upon which the worshipers presume to approach the holy table and receive the holy food. In that same prayer of consecration the worshipers associate with Christ's sacrifice, which has just been proclaimed, their own offerings of material goods, of praise and thanksgiving, of their souls and bodies. This total offering—the commemoration and pleading of the Passion, bread and wine, praise, self-oblation—is the eucharistic sacrifice.

In insisting upon the eucharistic sacrifice Anglicanism, as illustrated by the *Prayer Book,* clings to a Catholic insight. But also it affirms the Protestant insights that the sacrifice is not propitiatory and that attending it is no meritorious work. In the strongest and most explicit terms the prayer of consecration states that Calvary is the "full, perfect, and sufficient sacrifice, oblation, and satisfaction for the sins of the whole world." Article 31 affirms that it is "that perfect redemption, propitiation, and satisfaction for all the sins of the whole world, both original and actual, and there is none other satisfaction for sin but that alone." This same article condemns propitiatory masses for the living or the dead as "blasphemous fables and dangerous deceits." In Cranmer's term the eucharistic sacrifice is not propitiatory but "gratificatory": it aims not to appease God's wrath but to express our gratitude for the work of Christ. Unfortunately the term "sacrifice" in connection with the Holy Communion seemed to the continental Reformers inevitably to imply "propitiatory" sacrifice, and therefore to safeguard against that abuse they declined to use it at all; while Anglicanism has incorporated the truth for which the Reformers stood but, in order to preserve the truth of Catholicism, retained the word "sacrifice" even at the risk of the perverted connotation's being reintroduced. If I understand the ritual of The Methodist Church aright, the same doctrine is contained in the forms for the celebration of the Lord's Supper contained therein.

The *Prayer Book* teaches a doctrine of real presence. The prayer of consecration, after rehearsing the institution and commemorating the Passion and Resurrection, prays that the Holy Spirit will so affect the bread and wine that those who receive them may be partakers of Christ's body and blood. The words of administration call the elements "the body and the blood of our Lord Jesus Christ." The prayer after the people have received the elements gives thanks for being fed with "the spiritual food of the most precious body and blood of thy Son, our Saviour Jesus Christ." The first paragraph of Article 28 is to the same effect. The teaching is so strong that our Lord communicates himself to the faithful recipients that no standing room is left for Zwinglianism. In all this Anglicanism is catholic; not Roman, for it is at pains to repudiate Rome's perversion of catholicism, but catholic in the sense of trying to be in line with the Church of the New Testament, the early Fathers, and the early councils.

But at the same time the *Prayer Book* affirms the Protestant insights. Transubstantiation is categorically denied in Article 28 on the grounds that it is unscriptural, destroys the nature of a sacrament (by changing a means of grace into the grace itself), and is a cause of superstition. More than that, the bread and wine are not identical with Christ's body and blood but are the "outward and visible signs" thereof and the vehicles *through* which the gift is conveyed. Note that Article 28 declares that the body and blood are eaten only after a heavenly and spiritual manner, and the means by which Christ is received is faith. Article 29 becomes more specific and states that the wicked, though they eat and drink the sacrament, are in no wise partakers of Christ. The words of administration say, "Take and eat this . . . and feed on Him in thy *heart* by *faith* with thanksgiving." (Italics mine.) The service does not specifically teach that the elements are the body and blood of Christ apart from reception but rather that they are the channels through which that gift is conveyed to the recipients.

81

The result of asserting both the Catholic and the Protestant insights into our Lord's presence in the Holy Communion is that Anglicanism does not proclaim any one definite eucharistic doctrine. As Paul Elmer More wrote, it offers not a definition but a direction in which thought should move. It lays down limits within which it should remain but allows great latitude within those limits. In effect, as Dr. More further showed, it does for Eucharistic doctrine what Chalcedon did for Christology, saying that several things are true even if they are not reducible to a neat logical statement.[1]

Other things in the *Prayer Book* further illustrate Anglicanism's effort to hold together what is valid in both Catholicism and Protestantism. In the Catholic vein it maintained the church year; provided for the ordination of a threefold ministry; perpetuated the rite of confirmation by a bishop not only as a public profession of faith but also as a means of strengthening or "confirming" the candidate. In recent years there have been added forms for anointing the dying and special Collects, Epistles, and Gospels for Holy Communion when that service is used in connection with a marriage or a funeral. On the other hand, it took over two of Protestantism's chief contentions. The final authority of the Bible in all matters of belief and practice was asserted by the promises required of ordinands and by Articles 6 and 20. Following the same line of thought, Jewell wrote that the books of the Bible are "the very sure and infallible rule whereby may be tried whether the church doth stagger or err and whereunto all ecclesiastical doctrine ought to be called to account." [2] William Laud wrote that the difference between Anglicanism and Romanism was that the former taught the religion of the Bible, the latter the religion of the Council of Trent. The other Protestant insight taken over by Anglicanism, which the *Prayer Book* illustrates, is the doctrine of justification by faith only, which is asserted in Article 11; a conviction reasserted also by Jewel, Hooker, Andrewes, Laud, and others.

One further word about the *Prayer Book:* Many of us think that its unique value lies precisely in the fact that it was not written by any one man at any one time but is the product of centuries of Christian devotion. Thomas Cranmer chose, translated, and edited most of the contents of the book; but many men of many centuries and places wrote it. This, I think, accounts not only for its usefulness in corporate worship but also for the great value we find in it for private devotion. Furthermore, it makes it emphatically not the possession of the Anglican communion alone but of all Christians who desire through it to draw upon their spiritual ancestors. The Methodist Church, for example, has exactly as much right as we to the prayers and liturgical forms of which we availed ourselves, and I for one am delighted to find such similarity between the forms and orders adopted by the Uniting Con-

---

[1] More and Cross, *Anglicanism*, introduction, p. xxxvii.
[2] *Apologie*, p. 62.

ference at Kansas City and the services that, as an Episcopal minister, I must use. The *Prayer Book* is peculiar to Anglicanism only in the respect that that Church requires its use in public services.

THE HISTORIC EPISCOPATE

Another thing that throws light upon this Protestant-Catholicism, which is so central a feature of Anglicanism, is the historic episcopate.

However greatly they may differ in their interpretation of the episcopate, all Anglicans, I think, agree to the three fundamental propositions of the preface to the ordinal: that the episcopate has existed from the earliest days of the Christian Church; that it contains such values that the Anglican church will never give it up; that a bishop is a different thing from a presbyter with wide administrative powers—a difference indicated by saying that bishops form a separate order of ministry. I will return shortly to *why* Anglicans place so high a value upon it; but first I want to examine the *official* teaching of Anglicanism about it, for it is another example of that church's Protestant-Catholicism.

Anglicanism retained the historic episcopate as part of its Catholic heritage. Throughout the Puritan controversy it refused to give it up, even though it meant that the Church became so identified with the Stuart cause that during the Protectorate it was banned and had to exist precariously. The most Protestant-minded evangelicals were strong defenders of the historic episcopate. In the famous Chicago-Lambeth Quadrilateral it was made one of the four indispensable points in any plan of union to which the Anglican communion would agree.

But Anglicanism, it seems quite clear, has officially taught the historic episcopate to be of the *bene esse* rather than the *esse* of the church; and in this *interpretation* it has incorporated an insight of the Reformation. In the preface to the ordinal it is stated:

> To the intent that these orders may be continued and reverently used and esteemed in this church, no man shall be accounted or taken to be a lawful bishop, priest, or deacon in this church or suffered to execute any of the said functions except he be called, tried, examined, and admitted thereunto according to the form hereafter following or hath had episcopal consecration or ordination.

But nothing is said about the validity of other orders; only, that this church insists its ministers be episcopally ordained. It is a statement of the law of the Church of England, not an explanation of the nature of ordination. Furthermore, in all probability this preface was written by Cranmer. At least, it is certain that he approved it, and it is clear that neither he nor the other Reformers regarded all nonepiscopal orders as invalid. It seems clear that the insistence upon episcopal orders for the Anglican Church was originally a matter of discipline rather than doctrine.

The other thing in the *Prayer Book* which is sometimes quoted as proof that Anglicanism officially teaches a rigid doctrine of apostolic succession is a prayer in the office of institution of ministers, which reads: "O Holy Jesus, who hast promised to be with the ministers of apostolic succession to the end of the world. . . ." But here, again, two things should be noted: Nothing is said to deny that our Lord is with other ministers. Nor is it necessary to interpret "apostolic succession" here as implying the rigid view thereof; it can be interpreted as meaning ministers who belong to a succession that goes back to the apostles in respect of *continuity of office* rather than of episcopal ordination—an interpretation more in harmony with the preface to the ordinal, the office of instruction (p. 291), and Article 23.

I personally am convinced that the *Prayer Book* teaches the necessity of the historic episcopate as a matter of discipline, and that it is quite impossible to maintain that it regards it as a matter of doctrine. The preface to the *Prayer Book* states that "what cannot be clearly determined to belong to doctrine must be referred to discipline"; and, in my judgment, Anglicanism, thinking the rigid doctrine of apostolic succession unproved, has referred the episcopate to discipline. The historic episcopate is certainly of the *bene esse* of the church; it is not necessarily of the *esse*.

Three facts may be cited to substantiate the view that this remained Anglicanism's official position. In 1610 the Archbishop of Canterbury consecrated to the episcopate three Scotch presbyters without first ordaining them deacon or priest—this on the ground that their Presbyterian orders were valid. In 1662 an Act of Parliament ruled that thenceforward no nonepiscopally ordained minister might hold any cure in the Church of England *except* such continental Protestants as the King might see fit to license. The bulk of Anglican theologians from Jewel to the tractarians regarded Presbyterian orders as valid. There is no space to substantiate this last statement, but I am sure that it is correct.

In this respect, then, Anglicanism took over the Protestant contention that the Reformed churches, which had been obliged to separate from Rome in order to preserve the true biblical faith and had been unable to take any bishops with them, were still parts of the Holy Catholic Church; that orders were conferred by the Holy Spirit acting through the *Church,* of which the ordaining minister was a representative and agent; and that, therefore, what was necessary was that the ordainer should be the person or persons to whom his branch of the Church had committed that responsibility. Such nonepiscopal orders might be defective (or, to use a term of the sixteenth and seventeenth centuries, they were imperfect), but they were not invalid. The historic episcopate was of immense importance, but it was not so utterly essential that apart from it there could be no true Church of Christ. Such, I think, is Anglicanism's official teaching.

But there is no doubt that during the last century the rigid apostolic-succession view has gained considerably in Anglicanism. A larger proportion of its members now hold it, though, I think, they still are definitely in the minority. Also, the practice with regard to ministers seeking to transfer from other churches has been modified in two directions: I know of no nonepiscopally ordained man admitted to its ministry without reordination in the last century. Roman priests are now admitted without reordination, whereas up to a century ago some of them (I do not know what proportion) were reordained. These practices are interpreted by many as a matter of discipline, though those chiefly responsible for them regarded them as matters of doctrine.

If the bulk of Anglicans, who do not hold any rigid apostolic-succession theory, place so high an importance upon the historic episcopate that they would not contemplate abandoning it, on what is their estimate of it based? And in what do they think a member of this historic episcopate differs from a presbyter with wide administrative powers?

In the person of a chief pastor for relatively small areas we think that there is a religious and governmental feature for which no committee or executive secretary can be a substitute. A man can be a *pastor pastorum;* a committee cannot. A man who is also the chief liturgical figure, who ordained many of the clergy in his jurisdiction and perhaps confirmed them in their teens, can be a pastor to clergy in a way impossible to one who lacks this character. In addition to that, the episcopate has proved an inestimably important bond of unity. When the bishop is a real leader as well as pastor, his diocese is held together by the relation each congregation and each individual has to him. The bishops as a group are indispensable for uniting the dioceses that form any one of the various autonomous Anglican churches. For instance, the influence of the bishops was a major factor, if not the major one, that prevented any permanent split in the American Episcopal Church over slavery and the Civil War. And the bishops of the whole Anglican communion, meeting decennially at the Lambeth conference, have been an important factor in preserving and increasing the unity of Anglicanism's witness to the gospel, in co-ordinating the work of the different autonomous Anglican churches, and, by doing these two things, in strengthening the bonds that form these autonomous units into one communion. Furthermore, the office of bishop is a factor uniting us to the "Catholic" churches, even as synodical government is a bond uniting us to the Protestant ones.

Besides being a contemporary bond, the historic episcopate is an important link across the centuries, uniting the contemporary Church in fellowship and in witness to Christ and his gospel and in structure with the Church of every preceding age. Anglicanism insists that *continuity through the years* is as important as *unity today*. It believes that the Reformation did not begin a new church; it purified and re-formed the existing church, reaffirming the neglected elements of the early Church. It is concerned to preserve organic relationship in life and faith with the Church in the first and fourth and sixth and twelfth centuries as well as to achieve unity with those followers of Christ from whom it is unhappily at present divided. The traditional order of bishops is more than a *symbol* of this continuity; it is an actual preserver thereof. And this is true quite apart from any rigid or mechanical doctrine of apostolic succession. Take one illustration: Since the year 597 an unbroken succession of Archbishops of Canterbury links William Temple to Augustine. The lives and episcopates of these men, one after another, all of them guarding the integrity of the Christian faith and ethical norms, ordaining and confirming, administering church discipline, guarantee that their church is one throughout the centuries. And Augustine's consecration and mission, received from Gregory I, is a sign that the church in Canterbury is an extension of that in Rome, as that in Rome is of that in Palestine. We American Episcopalians think that our bishops, tracing their episcopal descent, through William White, Samuel Provoost, and Samuel Seabury, to two Archbishops of Canterbury, link our church with the Church of England and, through it, with the primitive Church. *An unbroken succession of men, all of whom have had the same office and done the same things, is an invaluable preserver of continuity between the Church of today and the Church of the earliest centuries.*

The bishops were—and, wherever the succession of bishops through episcopal consecration has been preserved, still are—different from presbyters who have been given wide administrative powers. Actually the executive authority of the bishop is the least of our concerns. In the early Irish church, for instance, the government was largely in the hands of abbots, and bishops were under their administrative control. In the American Episcopal Church a bishop has very little executive authority aside from his personal leadership. He always has to have the consent of some committee or group before he can act in other than a pastoral capacity; for while our fathers kept the Catholic office of bishop, they also took over the Protestant feature of synodical government.

What distinguish bishops from other ministers (in addition to being chief pastors) are the chief responsibility for witnessing to and guarding the integrity of the gospel; and the liturgical actions that have been traditionally reserved to them, namely, ordination, consecration, and confirmation. They are "sacramental persons." They are symbols and instruments of something much greater than they—the Church—as the Church is the symbol and instrument of the kingdom of God. The Church, temporarily and for particular functions, is, so to say, focused in the bishop; and the Spirit who resides in and works through the Church acts through him.

We do not claim that the episcopate is the only tie that preserves continuity between the earliest days and the present. We would stress the importance also of the same faith and Bible and ethical standards, the same sacraments, the ongoing life of the fellowship generation after generation, and the compulsion of the same mission to preach the gospel to all nations, as essential links across the ages. But, while insisting on these, we regard the traditional church order as part of the legacy from the past which is of the greatest value, of which we are not the beneficiaries so much as the trustees, and which, therefore, we are not at liberty to discard.

Toward Christian Unity

I have dwelt so much upon this holding together Catholic and Protestant insights for two reasons: On the one hand, as I have argued, it is the chief distinguishing mark of Anglicanism. On the other, it seems to me its most significant contribution to the Christian world as well as the source of its other major contributions. That one church should have declined to be exclusively Catholic or exclusively Protestant but insisted on trying to comprehend both strikes me as something of great moment in itself and perhaps also the most hopeful earnest of eventual Christian unity. Suppose, for the sake of argument, that the experiment should eventually fail: that would prove the complete irreconcilability of the two types of Christianity, would force all Christians into one or the other camp, and would forward thereby the search for Christian unity. Suppose that in time Anglicanism is enabled by God's grace to achieve a stable synthesis, in which each fructifies the other: that will point to others a way they may take toward the goal of a united Church spiritually greater and richer than either an exclusive Catholicism or an exclusive Protestantism. Don't misunderstand me. I do not for a moment think that all others will some day learn that they ought to become Anglicans; for if Anglicanism fulfills what I regard to be its peculiar mission of holding these two together till a genuine synthesis is found, I think it will thereby help toward the great and truly ecumenical Church of the future, into which it will fund its own life and tradition, losing its independent identity. That great Church will be a most precious gift of God to his children. Praying for its appearance and working to prepare for it along the lines we feel God has indicated for each church through its peculiar history are the indispensable conditions for receiving it.

THE INDEPENDENT TRADITION

Joseph Minton Batten

THE Reformation produced the cleavage of Western Christendom and destroyed the formal unity of the church. Since the sixteenth century Roman Catholicism and Protestantism have existed side by side in competitive rivalry. In this rivalry Protestantism has been handicapped by its divisive tendencies. The Reformers hoped that freedom from Rome would prepare the way for a new and lasting type of Christian unity expressed in terms of universal free communion, but they found themselves unable to curb the centrifugal tendencies of their age. The separatists from Rome, therefore, soon found themselves engaged in the task of forming distinct communions, which at first followed territorial and national lines. Ultimately the Reformation produced four major types of Protestant tradition during the sixteenth and seventeenth centuries. These types found expression in the Lutheran, the Anglican, the Reformed, and the independent movements.

Antagonism and rivalry often characterized the early relationships among these four branches of divided Protestantism. In the period of the Reformation and the wars of religion men found it difficult to appreciate all the values of these differing systems of Christian doctrine, polity, and worship. From this distance we should be able to survey that troubled era with calmer judgment and true perspective. Such a survey inevitably discovers major values in the teachings and practices of every branch of Protestantism. It serves to develop the fine art of appreciating the work of creative religious movements. It provides convincing proof that our common religious heritage is derived from many sources. Fuller realization of the sources and the values of this rich religious heritage can contribute toward intelligent good will and a spirit of co-operation among the various branches of the Church universal.

An Important Movement of the Masses

The recognition of our indebtedness to the independent tradition involves peculiar difficulties. The essential content of this tradition can be discovered only by due consideration of the contributions made to modern religious life by all those Protestant groups of the sixteenth and seventeenth centuries which remained outside the Lutheran, Anglican, and Reformed Churches. There were more than a hundred such groups. Their number and variety complicate the task of evaluating their work. Moreover, no great personality gave direction to the development of the independent movement. No dynamic leader, like Luther, guided its destiny during formative years. No able theologian, like Calvin, defined its doctrinal position. No master of prose expression, like Cranmer, taught its followers to voice their spiritual aspirations in words of common prayer. On the contrary, many leaders, usually men of limited gifts, guided the movement in various localities. These men helped to develop the independent tradition, but their leadership was of secondary importance. In reality this type of Protestantism developed out of the spiritual strivings of the common man. Its record can never be given in a biography or a series of biographies. It is essentially the story of the masses in search of a satisfying religious experience.

The spiritual quest that gave rise to the independent tradition is the most neglected phase of Reformation history. Research in this field has been handicapped by the fact that source materials have been scarce and, until recently, generally inaccessible. Textbooks in Church history usually allot the independent groups less than one twentieth of the space used to record the history of the Reformation. In many theological seminaries it has long been the custom to introduce these movements to students of Church history with a brief and contemptuous reference to their wide variety and their left-wing views and practices.

In thus discounting and discrediting the independent tradition modern historians are continuing a long-established practice. In the age of the Reformation scholarly opinion generally regarded the independent groups as by-products of an age of turmoil—useless and dangerous by-products that could have no lasting significance. Then Roman Catholics and the adherents of the Protestant State churches were always quarreling and often fighting, but these hostile factions repeatedly united in fervid denunciation and vigorous persecution of the independent churches. On the other hand, the advocates of the independent tradition, keenly conscious of the fact that their minority groups were being treated as the stepchildren of the Reformation, argued that all the Protestant State churches retained too much of Roman Catholicism. The independents regarded Rome as Babylon. They would break completely with the corrupt, medieval, and reactionary past in their haste to flee from captivity in Babylon. Their critics, in turn, charged that the independents were hurrying away from Babylon so fast they were in danger of running past Jerusalem.

Their Valuable Contributions

Despite the acknowledged extremist tendencies of some proponents of the independent tradition, the fact remains that they championed many ideas that have become treasured elements in modern Christianity. Carlton J. H. Hayes, a Roman Catholic historian, says:

In the long run the radical sects proved to be more characteristic of Protestantism than Henry VIII or Calvin or even a Luther. And, however transitory the tenets and practices of particular radical sects may have been, there can be no doubt that it was the succession of such sects which conferred upon Protestant Christendom the distinction of substituting individualist for collective Christianity. This was really a revolutionary Christianity.[1]

Writing in 1910, Adolf Harnack, one of the ablest Protestant Church historians, expressed this judgment:

Thanks to the research of recent years, we have been presented with figures of splendid Christian leaders from among the circles of the Anabaptists, and many of these noble and reverend characters come nearer to us than the figures of an heroic Luther and an iron Calvin.[2]

Since Harnack wrote these words, there has been an increasing interest in the independent groups. Every year research in this field has been facilitated by the publication of source documents, local histories, monographs, and biographies. Scholars have not yet combined this material into an authoritative and definitive history. However, there is a trend toward agreement on certain basic facts relating to the *sources* of the independent movement, the *environmental factors* that influenced its development, the *ideas* and the *activities* of the more important groups through which the movement found expression, and the *contributions* made by these groups to our common religious heritage.

All religious movements have roots that run deep into the historic past. This is especially true of the nonpolitical Protestantism of the Reformation era. As a rule its leaders were not men of creative religious genius. They borrowed ideas from many sources, and usually they borrowed without acknowledgment. There is circumstantial evidence that the independent thinkers were indebted to many ancient or medieval antichurchly groups such as the Arians, Albigenses, Petrobrusians, Waldenses, Lollards, and Hussites. But only in two of the independent churches—the Waldenses and the Unitas Fratrum—can proof be established of such transmission of ideas through a definite and acknowledged continuity. It is probable that the medieval mystics influenced independent thinkers both in their efforts to define the doctrine of saving faith and in their emphasis upon the importance of the "Inner Light." Certainly the Renaissance movement helped to prepare the way for the independent tradition by its championship of intellectual freedom and its exaltation of the worth of the individual.

The independent groups gratefully acknowledged their indebtedness to Luther and other Reformers who rediscovered and formulated the basic principles of Protestantism. They were quite willing to accept the doctrines of justification by faith, the priesthood of believers, the

---

[1] "Significance of the Reformation in the Light of Contemporary Scholarship," *Catholic Historical Review*, XVII (1932), p. 402; used by permission.

[2] Quoted by H. S. Bender, "Conrad Grebel, the Founder of Swiss Anabaptism," *Church History*, VII (1938), p. 157.

final authority of the Scriptures, and the right of the individual to interpret the Bible. But the independents were convinced that these principles called for more thorough reforms than those sanctioned by the State churches. Roman Catholicism had corrupted the original deposit of the Christian faith by its institutionalism, ritualism, scholasticism, and sacramentarianism. These corrupting factors were reappearing, they believed, in the State churches that had been established with the blessings of the major leaders of the Reformation. The independents found no hope for the future either in Roman Catholicism or in politically sponsored Protestantism. They regarded themselves as divinely commissioned to discover and restore the purity of primitive Christianity.

An Age of Confusion

In their efforts to secure the restoration of primitive Christianity the men who shaped the independent tradition were constantly influenced by environmental factors. They lived in an age of confusion. Thousands were deserting old loyalties to the medieval church. The Reformers were quarreling among themselves as to the nature of the new church that should replace the old. The arbitrary intervention of State authorities in religious affairs added to the bewilderment of the masses. Often priests or pastors were displaced without adequate provision for the religious needs of their people. Throughout all Europe simple folk, genuinely interested in religion but left as sheep without a shepherd, began to turn to the study of the Bible in order to find the solution of their religious perplexities. Each interpreted Scripture in his own way and discovered truths that appealed to his own interests. The resulting variety of religious opinions offered unique opportunities for zealous leaders to rally a following and establish group consciousness among people who found themselves in agreement on matters of faith and practice.

A rising tide of nationalism surged throughout Western Europe during the period of the Renaissance and the Reformation. Nationalism tended to discredit the medieval concept of a world State and a world Church. The outstanding Protestant leaders rejected the idea of a world Church governed by the Pope, but they sanctioned the organization of State churches and thus complied with the prevailing trend toward nationalism. The independent groups found no scriptural support for a world Church or a State church. They would build the kingdom of God without State authorization. They opposed the new nationalism, which regarded religious unity as a major support of political unity. Dissenting independents, therefore, frequently incurred the charge of treason and were often subjected to severe persecution by civil authorities, both Roman Catholic and Protestant.

Protestantism originated in an era of social revolution. The landed nobility had dominated the medieval social structure. The middle classes gained increasing wealth, power, and influence as a result of the rise of cities and the development of trade during the new era of geographical exploration and overseas expansion. The roots of modern capitalism spring from the changing economic life of this period. Class struggle was then the order of the day. Religious movements faced the necessity of defining attitudes toward the competing classes. The Roman Catholic Church, as the largest property holder in Western Europe, generally championed the continuation of the existing social and economic order. The Protestant State churches usually tended to give aid and support to economic systems dominated by the richer, capitalistic groups within the third estate. In contrast the independent churches, though sometimes led by upper-class individuals, drew most of their followers from the uneducated and poverty-stricken urban proletariat and the peasantry of the rural areas. The independent movement was therefore primarily concerned with workers' needs as seen from the workers' viewpoint.

These churches of the disinherited manifested a continuing interest in social reform. The independent groups, dissatisfied with the existing socio-economic system and inspired by a new idealism derived from the study of Scripture, committed themselves to the task of translating the New Testament teachings about the kingdom of God into present reality and practice. They conducted a constant series of experiments in social change. These ranged from watchful waiting for a divine intervention that would correct all the ills of the present world order to programs of Christian socialism and pure communism.

LIBERTY OF CONSCIENCE

In the Reformation era men were beginning to discover that the consciousness of the individual is the only creative faculty in life. Individualism involved responsibility for the use of reason as a criterion of right, truth, and goodness. The major Reformers, particularly Luther, distrusted the Renaissance appeal to reason, and the Protestant State churches curbed private judgment by imposing prescribed systems of belief. Only the independents consistently upheld the right of the common man to place his own interpretation upon Scripture and to seek the solution of all religious problems by the use of reason and the help of the Holy Spirit. In thus championing intellectual liberty the independents were following the teaching of Renaissance individualism to its logical conclusion, and they were anticipating modern views of the dignity of human personality and the trustworthiness of reason as man's guide in his quest for the abundant life. Most Protestant leaders thought that the new individualism had not developed sufficient standards of internal control, thus necessitating institutional controls. The independents would grant complete liberty of conscience to the individual, believing that the fullest individual development could be reconciled with the pursuit of social ends. They recognized more clearly than any of their contemporaries that the hope of the world lies in religiously motivated individuals who are free to devote themselves to group effort in building a world order that is in accordance with the will of God.

The Reformation gave expression to an ethical revolution of profound importance. The idea of justification by faith involved a new sense of the individual's moral obligation. In the national churches the full force of this idea was often nullified by efforts at comprehension which were designed to find a comfortable place for both nominal and real Christians within the State church. It was further weakened by the prevailing emphasis upon dogma at the expense of character. The independent groups were more concerned about the ethical revolution inherent in Protestantism. They usually proclaimed the freedom of the will, the duty of the Christian to imitate the life of Christ, and the necessity of good works as fruit of faith. Their emphasis upon self-discipline, supplemented by rigid group discipline in local churches, produced more zeal for righteousness than was usually found in State churches. This zeal was manifest both in teaching the ethical import of the Christian message and in the daily practice of the Christian profession.

Many groups held aloof from the great national churches. Recognition of their identity and their variety is the primary step toward the understanding of the independent tradition. Each of the independent churches can be differentiated by examining the circumstances of its origin, the sources from which it borrowed ideas and practices, and the environmental factors that influenced its development; and by the study of the direction it helped to give to the stream of Christian history. Only a few of the more important independent groups can be mentioned here. Two independent churches—the Waldenses and the Unitas Fratrum—originated long before the Reformation, but they associated themselves with the Protestant movement. Regardless of the changes wrought by the centuries, they still maintain much that is best in the independent tradition.

THE WALDENSES, UNITAS FRATRUM, AND ANABAPTISTS

The Waldenses trace their origin to the evangelical ministry of Peter Waldo, who was excommunicated by the Roman Catholic Church in the year 1184. This wealthy merchant of Lyons, France, gave up his business in order to devote his life to the rediscovery and restoration of primitive Christianity. He opposed the institutional and sacramentarian emphases in religion, proclaimed the Scriptures to be the only authoritative norm of faith and practice, encouraged the translation of the Bible into vernacular languages, and advocated simplicity in worship, lay preaching, and the imitation of the life of Christ. His followers, driven from their homes in southern France by relentless persecution, scattered widely into Spain, Germany, and Austria, but ultimately found their most congenial home in the Piedmont section of northern Italy. There they maintained their churches unchanged until 1532, when they formally adopted the basic principles of Protestantism. Though subjected to frequent persecutions, they have remained loyal to their original principles. Today they constitute the most significant Protestant church in Italy.

After the martyrdom of John Hus, in 1415, his followers were victimized by wars, confusion, and uncertainty. However, a remnant survived and, in 1457, organized themselves in an independent church, which was long known by the name Unitas Fratrum. This church, remaining thoroughly committed to the teachings of the great Czech reformer, professed acceptance of the Bible as the final source of Christian authority, practiced simplicity in worship, and stressed the necessity of Christian living as evidence of saving faith. Later adopting ideas from the teachings of both Luther and Calvin, the Unitas Fratrum became for a time the major religious organization in Bohemia and Moravia; but this era of prosperity was suddenly ended by Czech reverses in the Thirty Years' War and by merciless persecution at the hands of Roman Catholic and imperial authorities. Though weakened by its sufferings through the centuries, this church has achieved noteworthy success in its evangelistic, educational, and missionary work. The Unitas Fratrum, now known as the Moravian Church, later contributed the influence of its ardent evangelistic zeal to Pietism in Germany, to the Evangelical Revival in England, to the Great Awakening in America, and to Methodism around the world.

In the early Protestant movement the most numerous and influential advocates of the independent tradition were called Anabaptists, or "Rebaptizers." The name covers the widest range of religious opinion, as each Anabaptist exercised complete freedom in interpreting Scripture and in defining his own concept of the essentials of the Christian religion. Most Anabaptists were primarily concerned with the restoration of the beliefs and practices of primitive Christianity as described in the New Testament. Some despaired of the Christianization of the existing social order and centered their hopes upon the fulfillment of apocalyptic prophecies, the expectation of the Second Coming of Christ, and the manifestation of the glories of his millennial reign. A few placed major emphasis upon the use of reason in religion and applied rational tests to the traditional doctrines of Christianity, particularly the doctrine of the Trinity. Others developed an absorbing interest in Christian mysticism, listened to the voice of God speaking directly to their souls, and found a guidance and an assurance which confirmed their conviction that the possession of the "Inner Light" is the central fact of religious experience. Thus, Anabaptists may be classified as belonging to the biblical, apocalyptic, rationalistic, and mystical types. The influence of leaders and the interaction of varying cultural, racial, social, and economic factors further differentiated the Anabaptists of certain geographical areas. Consequently, we may trace the distinctive features of the Swiss-Moravian, the German, the Dutch, and the Italian phases of the movement.

Despite this confusing diversity most Anabaptists shared certain common beliefs. They were willing to accept the basic principles of Protestantism. They believed that the church should be a voluntary organization, composed of regenerate persons who seek to share its fellowship. Each local church should be a completely autonomous, self-governing unit. The practice of infant baptism was repudiated, and persons baptized in infancy were rebaptized on profession of faith prior to admission into church membership. Anabaptists united in the vigorous advocacy of the separation of Church and State, the right of liberty of conscience for the individual, and full toleration for all religious faiths.

There was also general agreement on the following views: Church government should be thoroughly democratic. The institutional and sacramentarian emphases current in both Roman Catholicism and the Protestant State churches should be rejected. Connectional bonds should be maintained between churches by the circulation of Christian literature, correspondence, and visitation by itinerant ministers. Lay participation in church activities must be regarded as essential to the life of the church. Religious emancipation must be granted to women. Christians should follow the teachings of Jesus in word and deed, especially by refusing to bear arms or take an oath. Each Christian should regard his property as belonging to God and held in trust under the obligations of stewardship. There were marked anti-Augustinian and anti-Calvinistic trends in Anabaptist theological opinion. Some followers of the movement held anti-Trinitarian views. A small minority developed the doctrine of the "Inner Light" into a pantheistic system of theology. There was a marked difference of opinion as to the right of a Christian to hold civil office. Some Anabaptists practiced immersion in baptism, but affusion and sprinkling were the preferred modes during the earlier years of the movement.

In 1525 the Anabaptists, encouraged by initial successes, had good reason to hope that they were sponsoring the most popular phase of the Reformation. But within less than a decade this type of Protestantism was weakened and almost destroyed by divisive factors, extremist tendencies, and State efforts to establish uniformity. In addition to the variations mentioned above Anabaptists soon aligned themselves into quietistic and revolutionary types. The leaders of the quietistic type, such as Conrad Grebel, Balthasar Hubmeier, and Hans Denck, attempted to leaven the religious life of the masses by the peaceful process of indoctrination in Anabaptist principles. Leaders of the revolutionary type, such as Melchior Hofmann and Jan Matthysz, combined Anabaptist ideas with a militant program for the overthrow of the existing social order.

Contemporary opinion, Roman Catholic and Protestant, regarded the Anabaptists as subversive rebels against a stabilized society. The tragedies of the Peasants' War in Germany intensified the public dread of radical programs. As champions of a left-wing movement in a troubled era the Anabaptist revolutionaries naturally attracted followers from the most rebellious elements in society. In 1534 a group of the most fanatical Anabaptist agitators went to the city of Münster and attempted to put their ideas into practice. The Münster experiment of 1534-35, conducted under abnormal siege conditions, involved a combination of radical social-religious practices which has seldom been equaled in history. Though the experiment ended with the capture of the city after sixteen months of siege, all Anabaptists were thenceforth regarded as fanatics who would, if given the opportunity, repeat the "Münster episode."

This unfortunate incident checked the progress of the movement. Its quietistic followers repudiated the Anabaptist name and gradually organized themselves into a number of denominations such as the Täufer, Mennonites, Baptists, Dunkers, and Schwenkfeldians. These churches have preserved to our day the best elements of Anabaptist teaching. One great leader—Menno Simons (1496-1559) — was the chief agent in purging the movement of extremist tendencies after the Münster episode. His followers—the Mennonites—helped to transmit Anabaptist principles to the English-speaking world.

Socinianism should be regarded as a distinct type of the independent tradition. This system of thought, as developed by Laelius and Faustus Socinus and formulated in the Racovian Catechism of 1605, involved a strange blending of rationalism and supernaturalism. Its proponents held that the truths of religion are discovered through divine revelation and human reason. They may be above reason, but they are never contrary to reason. Socinians, therefore, insisted on testing all religious beliefs by the norm of reason. On this basis they rejected the Nicene doctrine of the Trinity. Their anti-Trinitarian beliefs foreshadowed the rise of modern Unitarianism, but they made a distinct contribution to the independent tradition by their insistence upon a reasonable faith and by their revival of the New Testament emphasis upon the worth of human personality.

THE MOVEMENT IN ENGLAND AND AMERICA

In England the rise of the independent tradition is inseparably linked with the history of the Puritan party within the Anglican Church. After 1563 the English Puritans labored zealously but unsuccessfully to mold the State church in accordance with their ideas. Finally despairing of the reformation of the Anglican Church, some Puritans began to withdraw from its fellowship in order to form dissenting churches. In 1581 the rise of English Congregationalism set the pattern for the organization of nonconformist churches. Though suffering severe persecution, the Congregational, Baptist, Quaker, and other dissenting denominations gradually emerged to commanding prominence in English church life. Many of these denominations borrowed heavily from Anabaptist views as taught by Menno Simons and his followers—the Mennonites of Holland. The English Presbyterians also formed dissenting churches, but they hoped that the State church would ultimately become Presbyterian as a result of parliamentary victory in the civil wars. This hope was doomed to disappointment after Cromwell's rise to power.

English exponents of the independent tradition had almost unlimited opportunity for self-expression under the Commonwealth and the Protectorate. Unfortunately this new-found liberty encouraged the emergence of so wide a range of cults that public support for the independent tradition was alienated. Thus, a contemporary writer—Thomas Edwards—in his book *Gangraena,* was able to show the chaotic effects of independency by listing 199 current varieties of sects. Despite these disintegrating tendencies and the persecution of Dissenters after the Restoration the nonconformist churches continued to exercise a wholesome influence upon English life and thought. The transfer of these dissenting denominations to the New World was the most important single factor in shaping religious foundations in America.

All varieties of the continental and English independent churches ultimately found a congenial home in America. The State churches established during the Reformation period were also transported to the New World. Colonists from many lands brought their churches to their new home, thus giving to colonial and modern America more religious denominations than can be found in any other nation. The history of Christianity in America is the story of the transplanting of Old World churches to the New World and the development of Old World faiths under New World environmental factors. Each church, in its own way, has made its distinctive contribution toward the sum total of our American Christianity. The independent churches of the Reformation era have helped to type the distinctive characteristics, the form, and the power of American Protestantism.

Congregationalism, though undergoing a sea change in transit from Old England to New England, became the State church in several of the colonies. But the Congregational churches of colonial America preserved many of the basic elements of English independency, and they transmitted to the new nation the best Puritan standards of sound learning dedicated to the service of religion and the enduring influence of the Puritan consciousness of the supreme worth of ethical idealism. Likewise, Unitarianism, the modern counterpart of Socinianism, was brought to America from England. Unitarianism has exercised a wholesome influence far beyond the bounds of the circle of its own membership by its steady insistence upon a reasonable faith and its unceasing emphasis upon the worth of human personality.

The Quakers, likewise, have made a contribution to our religious heritage far out of proportion to their numbers. From the days of John Woolman to those of Rufus Jones they have provided unfailing testimony that the finest flowering of Christian mysticism bears fruit in an awakened social consciousness that pioneers in ever-widening fields of Christlike service in works of love and mercy.

Our indebtedness to groups that trace their rise to the Anabaptist movement is seldom recognized because of the persistent tendency to underrate the scope and influence of this significant phase of Reformation history. Many of the continental groups that trace their rise to the Anabaptist movement, such as the Mennonites and Dunkards, have brought to America the original Anabaptist emphasis upon the worth of the long-neglected but vital elements of simplicity of life and pure democracy, which characterized the Christian movement in the days of its origin. Moreover, many adherents of these churches have given and are now giving heroic witness to their conviction that war is evil. They have maintained their pacifist convictions when all the world about them tends to dedicate itself to the cult of Mars.

Of the American churches influenced by the Anabaptist movement the Baptists have exercised most significant power in shaping the course of American Christianity. Since the days of Roger Williams the American Baptist churches have ministered most faithfully to the religious needs of the common man. Increase in numbers in this great popular church has brought a corresponding increase in influence. American Baptist churches have shaped our common religious heritage in many ways, chiefly by their constant insistence upon the right of the individual to remain loyal to his own personal religious convictions, their constant emphasis upon the obligation of churches to follow the evangelistic and missionary imperative inherent in the gospel message, and their championship of the complete separation of Church and State. The Baptists, far more than any other denomination, are responsible for the provisions for the separation of Church and State which are now written in the federal Constitution and in each of the forty-eight state constitutions.

Each of the nonpolitical forms of Protestantism was independent in its origin. Each moved along its own line of historical development. All manifested innate weakness due to subjectivism, divisive tendencies, and the lack of effective connectional organization. All shared a fellowship of suffering because civil authorities, relying on what Roger Williams called "The Bloudy Tenent of Persecution," made oft-repeated attempts to enforce religious uniformity through repressive measures against dissenting groups. But these nonconformist churches kept alive certain basic religious principles that deserve a place in the co-operative Protestantism of the future. Recognition of our indebtedness to these varied groups must be combined with a consciousness of the values we have inherited from the Lutheran, Reformed, and Anglican types of Protestantism. Such recognition is deserved. It can advance co-operation among the churches and promote "the unity of the Spirit in the bond of peace."

PROTESTANTISM IN AMERICAN HISTORY

William Warren Sweet

It was just twenty-five years after Christopher Columbus discovered America that Martin Luther nailed his ninety-five theses to the church door at Wittenberg. Thus, the discovery of America and the beginning of Protestantism were contemporaneous events. For many years it was the custom of Protestant ministers in America, when making patriotic addresses, to stress this fact as clearly providential. It seemed to them perfectly clear that God had kept the very existence of America a secret until the fullness of time, or until Protestantism arose, so that in this new land, uncontaminated by the paganized Christianity of the Old World, Protestantism was to have its greatest opportunity of coming to full fruition. But, whether providential or not, these two events, coming as they did in close proximity, had large significance in making North America predominantly Protestant.

The dominant Protestant character of colonial America is indicated by the fact that of the 3,130 church congregations of all kinds at the end of the colonial period, from Maine on the north to Georgia on the south, all were Protestant, of one sort or another, except fifty. Of these fifty Roman Catholic churches all but two or three were located either in Maryland or Pennsylvania. Maryland, established by the Catholic nobleman Lord Baltimore as a refuge for his coreligionists, never had, even at the beginning, a majority of Catholics; and in 1701 the Anglican Church was established by law. In the middle of the eighteenth century the Catholics constituted only one twelfth of the population of Maryland, though many of these were people of wealth and influence. Outside Maryland, Catholic influence was negligible. Charles Carroll, the only Catholic to sign the Declaration of Independence, was undoubtedly the most influential Catholic in Revolutionary America; but his influence was due to his wealth and social position and was in spite of his Catholicism rather than because of it.[1]

In recent years, since Roman Catholics have become increasingly numerous as a consequence of immigration, Catholic writers have made larger and larger claims as to the importance of Catholic influence in the formative years of our history. A good example is the books by Michael J. O'Brien, official Catholic historiographer: *A Hidden Phase of American History* (1919) [2] and *Pioneer Irish in New England*

---

[1] For a well-documented statement as to the treatment of Roman Catholics in Maryland see Sister Mary Augustana (Ray), *American Opinion of Roman Catholicism in the Eighteenth Century;* New York, 1936; pp. 58-61.

[2] See J. Franklin Jameson's review of O'Brien's *A Hidden Phase of American History; The American Historical Review,* Vol. XXVI, July, 1921; pp. 797-99.

(1937). There is no doubt but that the Irish element in the population at the end of the colonial period was greater than is generally supposed, but these books are written in "the spirit of an advocate," and the sources and methods of using the materials are often questionable. A more recent book making large Catholic claims of this kind is *The Story of American Catholicism,* by Theodore Maynard.[3] A convert from Protestantism, the author shows an enthusiasm for his new-found faith which has led him to make sweeping statements that a less-prejudiced viewpoint would seriously question. He refers to the Protestant churches only to disparage them and gives credit to Roman Catholicism for practically everything of solid worth America has accomplished. Such history writing on the part of Catholics should serve as a warning to Protestants not to claim too much.

Two Types of Protestantism Transplanted

Two types of Protestantism came out of the Reformation. The dominant type is represented by the numerous national churches in the several countries of Western Europe. In England, Holland, Scotland, and in the German and Scandinavian states these national Protestant churches were established by law and, generally speaking, were intolerant of Roman Catholicism and of the sects that arose about them. They were the right wing of the Reformation. The left wing was made up of those people who were not satisfied with the right-wing type of Protestantism, which to their minds was only a halfway Reformation. Their chief concern was to revive ancient Christianity in all its purity and to do away with all the "corruptions" the centuries had added. The people making up the "sects" were generally humble and despised by the right-wing element and usually represented the lower economic classes.

Both the right-wing and the left-wing types of Protestantism were transplanted to the American colonies. Up to 1660 the dominant religious bodies in the colonies were the offshoots of the dominant religious bodies in Protestant Europe. This resulted in the establishment of Church-State relationships in all the colonies founded up to that time except in Rhode Island and Maryland. After 1660 left-wing Protestantism became increasingly important, and by the end of the colonial period American Protestantism was largely dominated by the left-wing element. To such an extent was this true that the statement is now frequently made that the left wing of the Reformation came to its completion and fulfillment in America.

The English colonies were as hospitable a field for experimentation as Christianity has seldom had in all its long history. The loose tie between the English colonies and the mother country, both politically and ecclesiastically, permitted the development of a large degree of self-

---

[3] See my reviews of Theodore Maynard, *The Story of American Catholicism* (New York, 1941) in *Church History,* Vol. XI, March, 1942; pp. 75-77.

government and an even greater degree of self-determination in religion. The American colonies were a haven for the religious radical from every country in Western Europe. In the colonizing century—the seventeenth—in Britain especially, the old political faith, as well as the old religious establishment, were under attack from every quarter. "Not only were many of the first American colonists dissenters from the established religion; . . . they were also, in large majority, poor men, dissatisfied with the whole economic and political order," and anxious, as Increase Mather states, to "shake off the dust of Babylon both as to ecclesiastical and civil constitution."

This was in striking contrast with the situation in Hispanic colonial America. Spain's colonial empire was so completely under the control of the mother country that there was no chance for new developments. Spanish Roman Catholicism was transplanted to New Spain and Peru with little or no change, and throughout the entire colonial period all other forms of organized Christianity were so successfully excluded that the various types of Protestantism arising in Europe were unable to gain even the slightest foothold. The Spanish colonies welcomed no religious refugees. The Council of the Indies saw to it that only Roman Catholics came out to the new American kingdoms, while the Inquisition in the Spanish dependencies was principally occupied with keeping out all subversive ideas. Absolute uniformity dominated the religious scene in Hispanic-America; religious diversity was the religious pattern in Anglo-America.

THE AMERICAN DEVELOPMENT

Of the right-wing churches transplanted to colonial America the most important was the Church of England. The Presbyterian was the state church of Scotland; but in North Ireland, from which most of the colonial Presbyterians came, it was a dissenting body, and the great flood of Scotch-Irish colonists leaned strongly to the left-wing position. The Church of Holland, or the Dutch Reformed Church, as long as the Dutch controlled New York was a right-wing body. The German Lutheran and the German Reformed Churches, while state churches in the Old World, became dissenting bodies in the American colonies. On the other hand, the Congregationalists, who were left-wing in England, became right-wing in New England, where they were established by law and supported by general taxation.

If the English government had any ecclesiastical policy at all relative to the colonies, it was to obtain the establishment by law of the Church of England in as many of the colonies as possible. This was accomplished, in a degree, in six of the colonies; but in none of them was its establishment complete, since there was never an Anglican bishop or an ecclesiastical court in colonial America. Even in Virginia, Maryland, and South Carolina, where it exercised its largest influence, it was vigorously opposed by a rapidly increasing number of dissenters. Royal governors and other colonial officials continually attempted to further its interests, while the Society for the Propagation of the Gospel in Foreign Parts, between 1701 and 1776, sent over 310 missionaries, who ministered to all of the colonies. Yet, in the long run, the special privileges the Anglican Church enjoyed and the official concern for its welfare which was so manifest proved a handicap rather than an advantage. At the end of the colonial era it ranked fourth among American religious bodies in the number of congregations.[4]

For the first one hundred years Protestantism in America was, in a large degree, a duplication of Old World patterns, though right-wing Protestantism in colonial America never became institutionalized, as in Protestant Europe of the seventeenth century. As the eighteenth century wore along, a distinctively American religious development began to be manifest.

One of the fundamental ideas coming out of the Reformation was that the individual could make his own approach to God; that there was no need of an intermediary priesthood, since each person could be his own priest. The doctrine of the universal priesthood of all believers[5] was held in a greater or lesser degree by all the Reformers and became an accepted doctrine of Protestantism. In colonial America, however, this doctrine had a much larger chance at fulfillment than in the Old World, for the very scarcity of professionally trained and regularly ordained ministers in a new land made necessary a larger degree of lay leadership.

In the Old World religion had become largely an institutional matter. There salvation was achieved through the church rather than through individual effort. People became members of the state churches more or less as a matter of course. In the colonies the exact opposite was true. There religion tended to become a personal concern. In the stress and strain of pioneering, in facing the hardships of everyday experience, religion came naturally more and more to concern itself with everyday needs and individual problems. Church membership came about, not as a matter of course, but through personal decision. Colonial preaching therefore tended to become personal, searching out the hearts and needs of individuals, and less and less a defense of a theological system.

The individualistic emphasis in the older American colonial Protestantism, together with the introduction of German pietism, with its emphasis also upon inner personal religion, and the growing concern over the decline in morals and religion generally, on the part of an increasing number of the colonial religious leaders, produced the great colonial awakenings. It is a remarkable fact that the great colonial

---

[4] See W. W. Sweet: *Religion in Colonial America;* New York, 1942; chap. II.

[5] Luther first set forth this revolutionary idea in his *The Liberty of a Christian Man.* He argues that the Scriptures make no distinction between men except that certain ones are set apart and called "ministers, servants, and stewards," who are to serve the rest in the ministry of the word. . . . "Though it is true that we are all equally priests, yet we cannot—nor ought we if we could—all minister and teach publicly." (See T. M. Lindsay: *A History of the Reformation;* New York, 1910; Vol. I, pp. 240-42.

revivalists were, without exception, Calvinists. But theirs was a modified and personalized Calvinism. The preaching of these colonial Calvinistic revivalists caused the people sitting in the pews to feel singled out. They brought religion down to persons. And when religion is personalized, it is automatically emotionalized. All the colonial Protestant churches, in a greater or less degree, participated in the great colonial awakenings. This was true even of the Anglicans, though their participation was slight and is represented almost solely by the activities of Devereau Jarratt. Thus, by the end of the eighteenth century American Protestantism had become essentially a left-wing Protestantism, stressing the inner and the personal rather than the formal and external, life rather than creed. And for more than a hundred years this emphasis characterized American Protestantism.

The personalizing of religion also accounts for the fact that by the end of the colonial period a larger proportion of the people was unchurched than was to be found anywhere else in Christendom. And the relatively small proportion of church members to population is still a characteristic of American Protestantism. In the United States the proportion of the churched to the unchurched is gradually growing and will continue to grow as the church becomes increasingly institutionalized. Or, to put it another way, church membership in proportion to the total population increases in direct ratio to the institutionalizing of the church.[6]

RELIGIOUS LIBERTY IN AMERICA

A notion widely held among Protestant people is that the Reformation brought in, more or less automatically, religious liberty; that Protestants of all kinds have always been more tolerant than Roman Catholics. But these are not historical facts. Protestantism and religious liberty are not synonymous. The Reformation resulted in the establishment of numerous national churches such as the Church of England, the Church of Scotland, the Church of Holland, and the Lutheran and Reformed state churches in the numerous German and Scandinavian countries. These Protestant state churches were as intolerant of Roman Catholicism as Roman Catholicism was intolerant of them. They were likewise often cruelly intolerant of the left-wing sects that arose about them.[7]

The triumph of individualized Protestantism in eighteenth- and nineteenth-century America underlay the achievement of the complete separation of Church and State. A significant contributing factor was the presence in the population of an overwhelming majority of un-

---

[6] Before the present war in countries such as Poland the population was at least 95 per cent Roman Catholic. Even in Chicago, where some five hundred thousand Poles reside, at least 90 per cent are Roman Catholic.

[7] For two different types of discussion of sects see J. M. Mecklin, *The Story of American Dissent*, New York, 1934, chap. II; J. L. Neve, *Churches and Sects of Christendom*, Burlington, Iowa, 1940; pp. 33-41.

churched people, or people who were without attachment to any one church.

The separation of Church and State in America and the winning of complete religious liberty were, in a large degree, an accomplishment of Protestant minorities. No majority religious body ever surrendered of its own accord its privileged position. The last stronghold of the Church-State idea in America was New England, where from the beginning Congregationalism had been the privileged body and had been supported by general taxation. It was not until well along in the nineteenth century that the religious minorities in New England, by combining, were able to disestablish Congregationalism.[8] It is also a fact that New England Congregationalism was the one American colonial church that had become, in a larger degree than any other, institutionalized.

Minority religious bodies are always in favor of a wide toleration, for their very existence depends on it. It is instructive to note how differently the same church bodies have reacted toward Church-State relationships when they are majority bodies and when they are minorities. The Episcopalians fought valiantly for the separation of Church and State in New England, where they were a minority body; they fought even harder to maintain a privileged position in Virginia, where they had long been a majority body. Roman Catholics are always strong protagonists of religious liberty when they are in the minority, as in the United States; but fundamentally the Roman Catholic position is one of intolerance, because it maintains that error has not the same right as truth, and since it holds that Roman Catholicism is the only true religion and all others are wrong, therefore, when Roman Catholics are in the majority, it is their duty to see to it that the true religion, or Roman Catholicism, triumphs and controls. Indeed, they hold that when Catholics are in a majority, it is the duty of the State to aid and uphold Catholicism as over against any other religious body.[9]

Not only was religious liberty and the separation of Church and State a Protestant accomplishment and based on a fundamental Protestant principle; but if it is to be retained, it must be retained by the united forces of Protestantism. Should the time ever come when the population of the United States would be overwhelmingly Roman Catholic, there is no doubt whatever but that the Catholic majority would attempt to place laws upon the statute books of the nation, making Roman Catholicism the favored religion and permitting non-Catholic bodies to carry on only "within the family" or in such an "inconspicuous manner as to be an occasion neither of scandal nor per-

---

[8] J. C. Meyers, *Church and State in Massachusetts from 1740-1833;* Cleveland, 1930.

[9] For a clear statement of the Catholic position on toleration see John A. Ryan and Moorhouse F. J. Miller, *The State and the Church,* New York, 1936, pp. 34-39. See also W. E. Garrison, *Catholicism and the American Mind,* Chicago, 1928; chap. V, pp. 98-122.

version of the faithful." [10] All Catholic authorities condemn what they call "indiscriminate and universal toleration." Pope Leo XIII specifically stated that "the Church . . . deems it unlawful to place the various forms of divine worship on the same footing as the true religion." It is only when the Roman Catholic Church cannot prevent it that it is considered permissible.

Educational Patterns

The educational and cultural patterns prevailing in America from the beginning have been and still are Protestant. A fundamental Protestant ideal is universal literacy. If the Scriptures contain all that is necessary for salvation, it becomes essential for all to be able to read the Scriptures. For colonial America the Bible was the principal textbook. Taking the colonial period as a whole, the Protestant Bible was easily first in moral and cultural influence upon the plain people of English speech. And the Bible in German, printed by the Dunker printer Christopher Saur, Jr., exercised a corresponding influence upon the growing number of German colonists. The Protestant Bible has also had an important part in every reform movement in American history. Unfortunately, also, it has been used to support glaring evils, to oppose progress, and has given birth to numerous erratic movements and, in many instances, to superstitious practices.[11] That, however, is one of the prices that must be paid for freedom of speech and conscience.

In the realm of higher education American Protestantism laid the foundations. Of the nine colonial colleges eight were founded by Protestant churches—three by the Congregationalists, two by the Episcopalians, one by the Presbyterians, one by the Baptists, one by the Dutch Reformed. The College of Philadelphia, now the University of Pennsylvania, was without denominational affiliation. It was established on the principle that all denominations were to have equal rights in the institution and that no one religious body was ever to control it. Of these nine colonial colleges five of them have developed into universities of world renown.

The educational function of the Protestant churches in America made its largest contribution in the pioneering stage. The great majority of the colleges founded before the Civil War were established by the churches on some frontier, one of the primary purposes being that of training a ministry for the rapidly expanding West. By 1855 of the forty thousand graduates of American colleges up to that time approximately ten thousand had entered the Protestant ministry—a striking verification of the dominant purpose of the college founders. It was the forces of frontier democracy, working in relationship with the young and virile Protestantism on the frontier, which determined

---

[10] Garrison, op. cit., p. 112.

[11] *Dictionary of American History*, Vol. I, article on "The Bible," W. W. Sweet, p. 181. See also P. M. Simms, *The Bible in America;* New York, 1936.

that higher education in the nation was to be democratized and that America was to be a land of colleges.

Even the new state universities being established in the West before the Civil War were dependent on the Protestant ministry to a large extent for presidents and faculty. Of the forty permanent colleges established between the years 1780 and 1829 thirteen were founded by the Presbyterians, five by the Congregationalists, six by the Episcopalians, three by the Baptists, one by the German Reformed, one by the Roman Catholics, and eleven by the states. And of the eleven state colleges all those west of the Alleghenies were under Presbyterian influence. Methodists and Baptists until about 1830 seemed to have accepted, more or less as a matter of course, the Presbyterian and Congregational control of higher education in the West, but from that time forward both Baptists and Methodists entered upon an unprecedented era of college founding. The Methodists did not have a single permanent college in 1830; by 1860 they had established thirty-four permanent colleges distributed throughout the country. The Baptists had four colleges in 1830; between 1830 and 1860 they had established twenty-one additional institutions of college grade. Besides the colleges all the evangelical churches had established a veritable deluge of lower schools and academies. Of the 182 colleges and universities established before the Civil War exactly 150 had been founded by the Protestant churches—thirteen by the Catholics and nineteen by the states.[12]

The great flood of Catholic immigration which swept into the country after 1830 led to the establishment of a Roman Catholic school system in America, now of tremendous proportions, ranging from parochial elementary schools to universities. To about 1840 practically every school in the country opened with Bible reading and prayer, and some elementary instruction in religion was given. In 1840 "the great school controversy" began in those sections of the country to which recent Catholic immigration had gone. The Catholics insisted that their schools receive public money, since they were assisting in the educational program of the nation. This they did not succeed in securing, but they did succeed in excluding the Bible from the public schools and then attacked the public schools for being godless. Unfortunately the accusation is too largely true, and American Protestantism faces no more serious problem today than that of finding a way to furnish something like adequate basic instruction in religion in the schools of the nation.[13]

---

[12] Donald G. Tewksbury, *The Founding of American Colleges and Universities before the Civil War with a Particular Reference to the Religious Influence Bearing upon the College Movement* (New York, 1932), pp. 84-87. See also article "Pennsylvania Men and the Church," by W. W. Sweet, in *The General Magazine and Historical Chronicle*, Vol. XLIV, No. III, pp. 348-57.

[13] For a recent discussion of the educational development in American Roman Catholicism see Maynard, *The Story of American Catholicism*, op. cit.; chaps. XXIII and XXIV, pp. 457-97.

WESTWARD ACROSS THE CONTINENT

The greatest single task that has faced Protestantism in the entire history of the American people has been that of following population westward across the continent and the bringing to bear upon a rude and uncouth society the softening and refining influence of evangelical Christianity. Barbarism, as Horace Bushnell pointed out in 1847, is the first great danger to a society in motion. The barbarizing effects of transplanting society have been illustrated over and over again in the long history of human migration. Within the last few years there has been the greatest unsettling of populations throughout the world that has ever taken place in so short a time; and we are bound to witness, for years to come, a deterioration in morals and religion among these great masses of transplanted people.

In combating these barbarizing influences in our own West evangelical Protestantism bore a good share of the burden. Those churches which developed the most successful methods of following population westward naturally became the most numerous and influential as well as the most typically American religious bodies. It is a significant fact that the two churches that occupied the most privileged position in the colonial period—the Episcopal and the Congregational—failed to retain their leadership in numbers in the face of the great western population movement. On the other hand, those churches which developed the most adequate methods of dealing with restless, rude, and moving populations in the early West became the largest Protestant bodies in America. The Baptists and the Disciples, with their farmer-preacher technique; the Methodists, with their circuit system and lay leadership; and the Presbyterians, with their schoolmaster type of ministry, proved most effective in meeting the needs of succeeding frontiers in process of settlement.

The older Lutheranism was handicapped in the earlier years of our national development because it confined its work almost solely to German-speaking people or to those of German background. The newer Lutheran churches, which arose as a result of nineteenth-century German and Scandinavian immigration, made no attempt to minister to a cross section of American society but have made their appeal almost solely to people of their own racial and linguistic background. Since the Civil War, Lutherans have profited more from immigration than any other Protestant body in America, and the Lutheran family of churches now constitutes one of the major religious blocs in our population. They have not, however, exercised the influence in American social and cultural development which their numbers would warrant.

All the more successful frontier religious bodies were revivalistic. They differed somewhat in method and in doctrinal emphasis, but the ends sought were the same—the reformation of life and manners. In the very nature of the case theirs was a practical emphasis: they faced a pressing need, daily manifest in the very life of the people about them. They were ministering to a democratic and individualistic society in motion. They were more concerned about people than creeds; their interest was in life rather than in theology.[14]

Colonial revivalism was in a real sense the first democratic movement in America. Its appeal was to high and low alike. Through revivalism religion for the first time reached down to the common man. The direct result of the colonial revivals was the large increase in the number of common people who became church members. For the first time the inarticulate plain people were welded together in organizations that brought to them a new consciousness of their own importance to society and to the State. The revivals also created a new type of leadership, political as well as religious. And frequently religious leadership led to political office, as in the case of Edward Tiffin, the first governor of Ohio, who, as a Methodist local preacher, had already achieved a place of influence. It has been pointed out that political independence was chiefly cherished among the dissenters of Virginia, the people most effected by the revivals, because they believed that with it would come the overthrow of every vestige of religious oppression. The political ideals of the revivalists were based upon the conception of the worth and equality of the individual, which is the very essence of democracy.

The types of independent church government which developed in the colonial period had a decided effect upon the development of political democracy. The religious temper and organization of America were undoubtedly one of the principal causes of the Revolution. In his famous speech on *Conciliation,* Edmund Burke stated that in America religious beliefs and practices were in advance of those of all other Protestants in the world. Their church organizations, he stated, were simple and democratic; and they were accustomed to elect and dismiss their own religious leaders. In short, at the end of the colonial period there was a larger degree of religious liberty in America than was to be found among any other people in the world, and the possession of religious liberty naturally led to a demand for political liberty. Thus, the growth of democracy in the churches was undoubtedly a basic factor in the development of political democracy.

It was out of this background of emphasis upon the practical and the experiential that the social gospel arose, and it arose to meet a specific problem and to deal with a present need. This is an emphasis that the European Protestant finds difficult to understand, and, not being able to understand it, he belittles it. American Protestantism has been accused of substituting action for meditation, activism for quietism. Pretty generally the Protestantism of the Old World has

---

[14] For a view of the frontier influence in American Christianity see W. W. Sweet, *Religion on the American Frontier:* Vol. I, *The Baptists,* New York, 1931; Vol. II, *The Presbyterians,* New York, 1936; Vol. III, *The Congregationalists,* Chicago, 1939; Vol. IV, *The Methodists* (in preparation).

had an attitude bordering on contempt for our American Protestantism. The American delegates attending the Oxford and Edinburgh conferences in 1937 noted the attitude of coldness and indifference toward American opinions. Unfortunately Europeans are almost totally ignorant of American Protestantism. The Master of Ridley Hall, an Anglican theological college in Cambridge, England, told me in the autumn of 1937 that he had never heard of the Disciples of Christ until the Oxford conference. Just now there is in preparation a book for the Cambridge University Press, attempting to interpret American religion to Englishmen. Let us hope that it will aid in piercing the almost total darkness. This situation has not been helped by the admitted dependence of American theologians on European leadership —a dependence that has been far greater in recent years than formerly. Indeed, it would seem that about the only thing we have been importing from Europe in recent years has been theology.

Another reason for adverse criticism of American Protestantism is the fact that it has divided and redivided into more than two hundred independent bodies. That is proof, at least, that we enjoy complete freedom of conscience and full religious liberty. And since religious liberty has been in such a large degree the achievement of minorities, we may well be thankful, even though our thankfulness may be somewhat tempered by shame, that in America religious minorities have the right to exist and carry on.

The very fact that American Protestantism is so much divided has been one of the reasons for the growing concern for ecumenicity. For the first time in the history of American Protestantism there is a compelling interest in "the Church." Formerly we were accustomed to think only in terms of "the churches." And this concern for a greater Christian unity in America has caused American Protestantism to take the lead in trying to bring about a world-wide Christian unity.

American Protestantism cannot and ought not be judged by Old World criteria, for it has developed in the New World, where a new spirit, a new emphasis, and new methods were a prime requisite.

SECTARIANISM RUN WILD

CHARLES S. BRADEN

SECTARIANISM is said to be the scandal of Christianity. But just for the record let it be said that sectarianism is not a peculiarly Christian vice. It is found in every religion that has developed far beyond the tribal stage. There are more than fifty sects of Hinduism in India. Buddhism is divided into two major schools and a great number of sects and subsects. The same is true of Islam, of Judaism, and of Shintoism.

Neither is sectarianism a peculiar vice of religions; it is rather a human vice that manifests itself in practically every important realm of man's organized life. There is sectarianism in art, with its various schools and cults. There is sectarianism in poetry, in music, in education, in philosophy, in medicine, in economics. And what shall we say of politics? How many kinds of Democrats are there and of Republicans, of Socialists, of Communists?

Or is sectarianism a vice at all? Should there be only one kind of medicine, one kind of music, of art, of poetry, of economic thought, or of government—that is, the right kind? But that is precisely, we are told, what the costliest and deadliest war in history is being fought for. We will not have just one kind of government—an authoritarian, totalitarian, one-party rule. We will have freedom—indeed, four freedoms—although it doesn't appear at the present moment that all the freedoms are to be extended to all the people, particularly the colonial peoples of the world.

Well, one of the freedoms, one of the most precious of all of them—the freedom of worship—is the very charter of sectarianism. We may not like the divisions that exist within the body of Christ; but so long as we believe in this particular freedom and actually permit it to all men, we shall have with us sects that we don't like and that probably do violence to Christianity as we conceive of it; which means, of course, "true Christianity!" Undoubtedly where freedom is allowed, it will often run over into license, but the cure of that is not to take away freedom but so to develop the human mind and spirit that it will act as its own corrective and so prevent the more extravagant forms of religious belief and practice.

SECTARIANISM A RESULT OF FREEDOM

It would seem to me that a healthy attitude to take toward sectarianism is first of all to recognize that it is the result of a principle that is one of the glories of our faith—namely, its freedom—and then to seek to understand the basic motives that underly its various expressions. My own

110

conviction is that most sects represent something real—the satisfaction of some fundamental need of the human spirit which, for one reason or another, is not being met in the groups from which the sects spring, or from which the people are drawn into the sects that already exist. I will go further and say that the formally expressed reason for division is not always the real reason; that sometimes an economic motive underlies a separation that ostensibly is a doctrinal split in an organization; and that had not the class spirit appeared in the denomination, it would have continued undivided. This may be to oversimplify any given case of a sectarian break, but that it represents something very real, I think, can be shown without great difficulty. Richard Niebuhr says that the divisions have occurred more frequently from the economic factor than any other.

Meanwhile, to see just how bad the sectarian picture is, let us look at the situation in the United States, where two factors have made for a greater diversity of sectarian expression, probably, than anywhere in the world. These factors are, first, that it is dominantly Protestant by tradition, and the Protestant principle of freedom to think has its logical outcome in just what has happened in America, where to that principle has been added the democratic freedom, particularly of the frontier. Freedom in a political sense is a dangerous thing, say totalitarian rulers; and freedom in the realm of religion is a dangerous thing, says the Roman Catholic Church. But in America we will have both. Sectarianism may well be the weakness of Protestantism, as Catholics are wont to say; but its freedom to divide may also be its strength if to the exercise of freedom there is joined the will to understand the needs of the human spirit and the willingness and skill to meet those needs in ways that will make no longer necessary the constant fragmentation of the Church which to many now seems to be a necessity.

The religious census of 1936, the latest available, lists 256 denominations or sects. How many there were in 1943, it is impossible to say, though the *Yearbook* of the churches lists 258. That does not mean that there are only 256 sects in America, but only that that many are reported on in the census. Elmer T. Clark asserts that he has compiled a list of at least one hundred which were not listed officially; and I myself know of many, usually small and insignificant groups that did not get into the official census report. Relying, however, upon the government figures and comparing successive reports by decades, one may get some picture of the growth of sects in America.

Before 1890 there is no dependable basis for comparison with later reports, and only since 1906 has the method of taking the census been sufficiently uniform to make comparative studies in most respects at all possible. The total number of sects reported in 1890, 1906, and successive decades is as follows:

1890	145	1926	213
1906	186	1936	256
1916	202		

This represents a gain of 73.7 per cent in forty-six years, the sharpest rise in the whole period being in the most recent decade—1926-36. Several denominations disappear each decade, some by union with other bodies, some by death. Some existing fail to make a census return. Also, each decade, a few begin to make census returns which were really in existence before the previous census and so appear for the first time. Some denominations represent only a split off an already-existing group, and some are a result of emigration to America of already-existing Old World churches. There were actually 61 listed in the 1906 census that were not in the 1890, but the net gain was only 41. In 1916, 31 were added with a net of 14; in 1926 it was 29, net 11; and in 1936, 57 with a net of 43. For the printed record I present in tabular form these and other interesting facts:

NUMBER

	Listed	Families	Separate denomin.	Added	Omitted	Net Gain	Exist before not reported	Uniting with other denom.
1890	145	18	25					4
1906	186	27	32	61	13	48	7	5
1916	202	24	44	31	17	14	5	9
1926	213	23	58	29	17	12	15	5
1936	256	24	73	57	14	43	24	4

	Formed by Division of Others	Newly Formed	From Immigration	Dropped as Nonexistent
1890				
1906	13	29	11	12
1916	3	14	5	7
1926	1	10	..	10
1936	10	21	..	10

It will be noted that in almost every respect the last decade showed the largest sectarian gains, the fewest reunions of sects. The periods 1890-1906 and 1906-16 show the influence of the heavy immigration of those years, 16 new sects (11 and 5 respectively) appearing during that time. This has now ceased to be a factor in the increasing number of sects. It will be instructive to see what kinds of new sects appeared in the latest period.

In summary, the 21 new denominations reporting in 1936 represent a total of only 580 churches with a total membership of only 51,984. Of these 9, with 392 churches and 25,988 membership, were of the Pentecostal type. Three were offshoots of the Eastern Orthodox Church, adapting itself to America, involving 34 churches and 13,704 members. Two were definitely not specifically Christian, one purporting to restore the ancient Mayan faith but in terms strikingly modern and scientific. One was a Seventh Day group. The others were essentially independent churches, one of them with only a single church, another with two; and there was one group of unorganized Italians of 104 churches. Finally, there was one new Methodist group—the Apostolic Methodist. You will be interested in the description of it given by the head of the church:

The Apostolic Methodist Church was organized in 1932 to provide for the spiritual needs of such persons as cannot conscientiously worship God in any system whose leadership or practical management invalidates the Word of God, the Holy Bible, or diverts the service and finances of the faithful to the proclamation of a so-called modernistic gospel, teaching such monstrous heresies as evolution, no need for blood atonement, salvation by works, mere moral science, social service, and the like. This church stands for the Bible as the pure and complete Word of God. This body has not grown rapidly (founded in 1932, it had two churches with total of 31 members in 1936) due to the inadequate finances of its members to undertake any extensive evangelistic operations; and due to hostility from ecclesiastical institutions whose apostasy its tenets condemn, and no less to the apostasy and godlessness of the general age and society now circumjacent.[1]

Proceeding backward, in 1926, of the 10 newly organized sects at least five, or one half, were of the Pentecostal-Holiness type, the Apostolic Overcoming Holy Church of God being one of them. Two colored churches are in general Episcopalian, though deriving their orders through the Syrian Church; one, Divine Science, is a healing church; and one, the Liberal Catholic, may be termed a liberal group.

In 1916 of the 14 newly made sects, 10 were of the Pentecostal-Holiness-Evangelistic type, including Church of God as Organized by Jesus Christ, which in 1916 had only 17 churches and 227 members and in 1936 had only 13 churches with 361 members. Two were branches of Catholicism, and two were national or language-group churches. None were liberal.

Of the 29 appearing first in 1906, 14 were evangelistic associations, several of them being of the more extreme emotional or Holiness type. At least 5 others were of somewhat similar nature. Two were foreign faiths—the Vedanta Societies and Bahai and definitely liberal; one was a Norwegian Free Lutheran Church; and most of the remaining, conservative groups emphasized some particular doctrine.

It is interesting also to note those which drop out, though that is not a part of this study. Of the 12 that dropped out between 1890 and 1906, 6 were communistic in character. Apparently the mortality rate of that type was heavy in that particular period. Nor, so far as I have been able to discover, have any new ones appeared.

THE DOMINANT TYPE OF SECTARIANISM

By way of summary, out of a total of 74 newly organized sects 43, or more than half, were of the Evangelistic-Pentecostal-Holiness type. Clearly we have here, then, the dominant type of sectarianism in America. If one were to attempt to characterize the group as a whole, prob-

---

[1] *Religious Bodies*, 1936, Vol. II, p. 1172.

ably about four words could be applied to them. They are extremely conservative, are Bible-centered, are millenarian, and stress personal religious experience, usually of a rather exaggerated emotional type, especially in the Pentecostal-Holiness groups.

Why, it may be asked, should there be so many sects of this type? I venture to suggest four possible reasons:

First, these sects are highly emotional. By that very fact they seem to me to be less stable than sects based mainly on some particular doctrinal teaching. Where the feelings are involved deeply, differences are not easily composed. The self-evidencing character of the emotional experience does not permit of rational argument. The natural result, therefore, is separation when sharp cleavages arise. As one reads over the statement of beliefs of these emotional groups, he is led to wonder why, since they are so very much alike in most respects, they do not get together. Well, of course sometimes they do, and probably geographical distances may have something to do with the continued separateness of some of them; but probably a more adequate explanation is that the small differences that do exist are points at which a great deal of feeling is involved, and this acts as a barrier to union.

Secondly, these sects represent a social and economic class of people who do not find themselves at home in the so-called "regular" denominations. Most of these groups draw their membership from what Richard Niebuhr calls "the disinherited." They are working people—people who live in the wrong part of town. In the cities—and they are urban in a considerable degree—they are found in the poorer sections, the industrial areas; seldom on the better streets. The comfortable middle-class churches maintain social standards they cannot keep up with. They find it difficult to hold up their end of the financial support of the church, and they are too proud to do less than their fair share. Few of our churches succeed in bridging the gap between different economic classes. Most of them are definitely class institutions. Methodism, which began in the eighteenth century as a church of the disinherited, has long since become a comfortable, middle-class church. The Salvation Army, you will recall, resulted largely because Methodism had already, in the time of William Booth, withdrawn itself from the disinherited.

Professor Anton Boisen recently made a study of religion today in the town in which he grew up, contrasting it with what it had been some forty years ago. At that time the people of the lower economic levels belonged to the Methodist, Baptist, and Disciples churches; the well-to-do, to the Presbyterian and Episcopal. Now, behold, the churches that minister to the lower economic groups—these on the wrong side of the tracks—are the Church of the Nazarene, the Church of God, the Pentecostal, et cetera. The Methodist, Baptist, and Disciples now stand alongside the Presbyterian and Episcopal churches. Their members are the solid, respected citizens of the city. The same story would be found to be true throughout the entire country. These sects are class groups designed to meet the needs of the disinherited, which are largely neglected by the "better" churches. Since this class, by its very economic condition, has been denied the advantages of an education, which might lead to a disciplining of the emotions, it is more easily subject to the exaggerated emotionalism characteristic of the groups as a whole.

Thirdly, following logically from what has just been said, these cults provide their members with an opportunity for emotional release which probably fulfills for them a genuine psychological function. The forms the emotional expression takes are too familiar to need elaboration here—shouting, hand clapping, dancing, jumping, rolling, speaking in tongues, getting the jerks, falling into prolonged trances. They undoubtedly serve as a kind of safety valve and relieve inward tensions and pressures, which the more orderly liturgical services of the "regular" churches do not serve to relieve in persons of pronouncedly volatile temperament, at least. Others, of more advantaged position, may find avenues for emotional release in other ways—in the theater, in social life, in sports, in travel, in literature, in art. But those who work long hours at humdrum tasks at little more than subsistence wages can ill afford such means of normal emotional release. For such religious emotionalism seems to provide the outlet they need.

Finally, these emotional experiences serve as a guaranty of the truth of the faith of these people and an assurance of their salvation. They provide unmistakable evidence that one has passed from death unto life, that one has been accepted of God. They bring a certainty of the possession of the Holy Spirit. There is here none of the tentativeness, the lack of positiveness, which characterizes so much of modern preaching in the established churches. These people know in whom they have believed as a result of an overwhelming personal experience, which, after all, is perhaps the most convincing testimony that can come to a man.

The fact that these sects are millennial and other-worldly in their emphasis fits well into the needs and hopes of economically depressed people, who hope in a world to come for what they have been denied here. But this is offered in many even of the "regular" denominations. The cogent thing about these cults is that to this general outlook they bring the corroboration of an overwhelming personal emotional experience.

RAPID GROWTH IN MEMBERSHIP

The growth not only in the number of this type of sects but also in the number of their members is a striking phenomenon of our time. An examination of the religious census shows some striking contrasts between the growth of some of these cults and the larger churches.

For example, the net gain of all the churches in 1936 over 1926 was 2.3 per cent. For a group of the larger churches, including the Methodist—there was a *loss* of 8 per cent. The Methodist Episcopal lost 14 per cent, the Methodist South, 17.1 per cent; the Presbyterian, 5.1 per cent; the Southern Baptist, 23 per cent; the Disciples of Christ, 13.2 per cent. Now look at the *gains,* not losses, of some of the smaller sects.

Arranged in descending order of percentage of increase between 1926 and 1936, the list is as follows:

	Per Cent
Church of God and Saints of Christ (colored)	450.1
Other Pentecostal Assemblies	264.7
Assemblies of God	208.7
Church of the Nazarene	114.3
Church of God	92.8
Pentecostal Holiness	60.0
Reorganized Church of Jesus Christ of Latter Day Saints	45.2
Christian and Missionary Alliance	41.4
Salvation Army	37.8
Pilgrim Holiness	33.8
General Conference of Mennonites	22.9
Seventh Day Adventists	20.0
Evangelical Mission Covenant Church	19.4

Of course, the number of members of most of these groups is not large. Those rather definitely perfectionist or Holiness numbered 286,110 in 1936. Those having Pentecostal in their official titles reported a total of 57,652. Thus almost 350,000 find their religious affiliations with these emotional sects. Probably if all were included which approximate this type of religious experience, even though that fact does not appear in the name, the number might exceed half a million—a large number yet small in comparison with the total in America.

To set the sectarianism of America in a proper perspective it should be noted that the vast majority of the churches and the members are found in a very small number of denominations. Thus, in 1926, 19 denominations represented 77.7 of all the churches, and 88.8 of all the members. In 1936, 19 denominations represented 73.8 per cent of all the churches and 88.7 per cent of all the members.

Ordinarily it is thought that the membership gains come through their aggressive and perfervid evangelism. It will come as a surprise to most of us, therefore, to discover that several of them have a much larger number of pupils in their Sunday schools than do the larger established denominations in proportion to their membership, and their Sunday schools seems to be on the increase generally, while just the contrary is true of many of the larger denominations.

For each 100 members in 1936 the Pentecostal Holiness Church had 187 pupils in Sunday school; the Church of the Nazarene, 166; the Christian and Missionary Alliance, 135; the Salvation Army, 119; the Assemblies of God, 117; the Church of God, 116. What of our own Methodism? Among the three Methodisms, since united, the Methodist Protestant for each 100 church members had only 88 in its Sunday schools; the Methodist Episcopal, 72; Southern Methodism, only 61. The Southern Presbyterians had 74; the Northern, 64 (the same number as the Disciples of Christ) ; while the United Lutherans had only 49, and the Episcopalians only 25. Concerning the quality of instruction or the methods used in their Sunday schools I ...ave no way of knowing, but it does appear that they have a wholesome regard for Christian nur- ure as well as the saving of the lost.

THE MORE MARGINAL GROUPS

Thus far I have spoken only of the cults that fall well within the framework of Christianity and differ mainly in that they are more conservative than the main group of Protestants. But I confess I am less troubled about these than I am about a considerable group that are more marginal in their relationship to the main line of Christian tradition or some of them clear outside of what may properly be called Christian at all. Yet some of these have drawn within their orbit in the last fifteen years probably more than all the ones we have been discussing put together many times over. Certainly this is true if the figures they quote as to membership are to be accepted at even half face value. Most of these are not even enumerated among the sects in the United States religious census. Here are the names of some of them: New Thought, Unity School of Christianity, I Am, Psychiana, Anglo-Israel Movement, Father Divine's Peace Mission, Ahmadiya Movement in Islam, Jehovah's Witnesses. The 1936 census indicates fifty-seven smaller or larger sects it made no effort to include in the enumeration.

The reason I say I am more troubled by these is that, it seems to me, their rise and rapid growth in the case of a few and their slower growth but continued existence in the case of others are symptomatic of the failure of the Church at significant points to satisfy certain legitimate human needs. For I hold that people do not join the cults, particularly those which entail a degree of social disapproval, without reason. To be sure, there is a much freer movement from one church to another than in an earlier day. This is due to a more tolerant spirit in the churches and, of course, to the great mobility of the population in recent years. But joining a cult is not the same thing. Often it means attending meetings in a rented room in an out-of-the-way place and, frequently enough, with a lot of queer people. No prestige—rather, the opposite—attaches to membership in it. There must be something a person greatly desires, which he is not getting in the ordinary religious groups, which leads him to try the cults. What are these needs?

Elsewhere [1] I have written at considerable length what I can only sketch here concerning the needs that, when not met in the churches, carry men and women out into the cults. There are, I venture to suggest, eight major needs, which are as follows: (1) the desire for novelty; (2) the desire for security; (3) the desire for health; (4) the desire for assurance of salvation; (5) the desire for emotional release; (6) the de-

---

[1] *The Christian Century*, Vol. 41, pp. 45-47; 78-80; 108-10; 137-40; Jan.-Feb., 1944.

sire for greater intellectual freedom; (7) the desire for a more central ethical emphasis; and (8) the desire for status.

Various less-important factors such as the lure of the mysterious and the occult, the glamour of the oriental, and the martyr complex seem also to have contributed to the exodus from the churches to the cults; but they are of secondary, not of primary importance.

All these major needs will be recognized as legitimate and even laudable needs, which ought to be met. Even the desire for novelty need not be met by following after alien fires but might be met within any of the churches that is ever seeking to present its central message and meaning in new and striking ways instead of eternally doing the same old things in the same old ways, and by keeping the Christian ideal a moving goal so that there is something always ahead worth seeking to attain without having to go outside the church.

Look again at the list. Is there any one of them for which the church ought not to concern itself? Is it not interested in the security of its members, their health and well-being, their assurance of salvation, their emotional life, their desire for freedom to think their religious problems through, their desire for a more profound and vital emphasis upon practical conduct, the desire of a person to feel that he belongs and that he has genuine worth? Surely these are or ought to be the profound concern of the churches. But the difficulty is that in being all-round in their interest they do not stress any one of these or all of them in a sufficient degree to meet always the need of individuals for whom some one of them is of paramount interest at a particular moment.

Here the cults have an advantage. They are not for the most part all-round in their interest. They put their major stress at some specific point, say health. Thus, they meet the sick person at the point of his greatest need—one that for the moment overshadows every other interest. When he is offered health—the thing he most desires—and when, as not infrequently happens, he is restored to health through the cult, it is little to be wondered at that he gives his allegiance to it rather than to the church to which he formerly belonged. Of course, when he is well, and his other interests again come to the surface, he may find little satisfaction in the cult, with its one-sided ministry, and may withdraw from it, as he actually does in considerable numbers.

I have already, earlier in this paper, discussed the cults that draw people into them who crave an assurance of salvation and a certainty of faith which are lacking in not all but many churches—people who find this, together with a needed emotional release, in the emotional cults, the most numerous among more recently formed American sects.

The healing cults are too familiar to this group to require extended treatment here. Almost all the cults, even the emotional type, profess to be able to heal, though only a few, such as Christian Science and New Thought groups and their offspring, make healing central. Why should it be thought necessary to go outside the churches for healing of body or of the mind? Do these cults have a monopoly on the healing processes of God? Is it necessary that people accept some philosophy alien to that of traditional Christianity in order to put themselves in the way of being healed? Psychologically it has been proved beyond a peradventure of doubt that the healing processes are in no way dependent on the particular content of the *faith*, which is the basic factor in the healing.

This is no plea for an abandonment of the aid of scientific medicine. Even Mrs. Eddy availed herself freely of its services in the later years of her life. It is a plea for the recognition of the tremendous value of a robust and healthy religious faith first of all in preventing much unnecessary illness due to worry and uncertainty and a sense of frustration, and at the same time in helping along the recuperative processes of those who are definitely suffering from serious illness, co-operating with and not displacing the skilled medical practitioner, who can undoubtedly also make a great contribution. It would be folly in the extreme to attempt to cure pneumonia by prayer or faith without the use of the sulfa compounds, which have so recently been discovered; but the sulfa compounds alone cannot be as effective as they can together with the ministry of the Christian faith.

This is a plea for recognition of the need of a type of training for ministers which will enable them to perform a ministry of health and healing for the minds and bodies of men as well as for their souls. When this is adequately done, we shall see far fewer people being drawn away from the churches into the healing cults.

Concerning the necessity of freedom to think, to integrate religion with the rapidly shifting scientific and philosophic thought of our modern age, little need be said to this group. We would not shackle the minds of men, denying them the freedom to examine critically any aspect of our faith, nor would we withhold tolerance of and respect for those who do not agree with us in our religious convictions. Thank God, Methodism has never been doctrine-centered. It can and does today have within its ample fold men and women of widely differing convictions concerning the details of the Christian faith. But the very existence of the cults which I would designate as the philosophic type is proof that not all churches are equally liberal and tolerant. I refer here to such groups as the Vedanta societies (which are, of course, just Hinduism in its missionary phase in America), New Thought groups, Rosicrucians, the neological societies, Biosophy, Theosophy, et cetera. All these make an appeal on the basis of their broad tolerance, their intellectualism, their purported complete harmony with modern science, although not a few of the groups actually have about them a large element of the occult and the miraculous, which are very far from squaring with science. It is amazing to me to discover just how much of the occult and the miraculous people in these cults are able to take who somehow are affronted by miracle in Christianity.

The Appeals of Security and Prosperity

Two appeals are probably drawing more people out of the churches into the cults than any other. I refer to the desire for security, which I interpret in two different senses, and an extension of it—namely, the desire for prosperity, wealth, abundance. There may well be a question as to what Christianity has to say about the latter; but concerning the desire for security in the sense of adequate provision for man's needs, not his wants, there can be little doubt that Christianity should have something very definite to say.

The first meaning I attach to security is not primarily economic, though the economic interest may also be operative here. What I mean is the desire to know what lies ahead or around the corner, doubtless with the hope of being able to prepare for it or to secure oneself against what threatens. It is a product of the precarious times in which we live. There is so much fear and uncertainty as to the future. Just out of a depression, with all its anxieties and forebodings, we are plunged into a war that touches almost every family and person in America. With so much fear, anxiety, foreboding, and uncertainty as to what lies ahead, it is not unnatural to expect that those who purport to be able to disclose the future should flourish now as never before. Some of these operate within religious cults, some outside; but all are today reaping a golden harvest. Never have there been so many fortunetellers, numerologists, astrologers, and their like, and never have they been so prosperous as they are now. There are in the United States about thirty thousand full-time practicing astrologers, to say nothing of the other numerous varieties of soothsayers. One author gives eighty thousand as a conservative estimate of full-time fortunetellers of all sorts. The astrologers are organized into regional groups like our Methodist conferences, one of them, the largest, being the American Federation of *Scientific* Astrologers. More than two thousand five hundred newspapers, daily and weekly, carry regular astrological columns; and newspapers don't carry material people do not read. Try to get as much space for religious news in many of these papers. The Better Business Bureau estimates that Americans are spending now at the rate of two hundred million dollars a year, trying to find out what lies ahead. In a day of the expenditure of billions in war such a sum does not seem large, but it is one tenth of what is spent for primary and secondary education in the entire country. It amounts to two fifths of all the expenditures of all the churches in America for all purposes local and missionary. It is nearly three times the amount spent by all the Methodist churches in 1936 for all purposes.

To be sure, astrology is not a cult with an active membership, though there are cults of which astrology is a definite feature, but the effect of astrology upon the churches cannot be lightly overlooked; for that many of those who purchase the numerous astrological journals and read the astrological columns in the press and write in for horoscopes are members of our churches there can be little doubt. Insofar as our people are led to seek freedom from fear and anxiety at the hands of what at best can scarcely be characterized as other than charlatanry it is a reflection of the inadequacy of the gospel we preach. Here is a door opening outward from the church into either the cults that specialize in the mysterious and the occult or out into a paganized secularism, which is perhaps a far more dangerous foe of Christian faith. Neither alternative can give any comfort to the Christian Church and its ministry.

The one religious group that ministers chiefly to this desire to know the future is the spiritualist. At least he usually cloaks his commerce with the unseen world with religion, sometimes, I think, sincerely, sometimes to hide behind the principle of religious freedom and carry on his exploitation of human credulity safe from the law. What a demand there is upon the medium today, with the mounting numbers of dead and missing on the battle fronts of the world! I have a medium friend who tells me that she has never been so busy in her whole experience. Of course, here two factors operate: the desire for certainty as to whether the missing are still alive and the desire for continued communication with those who have passed over. To this is coupled the desire to know what lies in store for those alive. It is a heartbreaking experience to hear the questions asked at the seances. What a picture of despair, hopelessness, anxiety, fear!

Why do people go to the spiritualist medium? Why not to the Christian minister in their extremity? Has religion no adequate ministry to such fear-ridden folk? I suggest that the fact that many do go to the medium is because they have not learned from their church a faith that is able to overcome fear and loneliness and defeat; that they have not found a philosophy of death and its inevitable place in the economy of life sufficient to see them through their admittedly cruel experiences of personal loss. Has the Church something adequate for these dread experiences? It is my belief that the Christian faith has, and that it alone has an adequate answer. But it must be confessed that it is not always found in the individual ministry of every local church.

Space permits only a very brief glance at a large number of cults that minister to the desire for economic security and even prosperity, which goes beyond the mere satisfaction of basic physical needs. Among them I would place I Am, which now claims more than three million followers, and it was begun less than fifteen years ago; Psychiana, the mail-order religion that claims over six hundred thousand in a little more than a decade; Father Divine's Peace Mission; New Thought, especially the Unity School of Christianity, which claims millions of readers for its periodicals. It is true that they do not limit their appeal to this one desire; they also stress health and freedom from anxiety. I pick at random a sample appeal from a publication of Dr. Robinson, of Psychiana:

Wealth or poverty? Happiness or despair? Health or sickness? Which do you want? Introducing to you an invisible Power that can bring to you now an abundance of everything you need. There is no limitation of this Power, because it is God.

This sort of appeal can be multiplied times without number. That it gets people is proved by the growth of this type of cult. It meets people where they are. It promises great things. How many are bitterly disappointed and thereby rendered even more impervious to the message of the Christian Church no one can say. But the cults stand indubitably as an indication of great, crying, felt needs of humanity. Has the Church an answer to these needs?

There is no easy answer to the questions raised by these cults. I have no panacea to suggest to ministers who are forced to deal with them. Of one thing I am absolutely sure: We shall know better how to deal with them when we understand them. And, understanding them, we shall then better understand the needs of people to whom we ourselves are ministers. The only cure for sectarianism and cultism, so far as I can see, is a full, rich ministry of the Christian Church to the whole range of human need. The cults perform a ministry to great groups for which the great churches apparently have little appeal or even concern. Until the "regular" churches find a way to meet the legitimate needs served by the cults and sects, the latter will continue to flourish. When these needs are met in a better way by the "regular" churches, they will cease to trouble Zion.

Part II

INTERPRETATIONS

CARDINAL PRINCIPLES OF PROTESTANTISM

ALBERT CORNELIUS KNUDSON

FIRST a word about the name "Protestantism" and the sense or senses in which it is used. There is general agreement in applying it to the great religious movement that had its chief source in the Reformation of the sixteenth century. But there has been and still is some difference of opinion as to the precise limits of the movement to which the name "Protestant" should be applied. Its first use was occasioned by the formal *Protestatio,* or protest, submitted at the Diet of Speyer in 1529 by the Lutheran princes and some free cities. This protest was a declaration of their refusal to carry out an edict, adopted by a majority of the diet, which aimed at checking and, to some extent, undoing the work of the Reformers. The protesters in this instance were called Protestants by their opponents; and this soon became the name commonly applied to Lutherans in general and accepted by them despite Luther's dislike of it. A little later it was extended to include the Zwinglians and Calvinists. And still later its meaning was gradually broadened until it came to include "all Christians (other than those of the Eastern churches) who are not in communion with Rome." [1] This is the sense in which it is at present commonly used.

There has, however, been some question as to whether the more extreme rationalistic groups in Western Christendom should be classed as Protestant. For a while the name was withheld from them on the ground that, judged by Protestant standards, they were not truly Christian. But more recently, insofar as they have claimed the Christian name for themselves, the tendency has been to include them in the Protestant family. Then, at the other extreme, we have, especially in the English Church, an ardent group of sacramentarians and sacerdotalists who do not wish to be known as Protestants. They are not in communion with Rome, but they feel a greater degree of sympathy with the spirit of Catholicism than with that of Protestantism and hence prefer the Catholic label. We usually refer to them as Anglo-Catholics. But in the light of the definition above given they still are Protestants, and it is hardly probable that out of regard for their sensibilities this definition will be amended so as to exclude them from the Protestant fold. Protestants may be catholic in spirit without ceasing to be Protestants.

Neither the Anglo-Catholics, however, nor the more rationalistic and humanistic sects can be taken as typical of historic Protestantism. The main stream of Protestant life and thought has been fundamentally evangelical.

---

[1] C. J. Cadoux, *Catholicism and Christianity,* p. 12.

125

Protestantism is a growing and developing movement, and we can determine its essential nature and its cardinal principles only by a careful and sympathetic study of its entire history.

If we are to understand Protestantism aright, we must take into account both its fruits and its roots, both its outcome and what it came out of.

In view of the changes and development that Protestantism has undergone and in view of its numerous divisions and the consequent complexity and diversity of its organization and teaching, it is no simple and easy matter to determine what its cardinal principles are and how they should be interpreted. We cannot accept without question the traditional Protestant views on the subject; nor can we altogether disregard the Roman Catholic contention that Protestantism has "no fixed and permanent character except hatred of Catholicism" and that "it has no principles, doctrines, or forms which, in order to be itself, it must always and everywhere maintain." [2] Then, too, we have to reckon with our own inherited prejudices and their effects upon our conception of the essential nature of Protestantism. These prejudices are to some extent unavoidable, and we need, so far as possible, to discount their influence. To give a truly objective and historical exposition of the cardinal principles of Protestantism is therefore a complex and difficult task.

THE RIGHT OF PRIVATE JUDGMENT

It has been customary for Protestant historians to say that there were two fundamental principles of the Reformation—a formal and a material principle. The former was the supreme authority of Scripture, and the latter the doctrine of justification by faith. These two principles are still commonly regarded as fundamental and essential to Protestantism, and neither could, in my opinion, be omitted from any adequate list of its cardinal principles. But they do not at present enjoy the almost unquestioned primacy they once did. It is now coming to be seen that they are not and never were the ultimate points of difference between Protestantism and Romanism. There was a deeper principle underlying them. This principle was the Protestant belief in the inspiration of the individual and the consequent right of private judgment. The real point of difference between Protestants and Romanists was not the inspiration and authority of Scripture but the question as to who is its true interpreter. Romanists said the inspired Church; Protestants said the inspired or enlightened individual. In other words, Romanists denied the right of private judgment in religious matters, while Protestants affirmed it. This has always been the basic difference between them.

On every other point of difference a compromise might conceivably have been effected. Numerous attempts in that direction have been

---

[2] *The Works of Orestes A. Brownson*, XII, p. 163.

made since the Reformation. But all have eventually broken down before the irreconcilable claim to absolute authority on the one hand and to the right of private judgment on the other. In both claims there has been more or less truth. Individualism needs to be balanced by authority, and authority by individual freedom. Both Roman Catholicism and Protestantism have in practice been forced to recognize this to some extent. But the emphasis in one case has fallen so largely upon the duty of submission to authority and in the other upon the right and duty of private judgment that an apparently irreconcilable difference between them has been created.

The right of private judgment, the most fundamental of the cardinal principles of Protestantism, carries with it the idea of tolerance and of religious liberty. But Protestants were slow to see this or, at least, to make the proper practical application of it. They resorted at times to coercive measures and to outright persecution, as Roman Catholics had done for centuries, and on the same ground. As in ethics freedom is a right accorded the moral, not the immoral, person, so, it was argued, in religion freedom is a right to which only the true believer is entitled—that is, the believer who agrees with the established ecclesiastical or civil authority. But the inconsistency in this position, so far as Protestants were concerned, gradually made itself felt until, finally, the logical conclusion was drawn from the principle of private judgment, and religious freedom and toleration became the accepted and avowed teaching and policy of Protestantism as a whole. In this development it was not the great national churches but the despised sects that led the way. And Roman Catholicism in this forward movement has naturally lagged far behind. In practice it has in Protestant countries been forced to yield to the new spirit of tolerance. But its teaching has in principle been opposed to the kind of toleration and religious freedom which the modern mind has deduced from the right of private judgment. Its official theory still is that the only true religious liberty is the liberty of true religion to propagate its faith; and by true religion is of course meant Roman Catholicism.

Justification by Faith

Next to the right of private judgment in the list of the cardinal principles of Protestantism comes the doctrine of justification by faith. This doctrine is not directly deducible from the right of private judgment, but the two stand in a sympathetic relation to each other. Both are subjective. Both put spiritual initiative and the sanctity of the individual conscience above submission to external human authority. Both make the inner attitude of the soul more important than compliance with external rules and rites. Both affirm the freedom of the individual. Indeed, in one respect the doctrine of justification by faith provides the firmest conceivable basis for religious freedom, for it makes the salvation of the individual independent of all human authority and independent also of his own natural weaknesses and

127

limitations. It puts his eternal welfare beyond the reach of all human tyranny and all enslaving human weaknesses and makes him, in the completest sense of the term, a free man. Salvation by faith and religious freedom thus go together.

But in thus emancipating the Christian soul from all tyranny of human origin early Protestantism fell into another tyranny—the tyranny of divine predestination. The doctrine of predestination or election had, it is true, an important practical purpose. It sought to impart to the Christian believer an indubitable assurance of his redemption by grounding it wholly in the divine will, thus eliminating any conditioning human factor that would render it in the slightest degree uncertain. It also sought to cut the ground from under all human pride and all human claim to merit by establishing the absoluteness of the divine grace. God, it was said, is the sole source of man's salvation. Saving faith is wholly his work within us. It is his will, and his will alone, that redeems us.

But while the doctrine of predestination thus had worthy practical motives and no doubt in many instances encouraged Christian humility and strengthened Christian confidence and hope, it had other consequences of a very different nature. It implied an imperfectly moralized Deity by limiting his redemptive grace to those whom he had arbitrarily elected and logically led either to indifference or to pessimism and despair by denying to men that freedom of contrary choice without which there can be no true moral responsibility and no moral ground for believing in the divine grace. Efforts were made to escape these logical consequences either by blinding one's eyes to them or by falling back upon the inscrutable mystery of the divine decrees. But these efforts could not permanently or universally succeed. Logic insisted on its rights; and the result was that the Reformation doctrine of justification by faith, with its predestinarian implications, led in some instances to antinomianism and in others to pessimism and a depressed state of religious feeling.

Such was, to a considerable extent, the situation in England in the early part of the eighteenth century, when John Wesley appeared upon the scene. He was the first great Protestant leader to break sharply with the predestinarian tradition, to dissociate from it the doctrine of justification by faith, and to carry on a popular religious movement of world-wide significance on the basis of a consistent freedomism. In so doing he influenced the religious life and thought of the Anglo-Saxon world more profoundly than any man since the time of the Reformation. A distinguished American theologian has recently, in a large two-volume work, characterized Methodism as a "belated pietistic-evangelistic sect." This is, I believe, his only reference to Methodism by name in the entire work. One would, however, like to know in what respect Wesleyan Methodism was a "belated" movement. If there has been any other religious movement since the Reformation more timely, better adapted to the needs of its own day, and more influential, it would be interesting to have it named. While not primarily a theologian, Wesley laid hold so firmly of certain fundamental but neglected or rejected truths concerning freedom, faith, and divine grace and proclaimed them so effectively that his long apostolic ministry became a turning point in the history of evangelical Protestantism. Before his time faith and the divine grace had in wide circles been so sharply distinguished from and so unrelated to human freedom and moral initiative that an almost magical quality came to be attributed to them. This nonmoral, if not antimoral, tendency in traditional evangelicalism Wesley corrected. He reinterpreted the doctrine of justification by faith in the light of a consistent freedomism and, by so doing, moralized the conception of faith and saved the operation of the divine grace from the just charge of being arbitrary and out of harmony with the principle of the divine love. This change did not weaken or contradict the doctrine of justification by faith, as many thought, but strengthened it by rescuing it from the realm of theological abstractions and grounding it in religious experience and in the moral nature of man.

Faith from this point of view is a human as well as a divine act. It is indeed the profoundest moral act of which man, enlightened and inspired by the Divine Spirit, is capable. And because it is such, it is also a justifying or saving faith. So profound is the act of will in Christian faith that God takes the will for the deed. That is what justification by faith means in moral and rational terms. And, so understood, this doctrine stands opposed to the superficiality, externalism, and irrationality of sacramentarianism, sacerdotalism, and ecclesiasticism. It is in itself a radically individualistic and spiritual doctrine.

THE SUPREME AUTHORITY OF SCRIPTURE

The cardinal principle of Protestantism which I place third in the list is the supreme authority of Scripture. This doctrine was for a time regarded as the basic principle of Protestantism, as the foundation on which the whole structure of its teaching rests. The Bible was held to be the one infallible source and ground of religious belief. But this point of view now belongs largely to the past. It has succumbed to the modern theory of knowledge and to modern biblical criticism. The theory of knowledge has made it clear that there can be no purely external or objective authentication of truth. The ultimate standard of truth must be found in the mind itself. The Bible or the Church cannot by its divinely inspired authority make a proposition true. If true, it must be such in its own right. This applies to Christian teaching as a whole. The Bible may mediate our knowledge of the right of private judgment and of the doctrine of justification by faith, but it does not validate them. These doctrines are true independently of their embodiment in Scripture. And tacitly, at least, the early Protestants recognized them to be such. Whatever finality they may have attributed to the letter of Scripture, they actually subordinated it to their own fundamental theological and ethical convictions. These convictions were of course not arrived at independently of biblical teaching. What made them living convictions was the fact that they were ratified in experience and by reason. It is only such ratification by the mind itself that can furnish a valid basis for belief. This truth, disclosed by modern epistemology, has rendered untenable the older doctrine of infallibility, both biblical and ecclesiastical.

But even if this had not occurred, modern biblical criticism would alone have had the same effect. For by its painstaking and thorough study of the biblical books it has showed by incontrovertible facts that these books are not all divine, that there is a large human element in them, that they represent different stages of moral and religious development, that their origin and structure can be accounted for by the same principles as those employed in the study of other literary works, that they represent the individual peculiarities and imperfections of their human authors, that there are in them numerous other differences in historical details and in religious teaching which are inconsistent with the theory of infallible dictation by the Divine Spirit, and that independent discrimination must consequently be exercised by the reader and student of Scripture if its unique authority is to continue to be recognized. A marked change has thus taken place in the conception of the inspiration and authority of Scripture as a result of modern biblical criticism and as a result also of developments in the field of the theory of knowledge.

But while this is true, while we no longer think of biblical authority as purely objective, absolute, and exclusive, while we attribute special divine inspiration to certain truths in the Bible rather than to the Bible as a whole, it does not follow that Protestantism has subordinated its authority to that of the Church or to that of human reason in the purely abstract and analytical sense of this term. As over against ecclesiastical tradition, on the one hand, and a shallow and barren rationalism, on the other, the Bible still remains the supreme norm in Protestant thought. It no longer, it is true, has the authority of force; but it does, on its higher levels, have the force of authority. And this it has, not because of any miraculous origin, but because it is the supreme expression in human history of that divinely inspired nature or reason which God has planted within us. There is such a thing as a religious reason as well as a theoretical reason, a moral reason, and an aesthetic reason; and the most perfect, the classic expression of this religious reason is to be found in the Bible. This is the underlying conviction of Protestantism, and in this conviction it has found and will continue to find a protection against ecclesiastical tyranny and corruption, against the arrogance of a superficial intellectualism, against fanaticism and superstition, and against other evils that spring up like weeds in man's checkered religious history.

THE SANCTITY OF THE COMMON LIFE

Next in the list of the cardinal principles of Protestantism I put the sanctity of the common life. This principle stands sharply opposed to both the sacerdotalism and the monastic asceticism of Roman Catholicism. As over against the exclusive claims of the Roman priesthood it affirms the universal priesthood of believers, and as over against the alleged superior sanctity of the monastic calling it affirms the equal, if not greater, sanctity of the various kinds of everyday work to which men are called in the normal relations of human life. This teaching was implicit in both the Old and New Testaments, but it became a revolutionary doctrine when Luther proclaimed it in such bold and aggressive terms as he employed in his famous address to the Christian nobility of the German nation in 1520. This address was a veritable broadside directed against the most characteristic features of both the ecclesiastical and ethical systems of Roman Catholicism. It rejected the unique and "indelible character" of the Roman priesthood and its mediating function. It set the individual believer in direct relation to God and restored his spiritual freedom. At the same time it broke down the middle wall of partition which had been erected between the sacred and secular and put back of the daily and essential tasks of mankind that sense of sanctity and that accentuated moral urge which had previously been largely restricted to ecclesiastical and ascetic vocations.

The ethical and social significance of this change can hardly be overestimated. Its immediate consequences, it is true, were not all that might have been expected. But as a long-range doctrine it has been and will continue to be of incalculable value both to religion and to civilization. It has served and is serving the same function as the message of the eighth-century prophets did in their day. It has been and is moralizing religion by attaching its primary sanctions to those elementary virtues which lie at the basis of every healthy and progressive society. At the same time it has emancipated the individual soul from bondage to ecclesiastical authority and given to it that freedom without which it could not attain to spiritual maturity. Emphasis upon the sanctity of the common life has thus been one of the major contributions made by Protestantism to Western Christianity and also to the social progress of mankind.

THE SELF-VERIFICATION OF FAITH

The fifth and last in my list of the cardinal principles of Protestantism is one that would be challenged by many. At least they would object to my phrasing of it. I call it the self-verification of faith or its autonomous validity. To some this phrasing of the principle, especially the second form of it, would be a veritable theological red rag. It directly contradicts, they would tell us, a fundamental tenet of Reformation Protestantism—the belief in divine authority as opposed to human reasoning or intuition. The latter, they say, is dubious and untrustworthy in the field of religion. It furnishes no basis for religious assurance. Only in the objective Word of God can such a basis be found. But this type of authoritarianism is, as we have seen, no longer tenable. It has, during the past century and a half, crumbled under the impact of biblical and philosophical criticism. And as it was gradually discarded, a new kind of authority took its place—an authority that was no longer regarded as external and coercive but as inner and spiritual. This new kind of authority is grounded in the uniqueness of religion and in its self-evidencing character and has never been without some degree of recognition. It was implicit in the individualism and subjectivity of such early Protestant doctrines as the right of private judgment, the witness of the Spirit, and justification by faith and in the Methodist emphasis on religious experience. But it was not until the time of Kant and Schleiermacher that it received what might be called official philosophical and theological ratification. Since then it has become increasingly clear to thoughtful people that religious faith does not need either an infallible Book or an infallible Church to establish its validity. It validates itself. So formulated, religious autonomy is, it is true, a modern doctrine; but inasmuch as the essential idea expressed by it has been implicit in Protestant teaching since the Reformation, it may properly be regarded as more or less characteristic of Protestantism as a whole and as one of its cardinal principles.

The chief significance of the principle of the self-verification or autonomous validity of religious faith is to be found in the field of apologetics. It renders unnecessary and untenable the type of authoritarianism which still persists as a fundamental principle in Roman Catholic teaching. But its significance is not limited to this point of difference between Protestantism and Romanism. It explains, in part at least, two other notable points of difference between them. One of these has to do with their relation to modern thought, and the other with their relation to the State and to the use of political means in propagating religious faith. Their differences at these two points are not sharply and decisively drawn either in theory or practice. They are differences of degree, not of rigid antithesis. Protestantism, for instance, does not wholly endorse modernism, nor does Romanism wholly repudiate it. Again, Protestantism does not in principle contend for the separation of Church and State, nor does Romanism in principle contend for their union. The differences between them are relative, but they are not on that account unimportant. Romanism is far more conservative both theologically and in its social theory than Protestantism, and it is also far more inclined to seek political aid in promoting its own interests.

These differences are due to various causes, but at bottom they seem to me to have resulted from different attitudes toward the independence and self-sufficiency of spiritual religion. Romanism has been distrustful of personal religious experience and its claim to autonomous validity and also distrustful of the free and untrammeled development of our other spiritual capacities. It has been fearful of new ideas and their possible evil effects upon religious faith. It has often resisted intellectual and social change in the interest of its own traditional beliefs, thus giving the impression of being opposed to true progress. Then, too, its distrust of vital personal faith has led to an undue stress upon the externals of religion, to efforts aimed at enlisting the support of the state in its ecclesiastical enterprises, and to dubious political methods in achieving its ends. This aspect of Roman Catholicism has done most to awaken antagonism to itself not only among Protestants but in nonreligious circles as well.

Protestantism, it is true, has not been altogether free from the foregoing faults. It has at times been reactionary in its relation to modern scientific and philosophic thought, and it has also at times been unduly dependent on the State and on special privileges obtained through political influence. But in general, whether in the form of a "free" or a "State" church, it has laid primary emphasis upon personal Christian experience, upon its independence, and upon its ability to maintain and propagate itself through spiritual means alone. It has had such profound confidence in man's religious nature, illumined by the Divine Spirit, that political intriguing and the fear of freedom of thought have been increasingly felt to be alien to its true spirit. If religious belief is to be vital, sincere, and intelligent, it is clear that it must relate itself to the changing thought of the world. It must have faith in its own rationality, in its own autonomous validity. It must in a word be progressive in spirit. This conviction lies at the heart of historic Protestantism and is one of its fundamental characteristics.

Conclusion

With this we conclude our survey of what seem to me to be the cardinal principles of Protestantism. Others would no doubt construct somewhat different lists. But in the end these probably would amount to about the same thing. The five principles I have selected differentiate Protestantism from Roman Catholicism; and on these points of difference Protestants are pretty well agreed, no matter how differently they may phrase and interpret them. Within evangelical Protestantism the deepest cleavage is that between Calvinism and Arminianism. But this has not prevented Calvinistic Presbyterians and Arminian Methodists from coming together in the United Church of Canada. As Calvinists and Arminians they have interpreted the doctrine of justification by faith differently, but they have nevertheless agreed in affirming this doctrine as over against the legalism and sacramentarianism of Romanism. There is also considerable difference of opinion among Protestants as to the interpretation of the doctrine of biblical authority, but on the doctrine itself they are fully agreed as over against the authority ascribed by Romanists to ecclesiastical tradition and to the church. The same might also be said of the self-verification or autonomous validity of religious faith. On the other hand, the right of private judgment and the sanctity of the common life have been generally accepted as both obvious in their meaning and distinctively Protestant.

From the Protestant standpoint there have been two great corruptions of the Christian religion. One is what has been called "theocratic imperialism" or what might be called ecclesiastical totalitarianism. The other is monastic asceticism. Both of these received their chief development in Roman Catholicism. And it was against them that the Protestant revolt took its rise. Since then the "acids of modernity" have co-operated with Protestant criticism in curtailing their growth. But in principle they still have their place and a vital one in the Roman Catholic system. This is especially true of its ecclesiastical imperialism or authoritarianism as embodied in the doctrine of papal infallibility.

As offsets to these criticisms Roman Catholic writers lay special stress upon what they regard as two critical, if not fatal, weaknesses of Protestantism. For one thing it is, we are told, "made up of negations without any affirmation or positive truth of its own." [3] It is "a negative product" of the Catholic Church, and its "principle of unity . . . is reaction against that institution." [4] In the next place Protestantism is said to be so extremely individualistic, so divisive in spirit, that it can never achieve that coherence and stability of structure without which no social or religious organization can permanently maintain itself. So it is claimed that both its individualism and its negative character spell its ultimate doom. Some Catholics speak of its collapse as "imminent"; others, less confident (as, for instance, Karl Adam), deprecate such language as "profane and unholy" and say that the future of Protestantism is "God's business." [5] This would seem to be the more reverent and objective attitude to take, and it is to be hoped that it will become more and more general in Catholic circles. The prevailing Catholic view, however, would still seem to be that Protestantism is a steep and slippery incline with rationalism and complete infidelity at its base. Its only hope as a religious movement, it is said, lies in its reunion with the Church of Rome. Eventually logic will require people to choose between the church and the world, Catholicism and naturalism, God and atheism. Protestantism, except as an antireligious movement, will disappear.

In the first of these two criticisms of Protestantism—that directed against its excessive individualism and divisiveness—there is, we will all acknowledge, an element of truth. The two hundred and more Protestant denominations or sects in this country are a scandal and a serious source of weakness to the Church. The world is too strong for such a divided Church as this. Some, it is true, have defended the

---

[3] O. A. Brownson, XIII, p. 167.
[4] Hilaire Belloc, *How the Reformation Happened*, p. 10.
[5] *The Spirit of Catholicism*, p. 5.

existence of these numerous sects on the ground that they represent an ecclesiastical application of the principle of democracy. But if so, it is, as someone has said, "democracy gone mad." A greater unification of Protestantism, in America and in the world, is an imperative need. In my opinion no more urgent and no more significant task at present confronts the Protestant churches as a whole.

But, while recognizing the weakness of Protestantism at this point, I see little or no justification for the charge that its message is wholly negative. Its cardinal principles and its four centuries of history are a decisive answer to this criticism. Both its faith and its works testify to the positive character of its teaching and its mission. Only on the assumption that religious truth in its purity is incarnated in the Roman Church, and in it alone, and that every departure from its teaching is an attack upon it could the contrary be maintained. Protestantism could live quite independently of Rome and to a very large extent does so. It does not need Romanism as a target to shoot at.

But, as an independent and self-sufficient entity, how should its relationship to Roman Catholicism be conceived? Thus far I have defined this relationship largely in terms of dissidence and conflict. But this is by no means the whole truth. In spite of all I have said, the points of agreement between Protestants and Catholics have been far more important than their points of difference, and in the face of the rising tide of secularism and paganism in the Western world they are becoming increasingly such. Protestants may call Roman Catholicism a perverted Christianity, and Catholics may call Protestantism a "curtailed" or heretical Christianity; but it is still Christianity that they both at bottom represent, and this is the most important fact with reference to each of them.

The cardinal principles of Protestantism, which we have discussed, are, it is true, expressive of significant differences between Protestant and Catholic teaching. But it is worth noting that they all had more or less rootage in pre-Reformation Christianity. This is particularly true of justification by faith, of the supreme authority of Scripture, and of the sanctity of the common life. And the other two—the right of private judgment and the self-verification or autonomous validity of faith—were implicit in the common Christian doctrine of spiritual freedom and the sacredness of personality. These five principles did not originate with Protestantism. What made them characteristics of Protestantism was the new emphasis and the fresh application given them. Here it is that we have the basic difference between Roman Catholicism and Protestantism. Catholicism interprets the fundamental principles of Christianity from the standpoint of a major emphasis upon the sanctity of the church, while the Protestant interpretation of them grows out of a major emphasis upon the sacredness of the individual.

These two viewpoints are not necessarily irreconcilable, but in Protestant and Roman Catholic Christianity they have been expressed in such antithetical terms and embodied in such mutually exclusive in-

135

stitutions that there is very little prospect that their differences will be composed on the basis of Christian equality for an indefinite time to come. No one can foresee what religious changes will take place in the centuries that lie before us. But this at least would seem to be clear from the last four centuries—that both Roman Catholicism and Protestantism have won the right to exist, and that in the world-wide mission of Christianity each has an important part to play. The time is past when we can look upon Catholicism as simply "a compound of stupidity, superstition, and lust of power." The Catholic Church, as Harnack said, is "the greatest religious and political creation known to history." She is our mother church, and a sympathetic understanding of her world mission is of the utmost importance. On the other hand, it is equally important that Roman Catholic scholars should cease to represent Protestantism as a willful and wicked revolt against divinely constituted authority and as owing its existence to the mere accidents of European politics. Each church has its own place to fill in the providence of God. The two are supplementary to each other.

This, of course, does not exclude the possibility of their ultimate union; but it does mean that this union, if achieved, must be a true synthesis and not an absorption or elimination of one by the other. The first great step in this direction must be the recognition of each by the other as a constituent and co-ordinate part of the true Church of God. Indeed, when that recognition comes about, true Christian unity will already in principle have been attained. But until that time arrives, Protestantism will continue to affirm its own cardinal principles in the profound conviction that they are essential to a complete and truly spiritual proclamation of the gospel, and that without them Christianity cannot hope to keep pace with the free and advancing thought of mankind.

PROTESTANTISM AND THE BIBLE

William G. Chanter

"Brother Martin," said one of Luther's teachers in the Augustinian monastery at Erfurt, "let the Bible alone; read the old teachers. They give you the whole marrow of the Bible; reading the Bible simply breeds unrest." Now, the rule of the Augustinians enjoined the reading of the Scriptures, so Luther had the letter of the law on his side. But he went at his reading so enthusiastically and took it so seriously that he astonished his preceptors. We may be sure that the worthy man who rebuked him was not the only one to be alarmed. For the fact was that the history of the Church showed that a serious reading of the Bible *was* apt to breed unrest. Wyclif, Hus, Savonarola, the Waldensians, and even, in a sense, the Albigensians had all appealed to the Bible to justify the positions they had taken. No wonder the tense young monk's assiduity in Bible study alarmed his instructor! Nor were the older man's forebodings altogether beside the mark. Luther's study of the Scriptures lead him to become the leader of the German revolt from Rome. The Reformation was born in a rediscovery of the Bible.

This is borne out by the story of the other great Reformers:

Zwingli was led to a separation from Rome even more pronounced than that of Luther by his study of the Scriptures. In the first great disputation in which he took part at Zurich in 1523 he made his main appeal to the Bible. Christ's "will and true service we can learn and discover only from his true word in the Holy Scriptures and in the trustworthy writings of his twelve apostles—otherwise from no human laws and statutes." He went on to accuse the bishops and priests of keeping "the pure and clear Gospel, the Holy Scriptures, from the common people. For they say it is not fit for any but themselves to expound the Scriptures." "Popes, bishops, prelates, and the big fellows in general will allow no council in which the Divine Scriptures were set forth in clearness and purity." [1] Taking the Bible as the supreme authority, he refused to accept as truly Christian anything not enjoined in it.

Calvin also, it is needless to say, was led by his studies in the Greek Testament to doubt the orthodox religious opinions of his day; and his doubts became more and more pronounced as he went on with his studies and compared the church as he knew it with Christ and his apostles as they appeared in the Bible. He discovered that many of the dogmas that were proclaimed as the very essence of orthodox Christianity had little or no warrant in the pages of the Bible. Before long he

---

[1] *Selected Works of Huldereich Zwingli*, edited by Samuel Macauley Jackson; Philadelphia, 1901, pp. 48, 55.

was a fugitive, condemned as a heretic because he was setting the authority of the Scriptures above that of the Pope and the church and expounding its teaching as opposed to that of the officially recognized theologians. For him the Bible was supreme.

As persons who are old, or whose sight has become dim, if you show them the most beautiful book, though they perceive something written, are scarcely able to read two words together; yet by the aid of spectacles, they will begin to read distinctly; so the Scriptures, collecting in our minds the otherwise confused notion of Deity, dispel the darkness and give us a true view of the true God. . . . Those who seek God apart from the Word wander in vanity and error.[2]

If Protestantism was born in a rediscovery of the Bible, it has been nourished on its study. The Reformation gave an immense impetus to the translation of the Scriptures into the venacular tongues, and the newly invented printing press was used so as to make them the property of the many instead of the few. The Bible became more widely read and known in Europe than any book had ever been before. Commentaries were multiplied, and preaching concerned itself with the exposition of the Scriptures. All the Reformed churches exerted themselves to see that their people knew their Bibles. Later the Puritans in England and America and the kindred movement of the Pietists in Germany and Holland found their inspiration in the reading and study of the Bible.

In more recent times the growth of the great Bible societies has testified to the vitality of the Protestant belief in the plain text of the Bible as the greatest single agency for the propagation of the gospel. It is a commonplace to say that the Protestant missionary entering a new field sees as one of his primary tasks the translation of the Bible into the language of the people among whom he is to work. In Protestant church schools the Bible is the main text. The Protestant minister who is saying good-by to a parishioner leaving for war service finds it the most natural thing in the world to give him a copy of the New Testament. In form, at least, the Bible has still a central place in Protestantism.

RECAPTURING A GREAT EXPERIENCE

Nevertheless, the essence of Protestantism cannot be contained within the covers of any book, even though that book is the Bible. After all, it was not in the rediscovery of the Bible that Protestantism was born but in the recapture of a great experience.

Luther was driven to the study of the Bible by a tormenting consciousness of his need of reconciliation with God, whom he beheld as justly angered and in righteousness compelled to exact from him the deadly punishment he fully deserved as a sinner. He was seeking for peace of soul; and since he could not find it in the ways provided by the church, he sought to go behind the traditional teaching to its os-

---

[2] *Institutes*, I: vi: 1.

tensible source in the Scriptures themselves. It was when he at last found his burdens lifted by a heart experience of the love of God in Christ that Protestantism was born. What is true of Luther is true also of Calvin. In a letter to Cardinal Sadoleto, in which he sought to defend himself from the accusation that he was a schismatic heretic, he wrote:

> When, however, I had performed all these things [confession, good works, sacrifices, and solemn expiations], though I had some intervals of quiet, I was still far off from true peace of conscience; for whenever I descended into myself or raised my mind to God, terror seized me—terror which no expiations or satisfactions could cure. . . . Still, as nothing better offered, I continued the course which I had begun—when, lo, a very different form of doctrine started up, not one which led us away from the Christian profession, but one which brought it back to its fountainhead and, as it were, clearing away the dross, restored it to its primitive purity.

With Calvin, as with Luther, the great turning point came in a moment of illumination when he passed from death unto life. In the preface to his *Commentary on the Psalms* he writes:

> God, by a sudden conversion, subdued my mind to a teachable frame. . . . Having thus received some taste of true godliness, I was immediately inflamed with so intense a desire to make progress therein that, although I did not leave off other studies, I pursued them with less ardor.

Thus it would seem that Sabatier is quite right when he says that the principle of the Reformation was simply "the primitive creating principle of Christianity itself," which had been so long imprisoned in an elaborate system of tradition, forms, rites, and priestly organization that its proclamation in its purity had all the revolutionary effect of an entirely new discovery. To quote Sabatier again:

> That which was new in the sixteenth century was the consciousness which Christendom then gained of the vital principle of Christianity, of its purely moral essence, and its absolute independence of all historical delimitations and realizations through which it had passed and might pass again. It was the incorporation of the Christian principle in the moral and religious consciousness of humanity.[3]

And this has been the real life of Protestantism all along. When this evangelical experience has been lacking, there has been a relapse into a formalism and legalism which differ very little in their essence from the system against which Luther and Calvin rebelled. On the other hand, when this experience has been common, Protestantism has been strongest. It was because a group of English clergymen enjoyed this heart-warming experience and went out to bring others to share in it that England's religious life was rescued from the stagnation of the

---

[3] Sabatier, A., *Religions of Authority and the Religion of the Spirit*; English translation, New York, 1904; p. 153.

early eighteenth century. It was by men of the evangelical experience that the modern Protestant missionary movement was launched, that the Bible societies were founded, that the Sunday schools were gathered. Without this immediate realization of the life of God in the soul the exaltation of the Bible degenerates into formalism if not into mere bibliolatry, and the Protestant churches into systems of ecclesiastical machinery.

Here we seem to have two opposed ideas of the origin and nature of Protestantism, one of which gives to the Bible a very modest place, while the other makes it central. But there is no real conflict. For the rediscovery of the Bible by the Reformers was a central element in launching them upon their careers of victorious and constructive revolution because it was part and parcel of their recapture of the first-century experience. Their discovery of the Bible was no mere return to the study of ancient documents at first hand, apart from official interpretations. It was no mere search for the literal meaning of the texts of the Old and New Testaments. The Reformers read the Bible not only for themselves but in a new way and with a new understanding. They discovered in it not only a new meaning but also a living word, which guided them into a new experience in which they found the satisfaction for which they had been longing. They found not the letter but the spirit that gave them new life. They found the word of God, which spoke to their souls. Sabatier well says that the Reformers were seeking to find the true way of salvation as provided by Christ and preached by his apostles.

[They] resorted to the original texts of the biblical books, just as the humanists were setting themselves to research and to the study of the ancient works to discover the true classic antiquity. . . . The Reformers traced the turbid course of the Christian stream to its source and there quenched their thirst for righteousness and peace. The new life they there drank in, filling them with joy and peace, was their sufficient and ultimate warrant that the waters of this spring had their source in heaven.[4]

The conflict between the Reformers and Rome was not caused by the fact that the Protestants appealed to the Bible and their opponents did not. For both the Scriptures were authoritative. But because they had two quite different ideas of what constituted essential Christianity, the Reformers and the Romanists had also two quite different ideas of the authority of the Bible. They looked to it for altogether different things.

For the Roman Catholic, Christianity was, in the first place, the acceptance of certain dogmas, revealed in the Scriptures, and systematically set forth by the recognized teachers of the church. The proper interpretation of the Bible, which made clear the doctrines belief in which was necessary for salvation, was the work of the church, en-

---

[4] Op. cit., pp. 155-6.

trusted to it by God himself. Only the properly trained theologian could hope to read the Scriptures intelligently, and even his training consisted in learning what the doctors of the church had taught. Hence it was that the ordinary man, even the man who made some pretension to learning, was apt to become confused and unsettled when he set out to interpret the Bible for himself. History showed that he was in the gravest danger of falling into error. Since saving faith was a matter of an intellectual belief in the right ideas, then errors in belief meant nothing less than damnation. Well might Luther's teacher be concerned when he saw his young pupil taking the first steps in the path that had so often led into grievous heresy. How could this young man hope to do for himself what had cost the doctors of the church so much labor? They had found the grand system of saving truth in the Bible, but certainly they had not found it on the surface, and the only safe way for the Christian was to accept the results of the toil of the ages as accepted and approved by the holy church and to confine his reading to the old books, in which the marrow of the Bible was to be found.

In the second place, religion meant for the Catholic of the sixteenth century the regular observance of certain practices, rites, and ceremonies enjoined by the church. Together with a reverent acceptance of the dogmas of religion obedience to these customs of life and worship made up the way of salvation. Luther's religious difficulties puzzled his superiors in the monastery because they seemed so groundless. Apparently he had little trouble over the orthodox dogmas, while he went to the extreme in devoting himself to all the prescribed practices. But it was all to no avail. He still did not find the peace for which he craved. His superiors found it hard work to be patient with his struggles for a divine forgiveness of which, on the orthodox principles, he should have been assured.

The fact was that Luther and the other Reformers could find no real value in the Roman Catholic conception of religion, which was a combination of intellectualism and formalism. Study of the accepted theology, the most extreme devotion to the observances of religion, all left them with a torturing conviction of spiritual bankruptcy. When, finally, they did find peace, it was not through finding a satisfactory scriptural proof of the truth of the dogmas of orthodoxy but through a deep and joyous realization that they could trust themselves to the power and love of God in Christ. The way of salvation was a matter of an immediate relation to God as known through his Son revealed in the heart. They had found the authority of the Bible, not in the fact that it enshrined a correct theology, but in its power to bring to them the truth that had set them free; not merely by enlightening their minds, but by warming their hearts and empowering their wills. The true interpreter of the Bible was not the orthodox theologian, nor was it the ecclesiastically commissioned priesthood. The only true interpreter was the Spirit of God in the hearts of his people, bringing to them the word of power to the salvation of their souls.

THE BIBLE A BOOK OF POWER

Thus, Calvin found the authority of the Scriptures in "the inward attestation of the Spirit, the personal conviction born of the inward contact of the soul with truth." [5] Zwingli pointed out how closely the perception of the living word was linked with the faith of the percipient:

Thou canst never know what is the Church, which can never err nor decay, if thou recognizest not the Word of God, who constituted the Church. The Word has the virtue of giving faith. . . . Only pious hearts know this, for faith does not depend upon the discussions of men but has its seat and rests itself invincibly in the soul. It is not a doctrine, a question of knowledge; for we see the most learned men who are ignorant of this thing, which is the most salutary of all.[6]

It was this conviction that the Bible brought to the faithful heart the authentic word of God that made the Reformers bold in insisting that the book be open to all men. No great learning but earnest faith was the primary condition of the proper understanding of the Scriptures. Hence it was that Luther could say, "The common man, the boy of nine, the miller's maid, with the Bible know more about divine truth than the Pope without the Bible." If the value of the Scriptures consists in their embodiment of a great system of intellectual propositions, this is nonsense. But if it is a book in which God tells of his redemptive purpose in an age-long process culminating in the story of his Son, then indeed the plain man who reads it in faith will hear his Father's voice speaking with an authority that cannot be doubted. For the Bible speaks with authority not only to the head of man but also to his heart, not only to his mind but to his conscience as well.

This means that to the Reformers the Bible was primarily a book of power and not a compendium of ideas about God, a source book for a complex theology. This conception was certainly not new with them. St. Paul, who knew that the letter kills, knew of a word that was power, that came with the demonstration of the Spirit. He had heard this word speaking with authority as he read his Bible, and he had seen its power at work in the lives of others as they received it from his own lips by the receptive hearing of faith. He had expounded the Scriptures again and again in the light of God's revelation of his Son in his own heart and had seen the mighty working of the word in the hearts of those to whom, as they listened, it brought a new life. The disciples who walked with their Master along the road to Emmaus felt their hearts burn within them as he opened to them the Scriptures, and their experience was repeated as the men and women of the

---

[5] Sabatier, op. cit., p. 163.

[6] Quoted, Sabatier, op. cit., p. 163.

Church read the old words in the light of their new-found faith. Luther was only following the men of the New Testament when he traced the power of the Bible to its testimony to Christ, to the fact that in it the deeps of human longing after God found an answer in the deeps of God's own love as revealed in his Word.

Of course, the Bible is not the only example of this literature of power. All our greatest literature does something more than provide information. Indeed, if any piece of writing does no more than that, it is a question whether it has much claim to be called literature at all. Great writing, whether it is prose or poetry, arouses the imagination, enlarges our view of life, stirs our hearts. But it does that only for those who come to it with at least a degree of sympathy and receptivity. The churl will not be alive to the nobility that speaks through great poetry, nor will the fool know the charm of the true wisdom that calls to ways that are ways of pleasantness and paths of peace only to him who has eyes to see and ears to hear. A page of Shakespeare is only a collection of words or, at best, the source of a moment's amusement for the shallow-minded reader. It is only to him who is awake to the wonder of the world that Shakespeare can tell the amazing story of life's infinite variety. The Gettysburg address can have its full meaning only for him who is himself moved by that dream of a nation dedicated to a great ideal that made the soul of Lincoln great and his words immortal. Shakespeare can be read for information about the Elizabethan age or as material for a study of the development of the English language. Lincoln's great words may be conned over as material for a history of political theory. And there is certainly nothing wrong with that. But he who can find no other use for these great classics is poor indeed. They belong to the literature of power and can never be read aright except by those who come to them with hearts astir and minds wide open.

But there is an immense difference between the Bible and other power literature. What that difference is appears in such a comparison as that between the Italian Renaissance and the German Reformation. For one the great works of classical antiquity were central; for the other, the Bible. Both were revolutionary in their effects; but while the Italian movement was certainly superior in grace and beauty to the German, in moral power it was far inferior. It produced a Leo X and made him head of the church, a true scion of the great family of the Medici in his ability, his artistic good taste, and his entire lack of comprehension of spiritual religion. His famous remark on being elected Pope summarizes his character and the frankly secular outlook of current Italian culture: "Now let us enjoy the papacy." While the German Reformers were by no means perfect, the movement they launched was a fountainhead of moral power that has never ceased to flow even in the dark days when Nazi paganism rules in Germany. The study of the classics produced a graceful humanism that highly exalted man but could not give him the power to support his new dignity. Ruskin once characterized the Renaissance spirit as compounded of "worldliness, inconsistency, pride, hypocrisy, ignorance of itself, love of art, of luxury, and of good Latin." The Reformers who centered their studies in the Bible gave to man a higher status than did the humanists. They called upon him to see himself as a son of God. But they gave him the power to live as became this more than royal station.

The Reformers, then, discovered the Bible as a source of power; and when they did that, they gave it its true place and acknowledged its true authority. Of what other book could be said what Prothero said of the Psalms:

> They translate into speech the spiritual passion of the loftiest genius; they also utter, with the beauty born of truth and simplicity and with the exact agreement between the feeling and the expression, the inarticulate and humble longings of the unlettered peasant. So it is that in every country the language of the Psalms has become part of the daily life of nations, passing into their proverbs, mingling with their conversation, and used at every critical stage of existence? [7]

Canon Farrar was using rhetorical language, but he was telling only the sober truth when he wrote of the Epistle to the Galatians:

> The words scrawled on these few sheets of papyrus were destined to wake echoes which have lived and shall live forever and forever. Savonarola heard them, and Wyclif, and Hus, and Luther, and Tyndale, and Wesley. They were the Magna Charta of spiritual emancipation. [8]

Matthew Arnold, scholar and critic, was measuring carefully the meaning of his words when he wrote:

> As for the right inculcation of righteousness we need the inspiring words of Israel's love for it—that is, we need the Bible—so for the right inculcation of the method and secret of Jesus we need the *epieikeia,* the sweet reasonableness, of Jesus. That is, in other words again, we need the Bible; for only through the Bible records of Jesus can we get at his *epieikeia.* [9]

LIVING WORD OR DEAD TRADITION?

The very essence of the relation of Protestantism to the Bible is in this insistence that it contains the word of God for those who come to it in faith. The purely intellectual approach can never know the truth that is in the Bible. That truth does more than inform the mind, because it liberates the soul. The story of the Last Supper can be read for the purpose of tracing the growth of Christian tradition or of getting at the historical origins of a great church rite, and such study has its place and an honorable place. But unless this story is read with kindled and reverent imagination, with a sense of the holy grandeur

---

[7] Prothero, R. E., *The Psalms in Human Life,* p. 2 (Everyman's Library).

[8] Farrar, F. W., *The Messages of the Books;* London, 1884; p. 258.

[9] Arnold, Matthew, *Literature and Dogma,* p. 342.

of what is read, with a gathering wonder of appreciation—unless, in a word, it is read with faith, there cannot be that living contact with the Lord Jesus by which he enters into life and makes all things new. And, contrariwise, that great thing is happening all the time to those who read aright. The Christmas story may be treated as a study in religious origins, and who would deny that this is a legitimate use of the early chapters of St. Matthew and St. Luke? But only to him who reads with something of the steady and ardent passion of the Magi, following the guiding star until it led where the young child lay, can come the ineffably glorious discovery of which the Christmas story tells. The expert scholarship of the chief priests and scribes whom Herod consulted found only a sentence in a book, you will remember. And the book had no power for them. They knew their Bibles, but they did not hear the word of God.

Unfortunately Protestantism has not always been true to its own peculiar genius. Indeed, in the Reformers themselves there were found the beginnings of a return to the very use of the Bible from which they had been turning away. For they were involved in heated and dangerous controversy, which was conducted under the rules of the only scholarship then known—the scholastic system. Hence, it centered around definitions, the formulation of theses, and appeals to the authority of church and tradition. Against such appeals the Reformers took refuge in citing the authority of the Scriptures, and they could not always maintain a consistent distinction between the authority of the letter and that of the spirit. They were in even worse case when they made the Bible the source from which they drew the theology they opposed to that of their opponents. Once they began to go to the Bible for proof texts, the importance of its literal and verbal inerrancy began to loom large in their eyes, and the necessity of an orthodox interpretation of its words seemed evident. Luther's famous insistence in his argument with Zwingli on the literal truth of the words *"Hoc est corpus meum,"* which he chalked on the table before him, shows this tendency. Calvin, of course, built up a complete system of theology and buttressed it with proof texts. This was all quite inconsistent with the freedom with which the Reformers at other times handled the Scriptures and with their insistence that their authority was not in the letter but in the spirit, which must be spiritually received. But when they were using the Bible as an authority for doctrine rather than as an inspiring answer to the quest of faith, the emphasis shifted to the literal meaning of the text and the need of a proper intellectual understanding of its theological teaching.

As the ardor of the evangelical experience cooled, it was inevitable that this shift in the emphasis of Protestant teaching should be more and more pronounced. The need of an infallible authority to which Protestants might appeal was all the more keenly felt as the inner testimony of an indubitable experience became less loud and clear. The Reformers had believed that the Bible was the source of authority because they found in it the divine word, which spoke peace to their souls. They had accepted that word, not because it was written in one or the other of the canonical books, but because it was validated by its power to stir the mind and warm the heart, because it spoke with the accent of the Holy Ghost. Their successors were found calling upon men to accept their testimony as true because they could appeal to the books accepted as canonical. They were laying themselves open to the taunt of their opponents that they had set up a paper Pope of their own in place of the Roman pontiff.

This was an abandonment of the true Protestant position in two ways: First, it led to the worship of the letter of the Bible. An infallible book, the verbally inspired revelation of God's truth, must be perfect in every respect. The logic of the case led inevitably to the statement of the Swiss churches made in 1675. In this it was solemnly declared that no barbarism or solecism could enter into the Greek text of the New Testament, and that the very vowel points of the Hebrew text of the Old Testament were divinely inspired. In the second place, the infallibility of the Bible, to which these Protestant theologians appealed, was in fact the infallibility of their own interpretation of it—the infallibility of a theological system they had based upon it. This amounts to a return to a religion of external authority. It is a retreat from the idea of the inspiration of the Bible as being evident in its gift of moral and spiritual power to those who read it in faith. It is a return to the idea of inspiration as assuring a correct statement of propositions about the nature of God and his commands to men. And that means a conception of salvation as creedal and theological belief on the authority of ecclesiastical interpretation.

It was this type of Protestantism which was terrified and angered when scholars applied to the Bible the methods of literary and historical criticism. It was this type of religion which rebelled against the rise of the scientific theory of biological evolution and had grave searchings of heart when the geologists began to estimate the age of the world in eons instead of in centuries. It was this type of religion which trembled before Robert Ingersoll when he pointed out what he called the mistakes of Moses. It is this type of Protestantism which usually takes the name of fundamentalism in an attempt to turn back all the clocks, apparently under the impression that in so doing they are coming nearer to eternity.

The Ever-living Word

But fortunately the genius of Protestantism could never be smothered in the authoritarian swaddling clothes in which misguided ecclesiastical nurses sought to wrap it up lest it should perish in the cold blasts of rational inquiry. The Bible could not be turned into a textbook of science or of history or of theology when it was loved and read by masses of plain people in their homes. Wherever the evangelical experience was found, wherever the Spirit of God opened the Scriptures to men of faith, there the Bible was known as the Living Word. In spite of the attempts of some excitable shepherds to stampede the flock with terrified shouts of alarm over theories of evolution, the discovery of a second Isaiah, or the heresies of the modernists, the sheep with a real taste for the green pastures managed somehow to find them. They were not even seriously disturbed by the vagaries of some scholars who explained the Bible in a manner that sounded very much as if they were explaining it away.

Methodism has been comparatively little troubled in these respects, because, after all, the Wesleyan movement was essentially a reassertion of true Protestant evangelicalism and has been quite amazingly successful in avoiding the contamination of rigid biblical authoritarianism. There have been lapses, but the history of Methodist theology is honorable evidence of the sanity and fidelity to experience which has characterized our communion. But what is true of Methodism is more or less true of Protestantism as a whole. In the large it is among Protestants that the work of biblical scholarship has been most vigorously and most fruitfully carried on. This is only natural, for the Roman Catholic is, after all, only mildly interested in the Bible. The marrow of the book is still to be found in the interpretations of the church, and it is in the acceptance of these interpretations and the due observance of the moral and ceremonial laws under the direction of the priesthood that salvation is to be found. It is not to be expected that either the church or the rank and file of its members should make the study of the Bible at all central. The Roman Catholic soldier is more likely to be given, as he leaves for camp, a prayer book or a religious medal than a copy of the New Testament. It is quite a different thing for the Protestant. For him the understanding of the clear meaning of the Bible becomes of primary importance, since it is through the simple story of God's gracious dealing with men that God's word may be spoken to him. For scholar and for layman alike the study of the Scriptures is a major concern.

Thus, it is by no mere chance that it is largely due to Protestant research that we now have a far better text of the Old and the New Testaments than as a church we have ever had. It is to Protestant scholars that we owe our present knowledge of the real nature of what used to be called New Testament Greek and our immensely improved understanding of it. The considerable number of new translations of the Bible into English is another testimony to the strong Protestant interest in getting at the plain meaning of the Scriptures. Even now we are awaiting with the most eager interest the appearance of the new edition of the American Revision, on which a group of distinguished Protestant scholars have been at work.

If Protestants have led the way in textual criticism—and the list of the leading textual critics is proof enough of that—they have held first place also in literary criticism. The spirit of free inquiry, which is at the heart of Protestantism, has never been willing to be bound by that theory of the Bible which turns it into an inerrant oracle and its authors into mere scribes, writing at the divine dictation. Once this theory of inspiration is subjected to rational scrutiny, it vanishes into the thin air of utter incredibility. The proper understanding of the Bible depends in part on a due appreciation of the character of the authors of the different books, the circumstances under which they lived and wrote, the immediate problems to which they addressed themselves. This understanding is no substitute for faith, but it is an aid no faith should scorn. True faith is the spirit of eager search. Criticism supplies it with the instruments by which the search is carried on. In the Scriptures, as Luther himself once said, there may be sometimes found "wood, hay, and stubble, and not always gold, silver, diamonds."[10] It is faith alone which can make sure of the distinction, but scholarship is an indispensable help.

True Protestantism is always fearless in its approach to the study of the Scriptures. It knows that the Word of God can never suffer from honest inquiry. But, also, it is sane and reverent; for it knows that the casket with which it is dealing contains jewels of infinite worth. The Protestant scholar has no need to fear that the jewels may be destroyed, but he takes care that he does not miss the chance of enjoying their beauty for himself and of displaying it to others. At its best, therefore, Protestant scholarship does not fall into the errors of a purely intellectual rationalism that deals with religion in an unsympathetic and therefore essentially unintelligent way. For example, evangelical Christianity saves scholarship from the amazing attempt to reduce Jesus to the rank of another great prophet or, worse still, to the status of a naïve young Galilean rabbi, who had some local influence but survives in history because he had among his disciples some men of real ability and, after his death, captured the imagination of a man of genius in St. Paul. Dean Inge characterizes the Roman Catholic scholar Loisy as representing Christ "as an ineffectual Mahdi, an agitator like Theudas."[11] But, after all, the Christ of the Gospels could be explained away without fatal damage to Christianity as Loisy understood it. He had the tradition and authority of the church upon which to fall back, and he was genuinely surprised when he was denounced by the Pope as a heretic. But there have been some theologians who were not Catholics who have done about the same thing with less excuse. Middleton Murry well remarks, "Criticism of this kind never seems to pause to think the obvious thought that if Jesus had been an ordinary kind of man, it would not now, nineteen hundred years after his death, be striving to prove that he was."[12] Sir George Adam Smith comes at once to mind as an example of a man who combined evangelical faith with scholarship of the first

---

[10] Quoted in Sabatier, op. cit., p. 159.
[11] Inge, W. R., *Vale;* London, 1934; p. 59.
[12] Murry, J. Middleton, *Jesus, Man of Genius;* New York and London, 1926; p. x.

order and, as a result, produced work that in his own lifetime became classic. Faith needs the help of scholarship, but how feeble a thing scholarship is without the aid of faith!

Needed: A Rebirth of Bible Reading

In very many ways, then, Protestantism has a special attachment to the Bible. In its spiritual interpretation it has found an unfailing source of power. Today we are proud of the activity of Protestant biblical scholarship, proud of the energy with which the Scriptures are being disseminated, proud of the fact that the Bible is a best seller in every Protestant land. Yet the cold fact is that we seem to be doing everything with the Bible except reading it. Our people do not know the Bible. A friend of mine who is pastor of a church situated under the eaves of one of the great American universities was moved last fall to gather a class for Bible study. He wrote me:

The results have been quite devastating. You may imagine my consternation when a full professor, a world authority in his field, with books to his credit which have been translated even into Japanese, asked me one day after I had been discussing the social idealism of the early prophets, "But, of course, these fellows had the writings of Paul to base their thought on, hadn't they?"

A professor in an eastern college found a boy in one of his classes, a lad who had been a regular attendant at church and Sunday school, who had not so much as heard of the story of the prodigal son. I can testify that in each of twenty years of teaching a class in freshman Bible, I found myself cultivating a virgin field. Yet my students were, nearly to a man, members of churches, the products of what is called religious education.

If our people do not read the Bible, neither do our preachers expound it. A reading of the topics listed in the church notices in the Saturday newspapers does not give much ground for believing that the exposition of the Scriptures is having a large place in our pulpits. In fact, expository preaching is apparently a lost art. Too often the procedure is, first, to prepare a sermon and, secondly, to hunt about for a text to fit it. This is called preaching the gospel, and perhaps it is. At least the text is likely to have some solid worth.

We have so many problems on our hands. We are like those tossed about "when there was midsea and the mighty things." All the problems of our complex and confused social order, which were difficult enough before the war, have been made menacingly acute. Then, there is the postwar settlement of the world to be reckoned with, and surely the Church must have something to say and to do about that. We cannot put such matters aside. The Church must serve the present age; and the present age is a time of crisis, a time of judgment, if ever there was one. It is a question whether we have time for the Bible in practice, whatever the theory of its importance may be.

All the while the Protestant churches show an alarming lack of power. An English psychiatrist of note—J. E. Hadfield, himself a devout Christian—wrote some years ago:

No reader of the New Testament can fail to be struck by the constant reiteration in different forms of the idea that the normal experience of a Christian at that epoch was enhancement of power. . . . Pentecost, the healing miracles of the apostolic age, the triumphant progress of the religion throughout the Roman Empire, the heroic deeds of saints and martyrs—all these point to the sense of a power newly discovered. In contrast, looking at the Church of today, one cannot but be struck with its powerlessness. It contains men of intellect, it produces a type of piety and devotion which one cannot but admire, it sacrifices itself in works of kindness and beneficence; but even its best friends would not claim that it inspires in the world the sense of power. What strikes one rather is its impotence and failure.[13]

Is it not possible that in our preoccupations with our many problems we have forgotten the basic problem that is ours as churchmen and as Christians? Our great task is to be effective witnesses for Christ in the world, to preach his gospel so that men may hear the Word and be saved—they and their social order. Our great need as Protestants is for a return to that essential experience in which Protestantism was born and in which it has always found its sources of power. In the sixteenth-century recapture of the first-century experience the Bible had a large part. To seeking hearts it brought a message—a word of God with power. Should we not turn to our Bibles in the spirit of hope and faith? Is it not time that as Protestants we laid claim to our Protestant heritage in the Scriptures? We have talked about the Bible. We have occasionally read it. We have even studied it. The toil of the scholar and the critic has given us a Bible freed from the encumbrance of false ideas of inspiration and authority, from the handicap of mistaken notions of authorship and history. Hasn't the time come when we ought to use it, to search in it for the sword of the Spirit, which is the word of God? It was in no less sober and factual a piece of writing than an encyclopedia article that Ernst von Dobschütz wrote:

Whenever a single individual, layman or theologian, has been enabled to draw fresh and full out of the Bible and present to others what he has obtained, the inward life of Christendom has been raised to a higher level.[14]

Surely these words are a challenge to us as Protestants to search the Scriptures with earnest expectancy that we may find the better for ourselves and our people that gospel which is the power of God unto salvation to everyone that believeth, in the twentieth century as in the first. In that power we shall be able to find a solution of our problems, as without it we shall most certainly fail.

---

[13] Streeter, B. H., editor: *The Spirit;* London and New York, 1919; p. 109. By permission The Macmillan Company, publishers.

[14] *Encyclopaedia of Religion and Ethics,* Vol. II: article on "The Bible in the Church."

CHRISTIAN THEOLOGY

HARRIS FRANKLIN RALL

THE terms "Protestant" and "Reformation" have become so firmly
established that they cannot well be avoided if we are to discuss the
great historic movement whose chief protagonist was Martin Luther.
It will help to clarity of thought, however, if we keep in mind that,
though these terms in form are negative ("protest," "reform"), the
movement itself was positive and creative. It was an attempt to re-
cover evangelical religion as this was set forth by Paul. In further explanation of our subject we must note two facts: (1) Protestantism did
not begin as a reform in theology. Unlike Roman Catholicism it has
no definitive and authoritative system of doctrine which its followers
are supposed to accept. (2) It nonetheless implies a very definite religious faith, and it has a positive and definite significance for theology.
This we are to consider.

But first we must indicate what we mean by theology. We may em-
ploy the word in two senses. (1) Used as a noun, theology means a
system of doctrine in which are set forth the beliefs of a given religion
or religious group. Frequently, though not necessarily, this is held to
be something fixed and authoritative, with the idea that Christianity is
primarily a sum of revealed doctrine given to the theologian either
through the Bible or in the creeds of the Church. (2) Used in the active
or verbal sense, theology indicates the continuing activity of the Church
as it seeks to understand the meaning of its faith and to relate this to
Christian life and work and to our total knowledge. It is in the second
sense that I am using the word in this paper, and this I take to be the
true conception of theology for evangelical faith.

Let me now, imitating Martin Luther, lay down certain theses that
underlie the discussions of this paper: (1) Christianity began as a
faith, a fellowship, and a way of life, not as an institution or a sum
of revealed doctrine. (2) Christianity produced organization, Scriptures, and creeds, and the religion became more and more an institution. (3) The Reformation brought a return to the living religious
center of Christianity, especially as a message of salvation. (4) The
theology that came out of the Reformation failed at two points, which,
in effect, are one: It did not apply the principles of evangelical Christianity to the whole range of Christian thought; and it carried over,
without the change these principles could have wrought, a great mass
of medieval traditional doctrine. (5) For the continuing work of
theology, in which the Church interprets her faith for each new day, the
evangelical principles of the Reformation can give us invaluable guid-

ance; but that will not be through a mere return to the traditional orthodoxy of yesterday.

Concerning the Beginnings

Christianity began, not as an ecclesiastical institution or as a sum or system of revealed doctrines, but as a faith and a way of life. More precisely stated, it began with a historic fact—the fact of Christ—his life, his teachings, his spirit, his death, his Resurrection, his creative presence in the fellowship of his followers. It was a fact with a meaning, and the meaning constituted the Christian faith: "God was in Christ reconciling the world unto himself." Out of that creative faith came an experience of God's saving power, a new way of life in the spirit of love, and a fellowship that was divine because it had the creative work of God's Spirit and human because it was a fellowship of men living in love and faith and service.

It is important that we see this simple religious quality of beginning Christianity. Religion, it is true, means many things; for it includes every human interest and every significant human question. It turns men to the Most High—that is, to what is highest in power and goodness, that in which men find at once the help for their needs and the rule for their lives. Religion is the only valid totalitarianism. Consider the questions it raises: (1) What is real? What is the power upon which all else rests and from which all things come? (2) What is the good for which we are to strive above all else and which has the right to our supreme allegiance? (3) Where are we to find the saving help for life? (4) What may we hope for, as individuals and as a race, in this life and for the life to come? All this belongs to religion. Yet religion, at heart, is simple. It is a circle that moves about the idea of God. God is the differentia of religion. To see all things in the light of God, to live by the help of God, to give our utter trust and obedience to God, is religion. Or one might compare it to an ellipse, with God and life as its two foci. Religion is man's search for life. God and salvation are religion's two great concerns. But these two are one for religion so that in the end God remains the center: the God from whom our life comes, in whom it finds its meaning; the God who is the light of all our seeing, the rule of all our living, and the hope of all our days.

The soul and God—that is the heart of religion. That is where it begins. And its great task is to bring men into the presence of God, that they may have life in him and with him and for him. Religion is a meeting of persons. It means "I and Thou." So it was with Jesus except that he enlarged the circle of persons. It was not with him, as with mysticism, the flight of the alone to the Alone and so the finite soul's losing itself in the abyss of the Infinite. Jesus added a third personal pronoun. When you pray, he declared, say "Our Father." The Lord's Prayer is all "we" and "our," not "I" and "mine." The command is "Love . . . thy God . . . and thy neighbor." "The Bible knows nothing of solitary religion." The reason lies at once in God's nature as love and in man's need of fellowship. If yours is this kind of God, the rest follows.

You will find at the heart of Paul's teaching essentially the same clear and profound concept of religion as with Jesus. Paul had a larger basis in history and revelation with which to deal. Christianity is more than the teachings and character of the historic Jesus; it is the whole Christ as the word of God to men and the deed of God for men. It includes the life of the early Church with the sense of his living presence, with its new experience of forgiveness and peace, and with the new life that was the work of the Spirit of God. Paul had all this to interpret. He gave the Church its first great interpretation of the Christian faith in its total meaning. I am not assuming that Paul's interpretation was absolute and final. Every interpretation, including Paul's, is historically conditioned and relative. Necessarily Paul was affected by the thought forms of his time, as in his idea of the visible return of Christ for judgment and the imminent end of the age. Yet in his central teaching Paul has the simplicity that was in Christ.

With Paul, as with Jesus, religion means "I" and "Thou" and "we"— man confronted with God, man living with men in the Spirit of his God and by his help. For Paul religion is not an institution with sacraments and priesthood. It is not a new set of rules superseding the old legalism. It is not a set of doctrines handed down by God or worked out by scholars or defined by Church councils or given in a body of Scriptures. Nor is it primarily an individual mystical experience. (1) It is the Eternal God, the God of holiness and mercy, coming to men in Christ; and the name for this God is *grace*, or love. (2) It is man's answer to this God—an answer of simple trust and utter surrender of will; and the word for this is *faith*. (3) It is man's life with his fellows; and the word for this, as with Jesus, is *love*. The surrender of faith is surrender to the spirit of love, which is God's Spirit. It is letting that Spirit rule your life and flow out from your life. Here is the same triad as with Jesus. Paul sums it up in the two pregnant words: "By grace are ye saved through faith"; "faith working through love"—grace, faith, and love. The first—grace—is the heart of Christian theology— that is, of its doctrine of God—not divine sovereignty but love. The second—faith—when rightly understood, as with Paul and Luther, is the heart of personal religion—that is, of our relation to God. The third—love—is basic for Christian ethics, though this love—the Christian *agape*—must be rightly apprehended.

What Christianity Became

Christianity began as a religion—the religion of a fellowship living in faith and love; it became an institution, with ritual and sacraments, officials and authority, laws and observances, authoritative doctrines and creeds. There is, of course, an ambiguity in the title of this section, for "Christianity" means two things. It is something divine: the word of God to men in Christ, the way of life in the spirit of Christ, the

153

presence of God's Spirit creating the fellowship of the Church and the life of God's children. But Christianity is also something human. It takes shape in human thought, which is expressed in human conduct, which appears visibly in society, which functions in history. Such a human and historical development was both inevitable and necessary. (1) Christianity was a word of God to men, a message of God's gracious purpose. The Church had to interpret that faith in its preaching. It had to conserve its great message and preserve its tradition in the writings of the early witnesses, in Epistles and Gospels, and in the history of the early Church. It had to define and defend its faith in doctrines and creeds. (2) Christianity was a fellowship. That involved organization, order, rules, authority, officials; and the common worship brought ritual, ceremonies, and the elaboration of sacraments.

But, though the task was necessary, its carrying out brought dangers with it. The first was that men should identify the human historical form with the divine reality. It was easy to argue that Christ had established the Church, that he had turned over to it his authority to teach and rule, that it had the guidance of the Spirit; and from this to move on to infallible creeds, infallible general councils, and, finally, to the infallibility of the Pope. What really happened was that the human was put in the place of God instead of serving in real, even if imperfect, fashion to point men to God. It was, in fact, idolatry. And the same happened with the theory of a verbally infallible Bible, where the sum of the words of the various biblical writings took the place of the word of God.

With this went the second danger: Men lost the simple way of faith and life which the Christian gospel had brought. For Paul faith was man's surrender in trust to the God who came in Christ. Now, *"the faith"* took the place of faith. *"The faith"* was the creeds that church councils had worked out with the instruments of ancient philosophy, ill adapted to express the truth of the gospel. Further, faith now meant believing a body of doctrine in submission to the authority of the church. There came in also a new legalism: God's free forgiveness was supplemented by complicated demands of penance and good works and church observances. Thus, the gospel tended to be lost in the law; and the "law of the Spirit of life in Christ Jesus," which made men free, gave way to a new system of laws, which kept them in bondage. And if legalism imperiled the gospel of grace, so did sacramentarianism. With its development grace ceased to be the simple word of forgiveness spoken to repentant faith; it became a reservoir of mysteriously—one might say magically—working power, administered by the priesthood and operative through the sacraments. So Christianity ceased to be a gospel and fellowship of love and became a great ecclesiastical institution, with a ceremonial-legal system not unlike the Judaism in which Paul had searched in vain for God and peace, joined to a magical sacramentarianism.

WHAT THE REFORMATION BROUGHT

The extraordinary fact about Luther is how little he changed in the total system of prevailing thought and how much that little meant. The larger part of the medieval system Luther carried over. He was essentially of a conservative nature, theologically and socially. One can see the latter from the violent way in which he broke out against the peasants and the small understanding he showed for their needs and hopes and their exploitation by their rulers. One can see the former from the way in which he accepted all the creedal formulations of the ancient Church. In part this was due to the fact that he was not primarily a theologian. But the principal reason was that Luther was concerned with one thing and so left other matters aside. That one thing was, indeed, the heart of the matter. Once more, as with Jesus and Paul, there stood forth the central issue of religion—the soul and God; and that issue was solved in the light of the gospel. Christianity, long an institution, once more became a religion. The whole complicated system of beliefs and rules, of sacraments and observances, of penance and absolution, gave way to the supreme question of a man and his God, to religion as a personal relation lived in faith and love.

It is a striking fact that in the history of Christianity the great revivals of religion and the great movements in theology have both been regularly related to Paul. So it was here. Luther had the double problem that faced Paul. First, to quote his own words, "How can I get me a gracious God?" Religion meant God, a holy God. Martin Luther was a sinner, and all his efforts to make himself the kind of man who could come before such a God had failed. The answer to that problem was the mercy of God as revealed in Christ. But still the second problem remained—the ethical. What about the demands of God, set forth by the church in its endless requirements of good works, of precepts to be kept, ordinances to be observed, and penance performed? Luther answered: Faith is the one demand of God. But this faith is no mere matter of beliefs or acceptance of the church's teaching. It is a self-surrendering trust in a Person—in Christ as God's word of mercy and as God's will for us. It is no single act but a consistent and continuing attitude, in which a man gives himself in utter obedience to God while at the same time he lives in trustful dependence on God. Faith, then, does not need morality as a supplement of good works, because it already includes this. Out of it there flows forth the whole Christian life as God desires it—the life of sons in the freedom of faith, the life of service in the obedience of love. Here was a great simplification of religion, yet at the same time a way to religious depth and power.

This, then, was the gift of Luther to the Church—not a system of theology but a rediscovery of the meaning of Christianity, going back beyond the creeds and beyond the institution to the Christian message of salvation, to God's word to man in Christ, and to the faith and life this word created. It was not a theology in the common sense; but it was a chance for theology to start afresh, a summons to theology to undertake its real task. For theology's task is not an independent one in Christianity. That has been theology's constant peril. The center of religion is the word of God to men in Christ and the faith and life it calls forth, and that is the real center and source of theology. Theology is the effort to understand and interpret this faith and life, to see what it means for our thought of God and the world and man and the way of salvation. Instead of that, theology has commonly sought other sources, using especially these three: the Church and her creeds, conceived as the result of special divine guidance; the Bible, viewed as a sum of inspired and infallible teachings; and reason, dealing with accepted first principles and developing these in logical-speculative fashion. These three forms—the confessionalian-ecclesiastical, the biblical, and the rationalistic—have been combined in varying fashion or opposed to one another, usually the first two to the last.

There are of course elements of value in these three approaches. Theology must always go to the Bible; for it is in this that the word of God in Christ comes to us, and here Christianity as a living religion is bodied forth. We need the Church, too, and her great tradition, bringing the fruits of long labor of thought and rich religious experience. The reason is needed also, for what is the work of theology but the mind setting itself to understand what God says and does? But theology is not the elaboration of doctrines given by an external authority, nor the product of philosophic effort nor the combination of the two, as in Roman Catholicism.

THE THEOLOGY THAT CAME OUT OF THE REFORMATION

We turn, then, to the theology that came out of the Reformation. It was produced less in Luther's day than in the years following. These comments bear primarily upon Lutheran theology; for while Calvin produced a more systematic and logical theology, its regulative principle of divine sovereignty fell short of Luther's insight into the evangelical faith. Supreme for Calvin was not the God of love, coming to men as grace in Christ, but the God of power, determining all things by his sovereign right. God was not love wielding power; he was power determining by sheer sovereignty what was to be right. He was not grace willing that all men should be saved; he was sovereign will determining by the "dreadful decree," to use Calvin's own phrase, who should be saved and who should be permitted to go to hell—and, indeed, to quote the *Institutes* again, not only foreseeing this but also "at his own pleasure . . . arranging the fall of the first man and, in him, the ruin of his posterity." Here the Christian gospel and the evangelical insight suffered from an emphasis that had another source.

The strength of post-Reformation Lutheran theology was in the central place it gave to justification by grace through faith. Its failure lay chiefly at three points:

1. It failed to make this central truth regulative for the whole range

of doctrine and so, in the end, compromised it, as our later discussion will indicate.

2. It returned to the principle of external authority. It did this in relation to the Bible and the creeds; and it must be added that Luther, inconsistent with himself, led the way. It has often been stated that the "material principle" of the Reformation was the doctrine of justification by grace through faith and the "formal principle" that of the authority of the Scriptures. The latter, to say the least, is inexact. Strictly the authority for Luther was the word of God in Christ as brought by the Scriptures. The final authority can only be the Living God himself, and the Christ of grace is the supreme word of this God. Further, Luther made a distinction between the books of the Bible, as, for example, in his reference to James and, more significantly, in the test of value he proposed: the way in which they present Christ (*wie sie Christum treiben*). Not the letter of the Bible appears here as authority, but the gospel, God's word to men. The recognition of this by such a leader as Karl Barth marks a notable and permanent gain made by Christian thought. But Luther needed an authority to set over against Rome's principle of church authority. So he resorted to the appeal, not to the word, but to the words of Scripture with the accompanying theory of verbal inspiration and infallibility—not a new position, of course, but one that here took a dominant role. The results we know: (*a*) It contradicted Luther's principle of faith and freedom. For he who in faith answers only to God is set free from bondage to human and external authorities, whether of pope or council, of creed or priestly command, or even of letter of Scripture. (Consider Paul's assertion at the last point in relation to the Old Testament, which was Paul's Scripture.) (*b*) It opened the door to all those extremist groups whose stock in trade is a collection of biblical texts, as well as to the atomistic and divisive trend in Protestantism. (*c*) It committed the Church to a position that could not be held in the face of honest historical study. The same authoritarianism appeared in connection with the place given to the creeds. Here, again, there appear Luther's ingrained conservatism and his fear of a radicalism that would endanger the Reformation movement. So he affirmed the authority of the Apostles' Creed, of Chalcedon, and of the Athanasian—"*rund und rein, eins und alles.*" And here, again, is a clear contradiction. The Athanasian Creed proposes its abstractions and fine distinctions, where "person," as Augustine recognized, cannot strictly mean person, and asserts damnation for those who do not accept. The evangelical faith requires neither philosophical acumen nor the sacrifice of the intellect in obedience to authority; it simply calls men to accept the grace of God in Christ in order to be saved. Here, rather than to Zwingli, Luther might better have said, "You are of another spirit." But this has already brought us to the next point.

3. Lutheran theology returned to the old creedalism, or orthodoxism—that is, the substitution of *the* faith for faith, the acceptance of doc-

trine on authority for the repentant, and trustful faith in a merciful God and surrender to him. The desire to maintain the gospel and its preaching in pure and true form was natural and needed. What happened was that the Church came to be more concerned with "pure doctrine" (*die reine Lehre*), which meant orthodox Lutheran theology, than with the gospel of grace to sinful men. Christianity was first of all a sum of doctrine.

TOWARD AN EVANGELICAL THEOLOGY

Our final question is: Along what lines should evangelical theology move today, and what help is there for us from the evangelical message of the Reformation?

1. The significance of the evangelical Reformation for theology is not in its contribution of any particular doctrine such as justification by grace through faith; it is rather in its conception of what our Christian faith is: that the God of grace in Christ brings men forgiveness of sins and lifts them into a life of fellowship with himself in faith and with their fellow men in love. But this central fact has profound meanings for the whole range of Christian thought.

2. Christianity, it follows, is a matter of personal relations and, first, the relation of God and man. God is personal Being, holy, righteous, and loving, not abstract principle, not bare sovereignty, not inscrutable will. Infinite and transcendent though he is, he is not for us the "totally other"; for he has made man a person, in his image, capable of fellowship.

3. But the personal means in Christianity the ethical and social. Our God is a God of holy love. Fellowship with such a God means sharing his spirit and expressing that spirit in all our life. An evangelical theology should not be individualistic, as Protestantism has often tended to be. It must demand that all human relations and all human institutions shall be shaped and ruled by the spirit of Christian love—the Christian *agape*, free, unselfish, all-including, holy, creative, redemptive.

4. From this there follows also the significance of the Church. Evangelical theology must recognize more fully the truth in the catholic tradition. It must protest as much as ever against the idea of a priestly-sacramentarian, legalistic institution and the claims of infallibility and absolute power. But it must see that the personal relationship in religion not only reaches up to God but also reaches out to men, that Christianity is fellowship-creating, and that the supreme human fellowship is that of faith and love in the Church that Christ is continually creating by his spirit. And we must make more use of "the great tradition," beginning with the Christian Scriptures but including also the treasures of the Church of the centuries—its saints and martyrs, its hymns and prayers, and its insights into Christian truth as they come to us in the historic creeds and the great Christian writings.

5. In all this, however, there must be for evangelical theology the principle of freedom. Faith and freedom go together. The organized

Church and the great tradition are not for us an external authority, nor is the letter of the Scriptures. They are here to serve us, not to rule us; to bring us God and his truth, not to take the place of God. Our authority is God—God as he comes in Christ to give us life and set us free.

6. The evangelical faith gives us guidance at the central point—the doctrine of salvation. Salvation is nothing less than God's gift of life bestowed when, by his grace, he forgives us, receives us into fellowship with himself, and then sets us in right relationship with our fellows and with the world of our daily tasks. It is not a mysterious transformation of soul substance by a sacramental process nor a forensic act by which a debt is paid or a punishment set aside nor a passing emotional experience; it is life from God and with God, carried over into all our life in the world.

7. The evangelical theology of today must do justice to a vital aspect of the doctrine of salvation which the Reformers neglected—that of sanctification. Man needs not only to be forgiven and reconciled to God; he needs to be made over in the spirit of Christ and to receive the power of a new life. And God's grace is equal to this. Here comes in the doctrine of the Spirit, not as a part of Trinitarian speculation, but as vital to the Christian life. This is the high point Paul reaches in Romans 8 following upon his great discussion of grace and faith. The gospel means not only grace for us but also grace in us, not merely mercy for the past but also the promise and power of a new life. John Wesley gave needed emphasis to this doctrine of sanctification and to the work of the Spirit. He cannot be said to have formulated them in a wholly satisfactory manner, but the Methodist contribution at this point has not received due recognition of its importance. Neo-orthodoxy, as it appears in Karl Barth's theology, illustrates the continuing limitation of traditional Reformation theology in this field.

8. Rightly understood, the evangelical faith gives theology the answer to the problem of how God and man work together. It has been a common mistake, following hard logic, to say God or man. So we have had a theology that saw the sovereignty of God and his absolute determining will set over a man who was a puppet, or else we had a humanism that had no need of God and could not conceive how God could work in man. But evangelical thought does not see in the meeting of God and man a mere confronting of impotence with power or a mutually exclusive activity. It knows neither a God dominating man nor a self-sufficient man in relation to God. Man is indeed wholly dependent on the grace of him who works in us both to will and to do of his good pleasure. But his grace is neither the irresistible power of a sovereign nor a mysterious sacramental infusion but comes in and through that saving fellowship of person with Person which is the center of evangelical religion.

9. An evangelical theology will take an attitude at once of regard and of freedom toward the ancient creeds of the Church. They will be highly regarded, for they represent the wisdom of the Church of the past in

its effort alike to voice the faith and to safeguard it. But there must be the attitude of freedom also. It must have a double concern: It cannot take as absolute authority what is itself a historical product and thus relative; it must not affirm that which in any way impairs the central place of the gospel message or makes supreme in theology that which is not required for saving faith. That appears at the crucial point of the doctrine of the person of Christ and the Trinity. An evangelical theology will begin here, where saving faith begins, where God comes to us in his word of grace and in his saving help. What is central and necessary at this point appears in the New Testament, which knows nothing of natures and substances and hypostases and which does not seek to analyze and define the inner being of God. It is sure of three things, and these are vital for its faith and life. (*a*) We have a Living and Mighty God, a God of holiness and grace and saving purpose. (*b*) This God we know in Christ. In Christ, God himself was present for our salvation. In Christ we know God and his purpose and see the light of the knowledge of his glory. (*c*) This one God, by his Spirit, works in us, creates his Church, and makes us over into the likeness of his Son. Here we follow the first and truest insight of Luther when he said:

For Christ is not called Christ because he has two natures. What does that concern me? He bears this glorious and comforting name because of the office and work he has taken upon himself. That gives him the name. That he is God and man by nature—this he has for himself; but that he uses his office to this end and pours out his love and becomes my Saviour and Redeemer—that is for my comfort and my good.

To this should be added the oft-quoted words of Melanchthon, prefixed to his *Loci Communes* in the first edition of that first Protestant theology: "This is what it means to know Christ: to know his benefits, not to contemplate his natures or the modes of his Incarnation."

WORSHIP AND THE SACRAMENTS

Oscar Thomas Olson

THE immediate motive that caused the early followers of Christ to form themselves into a Christian fellowship was the desire to worship God together in their special Christian way. The Church was primarily a fellowship for worship. The history of the Christian Church is the story of its attitudes and experiences in the worship of God as disclosed by Jesus Christ. It is not the function of this paper to trace the growth and development of the worship cultus of the Church through its long history. In general today, after twenty centuries of history, we see within Christendom two general types of religious expression: a religion of authority and a religion of the spirit.

In point of dignity, in numbers, in age, and in power we have to face the fact of the religion of authority. In its fellowship we find the overwhelming mass of Church membership. It holds that the essentials of Christianity are divinely fixed and constitute an unalterable system, which is not subject to common reason or dependent for its power and authority on spiritual insight. Superior to all that the mind and soul of man can perceive or discover, these essentials are arbitrarily and directly imposed by the will of God and are not to be disregarded, therefore, or set aside only on peril of eternal loss to the soul or the society that does so deal with them.

After sixteen centuries the fabric of the Church perfected its institutional and sacramental system with such weight of authority that without it salvation was not conceived to be possible. To this day there is no external assurance of the possession of a true and valid religion or of the impartation of divine grace outside the operation of this organized system. Catholic Christianity is a religion of authority. It mediates its salvation through the sacraments. The sacramental conception is older than Christianity. Underlying it is the notion of spiritual substance—the view that makes spiritual life something that can be imparted or transferred in a quasi-material form. This conception goes back for its roots to the eating of offerings and the Communion meal. There may be in it even dire and shadowy associations with the conviction, strong in primitive times, that the strength and courage of a brave man would take up their abode in the eater of his heart. The line between crude and crass superstition and high and lofty faith is not always easily drawn.

161

SACRAMENTARIAN RELIGION

Any sacramental system must be validated. Thus, we find the religion of authority setting up a highly articulated organization. If the sacraments are really a means of imparting divine grace, their celebration must be certified, assured, and safeguarded from falling into improper hands. How can they be thus protected from abuse save through an accredited priesthood? So arose and persists the elaborate organization of the Catholic Church, and the same insistence is found, in modified form, through all the sacramentarian branches of the Church—Roman, Greek, and Anglican. The emphasis is upon an ordered ministry, an unbroken line from the early Church, either through a historic episcopate or by some other divinely ordained means.

As a matter of history within two hundred years after the life of Jesus this type of sacramentarian religion was in full sway. This was the way of witness, which testified of grace coming from God to man through the right administration of the bread and wine of the Eucharist and the water of baptism. Down through the ages it has come, exercising mighty power over the souls of men. Even Luther did not succeed in breaking away from its influence. *"Hoc est corpus meum"* were the words hurled at Zwingli with as much vigor as any Roman cardinal could have proclaimed them.

Yet historic research and a clearer understanding of the purpose and message of Jesus make it clear that Jesus was no institutionalist in the sense of one who stresses the primacy of institution or ceremonies. For Jesus the two essentials in religion were revelation and faith—the divine disclosure and the human response. Beside faith all other human energies or institutions or observances are secondary. So the Protestant Reformation brought to the fore the conviction that the Church, with its worship and sacraments, is secondary, existing only to serve faith.

The Catholic claim, often put forth for these, that they possess within themselves a divine right, derived, not from their usefulness or effectiveness, but from their divine institution by Christ, has always been challenged by Protestantism. Protestantism seeks to witness, with the emphasis of Jesus, for the religion of the spirit. The chief difference between Catholic and Protestant worship is seen in the differing emphasis upon the word and the sacraments as the means of communion with God.

THE CENTRAL ACT OF WORSHIP

From the earliest days of the Christian movement the Lord's Supper has been the central act of Christian worship. The early Christians gathered in simple fellowship about a common table to bring their thanksgiving and praise to the God disclosed to them through Christ. But by the fourth century the simple worship of the early Church had grown up into an imposing structure of ritual. The order of Christian worship followed the pattern of the Jewish synagogue usage, to which were added various rites of a sacramental character. In this development the Eucharist, or celebration of the Lord's Supper, became the central act of worship. During the ten or twelve centuries of medieval history the Eucharist held the center of interest in Christian practice. It moved as a drama in two great acts. The first part of the Eucharistic service, often called the Liturgy of the Catechumens, consisted of prayers, psalms from the Old Testament or sometimes Christian hymns, Scripture lessons, and a homily sermon, or instruction. The second part of the service, which was called the Liturgy of the Faithful, were the oblation of the Eucharistic elements of bread and wine; the special prayer of consecration over them, including the words of institution, and the actual Communion in the elements. Through the entire history of the Church, from apostolic times into modern Protestantism, this usage and practice can be traced. Of course, there have been wide variances in differing rites, but essentially the basic pattern has remained. The great historic division between East and West, between the Greek and Roman rites, brought differing emphases; yet both had the noble and familiar words of the Preface, with the Sursum Corda, Sanctus, and Hosanna. The Sursum Corda appears in all the ancient liturgies of the Church and appears in the earliest complete ritual extant. At least 1,750 years of use lie behind this invitation to men and women to lift up their hearts in thanksgiving to God.

In the Greek liturgy the Holy Spirit is invoked upon the Eucharistic gifts. In the Roman Mass the consecration takes place simply through the recitation of the words of the Saviour (Luke 22:19), followed by prayers asking that the sacrifice be acceptable to God. In the Greek usage, after the Lord's Prayer, the priest elevates the bread, saying, "Holy things for holy people!" In the Roman ritual cup and bread are elevated, and the saying of the Lord's Prayer follows. The actual Communion is preceded in the East by an act of praise:

> There is one holy, one Lord Jesus Christ,
> To the glory of God, the Father,
> To the fullness of Holy Spirit.

In the Roman Mass the Communion takes place upon the note of supplication:

> Lamb of God that takest away the sins of the world,
> Have mercy upon us.

In both rites the Communion itself is much the same. It begins with the celebrant and may end with the people. In both instances it is followed by an act of thanksgiving and dismissal. In its practical outcome it became a drama enacted to be pleasing to God, altogether apart from any effect it might have upon the participant. Sharing in its efficacy through the celebrant, merit was earned, and God satisfied.

The meaning of this act of worship has been a center of conflict all through the Christian centuries. In the medieval Church the grace of the gospel became a thing, a divine stuff fused indissolubly with the sacramental act. In the act of consecration of bread and wine there was a transubstantiation into the actual body and blood of our Lord. The grace of God worked in a magically objective fashion on the soul of the communicant, without any necessarily corresponding faith on his part. The Reformation brought back into perspective the emphasis of the New Testament. The grace of God is the attitude displayed or disclosed in Christ toward sinful men. Faith alone appropriates it. The proper object of faith is this gracious attitude or will of God; and because the word is his uttered will, grace is supremely communicated in the word. It is mediated, not through the authoritative power that the sacrament of orders confers on the action of the priest, but through the Holy Spirit.

Protestantism does not keep the sacraments in the central position; neither does it dismiss them. It seeks to keep them as means of grace. Protestantism affirms that God's promises in his Word and the believing trust of men are the essence of Christianity. This fact was dramatized for me one summer when I was serving as the visiting minister in the Renfield Street Church, Glasgow, Scotland. Each Sunday morning, just before the service of worship, the verger used to carry the Bible into the sanctuary and place it upon the pulpit. One Sunday I ventured to ask him the reason for this custom. He responded by saying:

You know, in Roman Catholic practice the center of worship is the sacrament. At the climactic moment in Roman worship the priest turns his back upon the people, elevates the Host, the sanctuary bell rings, the congregation genuflects, God is present. *Hoc est corpus.* To Roman believers God is actually present. Worship is a contribution to God pleasing to God apart from any effect that it may have upon the worshiper. In Protestant worship the great moment in worship is in the opening of the Book of God on the pulpit, when the minister faces the people and brings the word of God. God is present when the man of God speaks the word with and for God.

In Protestant worship contribution is made to God of hearts in confession, supplication, intercession, adoration, and consecration. Protestant worship is a contribution to God from man, and it is also a reception of God for man. We shall not find the real genius of worship until we use it to get us God. Both the sacrifice symbolized by the altar and the instruction symbolized by the pulpit, both the sacrament and the word, are in our tradition and heritage.

WHAT WORSHIP ACCOMPLISHES

The truth is that men and women in our day need God. Worship is the accomplishment of something real—the effectual union of man with God. A church that does not emphasize worship as primary is trying to build the structure of spiritual society with the cornerstone left out. The old formal definition of worship called it "the response of the soul to the consciousness of being in the presence of God." A more recent definition approaches the experience psychologically and says, "Worship is the unification of consciousness around the central, controlling idea of God, the prevailing emotional tone being that of adoration." Worship is the appeal to the religious purpose through feeling and imagination. Worship is a creative act. Every act of worship seeks to bring forth a direct experience of God. It fixes attention before God as an object in himself supremely desirable. It brings all life into union with God, communicates power and results in a peace "that the world can neither give nor take away." In the words of Dr. Willard Sperry "worship is the adoration of God, the assumption of supreme worth to God, and the manifestation of reverence in the presence of God."

Our major difficulty grows out of the fact that the idea of God varies in the minds of different persons. Every man approaches God on the level of his own experience. With the colors of his own experience of thinking and living every man paints his own picture of God. The word "God" is a picture frame into which each person puts his own conception of the Eternal. A brilliant scientist says that for him God is "the unification in one conscious mind of the powers that act upon us for our own good." A contemporary philosopher says that for him God signifies "an Ultimate Reality in whom cohere ideals that press upon us for realization." Concede that these men are thinking accurately, but accurate definition does not necessarily help men and women as they lift the deep and genuine desires of life toward the Eternal. We cannot pray to one who is merely the integration of the powers that act upon life. We cannot lift voices of praise and thanksgiving to some general and vague embodiment of the laws of nature. Said a sincere and fine man, "I do not know of a more terrible feeling of loneliness than in the moment I try to unite with my fellows in public worship." The very fact that the ideas and conceptions of men are all so different makes it hard for many men to merge their devotion with their fellows. Their most sacred convictions are many times strained and harassed by the expressions or assumptions of their fellow worshipers. Thus, it has been easy in Protestantism to emphasize the inner aspect of worship, and increasingly there has been a growing inclination to regard the vital factor in worship as a matter intensely private.

Yet, despite all this, the need for public worship remains. The inspiration to creative growth lies in the awakening of life to the reality of a God who can be worshiped by men who share a common humanity. The God whom men of all families can worship is the living and personal God who feels and thinks and loves and wills. He is the Father of all men. No man lives who does not share the common need for the actual experience of God in the deep places of the soul. Worship should bring to the worshiper an awareness of the Living God.

When public worship is a corporate or collective assent to the purposes of the Living God, it becomes a socially creative act. Matthew Arnold was voicing the experience of the race when he said that while man philosophizes best alone, he worships best in common. There are two reasons for this. We recognize them immediately: (1) The movement of a group always lifts the individual into a deeper and more intense experience than would be his in isolation. One of my old teachers calls public worship "a gesture of Christian solidarity," an assertion of the reality of a common, collective faith. It is a declaration that the union of those who love gets its inspiration and validity from the God who is love. (2) The second reason why man worships best in common is more fundamental. A God who is love finds us readiest for his incoming when we are consciously sharing each other's hopes and aspirations. God fulfills his purpose, not through separated individuals, but through a fellowship of those gripped by his purpose.

The purpose of worship is to present to the mind, through the imagination, one idea, majestic and inclusive. If one reads the great prayers of the centuries, they indicate a sharing in this one idea— the life of God touching the soul of man. Take, for instance, this noble prayer from the *Service Book and Ordinal of the Presbyterian Church of South Africa:*

Almighty God, who art beyond the reach of our highest thought, and yet within the heart of the lowliest, we pray thee to come to us in all the beauty of light, in all the tenderness of love, in all the liberty of truth, and make thyself known to us. Mercifully help us in the struggle to be pure and good; encourage us in every effort to be true, loyal, and loving; to do justly, to love mercy, and to walk humbly with thee. Sanctify all our desires and purposes, and upon each of us let thy blessing rest. Amen.

Here is a prayer that fixes the attention upon God and invokes his presence as a source of power for life. The finest brief petition that I know, giving the steps in the unification of the soul with the Eternal Spirit through sublime emotion, is the prayer of St. Augustine: "Grant O God, that we may desire thee, and, desiring thee, seek thee, and, seeking thee, find thee, and, finding thee, be satisfied with thee forever."

Thoughtful men of our day want an assurance of God. We are mistaken if we suppose that men chiefly desire to be pleasantly entertained or extraordinarily delighted when they go into a church. They may not be able to express it, but they persist in going there because they desire to enter a Holy Presence; they want to approach One before whom they can be still and know that he is God. The things we may add to a service by the way of variety and color to catch the attention of the senses are, as ends, beside the point. We have advertised sermon themes and special music, usually to startle the pious and provoke the pagans. We have sought to arouse curiosity, to stir immediate interest, and to achieve some secular reaction. We do not announce that in our churches there is to be a public worship of God, and that everything we do will be in the awestruck sense that he is there. We are afraid that nobody would come if we really did that. What infidels we are! Why be surprised if the world passes us by? It knows that too often in Protestantism, Sunday-morning church is a this-world function, with pious gossip and a decorous sort of human friendliness, with a not-too-strenuous intellectual fillip thrown in. We try to make our services attractive to the secular tastes, to the nonreligious attitudes in man's nature. We have naturalized and domesticated our very offices of devotion. We call men to be listeners of contemporary event rather than participants in eternal purpose. Instead of bringing men face to face with God in awe and reverence we introduce an affable and comfortable season of spiritual entertainment.

NEEDED—A REVIVAL OF WORSHIP

We need a revival of worship at the heart of our Protestant churchmanship. A generation ago P. T. Forsythe suggested that "worship is a communion with the finished will of God in Christ." We get at what is meant here in that moving hymn of the Passion:

> "It is finished!" Man of Sorrows!
> From thy Cross our frailty borrows
> Strength to bear and conquer thus.
>
> Lifted high amid the ages:
> Guide of heroes, saints, and sages,
> May it guide us still to Thee.

The cross is central to every legitimate Christian experience of worship and adoration. Christ on the Cross is God's disclosure of himself at a focal point of history. Here man can never be uncertain as to the divine attitude toward him or ignorant of the conditions upon which he may commune with God. Here is the goal of man's hopes, to which every act of faith points. Here is where he discovers the sacramental quality of life. Here is where he finds an ineffable experience of something unworldly, mystical, spiritual, which brings the whole nature of man into communion with the whole nature of God.

It is hard for us to escape our tradition. For most of us our inheritance has given us a distrust of the altar and its liturgy. We are more familiar with the pulpit and its sermon. It is not easy for us to bring the sacrament and the word together. The Reformation brought us out of the Roman Church, where worship was regarded as an end in itself. To the devotees of the far-flung Roman Church worship is a contribution to God, pleasing to him apart from any effect it may have upon the worshiper. Upon the Roman altar there is a participation with the deed of God. Here, by an effective invocation, bread and wine are transformed into the body and blood of Christ, the very act of atonement is accomplished, and its virtue is imparted to the worshiper by the officiating priest. This is the priestly religion of authority in its clearest and most definite form. Of course, this theory of worship is open to grave abuse. It has led to indifference as to the effect of the worship upon the moral character of the communicant so that worship has been used, not to conquer evil, but to condone wrong, thus making sin as safe as it was easy. It has also degenerated into a sterile formalism until the *hoc est corpus* of the Mass has become the hocus pocus of the scoffer.

A thing we need to note is that even in so potent a conception as the Roman Mass a human means is used in communicating the divine. While we dismiss for very good reason all the superstition clustering about the Mass, in repudiating the defect we are likely to throw out the accompanying reality. I believe that modern psychology is going to teach anew the values and demand a fresh interpretation and more rational cultivation of the forms and ceremonies of liturgy and ritual which are part of our inheritance. Because they have been abused and have degenerated into empty forms and magical ceremonies, we have lost the senses of their inherent values and inspirations. By scorning and abandoning them in our Protestant reaction we have often poured out the baby with the bath.

Worship for us in Protestantism is not its own reason and its own end. It is valuable, as it is valid, because it is a chief avenue of spiritual insight, a chief means of awakening penitence, obtaining forgiveness, growing in grace and love, getting for us the Living God. These are ultimates. They are pleasing to him to whom we bring our adoration. The spirit of our tradition and heritage brings to us both the sacrament and the word. The sacramental symbol and the living word unite to speak to man today for God and of God. On the altar and from the pulpit there must be an uplifting of God in Christ, shedding his light upon life, individual and corporate, and claiming the reverent devotion of his children. We do not believe in repeating the actual sacrifice of Christ by a sacramental act like the Roman Mass. But we deem it essential that the experience of sacrifice be a continuing part of life. The divine does suffer in the human. It is not a matter of material elements which concerns us, but the spiritual insight of worshiping people.

We must cultivate the art of worship. Great music, noble liturgy, and worthy symbolism must be used to make men aware of the presence and reality of God. Both sacrament and word must be used to inspire awe and reverence, faith and trust. From services of worship where men have actually been brought into the presence of God they will go out into the world cleansed, uplifted, and inspired.

The preaching of the word must be sacramental. It must communicate God. It must be a breaking of the word of life if it is to impart life. In every era the way of uttering the word will vary, but the response to it will always be the same. This is how Thomas Olivers, one of

Methodism's first preachers, responded to the word preached by George Whitefield:

The text was "Is not this a brand plucked out of the fire?" When this sermon began, I was certainly a dreadful enemy to God and to all that is good and one of the most profligate and abandoned young men living; but by the time it was ended, I was become a new creature. For, in the first place, I was deeply convinced of the great goodness of God toward me all my life, particularly in that he had given his Son to die for me. I had also a far clearer view of all my sins, particularly my base ingratitude to him. These discoveries quite broke my heart.

PROTESTANTISM AND MUSIC

CLARENCE *and* HELEN A. DICKINSON

WITH the establishment of Protestantism the most important change in the character of public worship was the restoration of the service to the people. As Bismarck wrote, "The Roman service can be held by the priest without the people if need be; the Lutheran service can be held by the people without the priest if need be." This meant, naturally and primarily, that everything in the service must be put into the language of the people. Luther himself expressed his conception of public worship very simply and clearly: "Our dear Lord speaks to us through his Word, and we speak to him in prayer and song." It would indeed be difficult to find a more concise and simply inclusive description of a church service than that.

Now, that we may understand what God the Lord says to us through his Word, that Word must be translated into the langauge of the people; this is the primary necessity. When his worshiping people speak to him, the prayers and songs must be offered in their own language, that they may be understood of all the people; that even those "who sit in the seat of the unlearned" may say—or sing—"Amen."

Thus it was that, very early in the history of Protestantism, Martin Luther wrote Johann Walther, pastor at Zwickau: "I wish we had many German songs which the people could sing during the Mass. But we lack German poets and musicians—or they are unknown to us—who are able to make Christian and spiritual songs, as Paul called them, which are of such value that they can be used daily in the house of God." And again, "Unquestionably, in the early Church, the people sang much which only the priests and clerics now sing." We know that this was the case. The Council of Laodicea, in the year 364, had forbidden anyone to take part in the singing in church except those clerics who had the right to mount into the ambo.

At the earliest possible moment, therefore, Luther himself took up the task of providing music for all people to sing. In 1528 he wrote to Spalatin, chancellor of Frederick the Wise of Saxony, "I propose, after the example of the prophets and the early Fathers, to write for the people some German hymns and spiritual songs, that, by the help of song, the word of God may abide among them."

He associated with him Johann Walther, Michael Praetorius, and the venerable singing teacher Conrad Rupf. Under Luther's direction Johann Walther edited a hymnal for the new church, published in 1525, which contained thirty-eight hymns in German and but five in Latin, the latter bearing the indication "for the use of stu-

170

dents." [1] Luther was to live to see sixty collections of chorales published for the people to sing. From the first they were received with great enthusiasm. When the Englishman Roger Ascham visited Augsburg in 1551, he wrote home, "Three or four thousand people singing at a time in this city is but a trifle."

THE MASS IN CHORALE FORM

But not only were there many chorales written as we might write hymns for congregational use; all the invariable musical numbers in the Mass itself were translated into German verse and set as chorales for all the people to sing, the *Kyrie* as "Have mercy upon us, O God" (frequently sung, however, as a simple chant); the *Gloria in excelsis* as "All glory be to God on high"; the *Credo* as "We all believe in one true God"; the *Sanctus* as "These things the seer Isaiah did befall"; the *Angus Dei* as "O Lamb of God most holy" and as "O Christ, thou Lamb of God." Other suitable chorales could be substituted for these, as Luther did not urge an invariable form of service or the use of the same musical numbers in every service of the Mass. The significant thing was that the musical numbers in the liturgy, even those in the Mass, which for so many centuries had been reserved exclusively for clerical singers, had now come into the possession of the congregation: that all the people might "speak to God in song," "each in his own language in which he was brought up."

This, in turn, brought about certain changes within the music itself. The music to which the Latin words were sung had been (1) unison plain song or (2) contrapuntal music sufficiently involved to demand singers with considerable training in music for its presentation. Martin Luther set the canticles and hymns in harmony: "I have adapted them to four voices," he wrote, "for no other reason than that I wish that young persons who indeed ought to be educated in music and other right things should have something to sing as a substitute for loose and amorous songs."

PART SINGING; THE CHORALE PRELUDE

This meant the singing of the hymns in parts, whenever desired, rather than in unison. It meant, also, the participation of women in the church's song. Although they had taken part audibly in the worship of the early and post-Nicene Church, so that Gregory Nazianzen could describe as his ideal woman "one who stands like a pillar at the psalmody, and whose voice is never heard save in the responses in the service," their participation had been forbidden for about seven hundred years. Now, again, they had their share as all God's children sang together their songs in worship. And this brought about a change in the structure of the music itself or, rather, in the disposition of the parts. In earlier music the air was given to the tenor. His very

---

[1] Not the first hymnal, of course, but the first to include Latin hymns, the use of which was restricted to Protestant students.

name was derived from this fact—from the Latin *tenere:* to hold. He was the person or his the part which held the air. Now the air was taken from the tenor and given to the soprano—a measure that contributed greatly to ease and clearness in congregational singing. In his musical settings of French Calvinist psalms, for instance, Goudimel gave the soprano the melody in all except some half dozen numbers.

The singing of the chorales by the whole congregation offered opportunity for greater use of the organ as an instrument of accompaniment. Playing over the chorale on the organ before singing presently came to be customary and in due time gave rise to the practice of an announcement of the melody with embellishments and to a formal working out along structural lines. This resulted in the creation of one of the most important musical forms for organ—the chorale prelude, which has continually and vastly enriched organ literature ever since that time.

THE SINGING OF PSALMS

The Calvinist churches also laid great stress upon the use of music in the service. During the first years of his ministry in Geneva, Calvin seems not to have seen the value and importance of it. Preaching had his whole attention. The setting forth of the word of God in sermons was the chief reason for a church service. In *The Phenix,* published in 1770, there is reported a description written by a visitor to one of Calvin's early services in Geneva. "It was," he records, "a grave, demure piece, without either responses or psalms or hymns, but terribly fortified and palisaded with texts of Scripture."

But Calvin's year of exile and visit to Strassburg convinced him of the tremendous value of music in the service and that it did indeed "lend wings to the preaching of the gospel," as Luther said. When, therefore, he returned to Geneva, he enlisted the services of such poets as Clement Marot and Theodore Beza and such musicians as Claude Goudimel and Louis Bourgeois to make metrical versions of the Psalms and to set them to music for use in the church service. His first Psalter, published in 1539, contained fifty versified Psalms, the Ten Commandments, the creed, the Lord's Prayer, and the Nunc Dimittis. In due course the other hundred psalms received metrical translations into French and were set to music.

Calvin opened a singing school for the learning of this music and held those famous meetings which we nowadays would call "hymn sings" in his church on weekday afternoons, when the shopkeepers of Geneva closed their shops and the women their homes and all went over to Calvin's church to sing psalms. They sang so many, and so much time was consumed in announcing them, that Louis Bourgeois conceived the idea of placing upon the wall of the church a "hymn board," still used in almost every Protestant church, upon which was listed, in order, the number of each psalm to be sung. We are told that it was so great a comfort to the church that the congregation made Bourgeois the gift of a substantial sum of money, which the old chronicler tells us was most useful to him as he was about to set forth on a journey.

These metrical psalms were widely sung. In Holland, Peter Daten (Petrus Dathenus) translated them into Dutch for the Calvinistic Dutch Reformed Church; and such great composers as Sweelinck, who was appointed organist of the Oude Kerk in Amsterdam by William the Silent himself, used the psalm tune we know as "Old Hundredth" as the theme of his beautiful motet "Arise, O ye servants of God." As John Knox had been associated with Calvin in Geneva, it was natural that the Scotch Presbyterian Church should adopt the Genevan melodies for the Psalms. In England they were accepted with great enthusiasm. Bishop Jewel, writing to Peter Martyr in 1560, tells him that "at St. Paul's Cross, after service, six thousand people joined in praise to God, singing 'French' psalms."

With the formulation of the order of service to be used in the Church of England it became necessary that the canticles should also be translated into English, as we have seen that they had earlier been translated into German. This was not done at the very outset. There was not time for everything to be done at once. First must come the translation of the Epistle and the Gospel; then, bit by bit, of the rest of the service, including the musical numbers.

The Latin motet seems to have passed out of use in England early in the Reformation period, and it was not until the reign of Queen Elizabeth that we find the anthem mentioned as part of the service. The injunction sanctioning its use "in quires and places where they sing" specified that it must be in English: "An anthem may be sung, having respect that the sentence thereof may be understanded and perceived."

The French psalms had a more widespread influence upon hymn and psalm singing than had the Lutheran chorales; but the chorale has played a greater part in the creation of new musical forms such as the Passion and the cantata.

The Passion and the Chorale Cantata

The emphasis upon the death of Christ for the salvation of men as individuals, the inevitable central stress upon the fact that once and for all Christ died for man's redemption—"Christ our Passover, sacrificed for us once for all; for by one oblation hath he perfected forever them that are sanctified"—turned the thoughts of all people and, with them, the thoughts of all artists toward that act of redemption. Whereas in the Roman Catholic countries the Last Supper was the subject of countless pictures and, indeed, by far the most frequently depicted scene from the last days in the life of Jesus, artists in the Protestant countries represented it very rarely but painted instead countless pictures of the Crucifixion, filled with intense feeling, and, in series after

173

series, all the details of the Passion, which led up to that Cross on Golgotha.

In music, as in art, the Passion of our Lord became the chief great theme. The story of his Passion as told by one of the Evangelists had hitherto been chanted in Holy Week by the priest, like any other Scripture lesson, or slightly varied as the priest chanted the narrative and a choir of clerics interposed the questions of the disciples and the angry accusations of the mob in unison plain song. Now the "Passion" became a great musical drama in which the Protestant church poured fourth the intensity of its interest and its conviction; its penitence, its love, its hope, and its faith.

In the words of some one of the Evangelists scene followed upon scene. With each new development in the unfolding of the tragedy individual believers, therefore in solos, sang their passionate grief, their abject penitence, their loyalty. All people participated, men and women alike, in this consummate tragedy, as followers of the Christ or as enemies, the great chorus of whose singing makes vivid the power of evil to seem to destroy the incarnation of all good. And here, almost more than in the church service itself, we become conscious of the significance of the chorale as the voice of the Church, the bride of Christ.

In humility, penitence, love, and faith the Church comments upon each scene in the Passion; comments in the chorale, the musical language which has become the recognized voice of the Church, "which he has redeemed by his precious blood." So in Bach's great "Passion According to St. Matthew" the opening chorus calls the Church to witness the sufferings of Christ for her redemption; the sinless Lamb of God suffering for the guilty, the bridegroom dying for his beloved: "For our offense, for love intense, on the Cross content to languish"; and the Church, gazing upon this scene, overcome by a sense of its own sin, which has brought this anguish to its Saviour, breaks in even upon the choir, which is beseeching it to contemplate the unspeakable sacrifice being offered for its redemption—breaks in with the glorious chorale that the Lutheran Church substituted for the *Agnus Dei*, the great closing hymn of the Communion service for centuries past, now put into the language of song for the whole Church to sing:

> O Lamb of God, most Holy,
> The bitter cross undergoing;
> O Saviour, meek and lowly,
> Despite and scorn only knowing,
> The sins of man thou'rt bearing,
> Else were we left despairing;
> On us have mercy, O Jesus!

The Evangelist then begins to tell the story of the whole course of the Passion;

When Jesus had finished all these sayings, he said to his disciples, "Ye know that after two days is the Passover, and the Son of man shall then be delivered to be crucified."

The listening Church cries out in the chorale:

> O blessed Jesus, how hast thou offended
> That such a doom on thee has now descended?

When, at the Last Supper, Christ tells his disciples, "Verily I say to you, one of you shall betray me," and they begin each one of the disciples to say to him, "Lord, is it I?" the onlooking Church, in the chorale, sings:

> The sorrows Thou art bearing—
> On *me* they ought to fall.
> The torture Thou art feeling—
> 'Tis I that should endure it all.

And when the agonized, onlooking Church hears Pilate's question "What then shall I do unto Jesus, to whom they give the name of Christ?" and his enemies answer, "Let him be crucified!" the Church sings the chorale:

> O wondrous love, this sacrifice to offer,
> The Shepherd for the sheep content to suffer,
> The righteous Lord their debt for sinners paying!

And thus it goes throughout. As scene follows scene in the Passion, the Church, watching the unfolding, sings one of its great chorales as a part of practically every scene, even unto the death of Christ, when "Jesus cried aloud and departed," and the Church takes to itself this everlasting solace:

> When life begins to fail me,
> I fear not, having Thee;
> When pains of death assail me,
> My comfort Thou wilt be;
> Whene'er from woes that grieve me
> I seek to find relief,
> Alone Thou wilt not leave me,
> For Thou hast tasted grief.

Another smaller form of musical composition flowered directly from the chorale. This was the chorale cantata, for which the theme chosen was that of a well-known chorale. Such a cantata usually opens with the announcement of the theme sung to the music of the chorale melody by a chorus or by a soloist. Other soloists and choruses then comment upon the meaning and application of the text, expressing their personal reactions and pleading for God's blessing and the fulfillment of his promises to his children. The cantata usually closes with the singing of the chorale.

Such a cantata, for example, as Buxtehude's "Rejoice, Beloved Christians" opens with a soprano soloist singing to the well-known chorale melody:

> Beloved Christians, now rejoice.
> Sing joyously with heart and voice;
> For soon the Son of God will come
> And take us to his heavenly home.

The chorus eagerly responds with "Hear ye! Hear ye! The Lord cometh with thousands of angels, pronouncing his judgment upon all nations." A fanfare of trumpets is sounded, heralding Christ's approach. His voice is then heard (bass solo): "Behold, I come quickly, and my reward with me." The choir responds: "O come, Lord Jesus, quickly come, of evil make swift ending." A soprano and alto sing a joyous "Amen" to this, and the chorus of the Church breaks into the same chorale with the verse:

> Lord Jesus Christ, vouchsafe thy grace
> That we may see thee face to face.

The Bach cantata "Watch and Pray" opens with a chorus that sets forth the theme: "Watch and pray, for ye know not the day or the hour." A solo voice then calls upon the sinful to repent with fear, as the hour of condemnation draws nigh. A prayer follows, in aria form, that we may all turn to God and escape "this dread doom, the end of all." Another solo voice hastens to reassure the Christian that "if we but watch and pray, to us it shall be given one day to see the Christ," and that though "earth may pass and heaven fail us, the word of God endureth." The Church responds by voicing its eagerness for the coming of Christ, its joy and triumph, in the chorale:

> Saved by him from judgment sore,
> Jesus shall I leave no more.

THE SOLO CANTATA

This closeness of personal, individual relationship to God and Christ found expression, not only in the solos in the settings of the Passion and in those in the chorale cantatas but also in a new musical form—the solo cantata. The great Protestant composers in Germany, such as Heinrich Schuetz, Franz Tunder, Dietrich Buxtehude, and, of course, Bach, wrote such cantatas, which were sacred arias in three movements—*moderato, adagio, allegro*—with accompaniment of two violins or two flutes or string quartet with cembalo and organ.

Buxtehude's solo cantata "Lord, in Thee Do I Trust," for example, begins with a *moderato* movement of considerable breadth and calmness, expressive of confidence in God: "Lord, in thee do I trust: let me never be confounded." Then the thoughts of the petitioner turn suddenly to his own utter unworthiness, and a plaintive *adagio* movement sets forth:

Who is poorer than a sinner,
Than the soul that cannot see Thee?
Blind am I and sinful too.

This consciousness of need inspires the earnest prayer, in the third movement, that God will "heal my blindness, my weakness, and my sin"—a movement that increases in confidence as it goes on, becoming at last a joyful *allegro* of faith.

Some of Bach's solo cantatas have been fairly well known for some time, but we are just now becoming acquainted with such exquisite gems of sincere religious feeling and musical art as Heinrich Schuetz's "Dearly, Dearly Do I Love Thee"; Tunder's "Lord Jesus, Thy Dear Angel Send," for soprano and string quartet; and Buxtehude's "My Jesus Is My Lasting Joy," for tenor (or soprano) with two violins and organ. They are at once a great enrichment of our devotional literature and our musical art.

The most far-reaching influences of Protestantism upon sacred music were therefore the development of congregational singing in the church service through the writing of chorales in the language of the people, to be sung by all the laity, both men and women; the further increased participation of the laity in the service by the setting of the invariable (choral) numbers in the Mass in chorale form, to be sung by all the people, and not, as hitherto, by clerics; the giving of the melody to the soprano rather than the tenor and the encouragement of singing in harmony as well as in unison; the increased use of the organ as an instrument of accompaniment to the singing and the development of the chorale prelude as an instrumental form; the adoption of the chorale as the voice of the Church and the resultant important part it played in the development of the new form of the Passion and in the creation of the chorale cantata; the extensive use of the solo voice and the creation of the new musical form—the solo cantata.

Great as was the effect of Martin Luther's use of music in the Church upon the creation of new musical forms, possibly its most important and far-reaching influence was upon the whole development of German music throughout succeeding centuries. The musical historian Latrobe wrote:

A great deal of wonderment has been expressed as to how Germany achieved her musical superiority. It was because Martin Luther, by using good poems set to noble music, in the churches where all the people could hear them without cost and could learn to know them, cultivated musical feeling and musical taste practically universally, even in all the common people.

177

THE PROTESTANT EMPHASIS ON PREACHING

Halford E. Luccock

MAURICE EGAN, who was United States Ambassador to Denmark during the first World War, wrote in an article in the *Yale Review*, some fifteen years ago, that when the Protestant church should be found dead, the sermon would be the dagger in her breast. There, at least, is one dogmatic appraisal of the effect of the Protestant emphasis on the sermon.

The obvious answer to that is easy. Mr. Egan was a Roman Catholic, a scholarly and deeply religious man. It is natural, we say, for a member of a church in which the chief stress is put upon the sacraments to have a low estimate of preaching. While that does, in part, account for the estimate of the Protestant sermon as a death-dealing dagger, we would be far too complacent if we thought that was all the attention Mr. Egan's remark deserves. It is thrown up into visibility here, at the beginning of a discussion of the sermon in the Protestant churches, not at all for the purpose of approving it but for its vivid picturing of the fact that there are two sides—a debit and a credit side—to the emphasis that, historically, Protestantism has put upon the sermon and to the priority given to it. Mr. Egan's statement ought to open our eyes to the possibility that an overemphasis upon the sermon has frequently had crippling effects upon the church and the Christian religion. We must ask ourselves whether one agency of religion—the sermon—has not often been expected to carry a burden of religious influence which it cannot possibly carry alone. That leads us into the pertinent contemporary question of the true function of the sermon in relation to the other agencies of the gospel.

POSITIVE VALUES IN PREACHING

Let us begin, however, not with negatives, no matter how sharp or relevant a warning they may bring to the Church, but with the great positives, which are clearly to be seen in the history of the Protestant churches, in regard to the emphasis placed on the sermon:

Preaching is inherent and central in the Protestant conception of Christianity. The Reformation is inconceivable without a strong emphasis upon preaching. The insight that the just shall live by faith and not by the operation of sacraments, that the Christian religion is a matter of personal experience, a response of the soul to God, beseeching in Christ, "Be ye reconciled," demands the proclamation of the word of God. It is no accident that Luther was primarily a preacher. Scholar and theologian as he was, the center of the power that shook Germany

178

and Europe and the throne of the Pope itself was his preaching. It is likewise no accident that the "morning stars of the Reformation," such as Wyclif, Jerome of Prague, and John Hus, were primarily preachers. The new wine demanded and found the new wineskin of the sermon. Nor is it any accident that the great creative epochs of Protestantism found their supreme agency, both as cause and effect, in preaching such as that of John Knox, Hugh Latimer, Wesley and Whitefield, Finney, and Moody. Protestantism has been a religion of the word. When it ceases to be that, it may well cease.

In its tremendous emphasis on preaching Protestantism, as in some other things, was going back to the beginnings of Christianity. "From that time began Jesus to preach" (Matthew 4:17). "Go . . . and preach the kingdom of God" (Luke 9:60). St. Paul thus conceives of his great task: "For Christ sent me not to baptize, but to preach the gospel" (I Corinthians 1:17). He could not envisage the spread of Christianity without preaching. "How then shall they call upon him in whom they have not believed? and how shall they believe in him whom they have not heard? and how shall they hear without a preacher? and how shall they preach, except they be sent?" (Romans 10:14-15). Christianity began its evangelistic work, its outward thrust into the world, with a sermon—Peter's sermon at Pentecost. In the beginning was the word—of a preacher.

This emphasis, so deeply marked in the New Testament, was dominant in the early generations of the expanding Church. Jesus bade his disciples, "As ye go, preach." His disciples of the succeeding century, as they went, preached. In the first two centuries the spoken word was the chief agency, not only of evangelization, but also of edification, building converts up in the faith and the practice of it. It was not the only agency. There was the fellowship. There were the beginnings of forms of worship, the practice of sacrificial sharing, the instruction of converts. But preaching was the chief reliance.

The very character of the first church buildings is an evidence of this emphasis. They were designed for preaching. Hence, they did not follow the model of the Jewish Temple, which was split up into separate courts, or of pagan temples such as the Pantheon, into whose construction the need for preaching did not enter, but followed the model of the basilica, or court of justice, emphatically a place designed for speech. For this reason early Christian churches were called basilicas. The building was oblong in shape, with a raised platform at one end. These buildings were used for preaching, passing in time from the simple exhortations of the postapostolic years to the more polished and artistic sermons preached to thousand of hearers in the large basilicas such as those of Ambrose at Milan and St. Sophia at Constantinople. The outstanding names are those of great preachers: Origen, Basil, and Chrysostom in the East; Jerome, Ambrose, and Augustine in the West. This early era of preaching stands in glaring contrast with the darkness that descended over the Church in later

179

centuries, when preaching lost its place, particularly, in the almost complete black-out of preaching, beginning roughly about A.D. 600 and continuing, with local exceptions, until the first streaks of the daybreak of the Reformation. In its emphasis upon preaching, then, Protestantism made one of its great recoveries of early Christianity.

The great renewals of Christianity, its recurring springtimes, which make the most stirring and heartening chapters of history, have been accompanied, often started, by preaching. Men and nations and epochs have been transformed by the renewing of their minds through preaching. In depicting some of these great renewals through the grace of God and through the means of grace in preaching Silvester Horne, in his *Romance of Preaching,* has made a permanent as well as a glowing contribution to the history of preaching as a force.

The chart of the waxing and waning of preaching is parallel to another feature of Church history—that of the recoveries of Jesus in thought and life of the Church. Again and again through the centuries the central figure of Christianity has become clouded over and obscured. Such clouds veiled the face and personality of Jesus in the dark night of the Church from A.D. 600 on for six hundred years and in the eighteenth-century rationalism that swept into the pulpits like a dense London fog. As the ecclesiastical frame became more massive and ornate, the face of Jesus was lost. Then, again and again, the cloud lifted. Jesus was recovered. The light of the glory of God shown in the face of Jesus Christ.

So it has been with preaching. In the Reformation, in the Puritan movement in England, in the early days of Pietism in Germany, in the Evangelical Revival, in all great hours of recovery and renewal, preaching has been a creating power. There has been change and variety in the interpretation of the gospel and the type of preaching; but He who is the same yesterday, today, and forever has been presented as "the eternal contemporary" of each new epoch. In the beginning was the word. In every new beginning of Christianity there has been and will be an enthralled witness to the word.

The quickening contribution of the Protestant emphasis upon the sermon cannot be measured without some strong realization of the background against which it was set. The preaching of the gospel had disappeared in the Eastern church even more than in Latin Christianity. Torpor in the West and ossification in the East prevailed. The scriptural content of the sermon faded, and in its place there came, in the vivid phrasing of John Ker, "all the blind creeping things that spring up when life goes and corruption comes." Hard dogmas took on more and more the quality of lifeless, brittle granite. Polemics replaced evangelism. The Scripture was allegorized into ether. The minute details of ecclesiasticism often crowded out the words of eternal life. The Sermon on the Mount gave way to puzzles such as Gregory the Great proposed in a sermon: "What is the significance of the

153 fishes which Peter caught?"—surely a theme on which a man—even a Pope—could toil all night and take nothing.

Such a picture is admittedly incomplete and leaves out the gracious exceptions such as the preaching friars of the Franciscan and Dominican orders in the early days before the rigor mortis of monasticism set in; before, as in the case of the Dominicans, persecution of the Waldenses became a first concern and paved the way for the Inquisition. But the main outlines of the picture are correct. Against its somber background gleams the shining light of Protestantism, giving to preaching a role and a power it had not had since the earliest Christian generations.

This backward historical glance, all too superficial and brief, deepens and supports the conviction of the permanent, indispensable place of preaching at the center of a vital Christianity. If, as has been said, and I think truly, "Without prayer, God becomes a ghost," then without preaching the Church becomes a mausoleum. To quote John Ker once more, a major lesson of the Christian history is that "the church that cannot and will not preach, and preach well, will go down." If, on reading this, one asks, "How about the Roman Catholic Church?" one answer is that the strength of Catholicism as a vital religious force has owed much to preaching. It can also be said, with historical truth, that one of the great effects of the Reformation was the revival of preaching within the Roman Church. The classic age of French preaching, for instance—that of Bousset and Fénelon—owes far more to Luther and the Reformation than is usually realized or acknowledged.

The contemporary scene adds its tragic underlining to the overwhelming importance of affirmative Christian preaching today. There is intense need for the Church to be newly seized with a sense of the indispensable place of preaching, that it may exorcise the evil spirit of apology, which so easily besets us and dims the native resolution of both pulpit and pew. So much in our years of world convulsion conspires to induce an inferiority complex in the preacher. In a day when great impersonal forces are driving down the main avenues of life, it is not surprising that many in the Church should be oppressed by a feeling of being off on a side street, speaking in a muffled voice that cannot be heard above the din of engines and clashing of armor. Our day needs greatly a continuance and intensification of the Protestant emphasis upon preaching. We need the sense of being trustees of the only word of salvation in a world increasingly damned by its sin. The relationship of that word to our world was strikingly drawn in blazing letters more than a hundred years ago by a German Jew who saw with a penetrating eye—Heinrich Heine. He wrote in 1834, "Should that subduing talisman the cross ever break, then the old stone gods will rise from the long-forgotten ruins and rub the dust of a thousand years from their eyes, and Thor, leaping to life with his giant hammer, will crush the Gothic cathedrals." Has ever a prophecy been more literally and tragically fulfilled? The cross did break for multitudes in Europe, and Thor crushed the Gothic cathedrals. That sentence of Heine's states the case for the priority of preaching. It affirms that the proclaimer of "the talisman of the cross" is not marooned on a side road but is in the very center of the world's conflict and traffic.

When we consider the place that preaching, broadly defined, occupies in our world today, we must feel that this would be a strange time to relax the historic emphasis upon preaching which we have received through the Protestant tradition. Every great movement in history has been prepared for and partly, at least, carried through, by preaching—the beginnings of the Christian Church, the Crusades, the abolition of slavery, the Reformation and Evangelical Revival, the labor movement, communism, and German nazism—not, surely, always Christian preaching, but preaching as a powerful instrument. The present day also furnishes a powerful persuasion of the importance of preaching. For years we have been living in a world noisy with sermons. They blare through the radio, shriek through the headlines, are dropped by the ton over cities. They go, often, under the head of "psychological warfare"; but they are preaching just the same—arguments, persuasion, evangelistic appeals.

This is not the place for any detailed discussion of the content of Christian preaching, least of all for any tables of the law on the subject to be brought down from Sinai by the present writer. But two affirmations can and must be made to give proper definition to that word of large acreage: "preaching."

Preaching, if it is to have adequate depth and height and breadth, must be theological preaching—that is, with a definite core of Christian revelation. If preaching is not basically theological, if it is not the proclamation of a God who has acted in Christ but is merely an anthology of moral maxims, it soon comes to resemble the description of Matthew Arnold: a "mournful evangelist who had somehow contrived to mislay his gospel." Again, the gospel through the mouth and life of the preacher must be firmly set in the stream of modern life. It must not be allowed to be suspended, like Mohammed's coffin, between heaven and earth, without really touching either. It must be a Jacob's ladder, on which there is a two-way traffic, the ascent of the soul to God and the coming down of God's revelation in Christ to close relation to all the needs of men, individual, social, economic, and political. Thus, it may truly fulfill the purpose of Jesus, in our complex world, as he announced it at the beginning of his preaching, "The Spirit of the Lord is upon me, because he anointed me to preach good tidings to the poor; he hath sent me to proclaim release to the captives, and recovering of sight to the blind, to set at liberty them that are bruised, to proclaim the acceptable year of the Lord."

THE PERILS OF OVEREMPHASIS

Happy would we be if the whole discussion could be dropped here. But, as was suggested at the beginning, the liability side of the Protestant emphasis on preaching must also be considered. We forget it only at our peril. The history of the Protestant churches is strewn with many warnings against an overemphasis or a distorted emphasis upon preaching and placing a too-exclusive reliance upon preaching as the only agency in extending the kingdom of God.

Quite often Protestant churches and sects have been guilty of a gross violation of the second commandment in making an idol of the sermon. The sermon became a graven image, sometimes almost a minor god. Jesus said, "The sabbath was made for man." Often the practice of the churches has seemed to be based on the belief that man was made for the sermon. There it was, high and lifted up, and its train filled the temple. Its symbol was the hour glass on the pulpit, relentlessly turned over, often (as we know from contemporary records) to the inward groaning of the persons in the pews. When the sermon becomes an end in itself, it makes void the word of God by a tradition.

This undue elevation of the sermon as an end in itself has frequently prevented it from becoming a means of bringing Christ to people. The words of Jesus: "Whosoever will be great among you, let him be your minister" apply to the sermon as well as to the preacher. It is truly great only as it stoops down, puts aside the rhetorical sins that do so easily beset it, and serves men at a particular point of need. Take two instances—one from the seventeenth century in England and one from the nineteenth century, where preaching was remote from feeding the hungry sheep. Logan Pearsall Smith thus describes the "old divines" who flourished in the seventeenth century—the age of Hooker, Andrewes, South, Tillotson:

To the secular-minded the old divines, whose severe brows and square faces meet our eyes when we open their great folios, seem, with their imposed dogmas, their heavy and obsolete methods of exposition and controversy, almost as if they belonged to some remote geological era of human thought. We are reminded of Taine's image of them as giant saurians, slowly winding their scaly backs through the primeval slime and meeting each other, armed with syllogisms and bristling with texts, in theological battle to tear the flesh from one another's flanks with their great talons.

A long, long way from "Come unto me, all ye that labor and are heavy laden"! And just as far away from another aspect of Jesus: "Woe unto you . . . for ye devour widows' houses"!

From the nineteenth century listen to Professor John A. Rice, in his book *I Came Out of the Eighteenth Century,* describing the preaching of his uncle, a Methodist bishop:

To listen to him was like quietly getting drunk. He led his hearers by easy stages into an unreal world of effortless peace, dragging them gradually into unconsciousness by the melody that was himself. They went home to eat their Sunday dinners in dazed silence and remained befuddled until Monday morning, when they woke up and went about their business.[1]

The greatest hazard of overemphasis upon the sermon, however, has been pointed out in the words of Gaius Glen Atkins:

Preaching is having a hard time just now because too heavy a burden has been put upon it in our evangelical Protestantism. Preaching was never meant to carry out the program of an institutional church. It was never meant to do the whole work of making religion real.

Those words serve two purposes. They indicate some great changes that have come in the Protestant estimate of the sermon, and they point out fruitful lines of advance.

Many changes in a generation or more have been, over a wide area in the Church, in the direction of putting preaching into a co-operating place among other instruments and forces for furthering the kingdom. A fresh and deepened emphasis upon worship is one of the great recoveries of our time. Preaching is now set, not so much on a pedestal by itself, but as a part of worship. "The eye cannot say to the hand, I have no need of thee." Nor shall the sermon say to other elements of worship, I have no need of thee. The sermon has great need of worship, not as a "preliminary," of which the sermon makes a condescending and merely instrumental use to enhance its singular glory, but as a total experience, of which the sermon is a part.

The sermon is increasingly set in a network of Christian education and nurture. That is an ally, a coworker, of literally immeasurable worth. Here, again, preaching must not, cannot, be a sole agency of Christian teaching; it is a vital part of a wide and varied activity of education.

Another aid to preaching has been the increasing awareness to the social roots and causes of evil. This has been partly a real fruit of preaching; it is a continuous help in keeping preaching relevant to the basic issues of human welfare.

With this new vision of the place of preaching in relationship to the total impact of the gospel on the life of the Church, community, nation, and world, we may well respond with a deepened faith to the old words of commission: "As ye go, preach." As ye go into a devastated world, preach with a new conviction that the word must be proclaimed that there is no other foundation that can be laid for a livable world than that which is laid in Christ Jesus.

---

[1] By permission of Harper Brothers, publishers.

THE MYSTICAL SPIRIT

William Ernest Hocking

There was a time when it took courage to be a Protestant. And courage is poor business unless there is a groundwork of conviction to start from. The moral core of Protestantism is not any love of dissent for its own sake but a regretful sense of necessity because of what one surely sees to be true. We cannot understand the beginnings of Protestantism nor, indeed, the major part of its history unless we can discern the sources of the assurance that undergirded its tragic choice: "Here I stand. I can do no other; God help me!"

Now, assurance of a sort was abundant in the European world at the birth of the modern era. What *is* this modern era except a glorious burst of self-confidence, in which man notifies the powers above that he now proposes to take charge of his own destiny by the aid of science and has very little need for their further attention? This feeling has lasted well over three centuries and, after falling into shallows, is now going out in a pall of tragedy.

But the confidence of humanism and of the scientific spirit is not the confidence on which Protestantism has based its position.

And, indeed, so far as knowledge is concerned, self-confidence and self-management are only half the story of the modern spirit. It is astonishing how soon that rational self-assurance which worked out the principles of scientific method and summoned all theology to justify itself before a man-built theory of the cosmos began to share the field with symptoms of self-doubt. The modern era might as fairly be called an era of *distrust of reason*. For it created a new science—the science of knowledge, in which reason is occupied with pointing out the limits of reason. And it bred at least two new brands of skepticism—that of Hume, based on this theory of knowledge; and that of scientific relativity, based on psychology. John Locke, the ancestor of both of them, stands well toward the beginning of this great era.

And what is still more striking is the fact that the great critics of reason—Locke and Kant—as well as the great skeptics, spring rather from the Protestant than from the Catholic vein of modernity. How can it be that Protestantism, which could neither begin nor continue to exist without certitude, could even indirectly yield such fruits as these?

185

Protestantism's Certitude Is Moral and Mystical

The answer to this riddle has to be found in the fact that the certitude on which Protestantism builds is *not primarily rational but moral and mystical* and, at bottom, more mystical than moral. Let me briefly illustrate this point:

During the last century Protestantism, making valiant efforts to build for itself a positive theological foundation, has made much use of the distinction between affirmations of thought on one side and affirmations of our moral nature on the other. Religious faith was considered to be not an intellectual hypothesis but a decision, a launch of the will, an act of loyalty. Older writers had made much use of the Catholic Pascal's remark that "the heart has its reasons which the mind will never know." But the nineteenth century found greater help in Kant's famous distinction between theoretical and practical reason. It was said of him that he had "robbed reason to pay back to faith"—a statement that is roughly true if you are not very particular what you say. Kant, whose whole range of thought was deeply influenced by the Protestant Pietism in which his father's family was steeped, held that speculative reason could accomplish nothing in getting at the ultimate realities of the world —a fact that is perhaps fortunate if "dealing with reality instead of appearance" is something in which every man has a vital concern. There would be something wrong with a world in which finding God, if there is a God, would be reserved for men of high speculative talent. Our direct access to reality, Kant taught, is by way of our sense of duty, which is present in everyone. The most important truth is accessible on the most completely democratic terms. But in what sense does duty show us reality?

Schopenhauer had a simple answer to the effect that the will is the realest thing about us, as about all other living things, the intellect being but a servant of the will. When we "think," we are occupied with surfaces and symbols; when we act, we heave against the world, and we have to be as real as the world is. The will is therefore the place "where appearance and reality coincide"—a phrase of masterly penetration.

But Kant would not have endorsed without caveat this view of his ardent disciple. I think he would have foreseen the dangers both to theology in making thought a mere servant of a will power that must then be literally irrational, to religion in making faith purely a pragmatic choice or wager, and to civilization itself in making "I will" the ultimate ruler of the world. What Kant taught was that we are real, not because and when we "will" (that is, resolve, decide, act), but only because and when we will *according to duty*.

For when conscience speaks, and we acknowledge its authority, we are getting outside the will of our "natural man," which it is our business to master. The self of psychology, the stream of consciousness, is no more real than the stream of sensations that make up the apparent world of physical things. Both one and the other are "phenomena" and nothing more. But the whole issue of life is to keep these appearances in their place. Conscience is the awareness of our calling, or vocation, to master "nature" in ourselves; and to do this we must step over the boundary line from appearance to reality. It is only the man aware of duty who knows the direction in which reality lies. And, since duty is the place where the veil of appearance breaks, whatever is implied in duty must itself be real, including the being of God.

This searching and cautious analysis comes very close to the central vein of Protestant religious experience. Protestantism has not alone insisted that the fruits of religion are visible in the moral aspects of living and that the soundness of religion is to be tested that way, but also that there are conditions for perceiving religious truth which are primarily moral: "If any man willeth . . . he shall know." It is not surprising that a line of distinguished thinkers have seen first the philosophy of religion and then Protestant theology through this insight: Lotze, Ritschl, William James, and, to some extent, Josiah Royce. But I doubt whether this is the deepest source of Protestant certitude, nor do I think we shall find it until we realize how nearly Kant was a mystic; yet how clearly he misses what the mystic has given to the Protestant certitude!

The term "mysticism" has come to mean two distinct things in the Occident—a theory of reality and a doctrine regarding the way in which the human individual may gain union with reality. In the first sense mysticism is the theory that there is one all-inclusive real being, but that this being can have no further description. It is "ineffable" in the sense that all descriptives falsify its nature, even those which we take to be laudatory—such as "good," "holy," "omniscient," "Spirit," "Creator," "loving," "personal," "impersonal," "finite," "Infinite." The falsification involved in these epithets arises from what they deny, since every descriptive asserted carries with it the denial of its opposite. Thus, that which is "good," as we conceive goodness, cannot be not-good in the same sense; whereas the One cannot be assigned a quality, distinct from its being, to which our human distinction of good and not-good applies.

If the theoretical mystic were simply one who makes a thoroughgoing principle of being wary of the traps set by our "concepts," he would have a great deal of company in modern times. Bergson would join him on that ground, assigning all conceptual knowledge to the intellect, which has to be content with aspects of things, while the fullrounded truth, at least regarding everything that has life and "inwardness," can be had only through intuition, which can "coincide" with that inwardness. He would be joined also by a great group of thinkers and nonthinkers who, on various grounds, simply doubt that our minds were given us to know metaphysical reality at all. Dewey and James would unite here with Kant and Spencer and many of the "average man," for whom thought is a kind of adjustment, and truth a matter of getting a working hypothesis regarding the environment with which we actually deal—ergo, essentially "relative." These would agree with "logical positivism," and all with the mystic, that the question whether reality is "mental" or "nonmental" is "nonsense," because there is no way to decide between them. The real eludes our judgments about its nature; but this is another way of saying that it makes no difference to us what it is (since all significant differences can be embodied in concepts), and that we may as well ignore it entirely.

But the mystic is a better logician than all these. He has, in fact, made a fundamental logical discovery—that there is an important middle course between yes and no. If you ask the mystic whether there is a God, yes or no, he ought not to answer without knowing what you mean by "God"; at which point he should say, "No, not that God." He is not a theist. On the other hand, he is not an atheist; for he believes "that God is." He stoutly affirms "that" God exists while denying that he knows "what" God is. He throws himself open to the rebuke that if you have no idea *what* God is, your affirmation *that* he is becomes wholly meaningless; or, in other words, if you mean anything at all when you say, "God is," you must have some notion of God. The mystic replies that his affirmation is of the utmost significance, for (1) it saves him from despair regarding the reality of the world and, therefore, the seriousness of life; and (2) it keeps him in active search for that grasp of God's nature which no concept can contain. There must be, he maintains, some other way of apprehending God than by concepts.

The mystic has the better of the argument, and his final answer reminds us strongly of Kant's proposal that reason in metaphysics should be used to "regulate," not to "construct." It directs our thinking processes without offering us solutions. It commands activity without promising any goal. But it is at this point that *the theoretical mystic ought to turn into the practical mystic*, who has a way of gaining union with God other than by concepts. Indeed, it is only in the Occident that these two sides of mysticism fall apart. In the Orient speculative mysticism as we find it in the Vedanta, Taoism, and Mahayana Buddhism of the Nagarjuni school, are all ways of salvation. The theory is a mere auxiliary, explaining why the devotee carries on his peculiar way of finding God.

Now, practical mysticism continues to exist only because men in considerable numbers have come to believe that there is a mode of experience which can properly be called "an experience of God" or "an experience of union with God," and that this mode of experience is (1) of the utmost practical importance and (2) attainable by following the right discipline. Heroic leaders have found "the Way." Their instructions may guide their followers to a similar success. Here the mystic falls into war with the entire recent trend of modernity, since the trend of our time, looking at the mystic's person and his accomplishments (with special emphasis upon the oddity of the specimens chosen as typical), is to judge (1) that, far from being important, the mystic's achievement only makes him queer, subjective, and out of gear; and (2) that he has no way of distinguishing his "experience" from various types of autosuggestive exhilaration.

It is not my purpose to enter into this debate. The debate itself is a chapter little creditable to modern scholarship, whether in philosophy, theology, or science. For if there is any spectacle less edifying than that of the blind leading the blind, it is that of the blind fighting the blind. Those who disparage the mystic are in the position of denying something solely on the ground that they do not see it; which is not evidence in any court, whether of law or of science. The denial proves nothing but their own incapacity to see; which point might be conceded without any contest. The mystics, on the other hand, often treat their opponents with a certain arrogance as if to say that their mere assertion is itself a proof, whereas it can be nothing more than an invitation to test the matter by following the same path. Historically speaking, the mystics have not been free from the vanity of separatism. They have been inclined to turn the assertion "I have found a way" into the assertion "I alone have found a way, and it is the only way," and have called for exclusive following on the ground of this enlightenment or discovery or revelation. The position of mankind toward the whole wonderful history of mysticism would be vastly improved if attention were given to the extent to which the reports of the great mystics corroborate one another and indicate a common nature in the paths proposed; and if it were further shown how deeply the more extraordinary varieties of mystical experience are akin to very normal and, indeed, inescapable experiences of men everywhere.

In my judgment mysticism is strongest where it is most universal, and I believe that it is precisely here that it has had its great contribution to make to Protestantism.

The characteristic assertion of mysticism in all its forms is that there is a vitally important and nonconceptual experience of God available to men who meet its conditions. The simplest and most usual expression of this thesis is that all men at all times are directly dealing with God, whether they know it or not. They must breathe air whether or not they know it to be air; they must eat food whether or not they know that it feeds them; if they move, they must thrust against something that resists; if they have weight, they must be in a gravitational field; if they achieve effects, they must enter the network of causes. And if any of these appearances is a mere sign of some deeper reality (as, doubtless, they all are), then through those signs we are in actual traffic with that more real, just as through language we move the mind of our neighbor; and whatever is more real is embedded in what is Most Real so that the whole basis and response of their living is the Real. The mystic simply denies that this battle is with appearances—an absurdity equivalent to saying that because one's adversary is clothed, one fights *the clothes* of his adversary. The principle of the mystical consciousness is the *transparency of intermediaries*. Vital awareness deals with what intermediaries *represent*. And if the Real is God, it is with God that we have to do from moment to moment of daily living. For each action the world concentrates itself into a point of resistance and support; and that point is a Thou, not an It.

Kant missed this, because for him the intermediaries were not transparent. There they stood—the "phenomena"—and the mind of man could not peer behind them. Hence, for Kant, the best that man can do is to have an *immediate awareness of duty,* from which he may infer the existence of God. The mystic reverses the order. Man has (or can have) an *immediate awareness of God*, from which fact he perceives that he is under obligation and must live his life in careful listening to the voice of duty.

In my own view it is the mystic who is right, not Kant; and it is the mystic who speaks for the position of Protestantism and who represents the permanent inner strength of that movement. Let me develop this point in several special aspects of Protestant experience:

ON MYSTICISM AND AUTHORITY

The following statements are incompatible with one another, and all of them have been made by mystics of different types:

Man is always aware of God.

Man must struggle to become aware of God.

Man is neither aware of God by nature, nor can he win this awareness by his own efforts; but God must, by his own act, make himself known to man—the essential act of grace.

The tradition of mysticism, however, has shown itself capable of uniting these three positions, which have done so much to rend Christian bodies asunder. For (to speak of the second and third) the mystic has not infrequently asserted, on the basis of his own experience, that there comes a stage of effort in which effort must be set aside in favor of a purely receptive attitude. His effort has been chiefly (as the "negative path" suggests) to put aside the obstacles in his own nature to receiving that vision. He recognizes the danger that his "trying" may be a trying toward some preconceived goal and therefore impede his perception of the true goal, whose character is such that it cannot have been preconceived. He must render himself passive and wait in hope that God will vouchsafe to reveal himself.

It is the first assertion that appears to set itself most squarely against the other two. For if God is always present, it becomes foolish to make a problem of finding him. But this very sensible proposal forgets two things: first, that it is remarkably easy to overlook what is always present, just because it is an invariable element of experience: there is no absurdity—on the contrary, it is one of the commonest events—that we discover what it is that we have been presupposing or unconsciously relying on; secondly, that if the God found were different from the power that always surrounds and sustains our being (and in this sense is always "there") it would not be God that was found. In this respect there is an important truth in that somewhat misleading paradox of Pascal's: "Thou couldst not seek me, hadst thou not already found me." It is a question often put to the mystic by his psychological critics: "How do you know that it is God whom you experience?"; to which the apposite answer is simply that the object now so impressively discerned is *the same object* as that which he has always known in a far less adequate manner.

Thus, a fully understood mysticism may hold together what the accidents of Church history in the fifteenth and sixteenth centuries put asunder. The historic Church took the view that the life of God must be brought to individual men through the channels of revelation and the spiritual body of the Church. The Protestant view was that the life of God is already in the souls of men, and that this must be their guide in recognizing any outer authority.

It is sometimes held that mysticism is hostile to any authority whatever, but this is clearly not the case. As we have already seen, those mystics who announce their discoveries of "the Way" become authoritative to their followers. But, apart from this, the mystic, in claiming his own personal and original God-awareness, knows that this is only the beginning of his religious life. As his private religion it is a solitary religion. It has its own need of steadying, corroboration, interpretation, development. This he must find in the equally original experiences of other minds and in whatever has become for them the guide of the community. It is the Protestant position, certainly, not that authority is unnecessary, but that every man, since he has, by faith, his own access to the Highest, knows how to distinguish true authority from falsely claimed authority and knows how to use the authority he recognizes as valid. He has, for example, that in himself by which the Bible can be recognized as God's word and can be so read that God speaks personally to him through its language. In this sense it may be argued that the Protestant has *more use* for authority than anyone else.

But there is another sense in which the mystic is likely to be a thorn in the side of all existing authorities and so to be a person under suspicion.

The mystic experience of God's presence is either important to the mystic or it is fraudulent. It cannot be regarded by him as a commonplace. In principle it is *his* revelation and has the character of all revelation—that it authorizes him to speak, and with assurance. Perhaps, through him, God is attempting to open a new chapter of religious insight, as many in our time have thought—Mrs. Eddy, Joseph Smith, the prophets of Bahaism, the founders of new sects of Shinto, enthusiastic groups of all sorts from the peasants with whom Luther dealt so severely to Jehovah's Witnesses in our own day. The founder of Islam was himself a mystic of this type, wholly reverent toward earlier authorities except at the point where they declared the Book of Revelation closed. Bidden by the angel, he added to that book, revised its earlier statements, and then, not learning from his own experience the danger of premature closure, sealed the amended book, not with seven seals, but with seventy; in spite of which brave souls, equally respectful of their predecessors, continue to reopen and revise.

From the standpoint of the custodians of a finished revelation, therefore, the mystic is never a safe companion until he is dead. Not only may he add to the received truth, but he is bound to test the particular doctrines of earlier authority by his own vision of truth. This is that rill of "private judgment" which brings him into most frequent clash with the constituted religious channels and leads to division after division within Protestantism itself.

ORIGINALITY AND PRIVATE JUDGMENT

I shall not resolve the dilemma created by these corollaries of the mystic's certitude by trying to suppress any one of the three values involved—the actuality of certitude, the possibility of new religious insight, the importance of a stable corpus of faith.

As to certitude it stands at the opposite pole from that footless relativity—the moral disease of contemporary intellectual self-criticism, which neither has for itself nor allows others to have a point of solid ground on which to set their feet. The mystic is not in error in being certain; he may easily be in error in being certain of too much. When he is, the cure would lie in a firmer application of the mystic principle itself—the element of finality in all insight lies in the "that" rather than in the "what." It will lie, further, in a recognition by the mystic that his insight, while not achievable by pure reason, is not immune from criticism by the canons of reason. The convictions of its mystics are too precious for the race to lose even by the rational insistence that true insights must agree. But it belongs to the Protestant principle itself that the access to God's truth is democratic so that the long, slow suffrages of the race are pertinent to the ultimate judgment as to what is and what is not a truly interpreted word of God.

As to novelty in revelation this possibility is contained in the very center of Christian tradition. Jesus expressly taught that his teaching was necessarily unfinished, and that the process of leading his followers "into all truth" was a further work of God, which the Church, in view of the uniqueness of that teaching among organized religions, quite justly expressed in a symbol of the highest emphasis: they ascribed it to a third "person" of the Trinity. It is thus a fundamental disloyalty to the Christian tradition to regard that tradition as closed against growth.

We should not be too much disturbed if the implied "liberty of prophesying" does, in the course of history, lead to an amount of aberrant religious experimentation. We have every reason, however, to co-operate with the application of such criteria for distinguishing the true prophet, as the civil order and the common sense of mankind by degrees develop. There is no way to avoid the clash of mystic with mystic; neither, on the other hand, is there any way in which the bearer of a genuinely new insight can avoid the fate of the prophets even in a world where "freedom of speech" is promoted by the heirs of a Protestant disposition to give every new speaker the benefit of the doubt. Truth getting and truth spreading remain an adventure whose risks and prizes and penalties can never be reduced to the tame measure of "received standards."

But we have much to gain by distinguishing *originality* in religion from *deviation*. Christianity may be defined as the religion that insists upon the originality of the religious experience of each believer. Jesus was original in the sense that he took tradition for what it meant to him. He did not reject it; he relived it. He wanted no followers who were imitators. Whatever truth he had to give them had to be born in them anew. To be a follower of an original soul is to be original. This does not necessarily imply deviation; it implies verification from one's own center of life. Originality implies the *risk* of deviation in order that corroboration, when it comes, shall be the endorsement of an independent spirit. The Protestant, as mystic, stands for this originality, which is the charter of all true liberty; he has no stake in deviation per se.

When this is understood, Protestantism will be ready not alone to admit but also to assert our third value—the importance of a stable corpus of faith. Growth cannot be stopped until there are no more "accents of the Holy Ghost" for a heedless world to treasure; but growth can be *within* a body of truth as well as by addition or correction. Science may glory in the rapidity with which it discards old conceptions and frames new ones. Its "Principia" lose their pertinence and require to be rewritten. But religion's whole meaning to mankind depends on a contrast with this sort of supersession: Unless there is a truth that is changeless, religion becomes a branch of anthropology, chiefly of historical interest. So, too, the whole point of mysticism is that the individual mind, wherever it is in space or time, may have its own tryst with the eternal. While the vanity of man takes a pride in novelty and invention, the good faith of the mystic—and his true anchor—lies in his testimony to the underlying unanimity of the mystics. Through their freedom they can best confirm the stability of a central corpus of religious truth.

ORGANIZATION AND PERSONAL RELIGION

Where there is a consensus of faith in a body of believers who are also mystics—in the sense that their whole religious experience is contained within the frame of their own direct awareness of God as a constant presence—there can be a corporate mysticism as well as a private mystical experience. There are a few experiences in life in which a new perception is not "mine" alone but "ours," in which personal separateness is not destroyed but somehow outpassed. Augustine's memorable account, in his *Confessions,* of one such experience comes to mind. This is the purpose of *ritual,* which aims to conserve moments of common feeling and elevation within an existing community of many members and to reinstate them.

But the very ambition of ritual (usually set in opposition to the mystical element of religion) is so great and so difficult of realization that one may fairly say that it requires for its success a parallel development of private mysticism. It is for this reason that highly organized and highly ritualistic churches give rise from time to time, as if by reaction, to movements emphasizing "personal religion." It is for this reason, too, that the nonconformist branches of Protestantism, especially in England, including Independents, Puritans, and Quakers, have been most pronouncedly mystical in their beliefs and practices. The older Oxford Movement and the recent Group Movement have at least one thing in common besides the name—an attempt to reanimate the fundamental springs of religion in personal relationship to God.

If I were asked what qualities these mystical movements have lent to Protestantism as a whole, I should answer, seriousness, sincerity, dignity. The corporate life of the Church, not intentionally but by its very majesty, lifts something away from the individual feeling of responsibility. The mystic recalls himself to the thought:

> A charge to keep I have,
> A God to glorify,
> A never-dying soul to save
> And fit it for the sky.

There is a recovery of *seriousness*—that is, of the aloneness of destiny and of the mystery of individual calling, which made so much of the "character" of our American ancestry. Then, there is *sincerity,* which is closely allied: sincerity in the sense of an unwillingness to use general terms and ideals without a close inquiry to what extent I am carrying these out in my personal conduct. It is the disposition to bring my ethical code into direct relation with my religious experience. And there is *dignity,* which results from resuming, by the individual, of that role which ritual allows to become specialized— that of the priesthood. In Christianity the goal is that every man shall be the minister to all, and every man the potential priest to all. But

194

man attains his dignity only as he actually fulfills the function of priesthood, first in his own family and then for groups in which he may speak the reuniting word. This function has become difficult for the modern man and, I regret to say, for the modern Protestant as well as for others. But here Protestantism is false to its own deepest inheritance. It is its special mission to restore to our shallow lives the great qualities of seriousness, sincerity, dignity. And to do this it must renew its hold upon its birthright in the mystical spirit of the indivdual.

ETHICS

Francis J. McConnell

At first glance such a title as this may seem strange. The question at once arises as to what essential difference there can be between Protestant ethics and the ethics of the church from which Protestantism broke away at the Reformation. We may well ask whether Christian ethics is not Christian ethics wherever and whenever its problems arise.

On a little closer observation, however, differences between the two ethical systems become visible. In any ethical theory the question soon emerges as to the seat of authority, and the Roman Catholic Church always has claimed for itself the final authority in ethical concerns. On the other hand, students of Church history have repeatedly called attention to what they call the logic of Protestantism. They have insisted that as soon as any groups have broken from the parent church, they have yielded to a tendency that so puts the stress upon the individual conscience that there is no stopping short of an individualism that has little place for any religious authority that takes the form of organization.

It must be admitted that my statement here is an oversimplification. While the Roman Catholic Church insists upon its authority in ethical questions without any willingness to compromise whatever, as a matter of fact that Church does make ethical adjustments. The Romanist will have it that in the fields in which his church has succeeded, it has done so because of its insistence upon divine authority. So far as observation of church activities from the outside goes, we are warranted in believing that, no matter how large the claim for the divinity of the church may be, its practical procedure is one of extraordinary response to human demands. Admitting, to whatever extent we may wish, the divineness of the Roman Church, we have to recognize that its power is largely in the humanness of all its approaches to human society. No matter how complete the absoluteness of the church, its power lies in its realization of the relative nature of scores upon scores of ethical problems.

Penitence and Confession

To be sure, no one from the outside can speak with any positiveness upon what happens in Roman Catholic confession. Protestants have assumed that the Roman Catholic confessional is a realm in which the priest counsels moral delinquents or wrongdoers with profound psychological insight and understanding. Most priests, however, may protest that this is not at all the secret of the consolation found in the place and time of confession. The penitent believes that the priest is speaking as the actual agent of God and that when the priest pronounces forgiveness and prescribes the method of penance, the case is closed. This is probably the most profound psychological fact about the confessional. There is no need of the penitent's thinking of reopening the case. The priest considers himself as the spokesman of God. who is the source of all authority. The relief to the penitent comes from the official assurance that God has forgiven his fault.

On the other hand, the Protestant, confessing in his prayers to God or even to a discerning counselor, is never sure that the case is closed. The Protestant conscience, assuming it to be sensitive at all, is prone to review its own decision sometimes to the point of becoming morbid. In some cases a wise counselor brings relief to a penitent by showing that his wrongdoing may be partly the outcome of the working of an impersonal psychological law and is not to be taken as a divine voice intended directly and specifically as a rebuke for him. On the other hand, the counselor may soon show the confessor that his wrongdoing runs down into the deep centers and calls for a penitence that must virtually transform the entire life. We may claim a measure of truth for the statement that the Protestant whose religious life is serious at all is likely to take more responsibly the penitence for transgressions and adjustment of them than does the adherent of the Roman Church. The emphasis in the old faith may be more upon the external and artificial than in Protestantism. Here, again, I am in danger of oversimplifying. I am talking in general terms, but what I say is based upon some observation of the difference in moral opinion and attitude between the adherents of these different types of religious practice.

Almost all of us who are observers of various forms of religious activity and practice are quite convinced that the Roman Catholic fold has for one of its powerful appeals the sense of security which it grants its adherents. It appeals to and administers to the multitudes of believers who want to have problems settled for them. I am not now thinking only of ethics. This is manifestly more evident in the field of theology than in that of ethics. When the head of the church utters a judgment on a theological problem, that judgment settles the matter. Even in scientific pronouncements the head of the church is respected and heeded for his decisions as to what the believers may or may not accept. The vast advantages of this system are obvious. We live in a practical world, and somehow or other we must get on. The daily tasks have the right of way and cannot wait, so it is a genuine relief to hosts of faithful churchmen to have problems settled decisively and finally.

Returning to the moral realm, insofar as the individual conscience is concerned, the solution of one's personal secret and intimate problems by someone outside of oneself enables the penitent to get loose from the burden of a past, which may harmfully haunt his conscience by taking his mind off the duties that lie immediately before him.

Here, again, we must be careful to keep our balance. One cannot discuss the type of moral obedience which relies upon formal rules without making that obedience seem to lack a profound seriousness. So we always have to make room for necessary qualifications. At this point a good deal of offhand judgment has not been fair to the moral teachers of the Roman Church. In seeking to be guides to their people these teachers have prepared long lists of directions as to conduct under general rules. They have felt compelled to prepare exceptions to the rules. An enormous amount of intellectual energy in the history of the older faith has gone into such effort. The title we have given these attempts is "casuistry," which through the years has come to have an unfortunate suggestiveness, as if the casuist were one who spins out ingenious reasons for escaping moral obligations. In fact, such efforts have honestly aimed at the solution of moral problems which often involves making exceptions of the problems. It is difficult, of course, to make even an approach to a science of exceptions. Indeed, the exceptions themselves have often to be settled by an indefinable good sense, for which no convincing formal reason can be given.

It is interesting to note here that Richard Baxter, in the first century after the Reformation, attempted some casuistry for the believers who had broken with the Church of Rome. Among Baxter's discussions was one on the duty of landlords to tenants and others on such social themes. I believe that this is the only formal attempt by a Protestant leader to apply casuistry to moral problems of Protestants. I recall, too, that the late Bishop Gore remarked of Baxter's book that it was "entertaining," which surely could not be called high praise. Entertaining or not, however, Baxter's little book is full of sound social judgment and is itself by imitation a compliment to the Roman system, even though that system was largely the work of the Jesuit.

LINES OF MORAL PROGRESS

Moral progress can take one of three directions or, rather, must always keep in mind three points of view: First is the moral ideal. We sometimes call this the law of good will, which is absolute in that the moral man must strive always to keep the moral ideal before him in all his contacts. Wherever on earth or in heaven or anywhere else two moral agents meet, each owes the other good will—a requirement that is absolute. The second consideration is the relativity of moral judgment. This depends on circumstances of time and place and on scores of other elements, which condition the application of the absolute rule. At the risk again of oversimplifying, there are occasions in the moral life when the absolute becomes relative and when the relative becomes absolute. Circumstances may so change from one time to another or from one place to another that utterly contradicting forms of conduct may be equally consistent with the absolute law. The third factor is the expansion of the moral life to include more duties and to reach more persons. In a shorthand statement of this threefold obligation we may say that the Roman faith insists upon obedience to something like a military command, while the Protestant conception is that of the individual responsibility of the maker of moral choices.

Certain practical considerations at once come into our field of view. It is almost impossible to state the Catholic doctrine at all without overstating. If the Roman Catholic once accepts the church as his guide and shows that he sincerely intends to obey that guide, he can then do about what he pleases. This sentence would have to be subject to swarms of qualifications, but I am trying to make clear that tò those who are at least believed loyal to the church there is a flexible degree of freedom in private conduct.

Even if the transgression is quite serious, the penalty assessed is not so heavy as to hamper the spirit of the one who has transgressed and has been absolved. The situation here is somewhat the same as in some governments, which are looked upon as oppressive in their prohibitions of criticisms of the government. I am not now referring to present-day systems but am seeking to call attention to the historic fact that under some dictatorial systems a citizen who is loyal to the system has large freedom in his personal conduct. On the other hand, the Protestant seldom carries the principles of individual liberty of moral choices to its logical extreme. Among the factors that influence moral choices probably the most important is the social sentiment of the group to which one belongs. Conformity to this social sentiment, or expectation, of one's group, may stop far short of insistence upon extreme individual liberty. Probably there is here an element of social safety. We are familiar with the word: "Would God that all the Lord's people were prophets!" This is an entirely natural expression of high moral purpose, but only in the most favorable general moral conditions could any society that we have ever known flourish if all the individuals were prophets; for each individual would be likely to take his own path, to the harm of that like-mindedness which is necessary for social stability. Much can be said for Protestantism's creation of a wholesome social atmosphere, in which men conform without realizing that they are thus conforming. In sterner times the Roman Church had a most effective weapon in its claim to and use of the power of excommunication. It is interesting to note in reading the old-time histories how real the Roman leaders made the thought of hell. Hell was just around the corner as a literal, material fact. That period has almost wholly disappeared, and the compulsions of the Roman Church have become much milder and more reasonable with the passage of time. There is not much place in the Protestant system for formal compulsion. There are few expulsions from the membership of Protestant churches. Indeed, it would be today hard to get anybody to take such expulsions seriously. The social sentiment, however, which comes from the Protestant atmosphere is one of the most potent of all moral forces. It is really quite a question as to how extreme any personal individualism may be.

A New Emphasis

The ethical problem in the churches has had to meet a new emphasis within the last half century. Anyone who has paid any attention to present-day religious questions knows that for the time being the movement is somewhat away from the ethics of individual, personal conduct. It is customary to say that with the Reformation religious ethics started on this narrower movement in contrast with the teachings of the church before the Reformation. In the earlier days the church laid claim to control over what we now call the field of social ethics. The rulers of the church even told kings the conditions under which they could go to war and laid down the rules under which warfare must be carried on. The church even went into the market place and restrained the greed of dealers by the doctrine of the just price. Perhaps it was true that for centuries the church controlled the entire educational system of the various nations in which it was the official religion. With the coming of the Reformation, however, there was the beginning of a line between the more specifically religious obligations in the narrower, personal spheres and those in the larger social realms. One by one the so-called secular activities fell away from the Protestant church. By the time three centuries had passed, that line of cleavage between the sacred duties of the inner life and the secular activities of the outside world had become wide and deep. Even Luther so gave his chief attention to the individual demands of piety that he could in good conscience counsel the shooting of the laborers in the Peasants' War. When the prince of a realm who had favored Protestantism was charged with bigamy, Luther advised him to tell "a good, strong lie." This incident indicates the slighter importance in Luther's mind of a lie as over against the demands of an inner, virtually mystic piety. Of course, we all know that John Calvin put into effect what we today would call a social gospel when he went to Geneva and did so with an effectiveness that has made all such schemes since seem insignificant. On the whole, though, the general tendency has been toward the separation of which I speak. I do not mean that the believers themselves became indifferent to what we might call these outside interests. As individuals they stood for what their own consciences, as individuals, might approve; but I am thinking of corporative church action as such.

Church action as such is something different from the actions of individuals. There is a collective force about the action of the Church which lends a power lacking in the deeds of individuals. The new emphasis has put with increasing power the moral obligations of the Church to the world upon the consciences of the adherents of Christianity. There are difficulties enough in creating any moral sentiment in this direction, the chief of these being the fact that the Church, in its relations to politics and business and, indeed, toward all the outside social institutions, is not willing to take a very positive stand against what may be evil in those institutions. The Church lives in the world. It supports its agencies by resources earned in the world. The processes by which the earning is possible are in an industrial and commercial system far from completely in conformity with what would be high moral standards if such were proposed for individual moral guidance. The Roman Catholic Church has always taken such connections as inevitable and has accepted its share of the profits from the industrial system without much question. This acquiesence, however, is becoming increasingly disturbing to the Protestant conscience.

More and more the Protestant churches are becoming aware of their responsibility for doing the utmost possible to supply or to aid social agencies that will correct those conditions in our existence which do so much to prevent a really moral life. There are certain forms of emphasis today which are direct hindrances to anything like genuine moral growth. How can there be moral growth if the father of a working family does not earn enough to give his children the right amount and quality of food? How can there be any high flowering out of moral purpose unless there is a chance at the higher moral values that ought to be a part of every life? We admit that many material situations in our modern communities reduce the moral significance of individuals almost to the vanishing point. It is hardly to the credit of Christianity that, through so many centuries, it has preached the doctrine of triumph over adverse circumstances, often insisting that the blessedness of eternal life will adjust and compensate for all the hardships here. The fatal error here is in missing the fact that there are certain high values that ought to be seized here and now. I recently attended a ceremony in honor of the poetic efforts and achievement of the late Edwin Markham in behalf of the workers of the world. The theme of every speaker was some aspect of the significance of the poem "The Man with the Hoe." In much that was said the discussion stopped with the degradation that finds expression in the question "Who loosened and let down that brutal jaw?" and the reference to the degraded worker as "brother to the ox." To me the more significant point in the poem is reached in the lines:

> Slave on the wheel of labor!
> What to him are Plato and the swing of Pleiades?
> What the long reaches of the peaks of song,
> The rift of dawn, the reddening of the rose? [1]

Now, in these lines the poet has touched some of the highest values— the summit of the world's philosophy, the vision of the skies, the flights of poetry, the glories of the dawn and of the reddening of the rose. The tragedy of labor has so often been that the finer achievements of the mind of man mean nothing to him, and even the dawn and the reddening of the rose, with which he may come in daily view, mean nothing.

It is the duty of the Church to make, as I have said before, the conditions for the noble moral life. It is a waste of moral effort to have to struggle with basic hardships that block every advance away from the

---

[1] Copyright owner Virgil Markham. Reprinted by permission.

material. The worst materialism is scarcity, in which there is so little matter that the material means everything. We have much to say about the building of Christian character. Before the highest spiritual structures can be erected, the foundations have to be laid, and those foundations must be creative of co-operative social effort.

THE OPEN MIND

Ralph W. Sockman

Open-mindedness is a virtue all praise and few possess. Prejudice is a sin everyone denounces and almost no one seriously confesses. Prejudiced persons do not come crying to be saved from their bigotry. A closed mind is so cozy and comfortable to its possessor that he dislikes to be dislodged and driven out to the exposure of cold facts. And, just as the occupants of a crowded and closed room may become oblivious to the heaviness of the atmosphere which a newcomer detects at once, so those who dwell in closed minds may sit undisturbed until some fresh entrant opens the door.

The Gospels record the difficulty Jesus faced in gaining entrance into closed minds. The parable of the sower was occasioned by the hardened hearers who flocked to hear his words but refused to give a fair hearing to his truths. Afterward when the disciples asked our Lord why he spoke in parables to the multitudes, he said:

Because they seeing see not, and hearing they hear not, neither do they understand. . . . For this people's heart is waxed gross, and their ears are dull of hearing, and their eyes they have closed; lest at any time they should see with their eyes, and hear with their ears, and should understand with their hearts, and should be converted, and I should heal them.

Like our Lord we are baffled by those who come to hear us with their prejudices rather than with their prayers.

Sins of the mind are much more subtly dangerous than sins of the body. The latter, like lust or intemperance, usually leave their open marks and thereby are likely to induce a sense of shame and a spirit of repentance. But mental sins, such as pride or bigotry, beget no bodily brakes that serve to check their progress. For this reason Jesus had a harder time with them than with the flagrant vices of the outcasts and derelicts. In the presence of Jesus' purity Magdalenes grew repentant. In the atmosphere of Jesus' honesty publicans became conscience-stricken, but the hardened minds of the respectable Pharisees only grew harder. After the Master had tried vainly to pierce them with the shafts of his ridicule and to soften them with the warmth of his love, he said to them bluntly, "The publicans and the harlots go into the kingdom of God before you."

SOME COUNTERFEITS

But while the open mind is a necessary qualification for the follower of Christ, we must beware lest we be deceived by certain counterfeit attitudes that often pass current for open-mindedness. One of these is indifference. In opening the mind to the light of truth one does not need to open the windows and let out all the warmth of conviction. So far as religion is concerned, some minds are so open that, like my open-windowed room on a wintry morning, they are too cold to get up in—at least with enthusiasm. A biographer once said of Emerson that before he left the ministry, his attitude toward his message had become something like a yawn. When a minister reaches that stage of coolness, it is time for him to leave the pulpit. People will follow a fanatic whose zeal thaws out their icicled springs of emotion rather than a philosopher whose thought has become like winter sunshine—brilliant but cold. Great living can be inspired only by strong convictions. There is no tolerance worthy the name unless we care deeply about the issues involved.

We should take it as a valid rebuke when the man on the street hurls the charge against religion that its controversies generate more heat than do the discussions of scientists. That is natural. It is easier to keep cool and calm in discussing Einstein's theory of relativity than in discussing the religious heresies of one's relatives. Religious and moral questions are so intertwined with the issues of life and death that they stir our emotions. Christian open-mindedness is consonant with strong convictions, and cool indifference must not be mistaken for it.

A second attitude that must not be confused with open-mindedness is mental emptiness. Sometimes a man's conscience is clear mainly because his head is empty, and sometimes a person thinks he is broadminded because there is so little mental content to obstruct the horizon of what passes for his thinking. In *Main Street*, Sinclair Lewis said of the complacently conventional husband: "He believed in the church but seldom attended its services. He believed in Christianity but never thought about it. He was worried over Carol's lack of faith but was not sure just what it was she lacked."

Sinclair Lewis' description of Dr. Kennecott is too pertinent for us to dismiss. We Protestants pride ourselves that we are a teaching church in a degree not paralleled by our Roman Catholic brethren. Let us not boast too much about the religious knowledge possessed by our communicants. Few of the members in our churches really understand their own faith or could interpret it to others. Fewer still can distinguish what is fundamental in it from what is peripheral. Many do not even feel the need of trying to make such a distinction or, what is harder still, the need of understanding the convictions of those who follow a different way of life. Leading laymen may often counsel their socially minded pastors to "stick to the simple gospel," but they would be hard put to it if they were asked to define their terms.

204

The late Professor William Adams Brown asks why there are so many otherwise intelligent people who are strangers to their own religion. And he answers his own question thus:

I venture to suggest that it is because of a basic fault which runs through all contemporary education and is reflected in the teaching of the church— the loss of the sense of proportion. By this I mean the loss of the conviction that there are some things so important to successful living in any social order that everyone must know them, whatever else he has to leave un-learned.[1]

The empty mind is not an open mind, and the way to true tolerance is not by reducing our convictions to the lowest common denominator. Only as our own principles and beliefs are precious to us can we have the necessary respect for the convictions of others.

You naturally assume that a discussion of "Protestantism and the Open Mind" will assert the necessary link between the two. We of the Protestant faith regard ourselves as the champions of religious liberty and tolerance. And no doubt you are growing impatient for this paper to turn from the negative to the positive and devote itself to a discussion of what the open mind is rather than what it is not. But open-mindedness cannot be discussed or developed in the abstract. Virtues are not a set of attitudes that can be carried around like a plumber's kit of tools and used wherever there is a moral leak. Open-mindedness, like other virtues, is developed in life situations; and its application is conditioned by special sets of circumstances. A person may be broadly tolerant in his theology and narrowly opinionated in his politics. He may be brotherly in his ecclesiasticism and bigoted in his economics. Hence, in discussing open-mindedness we shall find it more profitable to consider specific areas.

How Can Churches Keep an Open Mind?

First of all, let us ask how Protestantism can preserve an open mind toward tradition. Protestantism began as a reformation in regard to the doctrine of salvation and as a revolution in regard to the doctrine of the Church. As a reformation of the doctrine of salvation it was a re-turn to and a renewal of what is regarded as Christianity's first princi-ples. This critical reduction to principles Luther accomplished by vic-toriously declaring that the Christian religion was given only in the word of God and in the inward experience that accords with this word.

For Luther the "word" did not mean Church doctrine, it did not even mean the Bible; it meant the message of the free grace of God in Christ which makes guilty and despairing ones happy and blessed.[2]

---

[1] *The New Order in the Church*, Abingdon-Cokesbury Press, p. 107.
[2] Harnack, A., *What Is Christianity?* p. 288.

Protestantism began by reckoning upon the gospel's being so simple, so divine, and therefore so truly human as to be most certain of being understood when it is left entirely free. It also counted on the gospel's producing essentially the same convictions and experiences in individual souls. But this was too much to expect. Whereas the Roman Catholic Church frankly admits that the Bible needs an interpreter and sets itself the responsibility of furnishing the guiding tradition, Protestants have no theoretical solution of the problem involved in the relation between the Bible and traditions. The Westminster Confession asserts that the Bible is its own interpreter: "When there is a question about the true and full sense of any Scripture (which is not manifold but one), it may be searched and known by other places which speak more clearly."

But when the Bible is left to be its own interpreter, divergences of views develop. These views crystallize into creeds and confessions of faith. The creeds then become the rocks on which communions have split and the barriers by which church membership has been denied. Thus, Protestantism has been involved in the inconsistency of advocating individual freedom of thought as a duty and often denying it as a practice. How open-minded are we as Protestants? How far can we carry open-mindedness without dissolving the cohesion of our communions?

When the American Presbyterians adopted their form of government in 1788, they put on record their conviction that while

they think it necessary to make effectual provision that all who are admitted as teachers be sound in the faith. They also believe that there are truths and forms with which men of good characters and principles may differ. And in all these they think it the duty both of private Christians and societies to exercise mutual forbearance toward each other.[3]

Alas, the need of mutual forbearance was somewhat limited in the fundamentalist-modernist controversies of painful memory.

Methodism began in a spirit of the broadest tolerance. Wesley's words are familiar:

One circumstance more is quite peculiar to the people called Methodists —that is, the terms upon which any person may be admitted into their society. They do not impose, in order to their admissions, any opinions whatever. . . . They think and let think. One condition, and one only, is required—a real desire to save the soul. Where this is, it is enough; they desire no more. They lay stress upon nothing else; they ask only, Is thy heart herein as my heart? If it be, give me thy hand.

It has to be observed, however, that this broad inclusiveness was not observed in the evolution of Methodism. And for this Wesley himself was

---

[3] The Constitution of the Presbyterian Church in the United States of America (Philadelphia, 1895), Form of Government, chap. 1, sec. 5, p. 283.

responsible. He early separated himself from the Moravians and precipitated a conflict with the Calvinists by his sermon on predestination. This cleavage was widened by Wesley's later pronouncement on justification. Although Wesley was sincere in welcoming into his societies all persons regardless of creed, he proclaimed far and wide the doctrine he held. He became the great doctrinal preacher of the eighteenth century. While Methodism may justly pride itself on its record of theological flexibility, we nevertheless aver certain doctrines as fundamental to our faith.

If the open mind means a purely individualistic freedom of thought, then Protestantism has demonstrated its impracticability. It would reduce the Church to the absurdity expressed by Coleridge when he said, "I belong to that holy and infallible church of which at the present time I am the only member." Writing in 1900, Adolf Harnack declared:

When we are reproached with our divisions and told that Protestantism has as many doctrines as heads, we reply: "So it has, but we do not wish it otherwise; on the contrary, we want still more freedom, still greater individuality, in utterance and doctrine. . . . .We want still more confidence in the inner strength and unifying power of the gospel, which is more certain to prevail in free conflict than under guardianship.[4]

The climate of Christianity has changed since Harnack wrote those words forty years ago. Adolf Keller tells us that in Europe, Protestant individualism and subjectivism are waning under the rising emphasis on the doctrine of the Church. Modern evangelical theology aims to be a theology of the Church. Considering the Church not as a subjective organization of the moment but a venerable fact in history, Church tradition is again becoming an important element of study.

This emphasis on the doctrine of the Church is paralleled in American Protestantism. Combined with it is the ecumenical movement, awakening us to the world-wide solidarity of the Church. By conferences such as those at Jerusalem and Edinburgh, Protestants are getting clearer light on the tradition that has been growing up since biblical times.

The road ahead for Protestantism lies between blind traditionalism and near-sighted individualism. Open-mindedness demands that we neither bow down to Church tradition nor bow it out. It requires that we give respectful attention to time-tested dogmas, as the scientists do to the findings of forerunners in their fields. The doctrines of the Church should be regarded as a heritage given over to us and not as a strait-jacket put over on us. We should give more study to doctrine and preach more doctrinal sermons. And if we keep our minds open toward the great corpus of inherited truth, we shall not run off on those in-

---

[4] Harnack, *What Is Christianity?* pp. 295-6.

dividualistic tangents which make much Protestant preaching theologically fragmentary, frivolously topical, and spiritually futile.

THE OPEN MIND AND OTHER FAITHS

Let us now consider Protestantism's open mind toward contemporary faiths. The open mind must first of all be open-eyed in facing the facts realistically. Today in some metropolitan centers the Protestant population is far exceeded by Roman Catholics and even by Jews. In New York City about 40 per cent of the residents are Jews, about 40 per cent are Romanists, and only 20 per cent have a nominal Protestant affiliation.

The Jews manifest an eagerness for education which wins admiration. Even ten years ago, when they numbered only 4 per cent of the nation's population, they comprised more than 11 per cent of the student body in schools of college grades. In one large eastern Roman Catholic college they have reached as high as 56 per cent of the entire enrollment. But their intellectual aggressiveness and business acumen have served to arouse an anti-Semitic feeling, which is one of the most sinister aspects of contemporary life and gives signs of still more tension after the war. And, with all the eagerness of the Jews for educational and social assimilation, we cannot blink our eyes to the fact that orthodox Judaism at least maintains a doctrine of cultural pluralism—a doctrine that insists on perpetuating the solidarity of a peculiar cultural and racial minority.

The Roman Catholics, in contrast to the Jews, have made prodigious efforts to avoid exposing their children to the public-school system of the nation in which they hold citizenship. They have set up parochial schools, secondary schools, and colleges in every corner of the land where their membership has become numerically important. In doing this they are acting under the direct orders and laws of the church. Canon number 1374 forbids Roman Catholic parents to send their children to a non-Catholic school if a Catholic school is available. Special instructions from the Holy See, dated November 24, 1875, describe the penalities for disobedient parents. Thus, it may be said that the school system of America has been open to the Roman Catholics; but they, in large part, have not been "open" to our free schools.

If the Roman Catholics had stopped at this point, they would only be in the category of other American citizens who exercise the right of sending their children to private schools of their choice. Unhappily, however, they felt it necessary, in their own protection, not only to create their own school system as completely as possible but also to protect those of their youth who did attend public schools from any contact whatever with Protestant teaching. They accordingly joined forces with the Jews, the narrower sects, and the left-wing educators in bringing political pressure to bear against all religious teaching in the public schools. As a result it is now possible for a student to move from the kindergarten to the Ph.D. degree without ever having heard expounded any part of the Christian doctrine or religious fundamentals on which this self-styled Christian nation was established.

DANGERS AND RESPONSIBILITIES

The thoughtful Protestant American, however open-minded, does feel concern when he sees the political action of his own country complicated by various decrees regarding education, social work, intermarriage, et cetera, issued by a spiritual potentate who is almost always an Italian and whose fundamental mentality is Latin and not Anglo-Saxon. He begins to wonder what will be the ultimate effect upon democracy if one group is educating its children for freedom, while an influential minority in its midst continues to educate its children in authoritarian modes of thought and action.

In this war we have abandoned the aim of twenty-five years ago to make the world safe for democracy, but certainly we have not discarded the goal of keeping America safe for democracy. This means, of course, keeping our democracy safe for racial and political minorities. Thomas Jefferson in his first inaugural address laid down the rule of conduct by which such safety is ensured. It is

the sacred principle that though the will of the majority is in all cases to prevail, that will, to be rightful, must be reasonable; that the minority possess their equal rights, which equal laws must protect, and to violate which would be oppression.

This is a principle that must be pressed home to those in the majority and also to those minority groups which aspire to become a majority. We cannot overlook the dangers that would imperil our free institutions if authoritarian types of teaching, now in the minority, should gain a numerical ascendancy. We must remember that the test of courage comes when we are in the minority, but the test of tolerance comes when we are in the majority. And any minority group that does not recognize this fact cannot be safely trusted with majority rule.

In face of this situation, difficult as it is, we Protestants must go the second mile in seeking harmony with other religious faiths, not only because we are at present in the majority, but also because we are the professed champions of the open mind and, still more, because open-mindedness is the Christlike attitude.

First of all, if our minds are truly open, we recognize the vastness of truth and the limitations of human reason. Our modesty should be akin to that of Sir Isaac Newton, who toward the end of his distinguished scientific career confessed that he felt himself only a child playing with the pebbles on the beach of the vast ocean of knowledge. We Protestants have not explored and charted the whole sea of truth. Ours should be the humility of the seeker. To use the term of Nels Ferré we should be liberal evangelicals

209

religiously committed absolutely and unquestioningly to the Christian love of God as the supreme revelation of reality and as the highest ideal for fellowship. Yet we must not become self-satisfied, narrow, or fanatical with regard to this truth, but must ever recognize that our human reason cannot initiate the revelation, cannot fully comprehend it, nor yet with full wisdom apply it.[5]

This mental humility, it may be said, is the greatest quality lacking in the sporadic Protestant sects and cults ever springing up in our midst. Their self-confident assumption that they possess the truth, the whole truth, and nothing but the truth gives their witness a pioneering zeal at the start but makes them ridiculous in the end.

Secondly, as Protestants we should try earnestly to understand those from whom we differ. What the average Protestant church member knows about Judaism or Roman Catholicism is gleaned from the literature of his own church rather than from the writings of the other groups. And very often, it must be admitted, he takes his supposed information from anonymous and irresponsible sources. And we can hardly suppose that the Jewish and Roman Catholic adherents are any better informed about us. In the absence of authentic inside knowledge regarding other religious faiths all sorts of rumors rise to prejudice and poison the minds.

It is being said that progress is being made in mutual understanding between Roman Catholics and Protestants. In the writings of recent Romanist spokesmen tribute is paid to vital religious experience to be found in the Protestant Church.

Catholics do not interpret the famous phrase *extra ecclesiam nulla salus* as meaning that no one can be saved outside the existing Roman Catholic Church. Catholics believe that there is a soul of the Church which takes in all those who, with the light they have, are loyal to their consciences; and they believe that among those are many loyal Protestants with whom they hope to have still closer fellowship in the life to come. Protestants, on their part, no longer believe that the Pope is "Antichrist." . . . They recognize that in the Catholic Church there is a stream of piety at which they are happy to drink and include among their choicest treasures the lives of the great saints who have found their inspiration in the Church of Rome.[6]

Undoubtedly the radio is also helping to break down the barriers of ignorance behind which popular misunderstandings barricade themselves.

Thirdly, if Protestants are to demonstrate their open-mindedness, they must co-operate in all areas where co-operation is possible without a betrayal of conscience. In the fields of scholarship and social service,

---

[5] Ferré, Nels, *The Christian Fellowship*, Harper's; p. 130. (By permission of the publishers.)

[6] William Adams Brown in *Religions of Democracy*, Devin Adair; pp. 238-9. (By permission of the publishers.)

in great moral and political issues, Protestants and Roman Catholics and Jews can and do work side by side. The recent pronouncement on peace principles issued by the official leaders of these three groups was a significant, perhaps epochal, manifestation of this possible co-operation.

Tolerance, as a merely passive attitude of noninterference, is not enough. The word "tolerate" often carries a connotation of condescension. A person frequently says, "I tolerate but—" and then follows the tell-tale confession of dislike. Religious toleration may be a long seamile from religious brotherhood. Nothing less than the sharing of mutual burdens can beget brotherhood. During the presidential campaign of 1860 Edwin M. Stanton said some harsh things about Abraham Lincoln. His aversion to Lincoln continued vocal during the early period of the latter's administration. Natural human emotions would have seemed to prompt the President to resentment. But Lincoln was above cherishing personal grudges. He might then have merely tolerated Stanton in contemptuous silence. But he did more. He eventually appointed Stanton to his cabinet. Later, when the martyred President lay dead, it was Stanton who stood by his bedside and said, "There lies the greatest ruler of men the world has ever seen."

It is co-operation that best begets sympathetic understanding. And in this Protestantism must lead, even though other groups sometimes fail to reciprocate. We must go the second mile even though we realize that our trust is often imposed upon. Men may laugh at our foolishness, thinking that we are deceiving ourselves in believing that there is a response from the other side when in reality there is none. But are we not consecrated to be fools for Christ's sake?

An Authority That Appeals to Free Minds

May I make a fourth suggestion as to Protestantism's open mind toward other faiths? Let us speed the spread of our own vital convictions by methods that appeal to free minds. The popular attitude toward authority manifests a pendulumlike swing. After the last war there was a swing away from all forms of authority. Youths felt they had been deceived by their leaders in the State, in the Church, in the schools, even in the home. The so-called revolt of youth led to an individualism about as atomistic as a sandpile. That uncharted freedom tired after a while, and we entered the era of dictatorship and totalitarianism. The atmosphere of the last decade has been congenial to authoritarian attitudes in religion, as in other realms. But the pendulum of popular mood will swing again. There will be a reaction from regimented thinking and living. Men will call for authorities consonant with free minds.

And there is such a type of authority. Let an illustration suffice. The president of a university at commencement time grants degrees, as he says, by the authority vested in him by the trustees of the institution and the laws of the state. That is authority by institutional investiture. But in that university is a professor, let us say, of English. He does not

211

take up *Hamlet* and say to his students: "By the authority vested in me I pronounce this a masterpiece of literature. Take my word for it without reading." No, he says: "Here is a work that the readers of three centuries have regarded as a masterpiece. Let us read it and see for ourselves." And under his guidance those students enter into the study of *Hamlet* until they, out of their own experience, say, "This is a masterpiece, and this teacher is an authority." Such is a type of authority resting not on investiture but on intelligence. And such is the form of authority that will appeal more and more as the pendulum of reaction swings away from the decade of the dictators and as liberal secular education lifts the thinking of our people.

Protestantism must demonstrate its religious authority by its spiritual power. It must vitalize its teaching function until it redeems its membership from their religious illiteracy. Its program of recruiting must be speeded up but on the principle of sharing rather than of propaganda. Its pulpits must preach more doctrine but not do it dogmatically. Its ministers must win respect for their right to be ambassadors of God, not because of the hands that were laid on them, but because of their ability to lay their hands with sure touch and healing power upon the ills and sins of men.

Let us briefly turn our consideration of Protestantism's open mind toward some other areas of prejudice. The contemporary test of the open mind is most acute in realms other than religious. We may be quite tolerant toward the beliefs and practices of the neighboring Roman Catholic parish; but when a member of that faith is nominated for President, religion runs into politics, and many a citizen is more sensitive about his politics than his religion. The antipathy toward the Jew is far more racial than religious; and into this racial prejudice the economic factor enters in a large degree. Whenever a preacher speaks out for fellowship with the Jews, he is usually met with some such remark as this, "But you don't work with them downtown"—a remark that reveals how far business rivalry colors the current race prejudice. Similarly into the relations between Negroes and whites: the economic factor is too apparent to need discussion. And how rife is the class prejudice that causes the poor to see red when they think of the rich, and the prosperous to see "reds" around every corner. Thus, prejudice forms a system of interlocking directorates, which hinder the free commerce of minds and spirits.

If Protestantism is the champion of the open mind, it must lead in the attack upon these stultifying prejudices. Its record in some zones, however, is not too reassuring. There are signs that indicate that the Roman Catholic Church is more successful than Protestantism in winning the confidence of organized labor in some sections of this country and also of the Negro groups in certain cities. Our talk about the open mind is not very convincing unless we can translate it into attitudes of tolerant living.

ERADICATING PREJUDICE

The open mind demands that we try to eradicate the roots of prejudice. Whence come these prejudices of men? It would seem, at times, out of nothing. As was said by one of its victims, "Prejudice, like the spider, makes everywhere its home and lives where there seems nothing to live on." But when we look more closely, we see that many of our prejudices came by social inheritance. It has been said that we are tattooed with the beliefs of our tribe while we are yet in our cradles. At a surprisingly early age children absorb unreasoned dislikes of the elders. It is therefore highly important that we should watch the juncture of the older and younger generations in order to prevent the child from catching the prejudices of the parents. We adults should not only endeavor to keep our prejudices from discoloring the fresh minds of youth, but we should cultivate the viewpoint of the young in order to emancipate ourselves from our narrow-mindedness. This was the aim of Jesus when he set a child in the midst of some bigoted Palestinian elders and said, "Except ye be converted and become as a little child, ye cannot see the kingdom of heaven."

Another source of prejudice is ignorance. Secular education and travel cannot be relied upon to develop the open mind. Education often serves only to rationalize unreasoned prejudices, and travelers generalize on such insufficient data. We of the pulpit must ever seek to be interpreters of those whom our parishioners dislike because they are unlike. When we meet in our service of worship and pray to the Father of all mankind, it should be as if we were in a room that had a mirror in the ceiling, which mirror would enable us the better to look down into the places of others, thereby sensitizing our imaginations toward the man whose color is black or the person who was born in Chungking or Tokyo, in London or Berlin.

Another source of prejudice is fear. As Herbert Agar says, we are a plot-haunted people. And he also avers that the well-to-do are more infected with fear of others than are the underprivileged. We Protestants, who, generally speaking, embrace the better-privileged, must be all the more alert not to foment this fear psychology. It is so easy and so cheaply popular. Not only must we refuse to play upon our parishioners' fears, but we should set ourselves to help rid society of those pestiferous writers, secretaries, broadcasters, and agitators who make a living rousing the prejudices of people by stirring up their fears of other groups.

We are the preachers of Him who "is our peace," having "broken down the middle wall of partition." As the Jerusalem conference, representing the churches, young and old, of Orient and Occident, said, "Our message is Jesus Christ." If our message can be kept Christocentric in spirit as well as in content, we shall be able to combine the glowing heart with a gracious inclusiveness.

In John Masefield's play *The Trial of Jesus* the wife of Pilate says

213

to the Roman official who superintended the Crucifixion, "What do you think of his claim?"

He replies, "If a man believes anything up to the point of dying on a cross for it, he will find others to believe it."

She then asks, "Do you think he is dead?"

He replies, "No, lady, I don't."

"Then, where is he?"

"Let loose in the world, lady, where neither Roman nor Jew can stop his truth." [7]

------

[7] By permission of The Macmillan Company, publishers.

Part III

OPPORTUNITIES

IN THE FAR EAST

KENNETH SCOTT LATOURETTE

IN THE Far East, Protestantism faces striking and critical opportunities. On the success with which the Protestants of this generation meet them depends in large part the quality of the future culture of the Far East and the future of world Christianity. By the Far East I mean primarily China and Japan; but in this region are also embraced eastern Siberia, Korea, the Philippines, Indo-China, Siam, the Malay Peninsula, and the East Indies. In this area lives approximately one third of mankind.

For several decades great changes have here been in progress. In the present century they have been markedly accelerated. The war in which we are now engaged is still further speeding them up. In these changes Protestantism has already had a significant part. It has been only one of many factors that have shaped events; but it has been and is a factor, in some regions and phases of life a very important one. The wisdom and devotion with which Protestants address themselves to the situation in the crucial days immediately ahead will determine in no small degree the character of the Far East that is even now emerging. What happens in the Far East cannot fail to influence profoundly the rest of the world and the world-wide Christianity we believe we see emerging.

If we are to understand the opportunities that confront Protestantism in the Far East, we must go back for a moment and see the historical background out of which they have arisen. We must remind ourselves of the nature of Protestantism and especially of the Protestantism that has been most strongly represented in the Far East. In this I shall be repeating, although in the briefest summary, something of what has already been said in earlier chapters in this series. We must also note the recent and present status of Protestantism in the Far East. With this freshly in our purview we can then go on to an appraisal of the door that lies open before Protestantism in that part of the world.

The term "Protestantism" is a misnomer. The Christian movement it is used to describe has been much more than a protest. Even at the outset the movement was positive. It was in part a protest and a reform, for it was an attempt to strip from Christianity the accretions that had accumulated in the Latin or Roman West and to revive the primitive gospel in all its early power and simplicity. It was also, and even more, a fresh burst of life. Its emphasis was upon the new birth wrought by God by his redemptive work in Christ through the Holy Spirit. It emphasized salvation by faith. The faith was that of the individual believer. As John Wesley found two centuries later, it was trust in Christ, and in Christ

217

alone. As an essential corollary there was the priesthood of all believers, the direct access of each Christian to God. This implied, as John Wesley also clearly saw and stated, the right and the duty of each believer to individual judgment on matters of faith and morals. In exercising that judgment the believer would seek the guidance of Holy Writ and of his fellow Christians. He would also not ignore the collective judgment of the Church. However, the responsibility was his.

PROTESTANTISM'S GROWTH

From Luther until this day Protestantism has been gaining momentum. For nearly three centuries it was a minority movement within the universal Church of Christ. The main stream of Christianity seemed to be flowing through other channels, notably the Roman Catholic Church. In the nineteenth century, however, it was becoming obvious that Protestantism had become the main current of the Christian stream. The currents represented by the Eastern churches have been dwindling. That represented by the Roman Catholic Church continues strong and has had something of a quickening in the present century. However, measured by inward vitality as displayed in new movements and the effects upon mankind as a whole, increasingly Protestantism has become the chief channel for the life of Christ in the world.

At its outset and through much of its development Protestantism has been closely associated with the peoples of Northwestern Europe. Luther was a German; Calvin a Picard, from northern France; and Wesley, English. Until the nineteenth century the overwhelming majority of Protestants were in Germany, Switzerland, Holland, Scandinavia, and the British Isles, with sprinklings in Hungary, Czechoslovakia, Russia, Transylvania, France, the East and West Indies, and South Africa, with a thin line along the Atlantic seaboard of North America. In the nineteenth and twentieth centuries great nations, predominantly Protestant and of Northwestern European stock, have arisen in the United States, Canada, Australia, New Zealand, and South Africa; and rapidly growing Protestant communities have been founded and nourished also chiefly by missionaries of Northwestern European ancestry in Latin America, Asia, and Africa.

Protestantism has become world-wide and is becoming rooted in many different nations and races. It is developing an ecumenical fellowship that is reaching out even beyond its own borders to churches of other traditions. The world-wide spread of Protestantism has been chiefly from the British Isles and Dominions and the United States. British and American Protestantism differs somewhat from that of the continent of Europe. It is freer from association with the state. It presents a greater variety. It stresses both individual and social transformation. From it have come the chief movements toward ecumenical Christianity.

It has been this Anglo-Saxon Christianity which has been most strongly represented in the Far East. Continental European Protestantism—Swiss, Dutch, German, and Scandinavian—has sent missionaries, but

218

they have been in the small minority. Only in the Netherlands East Indies have they predominated. There Dutch Protestants have carried the chief load, with German Protestants only slightly behind them in numbers and influence. Of Anglo-Saxon Protestantism it has been that from the United States which, especially latterly, has been predominant. In later decades Americans have been in a majority among the Protestant missionaries in China and British Malaya. They have been an overwhelming majority in the Protestant missionary body in Japan, Korea, and Thailand, and have had a practical monopoly of the Protestant missions in the Philippines.

In the Far East, Protestantism varies from country to country in its composition, its constituency, and its effect upon the country.

The Far Eastern Countries

In China, Protestantism is much younger than Roman Catholicism. In 1807, when Robert Morrison, the first Protestant missionary, landed, there were about two hundred thousand Roman Catholics in the empire. Today there are perhaps three and a quarter million Roman Catholics as against about three quarters of a million Protestants. Yet proportionately Protestants have grown more rapidly than Roman Catholics. Moreover, they have exercised a much greater influence upon the nation as a whole than have Roman Catholics. Of the Christians who are having such prominence in the leadership of the state, education, social reform, and medicine almost all are Protestants.

It is Protestantism rather than Roman Catholicism which has created the new medical and nursing professions, pioneered in the public health program, led in introducing secondary and higher education of an occidental type, and inspired general movements for moral reform such as the New Life Movement. Protestantism has had so little contact with Roman Catholicism that it is almost another religion and is in no sense a protest against the other. It has been planted chiefly by missionaries from Great Britain and the United States, and more from the latter than the former. It is varied denominationally, more so than Protestantism elsewhere in the Far East, and has been only partly brought together by the National Christian Council and the remarkable union movement the Church of Christ in China. It is also divided in its emphasis. Because of the Confucian environment and the heritage from the social gospel of the Occident one strong strain is toward social reform and the saving of China collectively from the ills that now beset that land. Because of the conservative background of many of the missionaries and perhaps because of the Buddhist portion of China's heritage, with its stress upon life after death, another strain in Chinese Protestantism emphasizes personal salvation and the life to come.

In Korea, Protestants are more numerous than Roman Catholics, although the latter have been in the country more than twice as long. Protestantism has been planted chiefly by missionaries from the United States, mainly Presbyterian and Methodist, the former predominating.

219

It has had a checkered and somewhat stormy history. The Protestant communities have been centers of opposition to the Japanization of the country and at times have been sources of active opposition to Japanese rule. The Japanese have accordingly viewed it with suspicion and in late years have taken stringent measures to bring its adherents into conformity with Japanese nationalism as expressed in Shinto and to incorporate it into the national structure of Japanese Protestantism.

In Japan proper Protestants are also more numerous than Roman Catholics, and that despite the fact that their branch of the faith has been there a very much shorter time than the other. They are also mainly the fruit of American missionary effort. They are mainly from the urban professional and middle classes. They have been progressive in achieving financial and administrative independence of the founding churches and latterly have almost all been brought together in the Church of Christ in Japan, a body that is more inclusive ecclesiastically than any other church in the world. In spite of its limited numbers and its brief history (for its communicants are less than half of 1 per cent of the population, and its first congregation was organized less than seventy-five years ago) Japanese Protestantism has exerted a not inconsiderable influence upon the life of the country in social reform and in shaping ideals.

The Philippine Islands have a large majority of Roman Catholics and a substantial minority of Moslems. However, Protestantism, although it did not enter until after the American occupation in 1898, was growing rapidly when, in 1942, the Japanese conquest largely cut off our information from the land.

In the Netherlands Indies, Protestants are more numerous than in all the rest of the Far East put together. They have been recruited chiefly from the animistic folk rather than from the Moslems, who constitute a majority of the population. Some of the smaller islands in the North are almost solidly Christian.

French Indo-China, although containing several hundreds of thousands of Roman Catholics, has almost no Protestants.

In Thailand, because of the strong hold of Buddhism, neither Protestantism nor Roman Catholicism has gained many adherents; but Protestants, chiefly the result of American Presbyterian missions, have had considerable influence upon the education and the medical service of the land.

In the British portions of the Malay Peninsula, including the Straits Settlements, as every spiritual child of John Wesley should know, Protestantism has been chiefly represented by American Methodism and has been particularly strong among the large Chinese elements of the population.

Outlook Toward the Future

This, then, is the current status of Protestantism in the Far East. In some extensive sections, because of the Japanese advance, we have little information since early 1942. There is no reason to believe, however, that the situation, so far as Protestantism is concerned, has been basically altered in that time. If the Japanese succeed in making their occupation permanent, fundamental changes will be wrought. If, however, as now seems probable, the Japanese are defeated by the United Nations, in no regions except Japan, Korea, and Formosa will the conditions that maintained two or three years ago be radically altered. It is upon the assumption of a complete Japanese defeat that the following appraisal of Protestantism's opportunities is made. If Japan is victorious or if the struggle results in a draw or in only a partial Japanese reverse, the conditions will be very different. Protestantism will still be greatly needed, but the conditions under which it must operate will be far other than those which now seem probable and which the ensuing paragraphs suggest:

Whatever the immediate or the remote future may hold in store for the Far East, the need for Protestantism will be great. The need is chiefly that of all men everywhere for the gospel of Christ. This might conceivably be met by Roman Catholicism, although, so we Protestants believe, nowhere nearly so adequately as by Protestantism. Protestant Christianity is especially needed because of its fruits in individual initiative and perseverance. One of the dangers in the Far East, as in much of the world today, is regimentation by the State and the curbing of the individual soul in its outreach toward God and the fullest life. This is strikingly the danger in Japan; but it is also present elsewhere, although not always in so acute a form. Against this Protestantism is a safeguard. With its emphasis upon the priesthood of all believers it is an enemy of tyranny of any kind. With its experience of the new birth and the empowering of the individual soul to undertake and carry through to completion apparently impossible tasks Protestantism, particularly that of Anglo-Saxon peoples, the kind that has predominated in missions in the Far East, has been the source of social reforms of unprecedented magnitude. As illustrations one need only recall that it was from Protestantism that the impulses issued which brought Negro slavery to an end and that from Protestants have sprung the most hopeful efforts for the curbing and elimination of war. It has been a matter of comment that from Protestant Christianity in China, although the constituency is small, has come a large proportion of those who have had the daring to dream of a remade China and the persistence and the disinterested loyalty to the welfare of the nation to pursue the incredibly difficult path toward making these dreams a reality. That contribution is to continue to be desperately needed if China is to achieve a unified, stable government that will bring economic, intellectual, and social opportunity and justice to all.

The thorough defeat of Japan in war will not alone solve the problem that nation presents to itself and to the world. There will be resentment and a passionate desire for revenge against Japan's former enemies, intensified by the incredible physical and mental suffering which the disaster will bring. Among many Japanese there will be disillusion in the

221

failure of the dreams on which they have been fed, distrust of the leaders and the system that have brought them to so evil a pass, and bewilderment. Among others there will be a fierce determination to recoup the imperial fortunes as soon as possible and renew the struggle. If Japan is to be made over into a nation that will co-operate with its neighbors on a basis of equality rather than of domination, it must be from an impulse from within rather than by force from without. If Japanese Protestantism can be sufficiently strengthened, it can make enormous contributions toward providing the necessary vision and leadership. Let no one deceive himself that the task will be either easy or brief. It is, however, imperative.

In Korea the world has a people occupying a peninsula that, because of its strategic position near three great empires, makes it a football in the stern game of international politics. Yet for a generation the Koreans have been without experience in self-government and in earlier decades were in the hands of a corrupt and inept governing class. Can the Protestant communities, small, latterly distraught by persecution, but with training in the conduct of their own affairs and with the heroic constancy and vision that their faith can produce, provide the leadership of which their nation so greatly stands in need?

In the Philippines there were, before the Japanese conquest, the promising beginnings of an autonomous democracy. If a true democracy is to emerge, with self-control, true unity, freedom from political corruption, and opportunities for the underprivileged, the Protestant elements must be greatly strengthened.

In the East Indies, Protestantism has been of immense service in stimulating and guiding the development of backward tribes. Of this the remarkable emergence of the Bataks is a striking example. Presumably Protestantism will still be needed for that and for other purposes as the many peoples of that vast archipelago grope toward the attainment of self-government and the solution of pressing problems of economics and overpopulation.

Can Protestantism be numerically and spiritually strong enough to give needed assistance in meeting the problems presented by the mixed population of the Malay Peninsula and the economic strains incident upon the rise of the synthetic-rubber industry in America, competing as that does with Malaya's chief crop? Will it continue and strengthen its already great services in Thailand? Can it be planted in what is now French Indo-China in sufficient strength to aid that region in meeting the difficult conditions of the uncertain future?

These are some of the challenges Protestantism faces in the Far East. Promising beginnings have been made in meeting them, but they are only beginnings.

As Protestantism seeks to meet the needs of the Far East, it is confronted with apparently impossible difficulties. The immensity and the complexity of the problems and the numerical weaknesses, amounting in some places almost to insignificance of the Protestant constituencies, are obvious. So, too, is the limited assistance in personnel and funds which is likely to come from the older churches of the Occident. Judging from the experience of the last twenty-five years and the situation that confronts the churches of the United States and the British Empire, no great expansion of the Protestant missionary forces in the Far East can be anticipated. We can look for their maintenance at their strength on the eve of the present war and probably to some additions. We cannot expect their great multiplication. Nor should we do so. Protestant Christianity in the Far East is associated with the United States and Great Britain. Any large increase in the missionary staffs from these lands would awaken fear in these lands, ill founded but no less real, which would see in it a phase of American and British imperialism. This will be especially likely if the United Nations are victorious. That victory will in a large degree be won by the United States and will be followed by the assumption by our government of responsibilities in the Far East in comparison with which our pre-Pearl Harbor activities will pale into insignificance. Any increases in Protestant missionary forces probably will be from the United States. We must take great care that they have as little association as possible with the extension of American political and economic power. Yet apprehension of possible resentment because of the supposed connection must not hold us back from our missionary task.

Then, too, there is always the unknown factor of Russia. So far as we can see now, Russia will come out of the war with enhanced power and prestige and will have greater influence in the Far East than at any previous time. That this influence will not be exerted in behalf of Protestantism or, indeed, of any form of Christianity we can be reasonably certain. We do not know whether it will be actively antagonistic to the Christian faith. It is no flattering or easy prospect that Protestantism faces as it attempts to meet the challenge of the Far East in the days ahead.

TURNING DEFEAT TO TRIUMPH

However, the difficulties must not deter us. From their very inception Protestantism and the Christian faith of which it is an active and growing expression have been confronted by obstacles that have seemed insuperable. Christianity has as its emblem the cross, itself a symbol of seeming initial and irretrievable defeat that was turned into triumph. At the very outset of Protestantism the defiance of Rome by Luther appeared utter madness. We need to remind ourselves that the first Protestant missionary to China—Robert Morrison—was confronted by a much more impossible situation than faces his successors today in that nation, and that he has been amply justified by the event in his calm reply when the owner of the ship on which he sailed scornfully said as they arranged the business details, "And so, Mr. Morrison, you really expect to make an impression on the idolatry of the Chinese Empire?" "No, sir, I expect God will." We need also to recall that the first Protestant missionaries to Japan were faced by a wall that appeared much more impenetrable than any blocking us today. We, as the heirs of these hardy pioneers and with the ample justification of their faith before us to hearten us, cannot be less daring and intrepid than were they.

Our generation has assets which the pioneers did not have and which, in their boldest dreams, they could not fully have envisioned. In every land in the Far East except French Indo-China there are Protestant churches. In the major and some of the minor lands they are vigorous and growing. The Protestant forces of the world are being knit together in an ecumenical fellowship that, for geographic extent and the variety of the forms of Christianity it embraces, is without parallel in history. Protestantism has had and is having a profound effect upon some phases of the newly emerging cultures of the Far East. With these foundations on which to build, Protestantism has a far brighter prospect in the Far East than in the days of its introduction to that region. In some regions, notably in China, it is in a better position to take advantage of the future than at any previous time.

Some of the main outlines of the program for Protestantism in the Far East which grow out of the present situation are obvious:

One of the most urgent tasks is that of reconstruction. In great areas congregations have been scattered and physical plants damaged or destroyed. There must be much of rebuilding. In many regions physical relief must precede reconstruction.

Clearly, too, there is the task of reconciliation. Strains and even bitternesses have developed between the Christians of the warring lands and will be intensified before the conflict is over. If the world Christian fellowship is to continue its promising growth, ties weakened by war must be reknit. We can do that even now, in part, through prayer. When such gatherings again become feasible, there must be an unhurried conference of the leaders of the churches in the various lands that fringe the Pacific for the frank facing of the sources of separation and ill will and for prayer, with the confident expectation that such breaches as have been wrought in the Christian fellowship by the tensions of our time can be healed. When reconciliation is effected, we must cement the ties among the Protestants of the various lands. Because of the divisiveness that springs from its nature Protestantism is tempted to become ancillary to nationalism. Fortunately, through the ecumenical movement, in these days of fevered nationalism Protestantism is more and more becoming supranational. We must do what we can to strengthen the trend. We in the United States must renew and continue our missions in the Far East. More and more we must give assistance, not on our own initiative, but at the request of the younger churches. Missionary personnel must go at the instance of our fellow Christians in the lands of the Far East and work under the direction of the churches of these lands. Missionaries will be asked for. We must be prepared to meet the requests as they come.

Where this fellowship across the waters of the Pacific will lead we cannot yet see. Unquestionably, as it takes firmer root in that area, the Protestantism of the Far East will become different from that of the Occident. This is what we should expect of the genius of Protestantism. Undoubtedly, too, if it is true to its essence, Protestantism in the Far East and the world around will preserve common characteristics. In its faith in Christ, in salvation by the faith of the individual believer, in the priesthood of all believers, it should not, if it is loyal to its genius and, we believe, to the Christian gospel, depart from its historic essence. It has contributed much to the Far East of our generation. It can contribute even more in the days and the years ahead. In its growing world-wide fellowship Protestantism can help to knit the peoples of the Far East into an inclusive and friendly neighborhood with the peoples of all the earth.

IN EUROPE

HENRY SMITH LEIPER

THE ONLY practical basis for an appraisal of Protestantism's opportunities in Europe is a factual one. And the unfortunate thing about the present from the would-be prophet's point of view is that facts are stringently rationed. They have to come to us through the iron curtain of censorship from churches that are prisoners of the censor as well as of the Gestapo. They come in ways that make difficult their verification. They come, furthermore, in ways that forbid the assurance of proper balance and proportion. One who has had an intimate contact with most of the European churches for a decade and a half knows just enough to realize how little he knows. He has seen the predictions of wise men with respect to the churches go wrong so many times that he distrusts generalizations and dogmatic assertions about the trend of church affairs.

Incalculable and imponderable factors abound. Not only do we *not* know as much as we need to know about the state of affairs in most of the European lands; but we cannot even guess what the political structure of postwar Europe will be and how it will affect the life of the Christians. A further complication that must be faced is the fact that Europe is not by any means homogeneous. What may be true of Finland is not necessarily true in any way of France. Estonia and England cannot be dealt with in the same breath. Spain and Scandinavia are utterly unlike. In the area we call Europe there are at least twenty-eight nations. Some of them can safely be grouped together because of their similarities; but most of them demand separate consideration because of their radically differing history, status, and probable future.

A book of at least a dozen chapters would be needed to do even elemental justice to the problems involved. But we have to compress our study into one chapter, which must therefore deal mainly with general considerations.

Nor does the fact that historically Protestantism has been so unimportant a factor in certain lands make it safe automatically to pass them by when writing about the future. An example of what I mean may be found by a look at Portugal. In a population of some seven million there are fewer than five-thousand Protestant church members. Yet in a recent census reported when I was in Portugal in 1942 well over a million persons stated their religious preference as "Protestant." The leaders of the brave little Protestant minority saw in that a great challenge and are pleading with stronger churches to help them prepare leaders for what they feel might be a great expansion among the unchurched. And as an indication of the contradictions and surprises to be found in Portugal, I need but mention the fact that in the office of the Unitarian Relief Committee I met the head of the Roman Catholic Mission to Jews and the head of the Vatican's special refugee service. Both of these men indicated that they were getting more help from this Protestant agency in Lisbon than from the authorities of their own communion.

UNPRECEDENTED CO-OPERATION

This mention of relationships between Catholics of different lands and of Protestants and Catholics within a given country leads me to deal here with one of the few things about which it is safe to generalize. Not since the Reformation has there been anything like the amount of co-operation now going on between these two historically antagonistic groups. Whether one looks at Norway, Germany, Holland, France, or England, one finds startling evidences of a new spirit and a kind of collaboration which would have been inconceivable before the war. The same cannot be said of Spain or Italy (which disproves the generalization), but it remains a general characteristic of the period, whose consequences for the future it will be very hard now to appraise with accuracy. From Germany itself we have the striking testimony of a Swedish newspaper man whose book is based on life in Germany from 1941 to 1943. Under the title *Behind the Steel Wall* he writes:

The clergy, both Catholic and Protestant, have shown great courage and tenacity in the struggle for freedom of conscience. They are co-operating in their resistance to Nazi pressure, and many barriers between Catholicism and Protestantism have fallen. Catholic priests preach in Protestant churches, and Protestant pastors expelled from their parishes have been supported by funds from the Roman Church.[1]

Even more significant, perhaps, have been the exhortations of Roman Catholic cardinals to their clergy to pray for the Protestants and the constant common planning of the leaders of both groups in the face of the Nazi effort to destroy Christianity root and branch. One of Hitler's early schemes was to detach the churches of Germany from all international connections and then to fuse them into one purely national church, which should be neither Catholic nor Protestant but "German Christian." In a manner he never intended, he has brought about a different kind of unity. But no one knows whether it will survive the emergency and what effects it will have upon the future of Protestantism in the postwar Germany. Similar tendencies are apparent in Asia.

From France, Norway, Holland, Hungary, and, of course, England, there come reports of similarly unexpected developments, frequent enough now to reveal a trend and so baffling as to discourage dogmatic predictions of the future. I myself attended a Religion and Life Week

---

[1] From *Behind the Steel Wall*, by Arvid Fredborg; copyright, 1944; by permission of the Viking Press, Inc.

observance in Manchester, England, in 1942, which ended with a great service, attended by seven thousand persons, at which the opening prayers were offered by a Catholic priest, the sermon preached by a Scotch Presbyterian, and the concluding worship led by a pastor from an English Protestant church.

Christians who see this during the crisis will expect continued breadth of spirit when the crisis is over. As one underground paper in Holland recently said: "When the time of the occupation is over, . . . churches will need deep insight into their vocation with regard to the whole life of a nation. One of the many miracles of these years is the discovery made by so many that the church is the conscience of a nation."

While reserving my opinion as to the probable course of developments in lands where the Roman tradition is dominant (except France) I think it is safe to say that one of the opportunities confronting Protestantism in Europe is that of a positive witness not characterized by anti-Catholicism. Without it what may happen is at least suggested by the reported trend toward Catholicism in Germany and the growing suggestions of the same thing in England. In the latter country we were told at the September meeting of the British Council of Churches, 1943, that persons converted in the general evangelistic services of the Religion and Life Weeks reported themselves dismayed by the sectarianism of the non-Roman Churches as they came to experience it while seeking to establish local church connections. They had been led to expect something ecumenical in emphasis. They did not find it in the evangelical churches and so were turning to Rome.

Canon Tatlow, in his Institute of Christian Education, which is training teachers for religious instruction in the British public schools, reported having observed the same trend, which he thought very significant. He found a return to Christianity among intellectuals, who had been deeply impressed by the heroic resistance of the churches to totalitarianism. But their efforts to find congenial lodgment within local Protestantism produced an unfavorable reaction because of the still-prevailing divisiveness and frequent preoccupation with denominational programs and points of view. Another generalization about European Christianity would be that the experience of persecution, beginning in Russia, where it seems happily to have run its course in almost exactly a generation, has produced results that will be highly creative and cannot be too much stressed for persons eager to take the measure of church life in the days ahead. Intellectuals, labor, youth, and other previously indifferent or hostile groups have almost without exception given evidence of being deeply and favorably impressed. And since, in general, their inner need is for spiritual freedom, the natural and congenial emphasis of Protestantism upon that element in life has had immense effect except where it tends, as I have sorrowfully noted that it sometimes does, to a kind of individualism gone to seed in denominational rivalries and sectarian extravagances.

My colleague Dr. Visser 't Hooft recently pointed out that evidences reaching the office of the World Council's Provisional Committee in Geneva show a *real and significant increase in active church member-ship* in almost all European lands. This is not likely to be reflected in church statistics, because in most of those lands the basis of census enumeration has been traditional.

EUROPE'S LOSSES

A third generalization may be ventured: It is that the drastic re-duction in the number of trained ministers will everywhere on the continent, save possibly in Switzerland and Scandinavia, prove a chal-lenging thing, both a danger and an opportunity of quite exceptional character; and the same will be true in England for somewhat the same reasons. Almost all classical education in the higher brackets has ceased. Theological faculties, even where they still exist, have fewer and fewer students to teach. The number of ministers killed in the ranks in Ger-many may well be over one thousand by this time. There were only eighteen thousand in the Protestant churches when Hitler came to power. The war left only a sparse 20 per cent of these at work. The decade has seen the steady decline of the prewar total from normal deaths and retirements and abnormal imprisonments and war casualties, without more than a trickle of new recruits. In the last year for which the figures are available the number of ministerial students for all of Protestantism in Germany proper was down to about forty for the first-year class against a normal seven hundred. The figures in England have recently become almost as startling, so far as recruits are concerned, although far fewer of the churches are without trained leadership.

Acute awareness of the seriousness of the actual and prospective lack of leadership on the continent has led the British churches to project some theological training schools in England for young German refugees, a project in which the American Committee for Christian Refugees is interested. Switzerland is moving in the same direction, and I understand that from Sweden as well we may expect some reinforce-ment of the German church leadership when the war is over. Persons who have not lived through these tragic war years with their brethren will labor under certain great disadvantages, but there will doubtless be places where they can serve effectively.

The recruitment and employment of large numbers of lay leaders, including women, which has been the answer of the churches in many lands to the dearth of trained ministers, may have produced results that will lead to some permanent changes in policy. But it is too soon to say much about that possibility. It should not be forgotten that in some of the most creative periods of the life of the early Church lay leader-ship was common. The same holds for the beginnings of Methodism in the days of John Wesley.

When one considers the loss of personnel in European Protestantism generally—and that is by far the most significant loss to be considered—

one is naturally led to think of the appalling material losses in buildings, libraries, and equipment. England's losses in this respect are known. No fewer than three thousand churches, not to mention auxiliary buildings, have been damaged or destroyed. What the numbers will be on the continent is beyond present calculation. At the very least the replacements required will be staggering in cost. Even if all of this loss could be replaced by gifts from outside, such a policy would most certainly be unwise. A good deal of study and consultation will need to be concentrated upon this problem as American churches formulate their plans for aid on the other side of the Atlantic. The almost incredible impoverishment of the churches over there will have to be kept in mind in all our thinking, and we shall need to realize that one of the challenging needs of the days ahead is for some manner of spiritually bridging the gap that will separate our relatively rich churches from their pitifully poor ones—all the more so since theirs will be amazingly rich in spiritual experience and deep faith wrought in the crucible of suffering, and ours will be, in relative terms, something far more conventional and superficial. No one can go, as I have in the last two successive war years, to share the life of the churches on the continent and in England without realizing that the spiritual atmosphere there contrasts at many points with the spiritual atmosphere here. And if that is true in lands where there has been no persecution, think of how much more widely it will be true of church life in such lands as have been under the most bitter persecution since the days of Nero. There will be no annual church dinners in Europe's churches after the war (there were very few before); and if there were such gatherings, they would not sing "K-k-k-katy" and "Sweet Adeline."

Some Opportunities

One of the opportunities confronting world Protestantism at the present time is that of being revitalized by the recognition of what the suffering and dying churches can give to those whose lives have been spared most of the worst kind of suffering and all of the dire poverty attendant upon this struggle in ancient Europe. We can share their sufferings even if, unfortunately, we cannot share our joys with them.

One of the further things we have the opportunity to learn is that modern men in mortal anguish are as sure to turn toward the treasures of the Christian gospel as were any in past generations. There is ample testimony to show that the amazing change which has come in Russia in the attitude of the State toward the churches is due in the first instance to the realistic recognition of the deep yearnings of a suffering people, in almost every one of whose homes there is a vacant chair. Political considerations and the like are undoubtedly concurrent factors in the situation. But more important than all else is the basic fact to which I have just alluded. Lenin said, "All religious ideas are an unspeakable abomination." Marx earlier had declared that religion is opium for the sufferings of the people. Stalin seems to have caught a gleam of the fact, which he once must have known when himself a student for the priesthood, that religion is the wine of the soul. He still claims he personally does not need it, but he told one of our American officials that he realized that his people do. How great is the change when it can be reliably stated that priests are to be officially permitted to work with the troops in the Russian armies, much as chaplains do in our own army, although without the same military status and government support! The new opportunity open to orthodox Christianity in Russia is likewise open to the relatively small Protestant bodies there.

It has been wisely said that many of the European lands have "lost their history" through the demonic onslaught of totalitarianism and its effect in the fields of education, culture, and the molding of the mind of youth. Russia shows more plainly than any other land "the return to history" and, with it, the return to the cherished memories of the church of bygone centuries. "Holy Russia" was never as holy as the romanticists like to make out, but there was in it a kind of religious aspiration and sense of dependence on God which the present sufferings of the masses have reawakened.

In Europe generally the vacuum created by materialistic humanism has for a time been filled with the politico-religions of totalitarianism, communism among them; but the faith inspired by totalitarianism has faded, and the old vacuum is again to be reckoned with. On this point may I again quote my colleague Dr. 't Hooft? He writes:

There is . . . a vacuum of frightening proportions. It is in the last resort a religious vacuum. The masses despair for lack of a real, substantial faith which holds on to the invisible realities. . . . But there is one hopeful thing about a vacuum—namely, that it demands to be filled.

One of Britain's most charming and spiritually dynamic Catholic laywomen—Miss Barbara Ward, editor of the *London Economist*, writing in the *Christian News Letter*, says:

Europe is like a country over which a tornado has passed. It has torn up all the landmarks and institutions and destroyed universities and schools. Practically speaking, the only institutions which remain as a continuous link with Europe's past are the Christian churches—the pulpit from which the German pastoral was read, from which Bishop Berggrav was able to read out his defiance of Quisling. . . . In a Europe from which all institutions have been wiped out there still exists a great network of organized bodies who speak with the voice of Europe and which still recognize these loyalties to freedom for which we say we are fighting.

Over against such fundamental upsurging of the human spirit as we have here been contemplating how petty a thing is denominationalism! And, one may at this point appropriately ask, how would any American Christian justify postwar attempts at proselytism among the churches of the continent as the contribution of American Christianity, as if Europe were a mission field in the usually accepted sense? As one who had to deal with it very directly, I recall with a sad heart the spiritual blindness of the small churches of foreign origin in Germany—mainly the result of American missionary effort—when Hitlerism was rising. To be sure, their record was no worse than that of many parts of the older Protestantism, Calvinistic or Lutheran. But light and leading came, in the fullness of time, not from them but from the ancient churches, over whose sufferings, in the dawn of Nazism, they had secretly gloated rather than protested. There is here material for sobering thought as we seek to point out future opportunities for the churches of our Protestant tradition on the continent.

Rebuilding the Moral Order

I have been speaking of Protestantism's opportunity in the largest sense, which in the North of Europe particularly is the great tradition of the past centuries—to give back to the Europe of tomorrow the best of its history. There is another related contribution of immense significance about which we must think. I refer to the rebuilding of the spiritual foundations of moral order, which everywhere must buttress civil order. Tracy Strong has been calling to our minds the fact that in most European lands now decent people have to keep their self-respect by evading or quietly breaking the immoral laws made by the Nazi conquerers. What is happening on a wide scale is that the best youth are themselves being taught by their parents, in the interests of decency and right, to break public law. What the effect of this will be no one can tell. It seems not unlikely that when just laws are once again enacted and upheld by government, the habit of mind acquired in this tragic period will remain. Whether it does or not, the fact is plain that catastrophic events have uncovered the ofttimes hidden relationship between law and spiritual faith. Judged even by the most realistic and hard-headed standards, the relevance of Christian faith, which knows that God is the sole author of moral law and that man cannot live by bread alone, is evidenced with startling clearness. No longer in Norway or in Holland, in Germany or in France, does one debate the relevance to modern life of the basic Christian view of life and destiny. Review, if you will, what we know of the trend of preaching on the continent, and you will discover this clearly enough. It is up to American Protestantism to understand this development, to interpret it aright, and to consider how we may not only profit from it ourselves but also aid our brethren on the continent in the reconstitution of civil order.

This is not a merely academic subject. Right here there is a very practical consideration I should not want to overlook. Our government and other United Nations governments will, in the not distant future, be responsible for the reconstitution of order in the lands of Western Europe. It ought to be persuasively brought to their attention that the churches of Europe, which have been the center of resistance to Nazi nihilism and lawlessness, should be taken into account from the very first in all plans for the new developments of order. All the United Nations governments, including our own, are busy gathering and publishing the evidence of the significance of spiritual resistance in Europe. But, unfortunately, there appear few evidences that our own government in particular is aware to the extent it should be of the meaning of this for the morrow. The voice of the church in America should be heard clearly and forcefully on this point before it is too late to affect the nature of our governmental plans.

Right here is perhaps the place to call attention to the fact that the opportunity of our Protestantism on the continent does not, in my judgment, include the opportunity to send over large numbers of enthusiastic young reconstructors and re-educators, many of whom have spent the war years sublimating their very wholesome distaste for war by cherishing the hope of taking over when the warmakers are through. There is not the least justification for assuming that they will be called into service in the immediate postwar years or later. I understand that there are now some fifteen hundred courses being offered to prospective reconstructors of Europe in the church schools and colleges of America. They represent a wholesome and welcome concern, but they do not represent realistic appraisal of what is at all likely to happen. England, which is much nearer the continent, has proceeded on a quite different assumption, recognizing that there will be need mainly for trained and *experienced* experts at a few points; but that in the majority of cases the work will have to be done by citizens of the respective lands. If no other factors needed to be considered, the shortness of food, the lack of physical accommodations, and the prevalence of unemployment locally when the fighting is over would preclude the bringing in of large numbers of foreigners with no knowledge of local conditions and precious little of the language or psychology of the people.

We can be thankful that the leaders of UNRRA are beginning to be aware of the place the Church may play in reconstruction and have made sincere efforts to secure the counsel and assistance of Church leaders in their planning and administrative procedure.

THE CHIEF OPPORTUNITY

What, then, at this point is the chief opportunity of Protestantism? I would answer in the best light that I can discover—emphasis upon a united program of reconstruction of the Christian institutions of Europe such as has been set forth on European initiative by the Provisional Committee of the World Council of Churches. This program, about which I wish in a moment to speak in some detail, recognizes at the outset the extreme sensitivity of the wounded European churches about foreign programs for their future, however well-intentioned and disinterested. It began by asking highly competent leaders of the churches in the main European lands what they consider needful and what lines Protestant planning in this and other lands should seek to follow. It recognizes the need for repentance and humility on our part and

233

the essential nature of the mutual aid that must be forthcoming and which ought to be a two-way process: our churches as eager to learn from the experiences of European Christians as they are to help them in physical and financial ways. It seeks to avoid patronizing, proselytizing, or condescending attitudes at all points, at the same time recognizing the basically denominational structure of our church life and the necessity for strictly respecting the independence and autonomy of the giving churches as well as those receiving.

The instrumentality proposed for the study of the needs in Europe, the framing of programs, and, in a degree, the administration of relief and reconstruction is a new department of the World Council for the reconstruction of the Christian institutions of Europe.

Those who planned this agency pointed out that the program of reconstruction must include:

a) Restoration of ruined churches and other buildings of Christian service.

b) Replenishing resources of churches and Christian movements whose funds have been confiscated.

c) Enabling Christian institutions of mercy, such as those which care for the sick, the poor, orphans, the aged, and refugees, to enlarge their work in view of the increased need for physical relief.

d) Reconstructing Christian youth organizations which have been disorganized, sometimes under coercion.

e) Providing for the training of a new supply of pastors and lay workers, now sorely depleted, including aid to theological schools and scholarships.

f) Assisting in the production of Christian literature, now almost at a standstill in several countries.

g) Re-establishing the foreign-missionary boards in countries where the home base has been undermined by the war.

Since one of the most remarkable evidences of the new unity of the Christian churches has been the "orphaned- mission" enterprise, whereby support has been provided for the thirty-five hundred continental missionaries cut off from their home-church support, this last would be a logical next step. Since we have had the vision and courage to forget denominational lines in the united support of the foreign missions of our sister churches of Europe, is it too much to hope that we shall have the good sense to refrain from carrying on proselytizing efforts within their natural home territories after the war? The absurdity, if not the insult, of such a procedure only needs to be stated to be obvious. Who can seriously contemplate sending missionaries to wean away from Bishop Berggrav in Norway the people of his land, who are over 92 per cent Lutheran by church connection and who have proved their loyalty to Christianity in the fierce fires of fanatical Nazi persecution?

But let me return to the general subject of which we were thinking and at this point quote the wise words of my colleague Dr. Samuel McCrea Cavert, general secretary of the Federal Council of the Church-

234

es of Christ in America, and a participant in the conference at Geneva in September, 1942, which produced the report from which I have quoted and to which in a moment I shall revert. He says of the program they envisaged:

So vast a program cannot be carried out merely on a denominational basis. It must be approached in a truly ecumenical spirit and be an expression of a Christian solidarity in which each group recognizes each other group as members of the one Body of Christ. All the churches which can help must help all the churches which need help, and that without any thought of proselytism. There will naturally be especially close relations between churches of the same confessional family. But every section of the reconstruction program must be co-ordinated with all other sections. The keynote of the whole effort must be not one of denominational extension but of working with and through the churches in each country in accordance with a general plan which is understood and accepted by all.

Pointing to the obvious danger of competition and overlapping, Dr. Cavert adds:

Fortunately the World Council of Churches affords the needed center for . . . co-ordination. Already most of the churches, both of America and of Europe, belong to its fellowship. Within this fellowship it will surely be possible to arrive at a voluntary correlation of efforts which will leave each church free to act within the framework of a generally accepted policy which all have helped to formulate. In this way it will be possible to avoid the impression that any denomination of any national group seeks to dominate the others; the spirit of mutual aid among all the members of the one Body can be visibly demonstrated.

The functions of the Department of Reconstruction of the Christian Institutions of Europe are therefore projected as follows:

a) to survey the needs of all churches and organizations which are members of or collaborate with the ecumenical movement;

b) to bring these needs to the attention of the churches which are able to help;

c) to register all projects of aid from one church to another and to co-ordinate these projects;

d) to formulate and develop relief projects in cases in which the help of several churches is needed;

e) to act as an executive agency of relief in cases in which it is asked to do so by one or more giving churches.

In order that this plan may be revised and improved and so implemented as to make for its largest effectiveness it is expected that immediately at the close of hostilities or as soon thereafter as may prove practicable an enlarged meeting of the Provisional Committee of the World Council, including representatives of all the co-operating agencies of the churches and other world-Christian movements related to them, will be held. That this may be in Sweden is a definite expectation. It would obviously be best held in some neutral land, to which representatives of nations on both sides of the world struggle might be able to come.

The program I have outlined is, however, in the way of being implemented now, and it ought further to be implemented in the immediate future if we are realistic about our desire to meet the opportunities open to us in Europe. Let me remind you of the steps that have already been taken:

RECONSTRUCTION STEPS ALREADY TAKEN

The Provisional Committee of the World Council, which derives its authority from the great world conferences of 1937 at Oxford and Edinburgh, has not been able to meet in plenary session since the proposals I have referred to were formulated at Geneva. But action has been taken by sectional meetings of the members and by correspondence to authorize the setting up of the new department in Geneva. Informal consultations have been held in America and in Britain with respect to the relation to be sustained by the Central Bureau of Interchurch Aid to the new and more comprehensive agency. Ultimate complete merger is hoped for and probable, although it cannot be achieved until the Central Bureau's own authoritative committee can meet and reach official decisions.

In Britain a special committee has been set up with the same name as that of the department. I attended one of its meetings and know from personal observation that it is making distinct progress in correlating the planning of British churches for their aid to the continental churches. Among other things, while recognizing the necessity to do certain kinds of work denominationally, they are proposing that a central treasury be used and that all funds allocated for expenditure in Europe be expended through that treasury, even when earmarked for exclusively denominational purposes.

It is interesting to note that this development in England was directly inspired in the mind of my late beloved colleague Dr. William Paton, who carried it through before his untimely death in the summer of 1943. He came to feel the necessity for it while participating in a series of informal consultations set up and chaired by Dr. Ralph Diffendorfer in New York City. This British agency is sponsored by the British Council of Churches and the British section of the World Council.

A more direct and immediate outcome of these same consultations has been the development in this country of the Church Committee on Overseas Relief and Reconstruction, commonly known as CCORR. It was sponsored here by the Federal Council of Churches and the Foreign Missions Conference and recognized by the World Council in this country as the official channel for all work with the new department in Geneva. Its chairman is Harper Sibley, and its secretaries are

Drs. Leslie Moss and Livingston Warnshuis. It differs from the British Committee in that it represents a correlation of nine existing agencies that have work overseas and represent, directly or indirectly, church initiative. (Examples would be the Foreign Missions Conference, the Central Bureau, the War Prisoners' Aid of the Young Men's Christian Association, and the American Committee for Christian Refugees.) It likewise differs from the British committee in that it takes into account Asia as well as Europe. But it will constitute directly and definitely the co-operative approach of American Protestantism to the continental churches.

By agreement when churches in this country set aside workers to become part of the staff of the Department of Reconstruction in Geneva, they do so by a process that includes the official action of CCORR so that, in effect, all Americans attached to the department in Geneva will be sponsored by CCORR as well as by their individual denominations.

Two churches have already acted in accordance with this part of the plan. The first to do so was the Congregational-Christian. The second was the Methodist. One devoutly hopes that this will have encouraged others to do the same in the not-distant future.

Instead of a series of rival surveys of the needs of the European churches, made by denominational agencies, it is hoped, although by no means yet assured, that the main survey of need and opportunity will be made through this united agency, representing all the member churches. It is likewise hoped that for purposes of information and mutual consultation the Geneva office will be a sort of general clearing house even for expressly denominational activity such as will of course continue. There would then be at least one place where it would be possible to learn about the whole activity projected and realized in the extending of aid to the stricken churches.

I should like to conclude this all too superficial and inadequate survey of a vital and complicated matter by reminding you that the primary responsibility rests upon the churches of Europe, and any efforts we make to be of help should be conceived in such wise as to strengthen and uphold them in their own approach to the fulfillment of these tasks and the meeting of these staggering opportunities.

May God give us the wisdom, the patience, the sympathy, and the faith to summon our churches for a great co-operative response such as the need of the times makes imperative. We have the beginnings of a real answer to the challenge; but much more needs to be done, and in particular there must be created in the rank and file of the church here in our land a true understanding of the requirements as well as the challenges of the situation among our brethren in Europe.

IN LATIN AMERICA

GONZALO BÁEZ-CAMARGO

PROTESTANTISM's opportunities in Latin America arise both from a divine command and from the actual facts. The command is final and unavoidable. The facts are pressing and challenging.

First, the command: "Go ye therefore, and teach all nations." Again, "Go ye into all the world, and preach the gospel to every creature." Latin American nations are not to be an exception. They need the gospel as much as do any other nations on earth. Then, the facts: Latin America's prevailing religion is leaving a multitude of souls in hunger and distress. A widespread spiritual longing is not adequately met. There is a vast field of human experience where the church has lost its influence, and extravagant substitutes are making their appeal. And even where that religion still holds its sway, so many spurious elements have been welded into the structure that the religious life of the average practicing Latin American becomes a mixture of vague Christian conceptions and motives, overwhelmed by superstition, bigotry, and nonmoralism—so much so that the church itself needs redemption and a conversion or reconversion to the gospel of Christ.

The validity of Protestant missions in Latin America, said to be an already Christian area, has been challenged at different times, but especially now, when the objection has taken a political turn. It is argued that Latin American countries are Roman Catholic countries, and that a sincere Good Neighbor Policy should see to it that the rule of Roman Catholicism in those countries shall not be disturbed by the presence and work of Protestantism.

But this idea of Latin America as an exclusive, "posted-by-law" hunting ground for the Roman Catholic Church or for any other religious body has been rejected by the Latin Americans themselves. There was a time when the claim to religious monopoly had a legal force. The early constitutions of most of the Latin American republics established Roman Catholicism as the religion of the State and prohibited the practice and propagation of any other creed. But long before Protestantism entered Latin America, this religious exclusivism was abolished, and, after successive reforms, the majority of these countries have accepted freedom of worship as one of their fundamental principles—written into their constitutions. Even where Roman Catholicism is still the State religion and is entitled to special protection from the government, freedom to practice and propagate other faiths is at least tolerated.

Protestant missions have as much right to exist in "Roman Catholic countries" as Roman Catholic missions in "Protestant countries." The

238

gospel message comes first to man as an individual, and it is as an individual that he is converted to it. The gospel is a personal appeal to a personal decision. It is not, therefore, a matter of having been merely baptized *into* a church, because salvation is not in church membership of any denomination but in a personal experience of the saving grace of Christ. Wherever there is a single individual, member or not, in a given church who has not reached this experience, the gospel must be preached freely.

On the other hand, a religious majority keeps its spiritual quality against the depressing effects of its own sense of security and predominance only by the presence of a dissenting religious minority. It is then forced to keep alert and continually to supervise its own position and life. A religious minority acts as a purgative and stimulant.

Protestantism in Latin America represents a higher form of morality and of spiritual life. Protestantism is needed in Latin America, first, for itself, because it gives room precisely for the type of spirituality which an increasing number of Latin Americans are seeking and see little hope of finding elsewhere. Secondly, it is needed because its presence, witness, and way of life may in the long run bring about, by emulation, a change for good in Roman Catholicism. The opportunities for Protestantism in Latin America are thus very great and challenging. They belong to the kind that dare not be ignored or deferred.

NOT YET CONVERTED TO CHRISTIANITY

There is a vast mass of population in Latin America, particularly Indian, which has never been actually converted to Christianity. To realize this fact one has only to watch their religious ceremonies and festivals and explore their conceptions and customs. Travelers and ethnologists are all of one accord that a strong survival of ancient pagan ideas and practices is blended into what is officially known as Roman Catholicism. Especially among the 15 or 20 per cent of Indians in the population fetishism, animism, demonolatry, and idol worship are deeply rooted and show extraordinary persistence.

To take a typical instance—that of the Tarascan Indians in central Mexico—this is what Dr. Lucio Mendieta y Nuñez, director of the Institute of Social Research of the National University, has to say:

Today, in spite of an intensive Protestant propaganda, Catholicism prevails in an absolute way in the Tarascan area; but reminiscences of the ancient cosmology are still preserved. The Tarascan Catholicism shows, also, certain special features. It cannot be affirmed that they have entered completely into the conceptions of the Catholic religion. It is not the worship of God but of the saints that has taken stronger roots in their souls. Each village has a patron saint, who is worshiped with idolatrous fervor; for even in the case of one and the same saint certain images or statues representing him are considered as of more virtue and power than others." [1]

---

[1] *Los Tarascos,* 1940, p. lvi.

The Tarascans burn incense to the household saints, each day at noon, "to feed them." During the big festival of the village patron saint they insist upon dancing within the church, because "the saint wants to see a dance." This festival lasts for several days "in the midst of great enthusiasm and general drunkenness." The funerals "preserve pagan customs." The Tarascans call the sun and the rain "Lord"—a polytheistic remnant. "All the Tarascans believe in magic . . . and they are very superstitious." Then comes a long list of superstitions about the dead, dreams, birth, ghosts, darkness, the devil, et cetera.

The Tarascan case is duplicated and, in some instances, to greater extent, by many other Indian groups in Latin America, as the very complete report of the Montevideo Congress on Christian Work clearly shows.

The reason for this persistence of heathenism and the lack of a real conversion of the Indians must be found in the missionary policy of the Roman Catholic Church.

In the first place, the Indians were joined to the church by the thousands through the mere rite of bapism. The classic story of friars and priests who in a single day and without a stop baptized Indian after Indian until they collapsed with fatigue illustrates this. "Mass conversion," of course, was only superficial, not followed by a real change of outlook and life. The indoctrination of the Indians was limited to the repetition of prayers and dogmatic formulas and to the attendance upon the ceremonies and the paying of tithes and other financial obligations. Then the children of these original "converts" became Catholics merely by baptism and tradition, generation after generation, up to this very day.

In the second place, in order to secure the most loyal allegiance from the Indians the church tolerated and, in many specific instances, even encouraged the persistence of ancient religious ideas and practices by giving them only an outer veneer of Christianity and incorporating them into the accepted practices of Catholicism. Thus the Indians felt themselves more "at home." Their inward souls, still pagan, were undisturbed.

The spiritual and social condition of the large Indian population of Latin America, among whom ignorance, superstition, poverty, and disease are the daily lot, is certainly one of the greatest challenges to Protestantism. This was undoubtedly realized by President Benito Juárez, of Mexico, and an Indian himself, who once said, "Upon the development of Protestantism depends the future happiness and prosperity of my nation," [2] and on another occasion remarked, "I wish that Protestantism would become Mexicanized by going to the Indian, because the Indian needs a religion which will compel him to read and not to spend his savings on candles for the saints." [3]

---

[2] John W. Butler, *History of the Methodist Episcopal Church in Mexico,* p. 35.

[3] Justo Sierra, *Mexico y su Evolucion Social*, Vol. II, p. 419.

EXTERNAL TRADITION RATHER THAN A LIVING FAITH

The spiritual situation is hardly any better outside of the Indian population. The contagion of many pagan and animistic beliefs common among the Indians has reached far and wide. Religion becomes, for a great majority, a mere routine, an idle fulfillment of external obligations. Revivals usually take the form of fanatical explosions of bigotry, sentimentality, and increased superstition, as well as hedonistic enthusiasm for the big festivals and luxurious demonstrations.

To the question whether or not there is a *Christian* tradition alive in Latin America, the great Argentinian scholar Don Ricardo Rojas answered, "*Catholic* tradition, as a matter of external formalities, is undoubtedly alive; but not so the Christian feeling as an inspiration of living." [4] Dr. Rojas describes Latin American Catholicism as "infused with Spanish fanaticism and Indian fetishism" [5] and sadly remarks that "the fetishism of the masses and the arrogance of the aristocracy are certainly not Christian; worship is practiced but its meaning unknown; charity is here nothing but selfish instinct or worldly ostentation." [6]

To many Catholicism is primarily a matter of social tradition and good manners, a sort of elegant conformity to socially approved standards, without which harm to business, loss of prestige, and social ostracism would be risked. Or the elaborate, colorful, impressive rites of the Church are practiced merely as a feast of the senses, an aesthetic enjoyment. Gabriela Mistral, the exquisite Chilean poetess and a Roman Catholic herself, wonders, "Is there not in many people's Catholicism a religion of esthetics, . . . much like Greek heathenism?" [7]

Some enlightened Roman Catholics admit this inner decay. The picture, given as early as 1866 by a Catholic paper in Brazil, of the condition of Catholicism can be applied to the present day and to all Latin America:

> . . . its despised episcopacy, the deplorable state of its clergy, a worship bastardized with pagan practices, beliefs either fanatic or skeptical, and asphyxiated as it is by the paralysis of crushing indifference. . . . The majesty of Catholic worship has been here reduced to practices not only idolatrous and heathenish but even of an absurd fetishism.[8]

This fact that has led the noted South American educator Dr. Juan B. Terán to the conclusion that "in [Latin] America . . . Christian preaching did not penetrate either the spiritual life or the customs. *The conversion of [Latin] America to Christianity is not a fact ac-*

---

[4] *El Cristo Invisible*, p. 258.

[5] *Ibid.*, p. 12.

[6] *Ibid.*, p. 261.

[7] Quoted by L. A. Sanchez in *Balance y Liquidacion del 900*, p. 194.

[8] Quoted by Braga and Grubb in *Religion in the Republic of Brazil*, World Dominion Press, London.

241

complished [9] during the conquest but a process that has not yet been completed, especially in the masses of people." [10]

Its own historic reluctance to change and the additional weight of a tradition of centuries make it very doubtful whether the Roman Catholic Church in Latin America will ever be able by herself to cure herself of these ancient and deep-rooted ailments. Those who know Christianity only as an outward formality, and not as a living, transforming faith, stand in dire need of the appeal of the gospel as preached in all of its redeeming force. This is the opportunity and task of Protestantism. And if Roman Catholicism is ever to come out of its present stagnation and to undergo a truly spiritual revival, it will be only under the impact and stimulus of a preaching permeated with the original spirit and stressing the basic message of the New Testament gospel. This, again, is the task and opportunity of Protestantism.

Throughout Latin America there are people who have no real concern about religion, no deep-seated interest in the spiritual life. These are found especially among the male of the species. They belong to two categories: first, those who are nominally affiliated with the Roman Catholic Church but leave the interest in and the practice of their religion to the women and the children; secondly, those who have given up religion of any kind openly and profess to be atheists or who hold a vague kind of naturalistic theism—that is, they say that to believe "there is a God," to be fair and kind to other people, and to respect the beliefs of everybody are all that is needed. The "scientific" snobs, who look down upon religious people because they think that religion is a symptom of primitivism and lack of culture, form a class by themselves and are very numerous among the Latin American intelligentsia.

The first group, however, is by far the more numerous—that of the nonpracticing Roman Catholics. Statistics fail to reveal their number. They register as "Catholics" when the population census is taken and thus help to raise the official proportion. But you have only to ask people at random about their religion to be surprised at the number who answer something like this: "I *am* Catholic, but . . . ." And then they begin to take exceptions to this or that particular thing that their church teaches or does or to what priests are and do, and to tell you that they attend church only once in a while for the sake of dear mother or wife and not to disturb the children too much. Finally, they apologize for their family, the "poor little ones," who are very fond of the church; and, of course, if they need it and find comfort in it, why not condescend and let them go and do what they please?

Many others stand for the preservation of Catholicism purely from patriotic and nationalistic reasons. Personally they are not concerned for that or any other religion; but they think that since it is something typically "ours," something that gives color and "unity" to the national

---

[9] Italics are mine.
[10] *La Salud de la América Española*, p. 69.

life, something that the mass of the people really need in order to behave—a "bridle," without which their instincts and ignorance would become dangerous to the other social classes—something that lies at the core of beautiful traditions, Roman Catholicism and all the uses and customs that go under its name should be earnestly supported. A prominent writer in Mexico, who has held very high positions, told me recently, "Personally I am not a Catholic but a freethinker, and I recognize that you Protestants practice your faith with more sincerity and purity; but I think that Roman Catholicism should be preserved because it is the cement of our national life."

In other cases it is merely the beauty and splendor of rites, the poetry in legends, and the simple fervor of the common people which hold their interest. Even a man like Ignacio M. Altamirano, prominent liberal and outspoken atheist, is said to have exclaimed, "Yes, but let nobody dare to touch the Virgin of Guadalupe." This Virgin is claimed to be the patron of Mexico and the symbol of its nationality and patriotism.

But this interest is only superficial. There is an appalling lack of real concern—that deep hunger of the soul, that inner wrestling of Jacob with the angel, that agony of the spirit out of which only a living experience of true religion can lead to God.

The case of a multitude of Latin Americans is one that may well deserve the description given by Unamuno, the Spanish writer:

For them there are no burning tears shed in silence, in the silence of mystery, because these barbarians think they have the solution for everything; for them there is no unrest of the soul, because they think they were born in the possession of absolute truth; for them there is nothing else but dogmas and formulas and recipes.

Ecclesiasticism, stubbornly standing in the way between the soul and its God, come in the end to place God far away and to stifle in the spirit of men the desire for an intimate and direct fellowship with the Living Lord. Often a reaction comes—the rebellion of those who want to think of God with their own minds and to seek for him in the depths of their own consciences. This carries them away into indifference, materialistic positivism, agnosticism, and extravagance. The religious quest is, in the long run, wearily given up, and the cold acceptance of the rules and dogmas of the church—or plain incredulity —is journey's end.

The only hope for these people is to challenge them with a faith that will not be afraid of the earnest exercise of thought but will encourage the right and the duty of every man to think out courageously his own doubts and to put to a test every single religious assumption; a faith that will make religion a vital, personal affair; a faith that will force men to a personal decision; a faith, briefly, that will stir up the innermost self in order to launch it upon the great quest for God. This is of the very essence of Protestantism, since a Protestantism that becomes dogmatic has lost its soul. Latin America offers here a very wide field of opportunity.

SEAGULLS AND CLOSED WINDOWS IN THE STORM

Don Luis de Zulueta, the former Spanish Ambassador to the Vatican, in writing about the many people who feel the appeal of Christianity but cannot find their spiritual home within the church, compares them to seagulls that in a stormy night seek refuge in the church, only to find its doors and windows closed to them.

There are many souls who feel that the Roman Catholic Church is no home for them, because it gives them no full satisfaction of their spiritual yearnings, no convincing answer to their inquiring intellect; yet they feel the appeal of Christianity, they respond to the subtle touch of Christ upon their hearts. They are sincere. They realize that they cannot be honest practicing Catholics, but they want to be Christians, to be with Christ, to belong to his fold.

Don Ricardo Rojas' experience is typical of many educated Latin Americans:

I was born into a Catholic family, with no immediate ancestors who were not old Christians—Christians in the orthodox way of the ancient Spanish America—and I was baptized by my parents' decision; I practiced the commandments of the Roman Church during my childhood; and although philosophic freedom took me away from Catholicism in later years, I never failed to feel myself deeply Christian in the widest sense of the word. . . . For years and years I have sojourned as a thirsty one in arid deserts, searching through the religious literature of all races for the fountain where I could quench my thirst. . . . Today I find in the Gospels my surest spiritual guidance. . . . My religious ideal . . . is no other than to revive the Invisible Christ in my conscience, through a spiritual mystery, in the heroic way of the old mystics. . . . I want Christ to be real in the conscience of every man.[11]

To these wandering souls Protestantism may come in order to confront them with the Living, Invisible Christ, who wishes to dwell in and become the Lord of their consciences. This Jesus, Lover of the soul, goes out, arms open, into the stormy night to seek those who, in sorrow, darkness, and yearning, are looking for him.

THE DOMINIONS OF THE SILENT CHRIST

One day I stood astonished in front of an image of Christ in the state of Michoacán. It was beautifully carved and dressed in white. But an ugly object disturbed the serene beauty of its face. It was an iron padlock, piercing his lips and closing them tightly. I inquired of a devout woman, kneeling close by, and she told me; "Why, it is Our Lord of the Padlock. So miraculous! If you have a secret, pray to him. He will hush up!" I noticed how the garment of the image was full

---

[11] Op. cit., pp. 119, 325, 329, 318, 333.

of tiny silver gifts pinned upon it. Hush money received by the silent Christ!

That sight pierced my soul. For there was the symbol of the Christ of Latin America. Beautiful, kept in churches superbly ornamented, candles lighted at his feet, silver and gold laid before him, and a padlock on his lips! For in no other area of the world, except in plain non-Christian lands, has the Word of God been so utterly ignored. For centuries it has been the well-known policy of the ruling Church to withhold the Bible from the common people. Church traditions, legends, catechisms, ceremonies, prescriptions, and dogmas have taken its place. The word of the priest is enough. There has been therefore a padlock on the Bible too. Editions of the Bible permitted by the church have been so costly that only the rich can place them as an ornament in their libraries.

The worst tragedy in the spiritual life of Latin America is that the prevailing religion has rendered direct study of the Word of Christ practically unnecessary. "Lord, Lord, we will worship thee; but keep silent"!

Is Latin America already Christian? How often we hear this question asked! It cannot be answered with a plain yes or no. We may answer yes in the sense that Christ is worshiped in Latin America, and that people are named after his name. We must answer no, because the Christ that Latin America worships and confesses is a dead and silent Christ.

Yet how many souls are longing to hear him speak! How many for whom the Word of Christ is the truth, the life, and the way!

One night I was the guest of a prominent professor in the National University of Mexico. He is not affiliated with any church. He led me to his library. On his desk there was a line of chosen books. He took one of them out. "Here," he said, "this is what I read every day—a Protestant New Testament in French."

A carpenter was working on some repairs in the evangelical bookshop in Mexico City, where phonograph records of hymns, Scripture readings, and short sermons are also for sale. Some of these records were being played for a customer. The carpenter listened. A year later he came to the bookshop again.

"I want some of those records," he said. "A year ago I listened to them, but I did not have a record player then. I have one now, and I want the records."

"Will you prefer some with songs and music?" the clerk asked.

"No," was the prompt reply, "I want especially the ones with the words of our Lord."

The Word of Christ! All the way down from the university professor to the carpenter, it is the Word of Christ they want—the Christ without a padlock.

"Mexico does not want more of . . . any instruction tainted by clerical influence," a former president of the republic said once. "If

245

the children of Mexico are going to be Christians, let them be so by imbibing the Christian doctrine at the pure fountains of the Word of the Master, which we find in the Gospels." [12]

Workers Away From the Master Worker

It has become a commonplace with students of Latin American life that the labor movement in these countries, holding under its influence several million workers, is drifting away from Christianity at a rapid pace. Perhaps this is a universal phenomenon. It exists in a large measure in countries where the Protestant faith is prevalent. But there is nothing to be compared with the tremendous situation in countries dominated by the Roman Catholic creed. One of the popes has called it "the scandal of our times" that the church has lost its influence in this field and that the workers are advancing along the road to social and economic justice under non-Christian banners.

This fact is particularly acute in Latin America, with its large population of depressed laborers and enslaved Indians. The fearful heritage of feudalism from the times of the Spanish rule still prevails in vast areas. And wherever this situation is breaking down, the revolutionary forces are taking on anti-Christian, certainly anticlerical taints. This is partly due to the fact that the Roman Catholic Church as a whole, especially its hierarchy, became divorced from the earthly needs of the people and tangled itself up with the old order. The church invested its great wealth in real estate and in loans to the landlords and thus became a part of the feudal system. When the claim for social justice sprang from below, the church found that although the gospel message it preached really meant justice for the poor and the downtrodden, the social and economic power the institution had achieved placed its interests upon the side of the powerful and the established order. With its soul thus divided against itself it was faced by the social struggle and forced to take sides. This it did inevitably against the people, so it became the most powerful conservative force. Social transformation, first neglected and then opposed by the church, has been going on under the force of a pressing social need. The result is that the working masses not only go away from the church but, carried still further by the natural force of their reaction, tend to consider Christianity itself as their social enemy.

Let us hear Gabriela Mistral describe this crisis:

A painful aspect of Latin America at this time is the divorce that is being made between the masses of the people and religion or, rather, between democracy and Christianity. . . . Unlike Anglo-Saxon Christianity our Christianity divorced itself from the social question. Not by tradition nor even by keen calculation has our Christianity known how to be loyal to the humble ones.[18]

---

[12] Emilio Portes Gil, 1934; statement as attorney-general.
[18] *La Nueva Democracia*, New York.

There has been a divorce between religion and ethics as well. Religion has had very little to do with morality. There is no practical connection between the rite and daily behavior. Religion is conceived and practiced as a system of external forms but does not pervade every order of life as a motive and inspiration of conscience. Even a superficial observer can notice how often religious fervor and disorderly conduct go together. Religious festivals easily become truly pagan orgies. Devotion to the saints as a means to attract success in crooked business is not uncommon. Divorce is repudiated as contrary to the commandments of the church, but there is a general indulgence in free unions and adultery. Religion becomes ritualistic, not ethical.

Protestantism has always emphasized the close connection between religion and life. It stresses ethics no less than doctrine and worship. While Roman Catholicism considers holiness as the possibility of only a few, Protestantism challenges everybody with the scriptural assertion that it is God's purpose that all be made holy. This creates in the believer a continuous striving after the good life. On the other hand, Protestantism brings up afresh the emphasis upon social justice and social cleanliness which Roman Catholicism in Latin America seems to have lost. It is therefore prepared to fill the gap so unfortunately wedged between religion and the individual and social conduct.

THE ESSENTIAL TASK OF LATIN AMERICAN PROTESTANTISM

So, as stated in the beginning, Protestantism's opportunities in Latin America arise both from the divine command to "teach all nations" and from the outstanding facts in the spiritual condition of that part of the world. These facts point to pressing needs. And the needs, in turn, involve a great challenge and lay down before Protestants a big and immediate task. In this task the following aspects are prominent:

First, *Protestantism must open up the Word of God to the common people by intensive preaching and an active distribution of the Bible and evangelical literature.* The preaching must be positive and must not indulge in bitter controversy. It must be Christ-centered: it must announce salvation in Jesus Christ. If this message is driven home to the hearts of men, it will tend to destroy unchristian and superstitious beliefs, no matter how deeply rooted in tradition they may be.

That this is a real opportunity is shown by reports from the Bible societies about the increasing distribution of the Bible in Latin America. The last report from the Mexico Agency of the American Bible Society shows an increase, in the last three years, of more than four thousand Bibles, more than two thousand New Testaments, and 100 per cent of Bible portions every year.

The Salvation Army in Mexico, with the co-operation of all the churches, is engaged now in a campaign to place seven million Gospels in the homes through direct, house-to-house visitation by trained corps of volunteers. At the time of this writing some 1,400,000 copies have been already distributed. Incidentally this campaign has shown how the Roman Catholic Church is being forced by Protestantism to lift its ban against giving the Scriptures to the common people. In answer to the Salvation Army crusade the Catholics launched a campaign in Mexico City to distribute twenty thousand Gospels in their authorized version. They openly declared that this was done to counteract the Protestant campaign. Some cheaper editions of the Bible and the New Testament have recently been put out by Catholic publishers, and also books on how to study the Bible. One of these books, printed in Argentina, begins with the statement that "the Bible is not a Protestant book."

Directly and indirectly Protestantism is thus giving the Word of God to Latin America.

Secondly, *Protestantism must demonstrate a type of Christianity closer to the sincerity and simplicity of the original.* As over against the great masses of human traditions that have been added to the doctrines and practices of the New Testament Church and the external splendor of an elaborate ritual, the Protestant churches in Latin America represent a return to the original sources. They represent the stress upon the inner experience rather than upon the sensual impressions, a religion of the spirit and in the spirit. It is true that the Latin American is fond of color and lights and pompous displays, but he is not deaf to the call of the spiritual when it rings the tone of sincerity.

Thirdly, *Protestantism must demonstrate a higher type of moral and spiritual life, the living witness to the transforming grace of God in Jesus Christ.* When visiting some Catholic sanctuaries in Mexico, Dr. E. Stanley Jones called attention to the fact that the miracles the people say they are thankful for have nothing to do with moral and spiritual changes in their lives. The task of Protestantism is to show that religion works; that it is not comfort, like a drug, or enjoyment, like a show, but a powerful force destructive of evil in individual and social life. And the only way to show it is by producing men and women whose morality is far above the average.

Fourthly, *Protestantism must give a living demonstration of the principles, ideals, motives, and deeds of a true Christian community; a sketch and pattern of what society will be at large if and when it accepts Christ as Lord; a sample in miniature of the kingdom of God on earth.* In Protestantism the Christian religion should demonstrate its power as a force for social reconstruction, not as an enemy of social progress. This means much more than the mere proclamation of "the social gospel" or a few benevolent works. It means a vigorous stand for social justice and sacrificial service to the community; a relentless campaign against all that is evil in the social life, against vice and ignorance; an ardent devotion to everything that makes for a better way of living. To Protestantism befalls, at this time, the sacred responsibility of restoring the faith of the common people, especially the workers, in Christianity as a social, redeeming force. In the midst of its social and economic remaking Latin America may be helped by Protestantism to see that religion has something to do with it—in fact, that there will be no successful social progress unless it is based on a spiritual revolution.

That Latin America welcomes and recognizes this type of help was proved in an impressive way by the decoration that the government of Brazil bestowed upon Dr. Tucker, the secretary of the American Bible Society in Rio de Janeiro, for his services to the country in the field of education and public health. Dr. Tucker distributes the Bible. He also shows the principles of the Bible in action. Again, in demanding freedom for the work of the Protestants in Peru, some deputies and senators of that republic commended the work Protestantism has done among the people, especially among the Indians. "Evangelical missions," they said, "have rescued many Indians from the most absolute ignorance and have made them forget the vices of alcohol and the narcotic coca leaf."

Finally, *Protestantism has an unparalleled opportunity, as President Juárez of Mexico said, to salvage the Indians.* About one fifth of the population of Latin America is Indian. They form the lowest social class and have been almost forgotten except as objects of mistreatment and exploitation. The Indians have never been actually converted to any form of Christianity. They are virgin soil for the gospel. To the extent to which it has been done, work among the Indians in Bolivia, Peru, Chile, Mexico, and other countries shows how fertile this field is for the planting of evangelical Christianity. If no other opportunity opened to Protestantism but the Macedonian call from the Indians, this would be enough to constitute a worthy challenge.

Latin America is undergoing a thorough reconstruction. This will be accelerated after the war. Protestantism may never become the religion of the majority in Latin America; but it has the splendid opportunity of becoming a real, living, decisive force in the moral, social, and spiritual remaking of Latin America's life.

IN AMERICAN EDUCATION

ERNEST C. COLWELL

IF PROTESTANTISM, as such, has an opportunity in the field of education, that opportunity must lie within the area of religion and religious interest. The great increase in vocational training even before the war cannot be identified as Protestantism's opportunity. Nor can the training of a quarter of a million men at government expense for specific military duties be recognized as the rosy glow of a new and better day's dawn for Protestantism.

It is probable that "education" is more widespread at the moment than it ever has been in this country before. More than 275,000 men in December, 1943, were being trained in the colleges in the Army, Navy, and Air Forces programs. Add to these the residue of civilian students, who still total more than a third of the prewar total. Consider the scope of the Armed Forces Institute, which has between 250,000 and 400,000 soldiers enrolled for correspondence work and courses taught in camps. Remember that 70,000 high-school upperclassmen took the qualifying test for the Army A-12 and Navy V-12 programs in November. Then realize that these numbers do not include the hundreds of thousands who have been trained and are being trained in radio operation and maintenance, aviation in all its branches, and a dozen other technological skills. But the presence of a million people in school for these purposes is not the educational opportunity for Protestantism.

The basic and general opportunity of Protestantism is the development and spread of "pure religion and undefiled." Wherever and whenever this can be developed, our churches have opportunities. I take it to be axiomatic that the development of true religion in school personnel or in the neighborhood of school buildings is an opportunity for Protestantism. But it is not the educational opportunity I have been asked to discuss. In fact, it is not an educational opportunity at all; it is the Church's age-old opportunity for evangelization and spiritual nurture.

I mean to urge at the outset that the employment of the finest student pastors or the most devout deacons as teachers in the public schools will not be Protestantism's adequate contribution to education in this country. I am heartily in favor of the items just mentioned. I believe that they are effective instruments in developing and maintaining the religious life of students. They are more effective than courses in Bible for this purpose, but this purpose is one that is collateral to education. The church's ministry to the individual should parallel his activities in school, as also his later activities in money-making. But this ministry is not education any more than the work of the local pastor is commerce.

Lest I should seem to be swinging a sledgehammer at an open door, let me remind you that the confusion of these two things has been widespread and long-continued. Less than twenty years ago a student in a course in Bible, which I was teaching, received a failing grade. His mother wrote me in great bewilderment and with equal force. She could not imagine, she said, what I could have against her boy. Was it a matter of personal dislike? How could he fail a course in Bible? He had always been a good boy and had not been late to Sunday school for thirteen years. Thus, also, students in a seminary are often puzzled because a course in the history of the doctrine of God does not increase their personal communion with the Deity. Today it is generally true that theological students substitute the study of religion for the practice of personal devotion. These false expectations are symptoms of a confusion in regard to religion and education that is widespread.

In spite of this confusion I am persuaded that religious people, and especially Protestants, have an opportunity to make a significant contribution to education—a contribution that will make education more religious. This hopeful view of mine does not rest entirely on the abstract speculations with which a professor is supposed to while away his time in the loneliness of his ivory tower. It is based in part on certain observations. The first of these is that there is a growing literacy in Protestantism. Evidence of this is to be found not only in general statistics, which indicate that more and more laymen are completing high-school programs and attending college, but also in the trend toward an educated ministry, even in conservative churches. The Nazarenes are beginning to appear in the denominational statistics of universities and liberal seminaries. Conservative Baptist and Presbyterian seminaries apply for accreditation to the Association of Theological Schools and Seminaries. A leader in one of the strongly anti-intellectual churches spent three days recently on our campus discussing the establishment of a program of ministerial training which would be academically respectable. There is a growing literacy in Protestantism, and this is a ground of hope.

One of my colleagues, who is actively engaged in the work of the ecumenical movement, reminds me, however, that there is still plenty of room at the top of the educational ladder for Protestants. He laments the shortage of Protestant scholars qualified to participate in constructive work in religion. If I am correct in assuming a large increase in college and professional training, there is hope that more Protestants will set themselves early to the arduous task of becoming scholars. The extension of graduate work in the South, for example, is both justifiable and inevitable, and Protestant institutions have the opportunity to make significant contributions in this area.

The opportunity to do something significant in education rests in part upon the increased popular interest in getting more religion into education. It is well known to workers in the field of education that this interest has been increasing steadily for the last ten years. This interest has manifested itself in demands that "religious instruction" be introduced in the program of the public schools. It has manifested itself also in new developments in the colleges and universities. Departments of religion have been established in both public and private institutions. In state universities two patterns have been extensively followed: One is the integration of religious instruction with courses in the humanities or, more specifically, with courses in literature or philosophy. Chairs of philosophy of religion are becoming a normal part of the academic furniture in state institutions. Other state universities have fostered an adjunct department of religion—outside the school, yet of it. There are several distinguished examples of this pattern in the Midwest. My hope rests not alone in these specific manifestations but also in the swell of popular interest out of which they come.

I see further opportunity for Protestantism to do something significant in education in the fact that we are at war. The great enemy of significant advance in the field of education is inertia. Education is rooted in the status quo and worships tradition. Since the days of John Locke education in England and America has paid careful attention to preparing the student for getting ahead in this world. The usefulness of the "contacts" made in some of our eastern schools has often been held to be an adequate justification of a college education. This tends to set up a closed circuit in education—a circuit that runs from the present leaders of industrial life to the college student through the professor and so on ad nauseam and add futility. Before the clergy cast the first stone at this aristocratic system, let them consider whether they have advised candidates for the ministry to stay within the denominational pattern of education for the sake of making contacts. Let them remember that closed circuits of theological education can be found in Protestantism—for example, in the colleges and seminaries of the Southern Baptist Convention, where the ministers and the teachers of the ministers are educated in religion without defilement by an alien, non-Baptist mind. The stultifying effect of such isolation has been stated in classical form by Professor Park in a description of Pasadena, California:

. . . Pasadena, where the rich and retired live in a seclusion so complete and so silent that in some of the residential hotels, it is said, one scarcely hears anything but the ticking of the clock or the hardening of one's arteries.[1]

Such systems of education lead to intellectual sterility, to complacency

---

[1] "Education and the Cultural Crisis," Robert E. Park, *Education and the Cultural Process*; edited by Charles S. Johnson; p. 104, *American Journal of Sociology*, May, 1943. (By permission, the University of Chicago Press, publishers.)

that defies improvement or extension. In them change becomes impossible.

But not in wartime! Then all is in flux. Change is the pattern of our daily life, and the protagonist of better education or of good education for more people need not waste his precious stock of energy in fighting entrenched interest. The trenches have been blown up in the explosion of civilian life in total war. Then the champion of religious education who knows what his cause is and who is unafraid has a chance.

Thus, increasingly literate Protestants may make education more religious with the support of popular interest and by taking advantage of the wartime fluidity of the educational structure. It is not partisanship to suggest that they owe this opportunity in part to the fact that they are Protestants. Their relative freedom in intellectual matters gives them an increased responsibility. Since they are capable of exercising toleration, they can take the initiative in general religious movements designed to improve education.

SHORTCOMINGS OF EDUCATION

In spending so much time in arguing that Protestantism has an opportunity to improve American education I have departed from the conventional outline of speeches in education. These speeches usually begin with an analysis of the educational situation—an analysis that shows that education is in dire need of help. I omit this analysis because it has been well done more than once by others, and the diagnosis of the disease is generally admitted to be accurate.

I shall therefore, after the manner of Cicero, pass on without mentioning that education in America is atomistic, without an integrating or synthesizing element. I shall not take time to say that the combination of scientism and pragmatism presents values in such a way as to suggest that all values are a matter of indifference to the educated man; nor shall I linger to point out that the nature of contemporary education makes a democratic society or a religious attitude to life equally difficult if not impossible.

All this has been said by others without refutation. There is disagreement on the cure but not on the nature of the disease. Mr. Hutchins' diagnosis has recently been repeated in effective fashion by Mr. Meiklejohn, and a score of others have supported this indictment.

The acceptance of this indictment by a score of leaders in the world of education should not be taken as evidence that the medicine has been prescribed and that the patient is now rapidly recovering. A recent incident is enough to demonstrate the contrary. The American Association of Teachers Colleges sent an appeal to the American Association of Universities for action that would change the education of schoolteachers in graduate schools so as to give them "a broad understanding of the complex interactions of human experiences, ethical ideals, social institutions, biological forces, and material environment."

At the recent meeting of the A.A.U. I spent a long evening listening to a group of graduate-school deans discuss the topic "Breadth in Graduate Study." The chemist pointed out that we could not expect the student to master *all* the divisions of chemistry because of the vast increase in knowledge of chemistry; the most we could hope for, he said, was that the quantitative chemist and the qualitative chemist would extend their speaking acquaintance. The physicist reassured us with the statement that physics still had its synthesis: it required the student to know the whole field of physics. The biologist felt that the inclusiveness and breadth that were possible in physics were impossible in biology. Nor did the other disciplines claim more. I am not sure that this discussion was intended to answer the appeal of the teachers colleges, but it clearly revealed the need for the appeal.

The lack of breadth in higher education is no more serious than the lack of depth in the entire educational system. Ever since the state took education away from the church, the slogan of educators has been toleration. But it is a toleration so negatively defined that it leads to indifference. If every man's opinion is his own business, the teacher has no right to influence that opinion even by reason. All the teacher can do is to say that truth is this to A and that to B, and that the student should have a clear understanding of both A and B. As the teacher scrupulously keeps himself outside the picture, the usual effect upon the student is to convince him that truth is neither A nor B nor anything else. This, and nothing else, is the Antichrist of modern education. No religious faith can rest upon the foundation that education of this type creates. Nor can a democratic state be nurtured thus.

PROPOSED CURES

Many specific cures have been suggested. The more specific they are, the less promising they seem. The most notable of these is the suggestion that religion should be included in the curriculum of the grammar and high schools. This suggestion has won extensive support and deserves discussion by someone better qualified than I am. All I can say is that I have seen nothing in it to waken enthusiasm and that the difficulties involved seem to me to be such as to prevent the success of the program as stated above. The difficulties can be summed up in the paradox that when religion is introduced into education it isn't education, and when education becomes religious it isn't religious.

When bona-fide courses in religion are introduced, they must satisfy the religious public that is being served. The least intelligent section of that public is often the most vocal and the most insistent upon having *its* religion taught in the schools. In a city high school that had proudly introduced courses in religion an inspection of their content revealed that what was being taught was Seventh Day Adventism and premillennial horrors. Nor is this determination of the program by the indoctrinators easily avoided by the released-time program. This often means that students are excused from school for work in religion which satisfies some church officials but could not satisfy the schoolman either in quality or conception.

When, on the other hand, the schools decide to make their education "religious" by inculcating personal and social values in the children, the result is religious only in terms of a lowest common denominator. It must shed every item that is distinctive of Christian, Jew, Roman Catholic, Baptist, or Methodist. I listened recently to a professor present such a program to some of his colleagues in the department of education. It was received with enthusiasm, since it showed that they had been engaged in religious education all the time without knowing it. Still later I witnessed the response of a group of professors of religion to the same program. They granted its moral and social values but could see nothing in it which they recognized as religious. If programs of this sort are to be the instruments for the introduction of religion into the public-school system, it should be clearly realized that what is introduced is not religion in any sense that will satisfy the public demand.

I realize, of course, that there are communities of a single faith, with intelligent leaders in church and school who have succeeded in introducing religion into the public-school system. There are also more complex situations in which significant progress has been made. But this is not a general condition in America.

A similar specific in the realm of higher education can be seen in the various insertions of religion into college programs. Attention has already been called to the increase in the number of departments of religion and chairs of religion in colleges and universities, both public and private. Instruction in religion is improving in quality and quantity in many institutions. Particularly noteworthy are programs being developed at Princeton, Colgate, and the Universities of Colorado and Oregon. Degree programs through an affiliated staff are carried on at the University of Missouri, the University of Michigan, and elsewhere. The typing of this article was interrupted by an appeal from one of our famous old colleges for assistance in selecting a man capable of establishing an effective department of religion.

This increase in courses in religion is paralleled by an increase in the number of college chaplains and gothic cathedrals, religious-emphasis weeks, and student Christian movements. But in this area I would still give the palm to the church on the edge of the campus and the Wesley Foundation.

All these activities are attempts to insert religion into the college as a gusset is inserted in the seat of a tight pair of pants. Insofar as they are a patch on the garment, they do not promise much. What is needed is a new pattern in the weaving of the whole fabric. The addition of gold buttons to a dress does not make a golden dress.

A third specific guaranteed to cure is Religious Education with a capital *R* and a capital *E*. When I was graduated from a Methodist seminary sixteen years ago, religious education was a siren that lured some of my classmates from the "traditional" pastorate to "a more significant vocation." "R.E.," as we affectionately called her, was the minister's ideal helpmeet and would make the education of the American people religious. But that was sixteen years ago, and the old lady is no longer the glamour girl she once was. Most of her ministerial boy friends are a little self-conscious about their former intimacy. Yet a master-of-arts degree in religious education for the lay worker (so some of our leaders think) may succeed, even though it failed with the clergy. Overconcentration on methods—on the *how* of education—and a too-easy acceptance of a philosophy of education which could not support religious values doomed religious education then and limits its usefulness now.

The successor to religious education's messianic role in education is counseling—a curious hybrid produced by grafting Freudian psychiatry onto a call to the ministry. Among religious workers in education, seminary students and faculty, teachers of religion in college, et cetera, the favorite fad of today is counseling. The same extravagant claims are made for it which were made for religious education in the twenties. The same frenzied efforts to make a profession out of a part-time activity are now directed to this new end.

But time would fail me, as the Scripture says, if I were to speak of work camps and caravans, of clinical training and vocational tests. My quarrel with all these is not with their specific virtues, but with their limited specific nature. What is needed is a general transformation of education. The causes I have mentioned are (with one possible exception) incapable of affecting education in general. We might as well hope to dig the Panama Canal with teaspoons as to attempt to improve education significantly by these methods.

NEEDED: A GENERAL RELIGIOUS VIEW OF EDUCATION

What Protestantism wants is a general religious view of education. It is Protestantism's great opportunity that it can help to shape both our society and our educational system so as to make this possible.

A religious view of education sees education as designed to serve society. This does not mean the service of some special social group. The best education is not to be offered to the children of the wealthy but to the children of all classes. Education is the preparation of the child to take his place as a member of the world's largest fraternity—the brotherhood of men. Ideally this means schools where all classes and both sexes pursue a common education. The length of time spent in school by any child would be determined by his ability and his inclination, not by his father's financial resources. For the Protestant this devotion of education to the purposes of human brotherhood, to the common good, finds its ultimate justification in man's relation to God.

Education cannot prepare individuals to serve the common good unless it is a broad education in which the culture of this country—science, literature, thought, art, religion, government, etc.—is presented comprehensively. Schools throughout the country are making significant progress in that direction, although the ghosts of the free-elective system and early specialization still frighten the timid from making the maximum advance.

Education cannot prepare students to serve the common good unless it is drastically changed so as to teach that there is not only *a* good or *goods* but also a common good, and that man's supreme obligation in society is to this common good.

It is at this point that modern education is an inglorious failure. The cult of objectivity still rules most of the sciences, including the social sciences. They will have nothing to do with any discussion of values or goods. They are concentrated upon a method of description and prediction which will create effective tools for man to use for any purpose. They, as scientists and scholars, are unconcerned with questions of ends. If the prediction is accurate, the method is sound, and that is progress. Thus, brilliant social and scientific technicians are trained every year. At commencement time they stand in the market place, waiting to be hired by those who are concerned with ends. It is not an overstatement to say of many of the graduates of our colleges and universities that they are sophisticated prostitutes of the intellect, so devoid of any truly objective criterion of value or subjective commitment to it that they will stoop easily to any low purpose.

This is true to some extent even of students of the humanities and of religion. In these areas values are studied. But no single theory of value can be adopted officially by a school to be presented exclusively to its students. If all God's children were Methodists, and all Methodists had the same knowledge of God's truth, *the* truth could be taught in all schools without difficulty. But even in Georgia, a state God has blessed with an extremely large number of Methodists, there is an enormous number of Baptists. Thus, Georgian education must be fair to both Methodists and Baptists. At the college and university level the number of clashing values that must be fairly dealt with is greatly increased. The result is a dispassionate presentation of this view of truth and that view of truth from which the teacher so carefully dissociates himself that the student gets the impression that the teacher himself has no sense of values but is an amoral person. The result is a conviction on the student's part that it is important to *understand* all conceptions of value, but that the *possession* of a theory of values for oneself is a matter of indifference and of no importance.

A Better View of Tolerance

In the religious view of education that Protestantism should champion this is the problem that should be attacked. Part of the solution is to be found in a reconstruction of our conception of toleration, which has implications for the Protestant conception of Church and State, especially in regard to education. Our present conception of toleration is a negative and, if I may say it without animus, a Catholic one; it should be changed into a positive, Protestant conception.

The present, negative doctrine of toleration runs as follows:[2] Toleration is not based on hope of agreement but on despair of ever reaching agreement. It accepts differences of belief as final. It does not regard men as working together in a common cause but as working separately. Each man makes his own interpretation of the world for himself. It is a sort of personal noninterference pact. If you'll agree not to do anything to affect my beliefs, I'll agree not to do anything to yours. The slogan is either "A man's opinion is his own affair" or "the sanctity of the individual's beliefs." In education it extends this to irrational lengths to mean "Nothing is to be studied or taught which might influence opinions or beliefs." Where this is rigorously applied, education cannot be important, let alone religious.

To change the American conception of toleration from this negative, privative one is a responsibility of Protestantism. Protestant insistence upon the individual's religious freedom involves a sound doctrine of tolerance. Such a doctrine requires the common pursuit of truth, which will have value for all. It invites students to join in this common quest in the hope that a common goal will ultimately be reached. It urges the study of different positions in the realization that one must come to terms with what others have learned so that one's own grasp of truth may be increased. It will *not* respect other men's opinions unless they can be shown to be respectable.[3] It will try to influence all men by reason and will subject itself to a reasonable argument from any man. Johann Amos Comenius, the great Protestant educator, preached this type of toleration, because he said, "The Christ whom I serve knows no sect." Toleration of this sort is a constructive force. If the American people thought of toleration in these terms, religion could be taught in all our schools.

But the American people know only the toleration of indifference. The ultimate goal, therefore, is the transformation of the minds of the laymen in the churches. The laymen cannot be led to see education in religious terms except as they are influenced by the ministers; the ministers will not see this opportunity unless their own education prepares them. But the change in the educational system waits for the people.

THE CHURCH-RELATED COLLEGE

This vicious circle can be broken in the church-related college and the seminary. These relatively independent institutions can exert an influence upon American education in general if their leaders have the courage and vision to make the education found in their institutions truly religious. This will mean that the colleges stop insisting that there is no difference between them and the state university and that the

---

[2] For many of the ideas presented here I am indebted to Alexander Meiklejohn: *Education Between Two Worlds* (New York, Harper's); pp. 58-60.
[3] This does not mean that force would be used to change opinions.

seminaries must find a higher model than the medical schools. This change can be made effective only by strong schools, and it is not necessary to wait for the millennium to begin. Strong leadership in administration can do much if it is clear as to its goals and is unafraid. My experience in educational administration has not been extensive; but it has gone far enough to show me that idealism, clarity, and courage are great virtues, and that the greatest of these is courage.

It is still the ministers who will do the ultimate task—the transformation of the thinking of the people as to the nature of education and of religious education. It was for this reason that I included seminaries with the church-related colleges as a possible resource. In the seminaries the pattern of religious education should be drastically changed. Technique and measurement should be given the minor place they deserve. Definitions and goals should be studied carefully against the background of the best religious thinking of today and of yesterday. The seminary in the university should pioneer in the meaning of religion for higher education. It should attempt to demonstrate on its own campus a religious education, an education in which religion is not a single subject among its peers but the map of the whole institution. Thus, as Arnold Nash says, the university itself will be a witness to the glory of God.[4]

American education stands in dire need of a service the church schools can render. Their traditional heritage and their freedom set them apart for this task—the demonstration of an educational experience that will support a democratic society and a Christian faith. This is no small opportunity, and it is an opportunity that is open to Protestantism.

---

[4] Nash, A. S., *The University and the Modern World*, New York: Macmillan Company, 1943.

OUR RESPONSIBILITY FOR A NEW WORLD

Paul B. Kern

THE early Christian Church began its life with a vehement protest against things as they are. The divine yes had sounded in Jesus Christ, and the affirmation of God's revelation to mankind laid upon the early disciples certain moral obligations. If God was in Christ reconciling the world to himself, it was evident that the world was not fashioned after the pattern of his will. The early Christians protested the paganism of the Roman Empire. When Peter stood up on the day of Pentecost and indicted his Jewish listeners, it was a protest against their sins, against their spiritual obtuseness, and against their hide-bound traditionalism. Protestantism is not so much a movement as a spirit.

When Martin Luther personalized the Reformation and launched his theses against the Roman Catholic hierarchy and autocracy, he was moving in a long line of men who had protested the deadness of a formal religion, and he was within the orbit of Jesus' violent denunciation of men who lay burdens upon others but do not themselves conform to the law they require of their disciples. The Reformation moved on through the years into power and influence because the age in which it voiced its protest had become senile and atrophied. The reformers stand out in lonely and prophetic solitude discerning the Spirit of God as he moves across the ecclesiastical valleys of dry bones. The right to protest thus becomes a divine imperative.

John Wesley was not always conscious of his Protestant leanings. His spirit of catholicity gave place to every vital spiritual movement of his times, but Methodism came to birth as a flaming protest against deadness and formality in the Church of England and a kind of weird and mystical sacramentarianism in the Roman Church. We should never have had the spiritual upheaval of the eighteenth century if men, under the influence of the Spirit of God, had not protested the rigidity and the irrationality of the theology that had grown up during the centuries after the initial Christian movement.

What is Protestantism's place today? In many lands and continents we constitute a minority. Numerically we are often overwhelmed by the strength of other branches of the universal Church, yet the light of Protestantism is not put out by the traditionalism and darkness of religions that surround it. It is still a faith of protest. It still lays its emphases upon reality, genuineness, honesty. It still believes in the priesthood of the believer and the accessibility of grace to every believing heart. It still insists that salvation is not by merit but by grace through faith. Its ancient thesis was never more pertinent than it is in this day, when men are forced to re-examine the foundations of faith and search for a creed and an experience able to bear the weight of a new world order, which is coming so rapidly to birth.

Protestantism is not without its weaknesses. While we are not the only great section of the Church which has different theological camps, we have presented a divided front far too long. We rightfully turn away from the formal unity that is made mandatory by the genius of Catholicism. As we exalt the individual and seek for authority in the domain of one's own personal experience, we must face the fact that such approach denies to us the outward unity that is possible to less-responsive religions. While we may agree that our weaknesses are at least the result of our virtues, we can only deplore the fragmentary schisms that have too long characterized the body of Protestantism. As we move into the future, these dividing lines are fading, the walls of doctrine and polity which have shut us out from the unified body of Christ are becoming lower and lower, and the spirit of co-operation is moving upon the life of the evangelical churches.

Sometimes we yearn in our hearts for the restful satisfaction of an authoritarian religion. It is a luxury for the human spirit not to have to struggle for religious positions that can be mediated by a papal pronouncement. But our faith in God is not primarily intended to produce a static dependence on some outward authority; the fiery urge within our souls makes us seek the face of the Everlasting Father and Jesus Christ, his Son. It is the old struggle between the religion of the spirit and the religion of the letter. The former brings life, the latter spells death; and no amount of human assumption upon the part of a church dignitary can answer the hunger of our own souls for the Living God. This may be the long road to the end of human freedom; but it is the only road that we can believe is blessed of his Spirit and will so transform the human individual that he can be conscious of his sonship with God and his responsibility for the building of a new kingdom of righteousness.

THE WORLD THAT IS TO BE

To prognosticate exactly what kind of condition we shall confront when the guns stop firing and the armies are demobilized is highly presumptuous. No man knows what the morrow may bring. Society is in convulsion. Old things are passing away. Out of the cauldron of our agony a new world may be born. No one is wise enough to blueprint it now, but certain great principles stand out as inescapable when we begin, with bleeding hands, to mold the clay and fashion the pattern of our new world. Some things are eternally in the moral order of the universe. They are not affected by whirlwind and fire and sword. Just as the love that was revealed on Calvary could not be overcome by the hate of the murderous enemies of God, so neither can the light that shines in men's hearts and the principles of the spiritual world order be blotted out by the gathering darkness of these ghastly days. Protestantism will live in the world of tomorrow only as it answers the fundamental quests of the human spirit and satisfies the longing of men for that reality which is God.

Let us now look at some of the distinctive contributions Protestantism will have to make to this new world order. And let us not forget that if Protestantism has what the world needs, she is under a high responsibility effectively to proclaim and to practice these fundamental principles. This is not for her own self-preservation; she can live only as she meets fundamental spiritual needs and fits into God's unchanging scheme for the redemption of mankind.

1. It is in the heart of the Protestant faith that the spirit of free inquiry and research finds its most hospitable home. As men feel their way into the mystery of life and search for truth on every page of God's unfolding revelation, they must be untrammeled and unimpeded by any authoritative mandate. We have discovered only a fragmentary part of God's revelation. In the shadows of tomorrow lie unexplored realms that invite the adventurous footsteps of men who love truth and who are willing to spend and be spent for its discovery and its integration into human life. When Protestantism broke away from the traditionalism of the parent church, she lifted her banner in every field of science, of philosophy, and of revelation and asked only that she might be guided into the discovery of truth itself. This search cannot be made if men must always be conscious of having to defend a dogma or the structure of an ecclesiastical polity. One recognizes with appreciation the contribution our sister communion has made and is making to the sciences; but this does not invalidate our insistence that the future belongs essentially to those who are unencumbered by any kind of ritual or doctrine and who are free to explore in the spirit of untrammeled freedom, searching for the truth that makes men free. The imagination staggers as one thinks of these undiscovered lands in the continents of truth which are out before humanity in the world of tomorrow. We are but children picking up pebbles on the vast shore of knowledge. No religion can be the friend of mankind which does not bid the explorer and the scholar and the scientist to go anywhere in the world for new concepts and patterns of thought. This whole process is invalidated if the discovery that may come must be stifled because it upsets some kind of religious status quo. The final authority is in the universe itself, and those who are humble searchers and faithful friends of this cosmic reality that is behind the outward shape of things will be God's prophets tomorrow.

2. A phase of this search for truth which is pertinent to this discussion is the way in which men find religious peace and satisfaction. One can but recall those pastoral days in Palestine when the Carpenter of Nazareth bade men "come and see"; when he told them that it would be the truth that would set men free; when he sent them out on their own, panoplied only by a divine passion for men; and when he blessed them because they had not been like the scribes and the Phari-

sees. The old, authoritative approach to religion is dying. It crumbles together with the other totalitarianisms of our modern world. The pomp and glory of high-flown ecclesiasticisms are suffering the same fate as kings and emperors. Their day is over past. The human spirit is in rebellion. Men must come to God, not through the mediation of some human priest, but through the wooing of the Spirit of God within their hearts. The answer to troubled hearts is not some priestly word of absolution but the answer to the heartfelt cry of repentance: "Have mercy on me, a sinner." Along this line is comfort and peace and redemption; along the other line is the false security that belongs to those with whose souls human hands have dealt.

3. The family is the basis of human society. As the home life of a nation goes, so will its moral life go. Civilization confronts no more acute problem than the threatened disintegration of the home. The family is the unit of society. It is the supreme sacrament of human life. Protestantism, with all of her shortcomings, has always recognized the normality and the spiritual quality of this union of two souls. And Protestantism has steadfastly refused to invade the sanctity of the marriage vow for the interests of the church. The home of the future must be a more religious institution, but it must also be free from pressures exerted upon it in behalf of one theological system as over against another. The celibacy of the clergy in the Roman Church has many advantages, but it also carries grave handicaps. At the top of the structure there is an abnormality that blights. To deny the fundamental law of human society, even in the interests of religion, so called, is very questionable. The battleground of the future is likely to be in the domestic field. Protestantism stands equipped to deliver her message in this area with effectiveness and redemptive power. If we can make these sheltered citadels of love radiant with piety and religious devotion, we need not fear the collapse of our civilization. The world of tomorrow will require of those who seek moral leadership that they shall have an effective answer to this fundamental and acute human problem. I verily believe that Protestantism has this answer.

4. Ethics may not be the whole of religion, but it is the flower of faith. If men believe in God and then violate the fundamental ethical ideals of Jesus, their faith is vainglory and blasphemy. The Christian community must live differently from the surrounding paganism. Unless certain standards of practice become impossible to us because of our oneness with Christ, we confuse the whole meaning of religion, and men tend to look upon us as a system of priestcraft. Protestantism, while she has not always lived up to the highest standard of ethical conduct, still confronts a world of evil and claims her right of protest. Giant social evils in our land call for denunciation. Gambling, which violates the Christian principle of property; intemperance, which is an offense against the body and soul of mankind; the artificial computation of merit, which is put over against the grace of God as the

basis of forgiveness—these and many other current iniquities cry out for a prophetic voice, for men and women who refuse to be outwardly religious but who are, in reality, covering up, like whited sepulchers, the corruption of questionable ethical attitudes. No society can rise above its ethical ideals because those ethical ideals find their verification at last in the gospel of Jesus Christ. Other religions have found themselves judged by the ethical standards of Protestantism. That faith will control the future which is most faithful to the ethical sensitiveness of Jesus and the disturbing attitudes of New Testament moral ideals.

5. A vast proportion of the world stumbles on in the darkness of ignorance. When one contemplates great continents and great races and realizes that not more than one out of ten people has even the elementary basis of an education, one is overwhelmed by any philosophy of life that is for a moment complacent with this sin against the mind. There are lands that have had religion for a long time. There are lands in which costly cathedrals have lifted their spires to the sky, but all around these stately edifices people are living in poverty and ignorance and misery. To offer men a mystical service of worship when what they need is a gift of enlightenment and knowledge is giving people a stone when they have asked for bread. It may be that this whole question is bound up with democracy, and democracy is tied up with Protestantism. A class society, in which there are the rich and the poor, the privileged and the unprivileged, the trained and the illiterate, is not a society in which Jesus can find his will and pleasure. He who noted the fall of a sparrow and placed the essential worth of every human spirit at the top cannot be content with any kind of social order in which the latent possibilities of any child are stifled by the indifference of those who are responsible or by the hoary prestige that can maintain itself only upon the shoulders of an ignorant multitude. If this is the century of the common man, the child of every common man is entitled to free education. This is the attitude of Protestantism wherever she has gone. If she has gone to a Mohammedan country, she has built a school. If she invades Buddhist territory, it is in the interest of free and undictated learning. If she comes into a Catholic-dominated continent, her ever-increasing institutions of learning are the pledge that in her mind the future is bound up with an equal chance for all God's children. Nothing less than this will suffice tomorrow, and no religion can be called the friend of man which does not seek to disfranchise the serfs of ignorance and open the door of knowledge in every land and among every race.

6. We talk a great deal today of the common man. As Abraham Lincoln once said that God must love the common people because he made so many of them, so today the vast multitude upon this globe is made up of people who must struggle and suffer and climb and love and live and die. Jesus looked out upon them one day and had compassion. They were without a shepherd, and he would be their guide.

There are more lost people in the world today than ever before. The unshepherded move through every avenue of life. These men and women are the stuff out of which tomorrow's world will be built. If justice is denied to them, there will be no justice in any world order. If their essential hungers are not satisfied with a reasonable share of this world's goods, their cry for bread will overturn kingdoms and undo governments. If they are not granted an order of life in which, periodically, they do not have to sacrifice everything upon the battlefield, there can be no peace on earth.

CHALLENGING TASKS

Certain grave responsibilities rest upon world Protestantism if she is effectively to influence the course of events in the postwar world. The tasks the times are imposing upon us must be met with forthright courage and intelligence. In both Great Britain and the United States groups of Protestant leaders have been facing the task of the Protestant faith in the world after the war. Much bold and untraditional thinking has been done. It would be well for us to review some of the areas in which apparently Protestantism holds a unique responsibility.

The Delaware declaration reasserts that "moral law, no less than physical law, undergirds our world. There is a moral order which is fundamental and eternal." If the world of tomorrow is to be secure and to escape these recurring orgies of blood and destruction, that moral order must be recognized. The present sickness of our civilization is due to our disregard of this inescapable moral law.

The Church must proclaim this fundamental basis of society. It is not recognized by a secular society that surrounds us. Lincoln declared that this is a nation "under God." Until the life of the world is brought under the sovereignty of the Eternal God and his law, there can be nothing other than chaos and confusion. Paganism and materialism simply cannot build an enduring social order. The universe is against such partial and self-centered interpretations of its life. It is for the Christian evangel to proclaim the ultimate authority that is greater than the kingdoms of this world—namely, the authority of God and the laws of his kingdom. "The government shall be upon his shoulders."

Protestantism must tackle another gigantic task: "to create a worldwide community in Jesus Christ, transcending nation, race, and class." The basis for this world unity lies in the gospel proclaimed by the Christian Church and in the New Testament record. That God is no respecter of persons, that all men are his children, that each is of inestimable preciousness—these are Christian truths that must come to common acceptance. The politician and the statesman have never accepted them. It will be only as the churches purge themselves of racial prejudice, abandon narrow sectarianism, and exalt the universal Christ above the petty gods they have worshiped that this ideal can come to reality. As was declared in the Malvern manifesto, "the Church is not an association of men gathered together by the act of their own wills, but is a creation of God in Jesus Christ, through which, as his body, Christ carries on his work for men. It has the duty and the right to speak not only to its members but to the world concerning the true principles of human life." The acceptance of this eternal mandate will make the Church the most powerful and dynamic institution in the world; the denial of this responsibility will leave the world without guidance in a twilight of gathering gloom.

I cannot here discuss the intricate problems connected with the economic life of the world. It has been through the ages an arena of conflict. The forces of secularism have striven to divorce the gospel from this area of life, and too many times they have succeeded. Chaos and deep discontent are rampant in the economic life of mankind. I recall the discussions at Oxford during the Conference on Life and Work. Boldly there it was declared that the economic life of the world was properly to be regarded as an activity of the kingdom of God. Society cannot be Christian in worship and pagan in business. This realm must be brought under the sway of Christian principles.

Here will be our battlefield. Much of our international strife has its roots in economic inequality. The raw materials and world markets are the possessions of the despotic strong. Millions go hungry and unemployed, while a minority bask in vulgar riches, which they refuse to share. An economy of scarcity brings wealth to the few and poverty to the many. The abundant life for which Jesus pleaded is not known by most of God's children. Only when the economic processes, both domestic and international, can be made to conform to the fundamental laws of the gospel can there be a hope for a just and enduring peace. But the Church must take her courage in her hand when she goes into that jungle.

Into the building of the structure of such a world Protestantism moves. God touched her with light in the days that were gone. She became a fire in the bones of men. She became a dream that pointed to human freedom. She preached a gospel to them that are in prison. And she opened doors of liberty and of life, of human grandeur and divine fellowship, to all those who heard her gospel. That gospel was never needed more than it is today. Our church does not possess all the truth; but the spirit that moves in Protestantism is akin to the Spirit of God, and God will need those who profess her faith in the world of tomorrow.

To keep alive faith in humankind, to battle for eternal principles that the centuries do not control, to believe in the ultimate sovereignty of God over all life—these are some of the Church's high imperatives in these stirring days. Behind her struggle stands the figure of the Christ. He is mankind's hope for a better world. He is the power in which humanity struggles forward, and his kingdom is the dream, foretold by bard and prophet, which shall some day be the last and best reality.

A GROWING ECUMENICITY

Henry P. Van Dusen

Those who live under the shadow of recent events lack perspective rightly to appraise their significance. However, it is not improbable that future historians, looking back from a perspective that is not ours, will discern clearly that all through the nineteenth and the first quarter of the twentieth centuries the life of the Christian churches was marked by two major developments. These two developments together indisputably constitute the most notable feature of Christianity in the modern era and give to this period of a little more than a century a character as distinctive and as distinguished as any previous great age of Christian faith—the early Church, the Middle Ages, the Reformation.

One of these developments has been *a movement of expansion*. Its aim has been to extend the reach of Christian allegiance to the farthest corners so that Christianity might truthfully claim to be a *world* reality. The other has been *a movement of consolidation*. Its ultimate objective has been the co-ordination and unification of the innumerable and varied organizations and agencies of Christian influence into a single effective organism so that Christianity might rightfully be recognized as a world *community*. The movement of expansion, in its major manifestation, is the enterprise of *Christian missions;* the movement of consolidation is the effort toward *Christian unity*.

Moreover, by a coincidence that later vision may recognize as of providential determination, each of these two developments came within sight of a preliminary achievement of its goal literally on the eve of the present conflict.

Only in most recent years has the Christian mission penetrated to the farthest reaches of the earth so that today there are vigorous, if sometimes tiny, branches of the Christian Church among every people and in literally every land save two. Only in our day has Christianity become for the first time a *world* reality. That fact received graphic demonstration at Christmastide, 1938, when delegates from seventy nations gathered at Madras. There the most representative assemblage of men and women which had ever come together met under the only auspices that could have summoned so representative a gathering, especially in the fevered days of late 1938—the Christian world mission.

Likewise, only in most recent years have the fumbling and varied efforts of Christians toward greater co-operation and even unification crystallized in a proposal to create a single body that, when fully constituted, should gather up into unity most of the earlier essays toward Christian collaboration and be empowered to speak and act for the whole of Christendom (except the Roman Catholic communion) in a measure never previously paralleled since the original great division into Eastern and Western churches in the eleventh century. This fact took concrete form when representatives of virtually all non-Roman Churches met in Holland in the summer of 1939, as the Western world was teetering on the brink of war, to draft a constitution for a World Council of Churches and invite adherence to it. Only in our day has Christianity become in a significant sense a world *community*.

Through most of the last century each development has been pursuing its own course with little apparent relation to the other. In the last decade they have deliberately drawn closer and closer together until today they constitute two intimately related and fully co-ordinated arms of one organism.

It is this inclusive development in its two intimately correlated phases which is coming to be known by the phrase, still stumbling for Anglo-Saxon tongues but of majestic tradition and meaning— "ecumenical Christianity" or the "ecumenical movement." For "ecumenical" means, precisely, "universal." It implies a reality that is both world-wide and united.

At the Dawn of the Nineteenth Century

Consider the facts:

A visitor from Mars who had chanced upon this planet at the dawn of the nineteenth century would hardly have entertained good hopes for the future of Christianity. For more than a century previous, in both faith and life the Christian Church had suffered deepening strain, weakness, and loss. In area after area to which Christian missionaries had ventured in the preceding era of vigor and extension their fragile young churches had sickened and died. In Latin America, the scene of most striking recent advance, Spanish and Portuguese adventurers who had sought to subdue a continent under the joint aegis of sword and cross had wasted their strength through lust and greed and had brought corruption and disrepute upon the Roman Catholic missions, which their conquests had sponsored. Australia and New Zealand and most of the lesser inhabited islands of the Pacific as yet knew nothing of Western culture and religion. In Japan, Christianity had been driven wholly underground. In China and Korea persecution had almost exterminated the weakling Christian communities. Here and there, along the seacoasts of Africa, in India and Ceylon, at a few centers in Malaya and Indo-China, on certain Pacific islands, small and seemingly unimportant Christian outstations might be discovered. But these Christian missions were usually spiritual adjuncts to the outposts of European military and economic dominance. Christianity was still quite definitely a European faith. Its fate as a world religion appeared linked to the future of European conquest.

But throughout Europe, the only continent where Christianity had established itself as the dominant religion, the Church was speedily losing its hold upon the common people. Its claim to the convinced allegiance of the educated and privileged classes seemed already gone. Much the same condition prevailed on this continent. Many Americans of today entertain a somewhat exaggerated impression of the influence of Christianity upon the birth and childhood of their nation. The period immediately following the Revolution and the Constitution was not notable as an age of faith. A famous item records that in Yale College, in an early year of the nineteenth century, not a single student could be discovered who would admit that he was a Christian. Meantime the only civilization in North America was concentrated in scattered white settlements fringing the Atlantic seaboard. Beyond, clean across the continent, stretched a vast Indian population virtually untouched by Christianity. In the midst of the white settlements dwelt a rapidly multiplying population of Negroes, still largely heathen.

Meanwhile the impulse toward infinite partition and proliferation, which has been such a marked feature (many would say, curse) of Protestantism since its beginnings, continued apace. The two most recent divisions had given birth to two new sects, which were destined to develop into two of the largest and most powerful branches of Protestantism, especially on the North American continent—Methodism and the Disciples of Christ. And the end seemed not yet.

Such were the condition and outlook for Christianity at the close of the Napoleonic wars. These facts could hardly have failed to paint the main features of the picture for the man from Mars. As he turned away for the return journey to his planetary habitat, he might well have left a sympathetic message of condolence for the leaders of a movement that once had seemed to possess such vitality, such promise for mankind, but which obviously was now doomed to inconsequence, possibly to extinction.

A CENTURY LATER

Let us imagine this same Martian traveler in his perennial youth, or his great-grandson, returning for another visit a century later.

By now Christianity had become the professed faith of the Western Hemisphere—the whole of the vast continents of North and South America, with their more than two hundred million people. In the Pacific basin the continents of Australia and New Zealand and certain of the lesser islands were inhabited by predominantly Christian populations. In Africa, Christianity had worked inland from the seacoasts to establish sizable and vigorous churches among the native tribes. Indeed, as we have already noted, at least some beginnings of a firmly founded native church were to be discovered in every country on the face of the earth except two. Only Afghanistan and Tibet still forbade admission to Christian missionaries.

Perhaps most noteworthy of all, among the most advanced peoples of Asia, those most deeply rooted in ancient and mature oriental cultures—India, China, Japan—the Christian movement, although numbering in its membership an insignificant minority of the populations (not more than 2 or 3 per cent), was now flourishing under the ever more vigorous leadership of native Christians whose influence upon national thought and life was all out of proportion to their numbers. In those lands Christianity was generally regarded as a factor of first importance for the physical, intellectual, social, and spiritual advance of their peoples. Thus, Christianity had become, for the first time in the nineteen centuries of its history, *a world religion*. More than that, there had emerged the promise of a Christian faith which should be truly universal, embracing men and women of every race and culture and stage of civilization from the crudest tribesmen just wrested from cannibalism to the most cultured and sophisticated descendants of sages who had achieved civilization centuries before Christ was born and millenniums before our ancestors left their tree huts and barbarous folkways.

By any reasonable test the nineteenth century was by far the greatest in Christian history. In terms of geographic expansion the Christian Church had reached to the ends of the earth, penetrating every continent and touching almost every people. In terms of numerical growth the Church had multiplied its membership manyfold. In terms of influence upon the whole life of humanity Christian ideals and spirit had effected greater reforms and improvements in the lot of all sorts and conditions of men than had ever been wrought by any single influence in any previous epoch of history.

CENTRIPETAL FORCES

Again, these facts could not have escaped the attention of the traveler from Mars on his second visit. One of the most manifest and astounding changes wrought in the life of the world by the intervening century was the radical alteration in the position of the Christian religion with respect to sweep, vitality, and promise.

It is by no means so certain that his notice would have been caught by another and companion feature of Christian development, centripetal rather than centrifugal in character. It is not even sure that it would have been pointed out to him by whatever human beings might have proffered their services as guides and interpreters of the times, even mentors drawn from the churches. Here was a development less striking, less spectacular, but perhaps not one whit less significant for the future of Christianity—advance in Christian unity.

All through the latter half of the nineteenth century Christians in different lands and of manifold traditions were reaching out toward

270

closer acquaintance and deeper fellowship and co-operation. These approaches were along many different lines. Some of them concerned Christian bodies within individual nations; others were world-wide in scope. Some involved Christians within a single communion; others were interdenominational in character. Altogether they were of five main types:

Earliest were ventures toward international fellowship among leaders of single communions from different lands. By the dawn of this century almost every major denomination—Anglican, Baptist, Congregational, Disciples, Lutheran, Methodist, Presbyterian, and Reformed—had created some form of world fellowship, with standing officers and periodic meetings.

Next came the birth of world alliances or federations of the several principal organizations especially concerned with the enlistment of Christian youth—the Young Men's and Young Women's Christian Associations and the student Christian movements.

Then there came into being several bodies of world-wide scope which brought together for consultation and common planning Christians united by some particular emphasis or interest. As early as 1889 the first *World Sunday School Convention* met in London. *Temperance* linked Christians of many lands. Out of the great World Missionary Conference at Edinburgh in 1910—the forerunner of the sequence of great ecumenical conferences of our own time and, in many respects, the grandparent of the ecumenical movement—there developed the *International Missionary Council*. On the very eve of the first World War, in the summer of 1914, through the generosity of Andrew Carnegie, leaders in the crusade for world peace were enabled to launch the *World Alliance for International Friendship Through the Churches*.

The years following World War I witnessed a marked acceleration in every type of impulse toward international Christian understanding and co-operation. In part this was a reflection within the churches of tendencies powerful in every sphere of the world's life; in part it sprang from chagrin and penitence among Christian leaders that the churches had proved so impotent to avert world conflict. In consequence two new world Christian bodies of a fourth type, conceived on bolder lines than ever before attempted, were brought into being. They were distinguished from all earlier efforts in that they sought to join in conference and in united action official church bodies from most of the major communions. These were the *Universal Christian Council for Life and Work* and the *World Conference on Faith and Order*. They became the immediate parents of the World Council of Churches.

Progress in world-wide co-operation was expressed and advanced through the series of great ecumenical conferences whose achievements are so familiar a story—Edinburgh (1910), Stockholm (1925), Lausanne (1927), Jerusalem (1928), Oxford and Edinburgh (1937),

Madras (1938), Amsterdam (1939). But behind these public and structural achievements and probably more far-reaching in ultimate significance were many smaller and more intimate consultations among Christian leaders of all lands representing the various world Christian bodies. Thus understanding and profound personal trust were achieved, and a united strategy was hewn out against the threatening day of testing.

Meantime a fifth series of developments were in process within individual countries—those which aimed to join in organic mergers previously separate communions. In the decade from 1927 to 1936 fifty-three such approaches toward church unity were undertaken, involving representative branches of most of the major communions of Protestantism and several of the Eastern orthodox churches. Fifteen full and final mergers were the outcome. Some united church bodies of the same family—episcopal, presbyterian, or congregational. But, contrary to every law of logic and normal expectancy, more than half took place between churches of unrelated types. Seven of the fifteen occurred among younger Christian churches of mission lands.

I have thus detailed the evidence in almost statistical summary because only when the many varied aspects are placed side by side and discerned to be manifold expressions of a single underlying impulse, contrasted essays toward a single ultimate goal, can we gain an adequate recognition of the breadth and depth of the growing ecumenicity. One feature of the record merits repeated underscoring. During the early years and most notably during the first of the two decades of uneasy respite between the World Wars, Christian efforts toward world cooperation were supported by general centripetal tendencies in the minds of men and the relations of nations. Indeed, Christian internationalism might have been interpreted as one illustration of the prevailing cultural drift. But throughout the second decade between the wars the continued—yes, accelerated—advance in Christian unity ran straight against catastrophic centrifugal tides in the world's life. "Let the Church be the Church" was a watchword proclaimed by the Oxford conference of 1937 and re-echoed from end to end of Christendom. As a result, when conflict again broke, Christian leaders of all lands faced it more nearly one in mind, in mutual trust, and in united provisions to outride its hurricanes than had been true of the Christian movement since its first great schism nine centuries ago. This was the justification for the sober declaration of the Madras conference, now often quoted: "The decade since last we met has witnessed the progressive rending of the fabric of humanity. It has witnessed the progressive unification of the Body of Christ." This was the record that prompted Professor Ernest Barker to write in the *London Times* in the summer of 1937 words also often repeated: "Our century has its sad features. But there is one feature in its history which is not sad. That is the gathering tide of Christian union."

WORLD CHRISTIANITY TODAY

Here, then, was the situation at the outbreak of the present conflict. What of the record of these last five years? What has World War II done to ecumenical Christianity? In a single sentence ecumenicity has pressed steadily forward, painfully but determinedly and surely, in its every aspect from week to week and month to month.

Step by step, progress in the organic unification of church bodies has continued. We noted that the decade before 1936 recorded fifty-three approaches toward church union and fifteen consummations. Since 1936 fifty further advances have occurred, and eight new instances of actual mergers, the two most recent being in Italy and Japan. From the point of view of church union this short period has witnessed a greater advance than any other like period in Christian history.

The World Council of Churches, projected when war already lowered, increasingly takes form and reality. Month by month, as the storm darkened and spread and finally broke, one after another communion voted adherence. Today its membership totals more than eighty churches from thirty nations, the latest additions being from Hungary and Ireland.

At Geneva, where most of the world Christian bodies have their principal headquarters, their leaders are welded in ever more intimate and effective collaboration so that today their organizations are in fact functioning as a single ecumenical Christian movement. From their base there they are unitedly carrying on, in behalf of all the churches, not only the normal activities of world Christianity, but also numerous emergency wartime ministries in behalf of prisoners of war, of refugees, of evacuees, of Jews, of youth. Through the several ecumenical relief enterprises—War Prisoners' Aid, World Student Relief, the Central Bureau for Interchurch Aid, Christian Relief and Reconstruction, the Orphaned Missions Fund—financial contributions flow steadily from Christian groups on every continent into central treasuries, and thence are distributed to the distressed and destitute of whatever nation, race or creed. Through the last named—the Orphaned Missions enterprise—a bafflingly intricate but shrewdly conceived and skillfully directed network of relief, resources from well-nigh the whole Christian world are pooled, across all barriers of theological and denominational cleavage and all chasms of political enmity, to succor and sustain isolated and imperiled cells of the world mission. It is one of the most notable and glorious demonstrations of common responsibility and mutual aid in the whole of Christian history.

Many of the most heartening manifestations of practical ecumenicity are occurring, however, not on a world scale, but within individual countries and in particular situations. Indeed, some of the most heroic and hazardous chapters of the story are being written within Germany and Japan. Many of them cannot yet be told. In Germany churchmen are operating "underground railways" to speed the escape of imperiled Jews and are shielding and supporting those who cannot flee. Christians within the German armies and administrations of occupation have been assisting Norwegian and Dutch Christians to organize the daring programs of effective resistance which are a principal glory of those churches in captivity, of course with certainty of death should their activities be discovered. In Japan the Christians strengthen the structure of their new united church and hold its basis and spirit loyal to the universal Church. And throughout the vast territories of Japanese occupation, where stripling young Christian churches had relied upon counsel and support from Britain, the European continent, and America, it is clear that both native churches and missionaries are being protected and assisted by fellow Christians of the "enemy" nation. Thus, ecumenical Christian fellowship and collaboration are established and strengthened amid war's starkest cruelty and fiercest hatreds.

Meantime, through the two great neutral oases of Sweden and Switzerland, continuous communication is maintained between church leaders of all lands and on both sides of the conflict, excepting only Japan. As Christian opinion, especially on issues of postwar reordering, takes shape in one country, it is made available through channels, which cannot be named, to collaborators within the iron silence of censorship. A recent careful compilation, by the Geneva staff, of documents and declarations reaching them from all over the world reveals that today there is actually more nearly a united Christian mind concerning political and economic order than there was on September 1, 1939, or at any previous date. Could there be more striking and significant proof of a growing ecumenicity?

From this wartime record three lessons stand forth with special meaning for our theme:

1. It is a record of churches, rather than of individual Christians, and of *churches united*. Indeed, fidelity in witness and effectiveness in action have been in direct ratio to the massed unity of all Christian groups. Nothing less than the *whole* Christian community is able "to withstand, and having done all to stand."

2. It is a record of Christians and their churches, living, acting, and standing steadfast within the vivid consciousness of their membership in *a world community*. In a profound sense it is a record not of individual churches but of a world Church. Only a world Church is adequate to a global age.

3. It is a record of a world community brought into being as a direct result of the Christian world mission.

LOOKING AHEAD

Finally, what of the future?

All through these latter years—not merely the last four years of war, but thirty years of war, respite, regirding, and war resumed—a single word has chorused through the vocabulary of mankind until we weary with its reiteration. It is the word "crisis." It has been thus re-echoed because it so accurately describes the deeper character of our times. More recently the Chinese transliteration of that word in its double meaning—*peril* and *opportunity*—is becoming almost equally familiar and for the same reason.

That word, in its double connotation, likewise defines the future for the Christian Church—*peril* or *opportunity*. One thing only appears certain: Like the culture in which the contemporary Church is set, we shall not resume the old days and ways. Either we shall go forward to new and greater possibilities, or we shall certainly slip down to a sadder destiny than Christianity has known in our lifetime.

Whether we shall be successful in weathering the *crisis*, in redeeming its *opportunity*, would appear to depend on two factors: how far the Christian churches are *united* and whether or not they are *revived*.

The first clear lesson from the recent history is this: The churches are strong in the measure that they are *united*. We need not argue the teaching on the face of the record. There is every reason to believe that this law of the Church's health in wartime is no less a condition of the Church's significant survival in the hardly less hazardous days of coming "peace."

This does not require a single organic Christian Church for all Protestantism, though we have observed actual church unifications as one of the most promising portents of these latter years. It does not imply surrender of the distinctive marks and gifts of each communion. What would the Christian missionary enterprise be without the special contributions of the finest Methodist missionary, whom one of their own number has rightly defined as a union of John Wesley and P. T. Barnum? It does demand far more cohesive and effective working unity than Protestantism has ever known.

Let us recall that the motivation impelling unity is twofold. In part it is *defensive, practical, expediential*; in part it is *positive, theoretical, ideal*.

We must have unity, because none of the churches' greatest problems can be adequately met by individual churches or separate communions but only by the total resources and power of the whole Church of Christ. That is manifestly true of the churches' world mission. It was inescapably revealed in the discussions at Madras. Christian missions cannot begin to meet any of the clamant practical tasks ahead—education, literature, theological training, evangelism, relations with governments—except through a unified strategy and united mustering and deployment of all available resources. This is no less true of the churches in America. Those churches cannot bring significant impact upon any one of the great problem areas or pioneering tasks—secularism, relations with government, the Roman Catholic problem, outreach and occupation, the social order—unless they act unitedly with every resource at their pooled command. It is no less true of each local community. Whether we have in view an effective tackling of great corporate diseases or a worthy meeting of the by-passed challenge of the unchurched, there is only one answer—the massed Christian strength of the community directed unitedly upon common responsibilities. Unity is, first of all, the clear counsel of expediency, of *practical statesmanship*.

On the other hand, unity is, no less clearly, *the command of Christ*. It is increasingly evident that the churches of Christ have no right to rebuke the world of nations for their disunity or to profess to bring significant healing to the world's divisions unless and until they can cast the beam of division from their own vision, unless and until they speak and act unitedly. That this is discerned most clearly and poignantly by the youngest Christian churches is only further evidence of keener sensitiveness to the mind of the Master at the frontiers of the Church's life, of the priceless gifts of the world mission to the world Church. Nothing less than the *whole* Church of Christ is adequate to the needs of the hour or worthy of the Church's Lord.

But there is a companion condition, less widely discerned and declared: The churches will hardly turn peril into opportunity fulfilled unless they be soundly and profoundly *revived*. This, too, is a clear teaching from churches in travail in wartime. At every point practical effectiveness and spiritual renewal have moved hand in hand. But here the wider record of the last half century is shadowed. There has been amazing advance in Christian outreach and Christian co-operation. There has been no comparable rebirth of Christian vitality. There has been no notable revival among the Christian churches of the world since that great movement of the Spirit in the closing decades of the last century which claimed as its principal channels Dwight L. Moody and Henry Drummond and which so largely empowered the advances since. The greatest single danger threatening the churches of Christ in our day is not contagion from the diseases of secular society nor even perpetuation of piddling divided ineffectiveness but internal sterility and shriveling through lack of indispensable spiritual renewal. Our greatest need is *revival*.

Yes, but, some will say, do not these two conditions—*unity* and *revival* —argue against each other? We unite on the lowest common denominator; we are reborn by a vivid, particular faith. Is not reunion always achieved on the basis of breadth at the cost of depth? And does not renewal always sacrifice breadth in the interests of depth and thus breed fresh divisions?

That is a general impression. On the whole, it *has* been the law of revival in Protestantism—until the last century. But in one of the unpublished conclusions from his monumental study of *The Expansion of Christianity*, Professor Latourette has pointed out that that was *not* the law of revival throughout the nineteenth century. The latest renewals of Christian vitality have not been divisive; they have been unifying. Indeed, the same springs that poured new life through arid organisms parented the great impulses toward fellowship and unity. That was true of Finney's revival in the early years of the century. It was abundantly true of the revival led by Moody and Drummond, which at once launched the greatest missionary outreach in Christian history and inspired the interdenominational student movements, principal training grounds of ecumenical leadership. The same movement has been nursemaid of both rebirth and reunion. Dr. Latourette says:

> The religious wakenings of the eighteenth and nineteenth centuries have been among the most potent sources of the growing movement toward Christian unity, which is so striking a feature of the life of the Church of our generation. The revivals cut across denominational boundaries. They were accompanied by common experience, conversion, and, to a striking degree, were based upon common theological convictions. . . .
>
> In summary we may say that, more than any of their predecessors, the revival movements of the nineteenth and twentieth centuries have contributed notably to Christian unity. . . . More than at any time since the third century the Christians of the world are drawing together. In this the Holy Spirit is clearly at work. We are living in one of the great days of the Christian Church.[1]

And today the voices that call Christian youth with greatest evangelistic power are, almost without exception, apostles of a united Christendom. Like their intrepid spokesman Kagawa they protest: "We are not interested in your damnations—I mean, denominations. We do not understand the necessity for your damnations in the cause of Christ."

The fact that recent revivals have furthered unity suggests that it has been *true* revival—revival in accordance with the mind of Christ. It may point to the largest importance of a growing ecumenicity—the most promising hope for a renewal of Christ's Church in our time.

---

[1] K. S. Latourette, *Divisive and Unifying Tendencies in Revival Movements.*

BIOGRAPHICAL NOTES

JOHN THOMAS MCNEILL has been professor of church history at the University of Chicago since 1927. He was born in Canada. He has degrees from McGill University (A.B., M.A.), Vancouver University (B.D., D.D.), University of Chicago (Ph.D.). He was ordained in the Presbyterian Church of Canada in 1913. Before going to Chicago he was professor at Queen's University and Knox College (Toronto). As this goes to press, his acceptance of a professorship at Union Theological Seminary, New York, is announced. One of his later books is *Makers of Christianity*.

MARTIN RIST has been professor of New Testament literature and interpretation at Iliff School of Theology since 1936. Dr. Rist was born in Illinois. He has degrees from Northwestern University (A.B.), Garrett Biblical Institute (B.D.), Iliff School of Theology (Th.D.), and University of Chicago (Ph.D.). He did special work with Dr. Goodspeed in preparing the *American Translation of the New Testament*. In the summer of 1943 he was visiting professor at the University of Chicago.

EDWIN PRINCE BOOTH, professor of New Testament at Boston University since 1925, was born in Pennsylvania. He has received degrees from Allegheny College (A.B., D.D.) and Boston University (S.T.B., Ph.D). He was ordained a Methodist minister in 1922 and has been pastor of the Community Church, Islington, Massachusetts, since that time. He is the author of *Martin Luther—Oak of Saxony* and editor of *New Testament Studies*.

ABDEL ROSS WENTZ has been professor at Gettysburg College and Seminary since 1909 and became president of the seminary in 1940. He was born in Pennsylvania and has received degrees from Gettysburg College (A.B., B.D., D.D., LL.D.) and George Washington University (Ph.D.). He has been treasurer of the American Association of Theological Schools since 1936. He is a member of the American Bible Revision Committee, the executive committee of the World Conference on Faith and Order, the organizing committee of the World Council of Churches, and the American Society of Church History. Dr. Wentz is author of several books, including *The Lutheran Church in American History*.

GEORGE WARREN RICHARDS, president and professor emeritus of the Theological Seminary of the Reformed Church in the United States, was born in Pennsylvania. He received degrees from Franklin and Marshall College (A.B., A.M., D.D.) and Heidelberg University (Th.D.) and studied at the Universities of Berlin, Erlangen, and Edinburgh. He was ordained a minister in the Reformed Church and served as pastor for nine years. He was a lecturer of the Biblical Seminary in New York, Sprunt lecturer, president of the Alliance of Reformed Churches, vice-president of the American section of the Continuation Committee of the World Conference on Faith and Order, president of the American Society of Church History, and vice-president of the Federal Council of the Churches of Christ in America. He is a member of the American Theological Society and chairman of the American Theological Committee on Faith and Order. Dr. Richards is author of several books, including *Creative Controversies in Christianity*, and is translator of sermons from German into English.

GEORGIA ELMA HARKNESS has been professor of applied theology at Garrett Biblical Institute since 1939. She was born in New York and has received degrees from Cornell University (A.B.) and Boston University (M.A., M.R.E., Ph.D., Litt.D.). She has been a teacher in public schools, an instructor at Boston University, and

278

professor at Elmira and Mt. Holyoke Colleges. She was a delegate to the Oxford, Madras, and Amsterdam conferences. She is a member of the American Association of University Professors, the American Theological Society, and the American Philosophical Association. Dr. Harkness is author of several books, including *John Calvin: the Man and His Ethics*.

ALEXANDER CLINTON ZABRISKIE has been since 1940 dean of the Virginia Theological Seminary, where he came as a professor in 1931. He was born in New York and has received degrees from Princeton University (A.B.), Virginia Theological Seminary (B.D.), Kenyon College (S.T.D.), and University of the South (D.D.) He was ordained a minister of the Protestant Episcopal Church in 1924 and served as pastor in New York City. He was secretary of the Executive Committee of the Forward Movement Commission of the Episcopal Church and now is a member of its Commission on Unity and its Commission on Evangelism.

JOSEPH MINTON BATTEN has been professor of church history at Scarritt College since 1924 and has been dean since 1943. Dr. Batten was born in Virginia. He has received degrees from Randolph-Macon College (A.B.), Princeton University (B.D., M.A.), and the University of Chicago (Ph.D.). He is an ordained minister of the Methodist Church and has served pastorates in Virginia. He is a frequent contributor to religious publications.

WILLIAM WARREN SWEET has been a professor at the University of Chicago Divinity School since 1927. He was born in Kansas and has received degrees from Ohio Wesleyan University (A.B., Litt.D.), Drew University (B.D.), Crozer Theological Seminary (Th.M.), University of Pennsylvania (Ph.D.), and Cornell College (D.D.). Dr. Sweet was ordained a Methodist minister in 1906 and served as pastor five years. He was instructor at Drew University and for several years professor and dean at DePauw University. He has written several books, among them *Methodism in American History*.

CHARLES SAMUEL BRADEN has been associate professor of history and literature of religion at Northwestern University since 1936. He was born in Kansas and has received degrees from Baker University (A.B.), Union Theological Seminary (B.D.), and the University of Chicago (Ph.D.). He was ordained a Methodist minister in 1912 and has been a missionary to South America, president of Union Theological Seminary of South America, and assistant secretary of the Board of Foreign Missions. He is a member and former president (1940) of the American Theological Society, a member of the American Oriental Society and of the American Association of University Professors, and the founder and editor of *World Christianity*. He is the author of several books, among them *The World's Religions*.

ALBERT CORNELIUS KNUDSON has been dean emeritus of Boston University School of Theology since 1938. Born in Minnesota, he has degrees from the University of Minnesota (A.B.), Boston University (S.T.B., Ph.D.), Allegheny College (D.D.), and Lawrence College (LL.D.), and has studied extensively in Europe. He is an ordained Methodist minister. After serving as professor at the University of Denver, Baker University, and Allegheny College, he became professor at Boston University, where he was advanced to dean in 1926. He is the author of many books, his most recent being *The Principles of Christian Ethics*.

WILLIAM GEORGE CHANTER has been professor of English Bible at Drew University since 1942. He was born in Canada and has degrees from Wesleyan University (A.B., M.A.), Harvard University (M.A.), Boston University (S.T.B.), Lawrence College (D.D.). Dr. Chanter served as a pastor, and for twenty-one years he was a professor at Wesleyan University. He is a member of the American Philosophical Association. His most recent book is *A Self Worth Having*.

HARRIS FRANKLIN RALL, professor of Christian doctrine at Garrett Biblical Institute since 1915, was born in Iowa and received degrees from the University of Iowa (A.B., M.A.), Yale University (B.D.), and the University of Halle-Wittenberg (Ph.D.). He has also received D.D. and LL.D. degrees. He was ordained a Methodist minister in 1900 and served as pastor in New Haven and in Baltimore and as president of Iliff School of Theology. He has been secretary of the Commission on Courses of Study since 1916. His most recent book, *Christianity*, had the distinction of winning the Bross Prize in 1941.

OSCAR THOMAS OLSON has been pastor of the Epworth-Euclid Methodist Church in Cleveland, Ohio, since 1934. He was born in Illinois and has degrees from Albion College (A.B., M.A., D.D.), Western Maryland College (Litt.D.), Mount Union College (LL.D.); and has studied at Union Theological Seminary. He was ordained a Methodist minister in 1912 and has served as pastor in Detroit, Baltimore, and Wilmette, Illinois. Dr. Olson was a member of the Hymnal Committee (1935 edition) and is now a member of the Commission on Courses of Study and of the Commission on Rituals and Orders of Worship of The Methodist Church. He is author of *Some Values for Today.*

CLARENCE DICKINSON, director of the School of Sacred Music of Union Theological Seminary and professor of music at Union since 1912, was born in Indiana. He received degrees from Northwestern University (M.A.), Ohio Wesleyan University, and Miami University (Litt.D.), and studied with several European music leaders He has served as organist of the Brick Church of New York City for more than thirty years. He is a composer and recently edited the hymnals of the Presbyterian Church in the U.S.A. and of the Evangelical and Reformed Church. He is a co-author with Mrs. Dickinson of *The Technique and Art of Organ Playing, A Choirmaster's Guide, Excursions in Musical History, The Troubadours and Their Music, A Treasury of Worship,* and *The Choir Loft and the Pulpit.*

HELEN ADELL (Mrs. Clarence) DICKINSON, lecturer on the history of art at Union Theological Seminary, was born in Canada. She received the M.A. degree from Queen's University and the Ph.D. from Heidelberg University. She is author of *A Study of Henry David Thoreau, Metrical Translations of 150 Ancient Carols,* and *German Masters of Art,* and is coauthor with her husband of a number of volumes.

HALFORD EDWARD LUCCOCK, professor of homiletics at Yale Divinity School since 1928, was born in Pennsylvania. He received degrees from Northwestern University (A.B.), Columbia University (M.A.), and Union Theological Seminary (B.D.) and has also received D.D. and Litt.D. degrees. Dr. Luccock was ordained a Methodist minister in 1910. He has been pastor, instructor at Hartford and Drew Theological Seminaries, editorial secretary of the Board of Foreign Missions, and contributing editor of *The Christian Advocate.* His book *In the Minister's Workshop* is a publication of early 1944.

WILLIAM ERNEST HOCKING is a professor emeritus of Harvard University, having served as professor of philosophy there from 1914 to 1943. He was born in Ohio and received degrees from Harvard University (A.B., M.A., Ph.D.), University of Chicago (D.D.), and University of Glasgow (Th.D.). Dr. Hocking has served as instructor in philosophy at Andover Theological Seminary and the University of California and as professor of philosophy at Yale University. He was a Gifford and a Hibbert lecturer. He is a member of the Congregational-Christian Church, of the American Philosophical Association, and of the Institute of Pacific Relations. His most recent book is *Living Religions and a World Faith.*

FRANCIS JOHN McCONNELL, bishop of The Methodist Church since 1912, was born in Ohio. He received degrees from Ohio Wesleyan University (A.B., D.D.) and Boston University (S.T.B., Ph.D.). He was ordained a Methodist minister in 1894 and, after serving as pastor, became president of DePauw. He has been president of the Federal Council of the Churches of Christ in America. He was the Beecher lecturer in 1930. He is chairman of the Commission on Courses of Study. Among his more recent books are *John Wesley* and *Evangelicals, Revolutionists, and Idealists.*

RALPH WASHINGTON SOCKMAN, pastor of Christ Church (Methodist) of New York City, was born in Ohio. He received the A. B. degree from Ohio Wesleyan, M.A. and Ph.D. degrees from Columbia University; is a graduate of Union Theological Seminary; and has also received D.D., Litt.D., and L.H.D. degrees. Dr. Sockman was ordained a Methodist minister in 1916 and throughout his ministry has been identified with Christ Church, serving first as associate and, since 1917, as pastor. He has been a Fondren and Beecher lecturer and is author of several books, latest of which is *Date with Destiny.*

KENNETH SCOTT LATOURETTE, professor at Yale University since 1921, was born in Oregon. He received degrees from Linfield College (B.S., D.D.), and Yale University (A.B., M.A., Ph.D.). He was ordained a minister of the Baptist Church in 1918. He has served on the faculty of Yale in China, on the faculties of Reed College and Denison University, and as a chaplain. Dr. Latourette has been a Lowell and a Noble lecturer. He is a member of the American Society of Church History, the American Council of the Institute of Pacific Relations, and the executive committee of the Student Volunteer Movement. His most outstanding work is *History of the Expansion of Christianity,* in five volumes.

HENRY SMITH LEIPER, American Secretary of the Universal Christian Council for Life and Work, was born in New Jersey. He received A.B. and D.D. degrees from Amherst College and the M.A. degree from Columbia University and is a graduate of Union Theological Seminary. He was ordained a Presbyterian but has spent most of his active years in the Congregational-Christian Church. He studied in China. He has served as traveling secretary for the Student Volunteer Movement, as pastor, with the Army Y.M.C.A. in Siberia, as missionary in China, and as associate editor of *The Congregationalist.* He is a secretary of the Federal Council of the Churches of Christ in America and of the World Council of Churches. He has written several books, one of which is *World Chaos or World Christianity.*

GONZALO BÁEZ-CAMARGO has been executive secretary of the National Evangelical Council of Mexico since 1940. He was born in Oaxaca, Mexico. He was graduated from the Methodist Institute, Puebla, Mexico, and from Union Theological Seminary of Mexico. Dr. Camargo has served as professor and vice-president of the Methodist Institute, as manager of the Union Publishing House, and as professor at Union Theological Seminary (Mexico) since 1941. He is a contributor to the religious and secular press, editor of *Luminar* (quarterly), and author of a chapter in *Christian Bases of World Order.*

ERNEST CADMAN COLWELL, dean of the University of Chicago Divinity School since 1939, was born in Pennsylvania. He received the Ph.B. degree from Emory University, the B.D. degree from Candler School of Theology, the Ph.D. from the University of Chicago. He was ordained a Methodist minister and has served as instructor at Emory and assistant professor and professor at the University of Chicago Divinity School. He is a member of the American Association of Theological Schools. He is the author of several books, one of which is *John Defends the Gospel.*

PAUL BENTLEY KERN, bishop of The Methodist Church since 1930, was born in Virginia. He received degrees from Vanderbilt University (A.B., M.A., B.D.), Duke University (D.D.), Emory University (LL.D.), and Ohio Wesleyan University (Litt.D.). He was ordained a Methodist minister in 1902 and served as pastor, as instructor at Vanderbilt, as professor and dean at Southern Methodist University, and as pastor at Travis Park Church, San Antonio. He has been a Fondren, a Cole, and a Jarrell lecturer. His most recent book is *Methodism Has a Message*.

HENRY PITNEY VAN DUSEN, professor at Union Theological Seminary since 1935, was born in Pennsylvania. He received degrees from Princeton University (A.B.), Union Theological Seminary (B.D.), and University of Edinburgh (Ph.D.). He was ordained a minister of the Presbyterian Church in 1924, and has served as instructor, assistant, and associate professor at Union Theological Seminary. He is a trustee of Princeton University and of Nanking Theological Seminary, and is a member of the American Theological Society. He is the author of several books, one of which is *For the Healing of the Nations*.